Jesus and the Religions

Jesus and the Religions

Retrieving a Neglected Example
for a Multicultural World

Bob Robinson

 CASCADE *Books* • Eugene, Oregon

JESUS AND THE RELIGIONS
Retrieving a Neglected Example for a Multicultural World

Copyright © 2012 Bob Robinson. All rights reserved. Except for brief quotations in critical publications or reviews, no part of this book may be reproduced in any manner without prior written permission from the publisher. Write: Permissions, Wipf and Stock Publishers, 199 W. 8th Ave., Suite 3, Eugene, OR 97401.

Cascade Books
An Imprint of Wipf and Stock Publishers
199 W. 8th Ave., Suite 3
Eugene, OR 97401

www.wipfandstock.com

ISBN 13: 978-1-61097-598-8

Cataloging-in-Publication data:

Robinson, Bob

    Jesus and the religions : retrieving a neglected example for a multicultural world / Bob Robinson

    x + 292 p. ; 23 cm. Includes bibliographical references and indexes.

    ISBN 13: 978-1-61097-598-8

    1. Jesus Christ—Person and offices. 2. Christianity and other religions. I. Title.

BT205 R55 2012

Manufactured in the U.S.A.

Contents

Preface vii

Acknowledgments ix

Introduction 1

1 Judaism and Gentiles: Jesus, Galilee, and Gospels 40
2 Some Key Encounters with Gentiles 81
3 Elsewhere in the Gospels: Purity, Temple, Parables 126
4 Samaritans and Jesus 167
5 Some Implications for the Encounter with Islam 200
6 Some Conclusions about Jesus, Gentiles, and Samaritans 228

Bibliography 271

Scripture Index 287

Subject Index 289

Preface

THE WRITER OF THIS book has one primary aim in mind: to persuade his readers that the *example* of Jesus has something fresh and helpful to say to those of us who wonder, "How am I supposed to live, as a follower of Christ, in a multireligious world?" I want to take something old—the example of Jesus—to say something new to our pluralist world. I want to do this by drawing attention to the example set by Jesus in the interreligious encounters of his day.

Most of the book examines the encounter of Jesus with Gentiles and Samaritans, and his varied comments about them. It asks, "What does a careful reading of the relevant Gospel passages disclose about Jesus and his attitude to non-Jews?" An interdisciplinary discussion then employs the exemplary Christology that begins to emerge to help answer the further questions: What might be the transformative implications of this christocentric example for an understanding of interreligious relations and mission in today's religiously plural world? In other words, what might it mean to "have the same attitude of mind that Christ Jesus had" (Phil 2:5) or to "live [literally 'walk'] as Jesus did" (1 John 2:6) in our contemporary multireligious setting?

Over the course of Christian history there have been a number of detailed exegetical studies of the encounter of Jesus with the Gentiles and Samaritans he met and spoke about. However, these studies (especially when written by Western Christians) rarely comment on the transformative and missional implications of the encounters for concrete interreligious relations today. When these encounters, and the comments by Jesus himself that they seem to have generated, are viewed through the lenses of recent hermeneutical approaches, they enable the retrieval of a rather neglected exemplary Christology. The example of Jesus does, it will be argued, model both an appropriately sympathetic and yet not uncritical appraisal of religion and the religions, and mission to the religions—and appropriate cooperation and dialogue as well.

There is, of course, *more* to Christian understanding of Christ than attending to the example of Jesus—the atoning death of Jesus, for example, is central to Christian self-understanding (even if discussion of it is beyond the intention and scope of this book). But that is no reason to ignore the example of Jesus, especially given the extraordinary claims about Jesus' identity embedded in his encounters with and teaching about the "others" of his day. These are to be found, as we shall see, in some of the most poignant and dramatic encounters and teaching in the Gospels: a synagogue address with near-murderous consequences, the healing of a pagan centurion's servant, the setting free of the afflicted child of a Gentile mother, a moving encounter at a Samaritan well, the unlikely story of a compassionate Samaritan—and more. As a notable missiologist asks, "What is it that gave rise to the many sayings, parables, and stories that seem . . . to nourish the idea that . . . one day, God's covenant will reach far beyond the people of Israel?" His answer, that "the primary inspiration for all these stories could only have been the provocative, boundary-breaking nature of Jesus' own ministry,"[1] is shared by this writer.

---

1. Bosch, *Transforming Mission*, 30.

Acknowledgments

THERE ARE ALWAYS MANY people to thank in the writing of a book. The leadership of Laidlaw College here in my native New Zealand offers regular study leave and professional development, and kindly gave me a reduced teaching load in 2009 to help with research and writing for the book. Classes at Laidlaw College and the Laidlaw-Carey Graduate School (especially the course R607) have enabled most of the book to be classroom tested and I am grateful for all the stimulating discussions they generated. Those who attended the conferences of the New Zealand Church Missionary Society over several years heard and responded to some of this material as incorporated into Bible studies. Study leave in 2004 took Heather (my wife) and me to the Mennonite Brethren Biblical Seminary in Fresno, California, where hospitality, academic interactions, and an excellent library enriched the book's preparation. Further study leave in 2008 took us to Singapore and Uppsala where Trinity Theological College and Johannelunds Teologiska Högskola provided not only hospitality, fellowship, study space, and stimulating discussion, but also the opportunity to test some of the material with staff and students, and (at Trinity) the honor of a public lecture. The generous provision of a month-long fellowship in 2010 by Calvin College, in Grand Rapids—part of their Communitas program—provided access to a wonderful library and much helpful discussion. Along the way, various individuals (Anne Aalbers, Nathan Askey, Jacqui Lloyd, Tim Meadowcroft, Richard Neville, Edward Sands, Jon Slack) offered research or editing assistance for which I am also very grateful. And, of course, there is my wife, Heather, whose caring support, patient sympathy, and gracious encouragement have lovingly nourished the pretensions of a would-be academic writer: thank you so much!

Acknowledgments

May those who receive and read this book find that—like the unnamed woman of Samaria—their hospitable reception of its words includes the perhaps unexpected gift of the water and Word of life in all its fullness.

Bob Robinson
Christchurch, New Zealand
June 2010

Introduction

Christian Concerns about a Pluralist World

FOR MORE THAN THIRTY years this writer has been trying to take the pulse of what Christians around the world think about the place of "Christ among the religions" (as the challenge of religious plurality might be described in a Christian context). The responses can be summarized as typically located along the following continuum of attitudes towards religious diversity:

> Celebration of plurality—sentimentality—curiosity—tolerance—accommodation—complementarity (naïve or principled)—diminished or abandoned belief—paralysis (indifferent or puzzled)[1]—anxiety—engagement (occasional or intentional)—triumphalism (principled or unreflective)—suspicion (principled or unreflective)—prohibition—fear and denigration—hostility and confrontation.

From a historical and global perspective, this range of responses is not new; both the religiously plural setting of the Bible and the religiously plural location of most Christians today provide many examples of how the people of God have lived among those with other religious allegiances. But the decline of Western hegemony, the implications of

---

1. By "diminished or abandoned belief" is meant reports that some individuals (perhaps best described as unprepared or even unreflective) have found their faith greatly challenged by the realities of religious plurality. By "paralysis" is meant the inaction or indifference that comes of despair at the difficulty of comprehending and assessing multiple religious claims. More than one Christian has simply given up trying to understand the place of Christ among the religions.

1

migration, the advocacy of pluralism (and its contemporary alignment with, or even nourishment by, postmodernism) and the ubiquitous presence and growth of Islam (and other religions)—these stimulate both interest and concern in Christian circles. Globalization is a more recent and particularly potent influence. "Radical changes in the political, economic, and cultural configuration of the world's nations make interreligious interchanges today different in both quality and quantity [from the past]. Christianity engages the world's religions on a playing field leveled by a global economic market, relative religious freedom, and a communications network that makes the whole world a virtual neighborhood. In most places today, Christianity not only confronts the world's religions, but it also coexists with them."[2] This religious diversity is visibly apparent in all the major (and many smaller) cities and universities of the Western world and well beyond.

Christ and Context, Mission and Interfaith Encounter

Most Christians continue to feel called by the "Great Tradition" of the faith to affirm both the uniqueness and finality of Jesus Christ, and mission in his name. But at the same time, they know that they are called to be good and loving neighbors as well; this is the second commandment from Jesus after the call to love God. The first of these callings can be described in terms of "christocentrism" and mission. Christ is at the very center of Christian self-understanding and identity—where he occupies a unique and irreplaceable position. For Christians, Jesus is not just "great" (comparable with, say, "Alexander the Great" or "Napoleon the Great"). "Jesus is not 'the Great.' He is the only. He has no peers, no rivals and no successors."[3] "Christocentrism" may not be an elegant word, but it well describes this traditional Christian view that the fullness of divine revelation, and the finality of humanity's redemption, center upon Christ. By christocentrism is meant those Christ-centered beliefs and practices that, however tolerant or positive their evaluation of the religions, and however warm their endorsement of interreligious encounter, nonetheless assert the traditional Christology of the Great

2. Muck and Adeney, *Christianity Encountering World Religions*, 15.
3. Stott, *Contemporary Christian*, 306.

Tradition of Christianity.⁴ One immediate advantage of the word christocentrism (especially in a pluralist setting) is its positive tone; the word strongly affirms the central affirmation of the Faith and for that reason is better than the term "exclusivism."⁵ What is meant by christocentrism can be summarized along the following lines: "Whatever statement we may choose to make about the character of God or the nature and destiny of human beings is ultimately grounded in and governed by the self-revelation of God in Christ."⁶

A number of criticisms have been made against christocentrism, especially the charges that it is morally inadequate (because it encourages triumphalism and intolerance), epistemologically naive (in its authoritarian view of religious truth), theologically deficient (in its high Christology), and culturally unacceptable (in its narrow-minded rejection of the pluralist paradigms of religious truth and interreligious relations and multiculturalism).⁷ But christocentrists are not found claiming an *exhaustive* knowledge of God and, fundamentalists excepted, are rarely found advocating the absoluteness of Christ. Rather, they argue that certain claims are accurate and true, especially as these center in one way or another upon the uniqueness and finality of Christ for Christian self-understanding. In the particular case of christocentrism, not only is that viewpoint epistemologically defensible, but it also appears to offer a more balanced representation of the biblical material than the theocentric alternative (the belief that all the religions revolve around "God" or some equivalent).⁸ Nonetheless, in recent decades, it has also often been asserted that such christocentrism is necessarily exclusivist and thereby impedes or even destroys the prospect of good

---

4. A comparison of the following confirms the ecumenically diverse yet shared assertion of this kind of christocentrism: the Anglican Archbishop of Canterbury, Rowan Williams, "Finality of Christ"; the evangelical Protestant theologian John Franke, "Still the Way"; the Catholic statement "Declaration '*Dominus Iesus*.'"

5. The word "christocentric" speaks of a centered set where Christ is the defining principle; an adjective like "exclusive" speaks of a bounded set where the organizing principle is who is "in" and who is "out."

6. McGrath, *Passion for Truth*, 51.

7. For a detailed discussion that attempts to answer these criticisms, and in the context of religious plurality, see Robinson, *Christians Meeting Hindus*, 240–64.

8. See, for example, the fine discussion in Wright, *Thinking Clearly*, 107–39.

relations with people of other faiths. This volume will argue a contrary view: that christocentrism rarely impedes good relations and dialogue and, in fact, actually *enables* a fruitful encounter (by following the example of Jesus in his encounters) in a way that diminished christological alternatives do not.

A claim of universal relevance and universal mission usually flow from the christocentric beliefs just described. This raises the question of reconciling the historical *particularity* of Christ with that other scandal (to postmodern ears): the scandal of the assertion of *universality*. But Christian mission to all people everywhere, whether conceived mainly in evangelizing categories or more holistically, flows naturally from belief in a unique Christ. And, alongside such a reason, a recent discussion (having emphasized a marketplace analogy in its analysis of the world of religions) adds "competition" as a reason for mission:

> Why compete? Because it is the very essence of the gospel to announce to the world the good news of what God has done through Jesus Christ. The Bible argues for competition on several different levels. On the emotional level, it is selfish to hide the light that radiates from the hope that is within us. On the theological level, it is disobedient to reject the call to teach and preach to all nations. On the philosophical level, it is arrogant to reduce all religions to a common-denominator rationality that denies equally the reality they all claim. Christian revelation demands competition. Buddhist dharma demands competition. Human rationality demands competition.[9]

At the same time, alongside christocentrism and mission, there is an equally clear call for Christians to love their neighbors as themselves—a call that ranked high on Jesus' list of priorities. In many places, these neighbors are increasingly likely to be people of faiths other than Christian. What does it mean to love these neighbors, and to act towards them with the grace that is another distinctive marker of Christian faith? At the very least it will mean talking with them, enquiring after their well-being, acting to help them and their families. It may

---

9. Muck and Adeney, *Christianity Encountering World Religions*, 29.

lead to invitations to their weddings, and funerals, and other events. Such encounters may lead to authentic and fruitful and even disturbing discussion in the midst of cooperation and celebration about matters both small and great.

There are both biblical and contextual reasons for such an emphasis and it is helpful to have the evangelical world in mind as our discussion develops. This is because, within the Christian community, it is usually evangelical or other theologically conservative Christians who display the greatest reluctance—or even opposition—to the sustained and intentional meeting with people of other faiths that is clearly needed in a painfully divided world. Such reluctance or opposition usually derives from anxiety that the meeting might in some way imperil their deeply held convictions about the centrality of Christ. Nonetheless, the consequences in the conservative Christian community can be considerable: ignorance or even misrepresentation of the beliefs and practices of others, tendencies towards indifference or willful neglect of the consequences of continued ignorance and misrepresentation, and even intentional negative confrontation. One example of recent research into Americans' responses to religious diversity shows that "support for the inclusion of non-Christians in community life is mixed. Theological exclusivism is consistently and strongly associated with *negative attitudes* toward religious diversity and *less willingness* to include Muslims and Hindus in community life."[10]

But at the same time, theologically conservative Christians—because of their numbers, global influence, and missional, activist inclinations—are often found at the interface between the Christian and other religious communities. There is, therefore, considerable public and even global benefit in offering to evangelicals, and others, a model for intentional interfaith encounter that:

- understands and respects the particularity and self-understanding of their (and other) faith communities;

---

10. Merino, "Religious Diversity" (quote from the research article abstract; emphasis added).

- does not relegate religious faith to the background during a search for any commonalities or any engagement in cooperative ventures;
- draws intentionally and deeply upon the example of Jesus himself in the interreligious encounter.

The Neglected Significance of the Example of Jesus

How then might contemporary Christians respond to the callings to be both christocentric and missional, and at the same time constructively engaged with people of other faiths? This writer has written extensively on the recent Christian-Hindu encounter in India. Because the work attempted a christological analysis of the encounter, I expected the example of Jesus in meeting people—especially Gentiles and those on the margins of Judaism—to feature as one of a number of Christian justifications of encounter and dialogue. However, during extensive travel and consultation in India itself, I found that the example of Christ to be almost completely absent from the discussions, even though the person of Jesus has long been known to be of considerable appeal to Hindus.[11] Nor is the example of Jesus much used in Christian reflection in the West. It is strange that, as Harvey Cox puts it, "Christians who think of Jesus as a model in other areas of their lives do not look to his example or teaching" when meeting people of other faiths.[12] There are a number of reasons for this neglect of exemplary Christology but one reason emerges as Korean theologian So Damon offers a critique of what he sees as the "dichotomy between the conservatives' emphasis on the death of Christ and the liberals' emphasis on the life of Christ" (a division that he deplores as "unnecessary and unbiblical") and urges the church to "recover the crucial sense of the unity between Jesus' life *and* his death, the holistic understanding of Jesus Christ in his whole missionary journey of being *with us* and *for us*."[13]

---

11. See the examples cited in Robinson, *Christians Meeting Hindus*, 209–10.

12. Cox, *Many Mansions*, 6.

13. So, "Missionary Journey," 139–40 (original emphasis); see also his *Jesus' Revelation*, 161–62, for further comment and analysis. The same dichotomy is criti-

Introduction

Jesus taught as much by his example and symbolic actions as by his verbal teaching. In the extremely large literature on Christology this exemplary dimension has received rather little scholarly attention. The NT urges disciples to "have the same attitude of mind Christ Jesus had" (Phil 2:5). It tells them that "whoever claims to live in him must live [literally 'walk'] as Jesus did" (1 John 2:6).[14] The suggestion of this volume is that disciples can discern something of the attitude that Christ had to the religions he encountered, or spoke about, by reflecting on the Gospels. Following the example of Jesus—what could be more Christ-centered than that? This "imitation of Christ" has always been the Christian way: from the apostle Paul ("imitate me as I imitate Christ," 1 Cor 11:1), to Thomas à Kempis in his *The Imitation of Christ*, to the contemporary bracelets inscribed with "WWJD" ("What Would Jesus Do?").

Biblical scholarship has revealed much about the encounters Jesus had with the Gentiles and Samaritans he met. In today's world Christians puzzle over how they should think about the people of other religions that they meet. This volume asks the questions: How did Jesus regard the Gentiles and Samaritans he met? How did he act towards them? What did he say about them? And, based on Jesus' example, what might we learn to assist us in our encounter with the "Gentiles and Samaritans" who are our neighbors in today's world? The twin callings to christocentric belief and missional action are part of the desire to be marked by both orthodoxy and orthopraxis: wanting to *believe* the right things and wanting to *do* the right things. For one writer, it is of considerable theological importance to insist that "it is not sufficient to discover how the person and teaching of Jesus Christ was significant in first-century Capernaum, or Jerusalem, but how it is consequential today."[15] In terms of the interreligious encounter there are a number of distinctly positive reasons for the encounter with people of other faiths to be approached in christological rather than theocentric, or pluralist, or other theological categories.

---

cized by N. T. Wright in his *Jesus and the Victory*, 14.

14. All translations of biblical texts are the author's.

15. Prior, *Jesus the Liberator*, 61.

Jesus and the Religions

Christianity has always drawn attention to the unique and irreplaceable position occupied by Christ in Christian self-understanding. There are distinct advantages in a concrete christological focus over appeals to "God" or "Spirit." These advantages are especially apparent when in discussion with most Hindus and with some Buddhists and with some followers of the "new spirituality" in the West—for whom the categories of "God" or "Spirit" can be construed in all manner of ways.[16] It can also be argued that it is the person of Jesus that, more effectively than any other aspect of Christianity, enables the Christian "word" to be understood. The primary focal or beginning point of any theology (or summary of Christianity) based on an appeal to the NT is the message of Jesus as presented in the Gospels.[17] It is the person and message of Jesus as remembered in the Gospels, then, that ought to play the central role in communicating the Christian message across cultural boundaries. This is because—to use a very helpful metaphor of Mark Heim—"people cross the membranes between different cultures more effectively than ideas or concepts do,"[18] and so to focus upon Jesus is to help enable the determining measure of Christian belief to take an appropriately central place in the discussion.

Mention might also be made of the fact that it is the person of Christ who accounts for the first major "interreligious encounter" of Christianity: its origins in, then separation from, Judaism. How did Christianity—a messianic sectarian version of Palestinian Judaism—transcend its Judean origins and ultimately establish itself in the Roman East as the multiethnic socio-religious movement we know as early Christianity? How did an initially Jewish, law-observant community in the eastern Mediterranean become a cosmopolitan religion? Or to turn the question a little, how did a non-halakhic and an increasingly non-ethnic Jewish movement end up claiming to be Israel? What accounts for the "Gentilization" of this Jewish movement (to use the neologism

---

16. This is not to overlook the ways in which an appeal to Jesus cannot be similarly misused but, generally speaking, it is more difficult to do this.

17. The point is well made by, for example, Räisänen, *Beyond New Testament Theology*, 182; and Matera, "New Testament Theology," 20.

18. S. Mark Heim, "Pilgrim Christ: Some Reflections on Theocentric Christology and Enculturation," in Das, *Christian Faith*, 119; see also 123.

coined by Terence Donaldson)?[19] The most plausible answer to these questions is that the changes derive, at least in part, from the person of Jesus and his attitude to Gentiles.

The Encounter of Jesus with Gentiles and Samaritans as a Paradigm for Interreligious Relations

This study begins with a contemporary reading, employing a variety of exegetical methods, of the encounter of Jesus with Gentiles and Samaritans, and his various comments about them. It asks, What do newer exegetical readings of the relevant Gospel passages disclose about Jesus and his attitude to non-Jews? An interdisciplinary discussion then employs the exemplary Christology that emerges to answer the further question: What might be the transformative implications of this christocentric example for a wider hermeneutical and theological understanding of interreligious relations and mission in today's religiously plural world?

There have been a number of detailed exegetical studies of the encounter of Jesus with the Gentiles and Samaritans he met and spoke about. However, these studies (especially when written by Western Christians), rarely comment on the transformative implications of the encounters for concrete interreligious relations today or for a contemporary theology of the religions. These encounters as recorded in the Gospels are few in number: for example, the Syrophoenician mother (Mark 7:24–30//), the centurion whose servant was healed (Matt 8:5–12//), the Samaritans (John 4:1–42). But each of them is significant because of the way in which they do involve genuine dialogue and some even appear to have Jesus changing his mind or, at least, stretching the received understanding of the possibility and place of Gentiles and Samaritans within the coming reign of God. Moreover, there are considerable implications to be drawn from didactic and narrative sections (besides the encounters) in the Gospels, for example: his teaching on purity, the temple action, and several parables (including the compassionate Samaritan). When these meetings, and the comments by Jesus himself that they seem to have generated, are viewed through the lenses

19. Donaldson, *Paul and the Gentiles*, xi.

of recent hermeneutical approaches, they enable the retrieval of a rather neglected exemplary Christology that offers substantial insights into, and for, contemporary interreligious encounters. In other words, the example of Jesus models an appropriately sympathetic, and yet not uncritical, appraisal of religion and the religions. The model advocated in the pages that follow calls for *engagement* modeled on the example of Jesus—a transformative model as Scripture inspires new perspectives and fresh insights. The dialogical model that emerges from one part of the discussion even suggests a constructive approach for one of the most challenging dimensions of religious plurality: the contemporary encounter with Islam.

This volume, then, offers something old (the example of Christ) as something new: a fresh way of imagining and living encounters in a multireligious world. It aims both to reassure and to challenge. It wants to reassure Christians that their response to the religions should and can remain both christocentric and missional. But it also wants to challenge them to undertake these callings in a neighborly, loving and gracious way—and to do this by following the example of Jesus himself.

Methodologies Employed

Methodologies help determine outcomes in every academic discipline. Much of what follows offers a contemporary reading of a number of passages in the Gospels. Such a reading makes use of the theological exegesis and interpretation of the Bible read as Scripture. It also employs a reader-response hermeneutic (alongside author- and text-centered approaches) with the "reader" located in a contemporary context of religiously plurality.

The Theological Exegesis of the Bible Read as Scripture

There has been considerable recent interest in the theological exegesis of Scripture. This is a cluster of approaches that begins by reading or "attending to" the biblical texts *as Scripture*.[20] Although there are a

---

20. Some of the range of meaning attached to theological interpretation is brought out in the (not uncritical) survey by Poirier, "'Theological Interpretation.'"

number of ways of reading the Bible, something specific is meant by reading the Bible as "Scripture." In particular, such an approach affirms that the Bible is understood and used in particular ways. It is seen as authoritative for the common life and beliefs of the church; "its use . . . is essential to establishing and preserving the community's identity."[21] As this identity is challenged by religious plurality (and the advocacy of religious pluralism, the ideological expression of that plurality), it is entirely appropriate that the Christian community turns again to the Bible as Scripture.

Theological exegesis implies a principled integration of theology and exegesis; such integration is a matter of what Walter Moberly calls "a *never-ending dialectic* and *a constant interplay* between text and rule of faith (i.e., prior theological commitments)." This does not mean that these "theological commitments" determine and control exegesis: "one indeed approaches the text with certain questions and assumptions, but these have to be tested and refined by the text itself in the well-known 'hermeneutical spiral.'"[22] An enormous amount of scholarly energy has been invested in the exegesis of a number of biblical passages related or potentially related to the interreligious encounter; but very little of that exegesis has had the theological and missional challenges of religious plurality in mind. The reluctance or inability or indifference of most exegetes (both Western and majority-world) to read the passages in the light of the contemporary context with its pluralist contours is apparent in most biblical commentaries, both academic and popular.[23] One of the identifying marks of theological exegesis is said to be its capacity to produce new insights into well-known texts; such exegesis "goes beyond repeating traditional interpretations; rather, . . . theological interpreters will produce *fresh readings*, new performances of Scripture's sense that

---

21. Kelsey, *Proving Doctrine*, 89. Among more recent treatments is Green, *Seized by Truth*.

22. Moberly, "Biblical Criticism," 83–84 (original emphasis).

23. The launch of a several new series of Bible commentaries—the Brazos Theological Commentary on the Bible (Brazos Press, 2005-) and Two Horizons New Testament Commentary (Eerdmans, 2005-)—and the *Journal of Theological Interpretation* (2007-), as well as growing number of individual volumes, should help correct this deficiency.

encounter the texts anew with eyes of faith . . ."[24] The (re)turn to theological exegesis offers exegetes and other readers of Scripture a renewed sense of confidence and expectation. What theological exegesis offers is an openness to the scriptural text bearing new meaning—but with the constraints imposed upon language and the tradition of interpretation in a given context, and "the possibility that through this very dialectic of openness and constraint, God might speak."[25]

A Reader-Centered Approach Alongside Text- and Author-Centered Hermeneutics

Related to interest in the theological exegesis and interpretation of Scripture is the contemporary hermeneutical conclusion that the meaning of Scripture is always a meaning for *readers*. In fact, one way of expressing a major concern of theological exegesis is found in a reader-response perspective.[26] The discussion of the various passages on the following pages will employ a reader-oriented hermeneutic (alongside author- and text-centered approaches) with the "reader" located in a contemporary religiously plural context. Biblical texts are not mechanisms that inexorably generate self-evident meaning; "they are not self-interpreting repositories of meaning insulated from outside influence."[27] This means that there is no "observer neutrality" or "value-free" perspective in the reading of biblical passages. Joel Green calls for "the recognition that all textual inquiry is shaped by the reader's context. Taking this observation seriously leads many to read NT texts in fresh ways at the same time that it raises for them a fundamental critique of the commitment to observer neutrality propagated in the practice of biblical interpretation in the modern period."[28] There is no "objective" reading

24. Hays, "Reading the Bible," 18 (original emphasis).

25. Le Grys, review of *Thiselton on Hermeneutics*, 164.

26. There is a considerable variation within reader-oriented approaches though they do "share a common, basic rejection of any portrait of the reader as a mere (potential) receptacle for meaning" (Green, *Hearing the New Testament*, 13).

27. Green, *Seized by Truth*, 118.

28. Green, *Hearing the New Testament*, 13. And, as one biblical commentator observes, reader response approaches can enable a healthy break with the subject-object dualism in which the reader (subject) has stood over the text (object) "with all

of the Bible given that "all interpretation is influenced and conditioned by the interests and social location of the interpreter."[29] All readers are self-involving; "where one stands *makes a difference* to what one sees," though it does not entirely determine it.[30]

Murray Rae calls for the acknowledgment that "[t]he meaning of a text . . . is a function of both authorial intention and reader reception. . . . [T]he meaning of a text is the role it plays in its context."[31] Meaning emerges from the dynamic interaction between author, text and interpretive communities of socially located and culturally embedded readers.

Some of these are readers of Scripture who face the questions and discomforts and opportunities of interreligious tension. They can and often do read the biblical accounts of interreligious encounters in quite different ways from those whose perspective is comfortably monocultural. Christopher Wright has provided a useful summary (with his own cautious approval indicated) of a reader-response hermeneutic in which he makes frequent reference to the religiously plural setting of both the biblical and contemporary worlds.[32] The meaning of the biblical text emerges from the interaction between text and reader, and Wright goes on to point out that this focus on the reader has facilitated fresh ways of discovering the relevance of the text in many contemporary contexts.

He also offers a warning: "We must get away from the Western superiority idea which was that we know the real meaning of the text—and everybody else has contextualised it! . . . Western biblical interpretation has no right to assume that all its insights are 'the standard', while those from other continents are 'contextualised'. . . . Recognizing this has led somewhat to the demise of Western hegemony over exegesis and the pseudo-scientific objectivity and superiority associated with the dark side of the Enlightenment" (Stibbe, *John's Gospel*, 8).

29. Green, *Seized by Truth*, 116.

30. Moberly, "Biblical Criticism and Religious Belief," 84 n. 17 (original emphasis); cf. Billings: "All interpretation is shaped, whether we recognize it or not, by the cultural context and social location of the interpreter" (*Word of God*, xvi); and Green: "The particularity of biblical texts and their origins is matched . . . by the particularity of readers and their locations" (*Seized by Truth*, 124).

31. Rae, "Texts in Context," 40.

32. Wright, "Interpreting the Bible," 48–51.

hermeneutics."³³ This hegemony may be one reason for the inability or unwillingness of Western interpreters to read the Gospels as if relevant to contexts of religious plurality; listening to scriptural interpretation that comes from the Global South may me one means of remedying this shortcoming.³⁴

One criticism of a reader-centered approach is the possibility that it can lead to a diversity of meanings if readers are located in varying locations. Clearly the imposition of arbitrary meaning (what Joel Green calls "a reading experience untroubled by outer limits"³⁵) overthrows the purpose of Scripture as one means of what we have noted Kelsey describing as "establishing and preserving the [Christian] community's identity."³⁶ The possibility of multiple readings does not imply the assignment of arbitrary meaning. Merely to be located in a context of, for example, harassment as a part of a religious minority, or self-satisfaction as part of a religious majority, does not in itself legitimate the taking of *any* meaning from biblical texts in order to help deal with those situations. The *possibility* of multiple readings does not mean that *any* reading is as legitimate as any other. "[T]he reading community known as the church has theological constraints on what biblical texts mean."³⁷

Nonetheless, Richard Hays can write that theological exegesis "is committed to the discovery and exposition of *multiple senses* in biblical texts. . . . Texts have multiple layers of meaning that are disclosed by the Holy Spirit to faithful and patient readers."³⁸ Daniel Patte (draw-

---

33. Ibid., 50; he goes on to point out to his fellow evangelical readers that "we cannot deny that when people read the text, its meaning for them will relate to whatever agenda is of vital importance to them. After all, on evangelical understanding, the Bible is God's word and it addresses us in any context and in relation to any issue. By the power of God's Spirit, words written in one context will 'mean' new things in radically different contexts as people read them" (50).

34. See the discussion in, for example, Treier, *Introducing Theological Interpretation*, ch. 6.

35. Green, *Seized by Truth*, 117.

36. Kelsey, *Proving Doctrine*, 89.

37. Green, *Seized by Truth*, 122. Rae discusses what he calls "the legitimacy of hermeneutical diversity and the limits to interpretive freedom" (Rae, "Texts in Context," 39; and later elaborates the limits on 43–44).

38. Hays, "Reading the Bible," 14. In a footnote he cites the fourth thesis of the "Scripture Project": "Texts of Scripture do not have a single meaning limited to the

ing upon a setting of religious plurality in the Philippines, and under the general heading "Acknowledging the Existence of a Plurality of Interpretations") can write that when there are "new interpretations," these "primarily reflect the believers' multiple interpretations." In reader-response terms, this is because disciples have varying needs; they are in a variety of different places as they hear Scripture.[39] As another scholarly comment puts it, "no one is native to the biblical text, no one reads only in the interests of the text itself."[40] Daniel Treier is also helpful; he searches for a middle ground between reader-response approaches and what sometimes appears to be a complete disregard for the "reader" in most conservative Christian hermeneutics. Treier argues for "interpretive plurality": "God makes humans as historical creatures, from which legitimate, loving plurality emerges as we understand texts in particular circumstances."[41] At the same time, risk is present. As Johannes Nissen points out, "our contexts can develop a life of their own, divorced from the biblical text and its critical challenge."[42] One safeguard against such a risk is the willingness to listen across cultures. It is not difficult to be critical of Western hegemony in the hermeneutical process; but caution must also be sounded lest situations of religious pluralism and even oppression lead to other distortions. If the hermeneutical process begins "with local experience and culture, we are in danger of reducing Christian faith to a human creation designed to solve problems humanly defined."[43]

---

intent of the original author. In accord with Jewish and Christian traditions, we affirm that Scripture has multiple complex senses given by God, the author of the whole drama."

39. Patte, *Challenge of Discipleship*, 44–45. He is at pains to distinguish between "the multiplication of readings" (which he rejects) and a "plurality of readings" or plural readings (which he accepts). What Patte wants to avoid is the arbitrary multiplication of readings but this does not rule out the possibility of a plurality of readings.

40. Athalya Brenner and Nicole Wilkinson Duran, in the Preface to Brenner, Lee, and Yee, *Genesis*, xii.

41. Treier, *Introducing Theological Interpretation*, 148.

42. Nissen, "Testament in Mission," 192. He goes on to quote Robert Schreiter: "We can create such powerful contexts in which to place scriptural texts that these texts can be muted and distorted."

43. Nissen, "Testament in Mission," 190–91. Treier suggests that "far from regulating biblical interpretation arbitrarily, doctrinal frameworks challenge new

Reader-response analysis, as the term implies, focuses on the kinds of responses a text evokes in different communities of readers at different times. The meaning of a text is not bound to its first readers, but is ever open to new responses in new communities. "The meaning of a text is . . . a function, ultimately, of the role(s) it serves in the divine economy."[44] It follows from this that, in a context of religious plurality, Scripture might well play a different role to that played in settings of secular hegemony or postmodern indifference. If texts play such multiple roles then multiple readings might well emerge. The text presents its own world of meaning to the minds of a reading community, affecting its readers through the shape of the text-world in dynamic interaction with the readers' own world. Proponents of a reader-oriented hermeneutic make no apology for the inevitable *multiplicity of meanings* a given text can present; such multiplicity of meaning offers legitimate alternatives to the gaps left by rigid historical interpretations born of monocultural contexts.

Michael Prior in his *Jesus the Liberator* provides a good example of an appropriate reader- and context-sensitive exegesis. For Prior, it is of considerable theological importance to insist that "it is not sufficient to discover how the person and teaching of Jesus Christ was significant in first century Capernaum, or Jerusalem, but how it is consequential today . . . . Exegesis within a community and tradition of interpretation ought not to be satisfied with a mere unearthing of the past, and an almost idolatrous veneration of the original historical context."[45] In Prior's case he is concerned that contemporary readers of Luke 4:16–30 hear the message of Jesus about the poor. But the points he makes are also particularly relevant to readers of the Gospels who find that their preunderstanding and predisposition is challenged—and not merely

---

generations to recognize their own cultural assumptions and to revise them in the light of how the church has understood Scripture as a whole" (*Introducing Theological Interpretation*, 77).

44. Rae, "Texts in Context," 40.

45. Prior, *Jesus the Liberator*, 61, 65. He goes on to urge that readers enquire of themselves whether their own prior expectations might help or hinder their hearing of Scripture "if it should invite a radical change of values and lifestyle. To be sensitive to one's own pre-understanding and predisposition may turn out to be more fundamental to 'understanding' a text than any enquiry into its putative meaning" (65).

Introduction

bored or irritated or infatuated—by contexts of religious plurality and pluralism.

A Cross-Disciplinary Approach:
Biblical, Theological, Contextual, Missional

Attention now turns, more briefly, to some other methodologies. This volume is consciously cross-disciplinary as it employs biblical, theological, contextual and missional discussions and analysis. At times, its approach is inductive: seeking to work from discrete biblical narrative and didactic passages in order to discern the attitude of Jesus to the Gentiles and Samaritans that he encountered. But it is also theological: seeking to rehabilitate an exemplary Christology and to use it to reshape a Christian understanding of the religions. The retrieval of such a Christology is also assisted by appropriate use of social-science analysis, narrative analysis, and analysis of place alongside the more usual historical and literary approaches to the Gospels. A deductive approach is also employed. Jesus is seen as an eschatological prophet called to the restoration of Israel and this has wide-ranging missional implications for the place of Gentiles and Samaritans in the Rule of God as announced by Jesus—and this influences the book's approach to Jesus' encounter with, and teaching about, non-Jews. At the same time, the biblical reflections do not attempt to be "neutral" and "non-theological": biblical texts do not signal their own meanings. Meaning emerges out of the author-text-reader dynamic—and all reading has a contextual edge to it. A cross-disciplinary approach offers the possibility of mutual transformation of understanding and requires interaction with a range of recent scholarship across disciplinary boundaries.

Recent Interdisciplinary Studies That Attempt the Cultural
Retrieval of Herodian Galilee and Their Implications for
Understanding the Relationship of Jesus to Judaism and to Gentiles

The past few decades have seen a rich proliferation of studies of Galilee and these studies, ranging across fields as diverse as archaeology, political and social-science studies, socioeconomics, and historical sociology, have contributed greatly to a more substantial understanding of the religio-cultural milieu of the region than has been possible on the basis of the literary sources alone. The "quest for the historical Galilee"—which has, at times, been strongly polarized—has centered on two major debates: the extent to which Herodian Galilee was Hellenized (and Romanized) and the kind of Judaism or Judaisms found there. The discussion may be framed by means of two questions: What was the extent of Jesus' encounter with Gentiles and Samaritans? And what was the kind of Judaism that might have helped shape Jesus' reaction to such encounters? The results of this research are discussed and followed by an attempt to draw out some implications for the study of Jesus and the canonical reports about his meeting with and speaking about Gentiles and Samaritans from Galilee and surrounding regions. Discussion and analysis of this issue is taken up in the next chapter.

A Contextual Frame: Growing Christian Interest in and Concern about the Religions

The model advocated on the pages that follow calls for an *engagement* that draws upon the example of Jesus—a transformative model as Scripture inspires new perspectives and fresh insights for the contemporary interreligious encounter. In the discussion of biblical texts that makes up a considerable portion of this volume, there is a double listening: an attending to the meaning of the biblical texts, and a theologically-motivated and theologically informed listening to the contemporary context that shapes and refines theological understanding. As Murray Rae points out, "God remains the Lord of revelation and uses particular texts, or not, in the working out of his purposes. That means that particular biblical texts may . . . in [certain] contexts . . . be given fresh vitality as instruments in God's communicative economy."[46] According to Michael Allen, in this way, "Scriptural reading in each context finds fresh meaning in the text, demonstrating God's faithfulness to speak to generation after generation in its own time and place."[47] In situations of religious plurality and interreligious tension, there is the hope that

---

46. Rae, "Texts in Context," 43.
47. Allen, "Divine Transcendence," 51.

one aspect of the meaning of Scripture (Jesus' appraisal of Gentiles and Samaritans) may, when read with prayer, be heard in new and fruitful ways and that new meanings will emerge.

Such an understanding will want to avoid any sense of interpretive closure—any sense that interpretive finality has been obtained.[48] This is because, as Rae puts it, such a claim "denies, effectively, that God, through scriptural texts, might speak a *new* word for our time not wholly envisaged by the authors of those texts."[49] One implication of this is to understand the appropriate Christian stance towards Scripture as "reading" rather than the more pro-active "interpretation" with its hints of mastery and control.[50]

There are, as we have seen, clear limits to how far diversity of meaning (Rae's "fresh vitality") may legitimately stretch, but considerable "freshness" may be overdue given the reluctance or inability or indifference of most exegetes (both Western and majority-world) to read the passages in the light of the contemporary context with its pluralist contours. The dialogical model that emerges from one part of the discussion is illustrated from the contemporary encounter with Islam. In other words, a new (but old) paradigm for interreligious engagement is advocated. In this writer's native New Zealand this "new look" has been welcomed at Anglican and Presbyterian study conferences where he has trialed it. Recent study leave was shared between Singapore and Sweden and, again, this exemplarist approach was welcomed among churches that struggle with the questions raised by religious plurality. Given an acute consciousness among many North Americans of the presence of Islam in the contemporary world, questions about the content and shape of a faithful, and yet appropriate, Christian response are increas-

---

48. There is a need to go beyond what Stephen Fowl calls the quest for the single and singular and supposedly "determinate" meaning of the text. For a trenchant discussion of the folly of such claims of interpretive finality see Fowl, *Engaging Scripture*, 52–54.

49. Rae, "Texts in Context," 39. Rae later adds: "Discerning the meaning of Scripture is . . . a pneumatic event in which God sounds his word afresh" (41).

50. For Webster, "reading Holy Scripture is 'faithful' reading: exegetical reason caught up in faith's abandonment of itself to the power of the divine Word" (*Holy Scripture*, 86).

ingly heard from them as well.⁵¹ New synergies are emerging for what the world is *becoming* and these have the potential to replace synergies related to how the world no longer is. The appeal to a neglected exemplary Christology offers both an appropriately sympathetic and yet not uncritical appraisal of religion and the religions.

Jesus and Gentiles and Samaritans: Too Few Examples?

Before considering the first of a number of passages in the Gospels where Jesus meets or speaks about Gentiles and Samaritans, the question might be asked: Can any safe or universal conclusions be drawn from the presence of so few examples? Is there any transferable learning possible from that ancient horizon across to ours given the small number of encounters? On the one hand, it might surprise some readers to find how many passages in the Gospels are relevant to the discussion. But another conclusion—for example, that of the distinguished missiologist David Bosch—is that the weight of Gentile references or encounters is so light as to confirm the bias of Jesus to the Jewish mission and so render as insignificant his Gentile references and encounters. Bosch likens the Gentile references to "golden nuggets" from whose rarity not much can be gained theologically or missiologically.⁵² But another approach is to ask whether Jesus is not, rather, indicating the extraordinary significance of the Gentiles (and Samaritans) by his setting their examples as signs and affirmations of the eschatological inversion of the present/coming Kingdom. In Luke 4 (as we shall shortly see) Jesus employs a principle of eschatological reversal when pointing to what might seem to be two rather minor and insignificant incidents centering on Gentiles to characterize the new eschatological age being inaugurated in him. Jesus employs a hermeneutical method that enables hearers (and read-

---

51. Responses to these concerns have begun to emerge within the North American evangelical community as well; see, for example, the constructive approaches modeled by the websites http://evangelicalinterfaith.com and http://www.sacredtribesjournal.org.

52. The "nuggets of gold" analogy is taken from Bosch, "Hermeneutical Principles," 439, where he minimizes (perhaps even dismisses) any importance to be attached to Jesus' Gentile encounters. I am grateful to my colleague Steve Graham for the reference, and for discussion about it.

ers) to see that the weight to be attached to the Gentiles far exceeds the actual number of the encounters.[53]

Having outlined a number of methodological issues, we turn to the first of a number of passages in the Gospels that illustrate the claim that that the example of Christ opens new possibilities for understanding and responding to the interreligious encounters of our own age.

Christ as Exegete: A Theological Reading of Luke 4:16–30

"Christ himself was an exegete, at Easter and even in the beginning."[54]

The church is well served by commentaries and other studies that probe for the meaning of this passage but what follows asks, "What might a contemporary theological reading of Luke 4:16–30 as Scripture bring to the mix?"—especially in the light of questions about a Christian response to contemporary religious plurality. Much of the material on the passage as found in commentaries and specialist studies is not repeated here. The text of Luke's Gospel is taken as canonically received with rather little attention paid to historical-critical issues and supposed redactional trajectories behind the text. The author of Luke-Acts undoubtedly helps to shape the text but of far greater theological significance is the way in which Christ himself is here presented as the principal exegete.

Luke 4:16–30: Jesus' Mission—Announced, Illustrated, Rejected

If Luke usually follows the order of his sources carefully, he appears to diverge from it here to enable this passage to become a significant programmatic statement of the gospel.[55] The passage opens with Jesus standing to read in his hometown synagogue:

---

53. Perhaps it is better to liken the relatively few encounters not to "golden nuggets" but to radioactive material whose significance is assessed not in terms of "weight" but in terms of long-lasting and highly potent emissions of radiation.

54. Bovon, *Luke the Theologian*, 120. Bovon has Luke 4 in mind in his mention of "the beginning."

55. Compare Luke's positioning with that implied by Mark 6:1–6 and Matt 13:53–58.

21

"The Spirit of the Lord is upon me, because he has anointed me to bring good news to the poor. He has sent me to proclaim release to the captives and recovery of sight to the blind, to let the oppressed go free, to preach the year of the Lord's favor. . . . Then he began to say to them, 'Today this scripture has been fulfilled in your hearing'" (4:18–19, 21). The clear reference to Isaiah 61 is a redacted quotation that comes substantially from the LXX of Isa 61:1–2 along with Isa 58:6 in which the prophet appears to describe Israel's future in terms of the year of Jubilee.[56] God's coming salvation is understood as the year of the Lord's favor towards "the poor" and Jesus presents himself as the anointed herald of such a Jubilee.

Luke continues with Jesus' acknowledgement that his prophetic identity and credentials are questioned by his contemporaries, and this is followed by a defense (or illustration) that appeals to incidents in the lives of the prophets Elijah and Elisha. Jesus appeals first to the narrative of the widow at Zarephath (1 Kings 17); she and her son are saved by the intervention of Elijah. The second story is about Naaman the Syrian leper (2 Kings 5); Elisha is not sent to heal the many lepers in Israel, but he is sent to a Syrian Gentile enemy whose leprosy added to his estrangement. In these two examples, those who recognize and benefit from prophetic ministry are Gentiles. Moreover, these Gentiles are among the socially weak (as a widow) and among the marginalized and unclean (as a leper). Their faith-filled recognition of the two prophets (and the blessing that follows) takes place in Sidon and Syria—areas regarded by Jesus' hearers with particular suspicion. In other words, when Jesus' credentials as a prophet are challenged, he exegetes what might seem to be two rather minor and insignificant incidents centering on Gentiles whose humility and faith characterize the new eschatological age being inaugurated in him.

Stung by the implication that they reject God's prophets, the crowd's rejection of Jesus boils over into murderous rage at these examples of Gentile recognition and divine favor at Israel's expense. An attempted execution follows, perhaps because of a conclusion that Jesus is a false prophet, deserving the harsh rejection of Deut 13:5–6. But

---

56. See Lev 25:8–17 (and cf. Deut 15:2); there were circles within Second Temple Era Judaism that read Isaiah 61 in this way.

Introduction

Jesus' attitude silences the crowd and he walks through it; in Johannine language, his hour has not yet come.

Christological Implications—both Narrative and Eschatological

One task of theological exegesis is theological analysis, so a theological reading might begin by attending to the succession of christological assertions in the passage. In its opening words there are three claims by Jesus: that he is anointed by the Spirit, that he is the prophetic figure who announces the arrival of a new eschatological age, and that he himself embodies the holistic salvation of the time of eschatological Jubilee and so is the very one who will bring the release that it promises. Jesus' statement in Luke 4 makes claims about the arrival of the Rule of God: not only is the divine promise fulfilled, the one who accomplishes the fulfillment announces it. The Judaisms of the time of Jesus had a clear image of the coming Rule of God but Michael Wolter points out how Jesus' own specific understanding diverged markedly:

"The essential difference is that the term 'Rule of God' acquires a very specific denotation, namely Jesus' own ministry. . . . Jesus defines his own ministry in Israel as the reality of the Rule of God that can be experienced here on earth. . . . Jesus claims for himself something that in the basic eschatological stock of knowledge of his milieu was reserved exclusively for God."[57] Moreover, the very way in which the pericope begins with biblical quotations is significant in itself; in Luke, such quotations are used to draw attention to the divine purpose that is being worked out in the narrative.

Rather than embracing the low or subordinationist Christology sometimes attributed to him, Luke has already made clear in the chapters before this pericope his view of the status of Christ. He is persuaded of Jesus' messianic and soteriological credentials[58] and his divine sonship.[59] For him, Jesus is clearly a prophet whose concerns "encompass Israel and more than Israel. The understanding of God's salvation as

---

57. Wolter, "Jesus as Teller of Parables," in Charlesworth and Pokorný, *Jesus Research*, 137–38.

58. See Luke 1:32–33, 46–55, 68–79; 2:4, 10–12, 29–35, 38; 3:16–17; 4:1–12.

59. See Luke 1:32; 2:49; 3:21–22, 23–38; 4:1–13; 4:14.

incorporating both Israel and the Gentiles is itself a prophetic motif, as Simeon makes clear in Luke 2:32 by means of Isaiah 9:6."[60] At the same time, Luke "is also insistent that Jesus is more than a prophet.... [T]he transfiguration places Jesus in the company of Moses and Elijah, yet the heavenly voice announces, 'This is my Son, my chosen one' (9:35)."[61] He is also clear about Jesus' close connection with the Spirit: immediately before the Nazareth event Jesus is said to have returned to Galilee "in the power of the Spirit" (4:14). So now, having been "empowered and sanctioned as God's Son, Jesus . . . performs as God's Son."[62] As he begins his public ministry (cf. 4:18–19), he is not only portrayed as someone who will depend on the Spirit of God but as one whose exegesis of the two stories results in what Michael Bird calls "a dramatic redefinition of who Israel is"—it is now, in his coming, reconstituted. "The identity of the captives to be set free is said to include traditional outsiders: widows, women, lepers and even Gentiles who respond to Jesus."[63] Such radical redefinition of the people of God is a task surely reserved for Yahweh alone.

Narrative is also an important category in theological exegesis[64] and a narratively constituted Christology also begins to emerge from a passage such as Luke 4. Terence Donaldson notes a recent shift from redaction to narrative criticism in the study of the Gospels, from the study of christological titles (for example) to the study of the *story* of Jesus—with the result that Christology becomes narratively constituted. The Gospel story is a narrative and so the identity of Jesus emerges from his actions as the Gospel writers provide an implicit commentary with value-laden descriptions.[65] A distinctive portrait of Jesus emerges from such a narrative analysis; it is seen both in the surprising elements of

60. Gaventa, "Learning and Relearning," 159.

61. Ibid., 158.

62. Green, *Gospel of Luke*, 203.

63. Bird, "Jesus and the Gentiles," 99.

64. One of the programmatic theses that summarize the hermeneutical conclusions of the interdisciplinary Scripture Project begins with the statement that "*Scripture is rightly understood in light of the church's rule of faith as a coherent dramatic narrative*" (cited in Davis and Hays, *Art of Reading Scripture*, 1; original emphasis).

65. Donaldson notes, for example, the role of *surprise* in the plot of the Gospels (Donaldson, "Vindicated Son," 100–111).

this story in Luke 4 (as we shall see in its many reversals) and elsewhere in the Gospels, in Jesus' (surprising) encounters with Gentiles and Samaritans and in elements of his teaching and actions that respond positively to these "outsiders." Rather than attempting to understand a topic such as Jesus and interreligious encounters in terms of theological propositions and ahistorical principles, a narrative approach helpfully points to the story told by Scripture—a story that contains Jesus' unexpected and surprising appraisal of Gentiles and Samaritans.

At the same time, it is a narrative that is exegeted by Jesus himself in eschatological terms. The time of eschatological Jubilee, with its promise of holistic "release," is embodied and fulfilled in him—and it is realized and accessible "today." As Bovon puts it, "[t]he soteriological activity of the Messiah fits into eschatology: the references to Isaiah 61 in Luke 4:18f and to Isaiah 35 in Luke 7:22 demonstrate this."[66] Or, to paraphrase Howard Marshall: Jesus does not de-eschatologize his ministry by separating it from the end times; he broadens out the time of the end so that it begins with his coming.[67] In the person of Jesus, the future breaks in from above—and these eschatological dimensions further consolidate a substantial Christology. Theological exegesis draws, then, on both the narrated text of Scripture and a theological understanding of that narrative—and from this narrative emerges the attitude of Jesus to the Gentiles and Samaritans whom he met and about whom he spoke. This, in turn, has wide-ranging implications for the discussion of interreligious relations, to which discussion turns shortly.

"Fresh Readings," "Fresh Meaning," and the Challenges of Interreligious Plurality

A further claim of theological exegesis is that it extends beyond the repetition of traditional interpretations; "rather, . . . theological interpreters will produce *fresh readings*, new performances of Scripture's sense that encounter the texts anew with eyes of faith . . ."[68] The turn to theological exegesis offers a renewed sense of expectation and an openness to

---

66. Bovon, *Luke the Theologian*, 298.
67. Marshall, *Luke*, 121.
68. Hays, "Reading the Bible," 18; original emphasis.

the scriptural text bearing new meaning. The very notion of canon (important in theological exegesis) also implies, or at least allows, that the *diversity* of biblical voices is to be heard. The canon may be likened to a polyphonic diversity that captures hearers in a way that a singular voice might not. So, such "fresh readings" imply an affirmative answer to the question posed by Charles Scalise, "Can Christian communities move beyond univocal interpretation . . . while retaining some hermeneutical control?"[69] As we have noted above, there are limits to how far the diversity of meaning within Scripture may legitimately stretch. The very notions of canon and canonical boundaries, not to mention the "rule of faith," clearly indicate some limits to theological speculation.[70] Nonetheless, the possibility of "fresh meaning" in the text moves hearers beyond any supposedly singular or final meaning of a given part of Scripture. In situations of religious plurality these insights from a theological reading of a passage such as Luke 4:16–30 suggest a number of implications and discussion now turns to some of them.

The Example of Faith and Humility in "Outsiders"

In the narrative in 1 Kings 17, many widows in the region suffer as Yahweh withholds rain because of the sins of Ahab and Jezebel. God chooses one widow to provide for her and for her, in turn, to assist Elijah, who miraculously restores her son. And, although Jesus' summary account itself does not emphasize the point, it is clear from the OT that the widow of Zarephath exercises considerable faith.[71] Naaman the Syrian is shown as an example of humility as he agrees to advice from a young Israelite woman, and as he submits, in faith, to ritual cleansing. He too is portrayed as a person of faith whose actions not only lead to

---

69. Scalise, "Hermeneutical Circle," 224.

70. Scalise's modified canonical approach incorporates "levels of meaning across the long history of interpretation of Scripture while employing the historical meanings of the canonical forms of the text for hermeneutical control"—an approach that "offers one way to balance creativity and control in the interpretation of Scripture" (ibid., 224).

71. See 1 Kgs 17:12, 16, 18, 24.

his healing but also, in his case, to a confession of faith as well: "Now I know that there is no God in all the world except in Israel" (2 Kgs 5:15).

It seems reasonable, therefore, to assess the two stories as examples of the kind of faith, humility, and praxis that Jesus affirms here, and will affirm again when he encounters Gentiles and Samaritans in person. Moreover, Jesus is willing to contrast such faith, humility and praxis favorably with what he finds "in Israel." In both stories Israel receives rebuke *from Gentiles* for the religious and nationalist insularity to which it was blind. The passage as a whole sounds a note to which Luke returns repeatedly: Gentiles and Samaritans respond to Christ or display behaviors of which he approves, while the chosen people hesitate or reject him.[72] The contemporary church might well consider the implications of such a rebuke for some of its own attitudes towards those of other faiths given that Jesus is seen in this passage (and others) to affirm at least some dimensions of the faith of "outsiders." As Donald Baillie once observed about the faith that Jesus commends in such people, "it is plain that Jesus came to single out this faith-attitude as a very vital one and to attach unlimited importance to it."[73]

A Great Reversal

One especially prominent theme in the entire passage is reversal on a significant scale. It is clear that Luke 4:25-27, with Jesus' invocation of incidents from the time of Elijah and Elisha, is about reversal. In fact, these verses (near the end of the passage) may be the interpretive key to the whole: John Poirier points out that the literature of the Second Temple Era, including speculation in the Qumran community, included repeated affirmation of significant allusions to Elijah in Isaiah 61.[74] The

---

72. Besides the passage under consideration, see also Luke 2:34; 3:7-9; 7:1-10; 10:25-37; 11:49-51; 13:6-9, 23-30, 31-35; 14:16-24; 17:11-19; 19:41-44. For Luke, the "times of the Gentiles" (21:24) are imminent.

73. Baillie, *Faith in God*, 78.

74. See the discussion of "The Elijianic Reading of Isaiah 61:1-2 in Jewish Tradition," in Poirier, "Jesus as an Elijianic Figure," 353-59. He writes that "when one reads [the passage] through the lens of first-century assumptions and exegetical complexes . . . this passage from Isaiah was understood to be very much about an Elijianic figure" (353). This insight illustrates the coherence of the passage. In fact, a

theme of reversal is also clearly apparent in the opening verses: the prophetic word from the anointed one is addressed to the condition of the poor. Their predicament is going to be *reversed*; they are promised release, recovery of sight, and freedom from oppression in line with the imagery of the Year of Jubilee in which all debts are also reversed.

A further dimension of the great reversal is seen in the contrast drawn between the particularity of the setting of the story and the inclusive tone of the message that emerges from it. It is a formal setting that parades the great determinants of Jewish identity: synagogue, Sabbath, Torah, chosen people. There may also be an implication that synagogue-centered religion, as typified by the Nazareth synagogue, was turning against Jesus. (It may be significant that in none of the Gospels do we hear again of Jesus entering a synagogue.) "However, these familiar forms affirming the identity and priority of the Jews are employed to reverse all expectations, proclaiming instead the inclusion of the Gentiles . . ."[75] The theme of reversal is also apparent as key words in the opening verses of the pericope are redefined by Luke to make clear the true status of Jesus. Although Jesus is rejected as a *prophet* in Nazareth (despite his self-identification in 4:21b as the fulfillment of 4:18–19) he is at least the equal of Elijah and Elisha as he defines himself as the agent by whom the boundaries of God's *patris* ("homeland") are graciously extended. The twice-mentioned *aphesis* ("release") in 4:18 has its extension into the cleansing experienced by Naaman as he is *released* from leprosy. And with the widow there is a similar "*release*, of divisions between Jew and Gentile before God, as she and Elijah share in eating together."[76] The sharing of food points forward to the table fellowship that characterizes Jesus' attitude to "sinners" who were also seen as outside the covenant boundaries but whose status is reversed by

---

theological reading of the passage helps to demonstrate its *structural* unity contrary to the assumption of many historical-critical approaches that see the pericope as a pastiche from a number of sources. In other words, the pervasiveness of the Elijah theme points to the compositional unity of the whole pericope; see also ibid., 363. Elsewhere, Siker also argues persuasively that, as he puts it "[t]he reference to the Elijah/Elisha stories in 4:25–27 provides the interpretive key to the whole passage" (Siker, "'First to the Gentiles,'" 74).

75. Siker, "'First to the Gentiles,'" 84.
76. Ibid., 85; emphasis added.

Jesus himself. The "acceptable" (*dektos*) year of the Lord (4:19) shows itself as "unacceptable" persons—the marginalized Gentile widow and the impure Gentile leper—receive release; and the word has overtones of the lifting of burdens as Luke incorporates or alludes to Isa 58:6 in the rendering of Isa 61:1–2.

The theme of reversal also continues as Jesus appeals to narratives centered on Elijah and Elisha. At a time when Israel had many famished and many lepers, the two prophets are sent to Gentiles outside Israel's borders. An initial distinction is made in 4:23–24 between Nazareth (Jesus' own *patris*) and Capernaum as a rival—a contrast that is then amplified by the contrast between Jew and Gentile in the stories about Elijah and Elisha in which God's *patris* clearly includes Gentile lands. God's blessing in "the year of the Lord's favor" is not confined to the ancient borders of Israel. "Thus the Nazareth/Capernaum reversal anticipates the Jew/Gentile reversal."[77] Jesus points to unexpected reversals of status in keeping with the theme of reversal sounded in his appeal to Isaiah 61.[78]

A final and related dimension of the reversal theme is seen as the people of the Nazareth synagogue reverse their initial approval of Jesus (4:22b) when they realize that this prophet's message includes some kind of affirming acceptance of Gentiles.[79] Jesus appears to juxtapose Isaiah 61 with the Elijah and Elisha narratives to undermine a privileged traditional view of election in which judgment is reserved for those outside the elect community. Jesus, in his exegetical appeal to the Sidonian widow *and* the Syrian leper, rejects that axiom. For him, the poor, captive, blind and oppressed represent not religious "outsiders" but the needy ones whom God favors. For those who expected eschatological revenge on Gentiles, "Jesus' point—that when Elijah comes he will act as he had previously and will bless outsiders—would have been offensive indeed." This explains the violent reaction to Jesus' words. His

77. Ibid., 84.

78. Luke repeatedly draws attention to such reversals. For him they are a significant indicator of the presence of the Kingdom; see, for example, Luke 1:52; 5:1–11, 12–16, 17–26, 27–32; 7:1–10; 14:7–14, 16–24; 15:25–32; 16:19–31; 18:9–16; 19:1–10.

79. Although, as Howard Marshall points out, "Luke 4:22 is ambiguous as to whether there is admiration of Jesus or the sort of amazement that is inherently incredulous" (*New Testament Theology*, 133).

hearers are greatly offended by his rejection of their understanding of the Isaiah text.[80]

The reversal leads to aggression and attempted murder; the long human history of religious rejection and violence is illustrated, not for the last time, on Palestinian soil. A link with the contemporary world might also note the continuing way in which notions of difference can and occasionally do lead to attempts at a range of coercive behaviors—even if there is no *necessary* connection between religious truth-claims and aggressive attitudes.[81] The considerable emphasis upon divinely initiated reversal has important interfaith implications. It identifies as important a number of transferable qualities including humility and a willingness to identify with and not to denigrate the poor and the marginalized; and it certainly requires the renunciation of all forms of religious or religiously linked coercion. The examples Jesus cites contain a message that is surprising and even disturbing to his hearers: the salvation of God is open to a range of outsiders, while insiders are left out. A Gentile woman and a Jewish prophet eat together: an example and a foreshadowing of the new eschatological age characterized as it is by the kind of surprising reversals signaled by the opening verses of the passage. The theme of reversal offers warning (and even reprimand) to those whose attitudes today display indifference to the faith of "outsiders" or whose self-assured confidence attempts triumphantly to exclude or denigrate or coerce others.

The Exclusion of Vengeance and the Sounding of a Note of Universality across Two Testaments

The two stories deployed by Jesus are examples to Israel of a sovereign display of Yahweh's universal compassion. The message of hope in Isaiah 61, originally intended to console returned exiles, is exegeted by Jesus as good news of reversal for *all* who are oppressed; it becomes a message of universal hope. Jesus omits the reference to the divine vengeance that follows in Isa 61:2b and it is often suggested that it is

---

80. Sanders, "From Isaiah 61 to Luke 4," quote from 65.

81. On the possible links between religion, mission and violence, see Kirk, *Mission under Scrutiny*, chs. 6 and 7.

this deliberate removal of any reference to a day of divine judgment on Gentiles that infuriates his Jewish hearers (Luke 4:28–30). The reason for the omission is contested among exegetes but is certainly in keeping with the Lukan theme that Israel's "enemies" (Gentiles, Romans, and also the marginalized and "sinners") are not to be excluded from God's salvation. If so, the "great reversal" theme continues as Jesus employs these examples as a direct challenge to the usual Jewish notion that the coming age would be characterized by Jewish vindication and rule, and Gentile punishment and subservience as the nations stream to Zion. The apparent attitude of Jesus contrasts strongly with, for example, the Qumran community, whose commentary (11QMelch) on the same text to which Jesus appeals (Isa 61:1–2) emphasizes judgment. The phrase "the day of vengeance of our God" (Isa 61:2b) is interpreted as eschatological judgment on all the enemies of Israel, including the Gentile nations. This very point may be reinforced by the reference to Naaman. As a military commander, he was one reason why "there were many widows in Israel in the time of Elijah" (Luke 4:25)—but this is not held against him. In fact the passage is a rather rare OT example of the love for an enemy that becomes a distinctive feature of Jesus' own message. The inclusion of this story suggests, therefore, that Jesus rejects the notion of eschatological vengeance on Israel's Gentile enemies; instead, he will offer healing and even inclusion to them.[82]

Further mention might be made of the theme of *patris* already discussed. Jesus' exegesis implies that God's land of blessing stretches beyond Israel's borders, as Jesus sees examples of divine blessing in the stories of Elijah and Elisha. Elijah, in being sent by Yahweh to Zarephath, is not only being directed to move outside of Israelite territory, but is led into what the hearers know to be a highly compromised and troubling location: the homeland of Ahab's new wife, the Sidonian princess Jezebel, the instigator of Baal worship. Elijah is led into the company of a pagan woman, a lowly and vulnerable widow in which his actions are suspect: he not only associates but also eats and lodges with the woman, who is nonetheless seen both to recognize and to accept a

---

82. The idea that Jesus deliberately intends to subvert the notion of eschatological vengeance towards Gentiles is cogently argued by Bosch in his *Transforming Mission*, 108–13.

prophet sent by God. Jesus' own journeys to the borders of Israel, and his encounters there, will demonstrate something similar; as his fame grows, people will come to hear him and to receive healing—they even come from Tyre and Sidon (Luke 6:17). Perhaps even more surprising is the disclosure that Jesus himself deliberately goes "to the district of Tyre and Sidon" (Matt 15:21).

In the passages mentioned in the previous paragraph, it is clear that God is at work in unlikely places and events. Yahweh commands Elijah to go to Sidon for "I have directed a widow there to supply you with food" (1 Kgs 17:9). Yahweh communicates his will to both Jewish prophet and Gentile widow; there is no doubt that "this Jewish-gentile meal in the midst of famine is arranged by God."[83] However, since for many contemporary readers of Scripture the currents of religious particularism and of soteriology swamp all others in their reading, it is helpful to consider the implications of Koskie's remark that one "theological way of reading would be to allow Scripture to change our questions and challenge us, bringing to our attention something other than the agenda we bring to it."[84] If religious believers are unable to recognize or even to consider the possibility of divine encounters beyond the covenant communities of faith (whether Jewish or Christian), is it because "the agenda we bring" to Scripture closes ears to it? Such an agenda might be generated by an over-preoccupation with soteriology (usually formulated only in individualistic categories).

There is an acute consciousness of the presence of other faiths in the contemporary world, and questions about the content and shape of an appropriate Christian response are increasingly heard. The example of Jesus in Luke 4 certainly implies a refusal to act from motives of vengeance or retaliation; it might even prompt a forgiving spirit, given the story of Naaman. The message of hope in Isaiah 61, originally intended to console returned exiles, is exegeted by Jesus as good news of reversal, freedom and Jubilee-release for *all* who are oppressed; it becomes a message of universal hope that excludes retribution. In other words,

---

83. Crockett, "Luke 4:25–27," 179.
84. Koskie, "Seeking Comment," 247.

Jesus clearly affirms that God's saving and healing presence is not confined to the ancient borders of Israel.[85]

From "the Margins of Scripture . . . to Center Stage": A Constructive Synthesis

In narrative terms, an earlier event in the scriptural text can assume new significance when, for example, it is reconsidered in a new context. This leads to a distinction between the "original meaning" of a text (derived from an understanding of authorial intent, historical setting, and original context) and the "full meaning" in a canonical sense; there is "new significance because of the way things turn out."[86] One example of this is the way in which occasional contact with Gentiles and Samaritans (in the OT, and in the Gospels) assumes greater significance in the canonical fullness of Scripture. As Scripture unfolds, the narrative and theological significance of the encounters enlarges. Luke seems to signal such an enlargement by redacting Luke 4 (with its appeal to encounters with Gentiles) into a significant position in his two-volume work. The theological significance of the canon, and canonical placement of material, have received considerable emphasis in recent theological exegesis but, included within this emphasis, is the call to resist the notion of a permanent canon within the canon. Instead, as Scalise notes, "at different moments in the history of the people of God, various parts of the canon are held up to challenge the . . . limitations of the traditions of the church. Although these parts of Scripture might formerly have been perceived as being on the margins of Scripture, they move to center stage to address the new issues of later centuries . . . ."[87] The encounter of Jesus with Gentiles and Samaritans provides an example of a "marginal" issue (the significance of Gentiles in the First Testament and the Gospels, and "outsiders" generally) that warrants elevation from a minor to a major key in the canonical mix—with this elevation signaled by Jesus in our passage in Luke 4.

---

85. The mention of Tyre and Sidon and, as we shall see, the encounters of Jesus with other Gentiles and Samaritans, points in a similar direction.

86. Leithart, *Deep Exegesis*, 46.

87. Scalise, "Hermeneutical Circle," 224. Scalise himself offers as an example the relevance of the book of Esther.

Theological exegesis also holds out the possibility of a certain kind of constructive synthesis: what Hays calls "the synthetic question of canonical coherence," by which he means that "theological exegetes will seek the big picture, asking how any particular text fits into the larger biblical story" so that "some sort of complex unity" is sought and articulated—rather than simply hearing a variety of biblical witnesses.[88] There is, for example, the problematical question of how Gentiles relate to the covenant people of God. The dominant answer in the OT and for Second Temple Judaism is framed in negative ways: the rejection of Gentile religion as idolatrous. But there is a minority position (seen in the affirmation of Melchizedek, Jethro, Naaman, Ruth, the Ninevites, and Job) that Jesus, by his appeal to the widow and Naaman, seems to embrace. The canonical fullness of the scriptural narrative enables the observation that Naaman's cleansing in the water of the Jordan, along with the story of Elijah and the widow, anticipates both the baptism of the Gentiles and a time when "Jews and gentiles may live, eat, and have fellowship together as one people."[89] It is, of course, the person of Jesus who offers the means by which this "complex unity" might be sought and found. He is the one who has "broken down the dividing wall, that is, the hostility between [Jew and Gentile]" (Eph 2:14; cf. 2:11–19); in him there is neither Jew nor Gentile (Gal 3:28). This is part of the "big picture" and the "complex unity" referred to by Hays.

Implications of an Exemplary Christology for a Religiously Plural World

One advocate of theological exegesis argues that "[t]he way in which the church witnesses, through its language and life, is perhaps the most important form of theological interpretation of the Bible. . . . The theological interpretation of Scripture is a distinct practice *of the church*, and hence it is regulated by the goods at which that practice aims."[90] One of those goods is faithful and appropriate Christian living in a religiously

---

88. Hays, "Reading the Bible," 13.

89. Crockett, "Luke 4:25–27," 182.

90. Vanhoozer, Introduction to *Theological Interpretation*, 19, 22; original emphasis.

plural world. One distinctive feature of the Bible understood as Scripture is that it is seen as authoritative for the common life and beliefs of the church: "its use . . . is essential to establishing and preserving the community's identity."[91] As this identity is challenged by religious plurality and religious pluralism, it is entirely appropriate that the Christian community turns again to the Bible as Scripture. In an instructive article that echoes this present volume's intentions, Steven Koskie argues that "to read the Bible as Scripture is to read as if it addresses us, the church. . . . Ultimately, it is about reading as if Scripture is addressed to the church that is reading right now."[92] Because the texts "being commented on are Scripture, then their presence in the Bible indicates that, whoever the original addressees . . . were, the church over time continued to sense itself addressed by God through them as part of the economy of salvation. . . . Or, to make an eschatological claim, the church at any point in history is always the native community of interpretation of its own Scripture."[93] So, what might it mean for the contemporary church, which is at one such point of history, to look for scriptural guidance as it faces religious plurality and a wider cultural pluralism? One possibility would be to embrace the exemplary Christology that emerges from Luke 4 (and from canonically subsequent encounters between Jesus and Gentiles and Samaritans). Discussion will return to this "imitation of Christ," to which surprisingly little appeal has been made by Christians entering interreligious encounters.

Although theological exegesis does enable a comprehensive means of understanding the biblical story, "this does not mean that every reading explicitly connects with an article of faith, for right confession is not the only reason the church reads Scripture. The church also reads for direction on how it lives out its life of witness in the world."[94] Luke 4:16–30 contains the beginnings of a theology of interreligious encounter, and some of Jesus' encounters with Gentiles and Samaritans (and teaching that relates to them) further develops such a theology. Jesus begins to model some contours of a distinctive approach to interfaith

91. Kelsey, *Proving Doctrine*, 89.
92. Koskie, "Seeking Comment," 243–44.
93. Ibid., 245.
94. Ibid., 247.

issues as he offers favorable comment on some Gentiles, and the passage does offer an example for the contemporary church of direction for "how it lives out its life of witness in the world" of multiple religious allegiances.

There are missional dimensions as well. The central component of Jesus' mission is identified as being sent: sent to proclaim good news, sent to proclaim freedom, sent to proclaim recovery of sight, sent to set free, sent to proclaim the Lord's favor. Moreover, Luke—as we have seen—is persuaded of Jesus' christological credentials. The focus of the missional intent is summed up in the opening verses of our passage as 'the poor' who are, for Luke, understood in "the holistic sense of those who are for any of a number of socio-religious reasons relegated to positions outside the boundaries of God's people."[95] The mission of Jesus also seems to include, or at least anticipates, Gentiles (and Samaritans) who fit this "outsider" category. A survey of theological exegesis by Michael Gorman concludes that it is made up of separate but interrelated tasks, of which "reflection on contemporary significance" is the fourth but from which a commitment to *mission* is absent. Concerning this absence of mission, Gorman goes on to note: "[t]heological interpretation must retain, or regain, its focus on the missional purpose of scriptural interpretation if it is to be truly ecclesial. Nothing is more fundamental to theological interpretation than its connection to the *missio dei*."[96] There has been considerable debate concerning the question of whether and what kind of Gentile mission Jesus might have envisioned. Nonetheless, for most commentators it is clear that Luke 4:16–30, because of its placement at the beginning of Jesus' public ministry, functions in a programmatic way for the Gospel of Luke and anticipates the Gentile mission that becomes a central dynamic in Acts. Moreover, the narrative perspective already mentioned has the further advantage of casting some aspects of Christology into a storied rather than an ideological framework, with consequential advantages in a postmodern and global setting. A narrative framework nicely accommodates the importance of

---

95. Green, *Gospel of Luke*, 211.
96. Gorman, "'Seamless Garment,'" 126, 128.

Introduction

witness as the church recounts—and "embodies" and "performs"[97]—the story of this Jesus.

The Character of the Triune God

Perhaps the most substantial claim made for theological interpretation is that, as Kevin Vanhoozer puts it, only such a reading does justice to the subject matter of Scripture—by which he means "God, the acts of God in history, the gospel . . . Theological interpretation of the Bible . . . is biblical interpretation oriented to the knowledge of God."[98] What is disclosed here in Luke 4 about the character of God? It is clear that the living God has a compassionate concern for the widow and Naaman who reside, geographically and spiritually, outside the borders of Israel. It is also apparent from the stories exegeted by Jesus that Yahweh has the ability to direct even the lives of such Gentiles. One distinctive feature of the Elijah narrative in 1 Kings 17 is "the remarkable way in which God is able to make himself known to persons outside of Israel, to command them, and to keep both the prophet and the gentile informed of what he is doing."[99]

Aspects of the Trinitarian character of God are also apparent in this passage. We have already noted that Luke is clearly persuaded of Jesus' messianic and soteriological status, his divine sonship, and his close connection with the Spirit. He is the one who lives and acts by the Spirit's presence and fullness (as the citation of Isa 61:1 affirms).[100] In the power of the Spirit, Jesus announces his coming as one sent by the Father; a christocentric approach is also, finally, a Trinitarian one.[101] The recent retrieval of a Trinitarian perspective in theology also reinforces the emphasis on mission that might otherwise be absent from theo-

97. Embodiment and performance are two images employed in the narrative theology already mentioned.

98. Vanhoozer, "Introduction," 20, 24.

99. Crockett, "Luke 4:25–27," 180.

100. See Luke 1:26–38; 3:21–22; 4:1–13, 14; 10:21. Luke "intends us to read the rest of his Gospel narrative with 'by the Spirit' as the proper modifier of all Jesus' mighty words and deeds . . ." (Fee, "New Testament and Kenosis Christology," 39).

101. For arguments to this end, see Padgett, "Canonical Sense of Scripture"; and Billings, *Word of God*.

logical exegesis; it enables mission to be situated within the Trinitarian being of God. In the words of David Bosch, "mission is not primarily an activity of the church, but an attribute of God. God is a missionary God."[102] The Father sends both Son and Spirit into the world; as John Flett comments, such an understanding of mission enables it to be seen not as attached to "the geographic expansion of the Christian faith from the West to the non-Christian world, but to its dogmatic origins, to the activity of the Father in sending his Son and Spirit."[103]

Theological interpretation, then, derives its essential characteristics from the *character* of the divine author/speaker who is disclosed on the pages of Scripture. Such interpretation has some distinctive characteristics: the author is the living God, and this author remains, by means of his Spirit, present to the reader. "The divine author of Scripture is perennially present and ubiquitously speaking."[104] Such a claim fits well with the presence and activity of the Spirit in Luke's narrative.

Conclusion: Christ as Exegete

A theological reading of the passage in Luke 4 that announces the mission of Jesus has fruitful implications for those who live in contexts of religious plurality. Such a reading notes that Jesus is heard affirming faith and humility in "outsiders" who model and foreshadow a new eschatological age characterized by a willingness to hear, respond to and not reject the prophetic word. A theological reading attends to themes of reversal and rejection, surprise and universality (illustrated by Gentile examples of faith and humility as God is shown to be able to make himself known to and even to command persons outside of Israel). It offers the beginnings of a theology of religion and the religions or, at least, the possibility of a shift in Christian attitudes towards people of other faiths. Such a theology might well enable a more fruitful inter-religious encounter than is sometimes found among those whose theology claims to be biblical.[105] From a theological reading of Luke 4:16–30

---

102. Bosch, *Transforming Mission*, 390.
103. Flett, *Witness of God*, 6.
104. Bowald, "Character of Theological Interpretation," 168.
105. Such a theology of divine initiative and human response might also want to

there are the possible beginnings of an exemplary, missional theology as the "marginal" position of Gentiles assumes a greater significance in the canonical mix and the flow of the narrative of Scripture. All of this is made clear by Christ's own exegesis.

In other words, in the church's continuing quest to be both christocentric and missional, neighborly and engaging with others, the exegesis of Christ in this passage is instructive. There is, of course, much more to be said about Christ and his mission in a multireligious world than our passage in Luke 4 discloses. But the "more" surely need not be *less* than is found here in the example of Jesus. Our reading of Luke 4 is a reminder that interpretive practices that allow Christian readers either to ignore (or only to comment critically on) people of other faiths are at odds with the example and commentary of Jesus himself. An exemplary Christology models not only divinely initiated reversal and universality but also affirms human responses as seen in faith, humility, and a willingness to hear and obey the prophetic word. All this is made clear because, as François Bovon puts it, "if the Spirit permits proper perusal of the Scripture today, it is because formerly Christ himself was an exegete, at Easter and even in the beginning." The divine purpose is disclosed as "Luke extols a reading illuminated by the Spirit and Christ."[106]

This is precisely the direction this book wants to take: to allow Christ to exegete our multireligious world so that his contemporary followers might also bring a word of insight, understanding and liberation.

---

appeal to both "general" revelation and even to a Logos Christology—but limitations of space preclude development along these lines.

106. Bovon, *Luke the Theologian*, 120.

1

Judaism and Gentiles: Jesus, Galilee, and Gospels

THE OVERALL INTENTION OF this volume is to argue that appeal to the example of Jesus can and does offer insight for Christian belief and practice in situations of religious plurality and even tension. But such an appeal is necessarily tied to the complex task of the retrieval of what Jesus said and did. Such a retrieval is, in part, an exercise in understanding the context in which he lived. Before a consideration of Jesus' meetings with and attitude to Gentiles and Samaritans, answers to two questions will set a necessary backdrop to the world in which Jesus lived—and add a helpful dimension to the encounters themselves. The first question is: "What was the attitude of the Judaism of the time towards non-Jews?"[1] One assumption of contemporary NT scholarship is that Jesus' teaching and actions are most likely to be best understood within his context as a Jew.[2] This is not to say that Jesus might not stretch or challenge some currents that flow within Second Temple Judaism—but that is the context that most reasonably ought to be scrutinized in order to understand him. The second question is: "What was the ethnic and religious mix in the Galilee of Jesus' day?" Having offered answers to these questions, discussion then moves to Jesus' interaction with Gentiles.

---

1. Almost all of what follows concerns Gentiles and "the nations." Attitudes towards Samaritans will be considered below in the first section of chapter 4.

2. See, for example, Markus Bockmuehl, "God's Life as a Jew."

Jewish Attitudes towards Gentiles[3]

Biblical Foundations, Historical Developments

Jewish attitudes toward Gentiles (Hebrew: *goyyim*) start with the Jewish self-understanding that "Jews are set apart from Gentiles and that this separation is of divine origin."[4] Yahweh chose Israel to be his own people and a holy nation. In return, Israel is required to worship God alone, to display loyalty to him alone (Exod 20:3), and to not follow Gentile practices. In the OT, circumcision is the covenant sign for this divinely chosen people (Gen 17:11)—a distinctive mark of their consecration to God (cf. Gen 17:1) and their exclusive covenant with him.[5] On the other hand, uncircumcision is symbolic of Gentile stubbornness, unbelief, and unholiness.[6] One consequence is that, as one writer puts it, "Gentiles as uncircumcision were indeed the people of rebellion and disobedience, and they were thus viewed with contempt."[7] However, the attitudes to

---

3. Although the word "Gentile" (*ethnē* in Greek) is very often capitalized in English, properly speaking it ought not to be—especially if that implies that Gentiles are the ethnic counterpart of "Jews." As Charles Cosgrove points out, the capitalization is "misleading if it gives the impression that Jews used *ethnē* as a proper ethnic name for non-Jews. Jews used the term *ethnē* at times of non-Jewish peoples generally and sometimes inclusive of themselves, inasmuch as they thought of themselves as an *ethnos*. Perhaps, in some usages, the term *ethnē* approaches the sense of a proper name as a counterpart to 'Jews,' but not as an *ethnicity* or *nationality* comparable to 'Jews,' 'Greeks,' 'Romans,' 'Scythians,' 'Ethiopians,' and so on. Another difficulty is that the English word 'Gentiles' invariably suggests a category of individuals, each of whom is a 'gentile.' But *ethnē* is, strictly speaking, the plural form of the noun *ethnos*, which means 'people' or 'nation.' As such, *ethnē* does not refer to a plurality of individual persons, 'gentiles'" (Cosgrove, "Did Paul Value Ethnicity?" 272, with helpful documentation; and see the whole of the section entitled "'Gentile' Is Not an Ethnicity"). However, the capitalization is very widely employed (for example, in the authoritative *Eerdmans Dictionary of Early Judaism*) and that convention is followed in this volume.

4. Gilbert, "Gentiles," 670.

5. For a survey of what he calls "the Primary History of Israel," ranging from Genesis to 2 Kings, and with an emphasis upon exclusivist covenant texts, see Wills, *Not God's People*, ch. 2.

6. See Lev 26:41; Deut 10:16; 30:6; Jer 6:10; 9:25–26; Ezek 23:30.

7. "Gentile" in Ryken, *Dictionary of Biblical Imagery*, 324; citing as evidence Judg 14:3; 15:18; 1 Sam 14:6; 17:26, 36; 2 Sam 1:20; 1 Chr 10:4.

Gentiles are not wholly negative. For example, Abraham is portrayed in the Torah as enjoying what one writer calls "normal relationships with diverse cultures and religions including Egyptians, Philistines and various West Semitic kingdoms."[8]

Two further important terms are the Hebrew words *nōkhri* and *zār*, which usually refer to non-Israelite "foreigners"—for example, to merchants and soldiers who come to Israel. The terms have an important psychological tone: "This is the most basic social, ethnic distinction that can be made—'not us' (rather like the Japanese term for foreigners, *gai jin*)."[9] In most passages, the terms have negative overtones. In the prophetic literature, the words are employed with reference to Israel's oppressors.[10] Such foreigners (and their nations) may cause Israel to fall into idolatry and other sins.[11] Israel is to avoid contact with them; in fact, after the return from exile, "those of Israelite descent separated themselves from all foreigners, and stood and confessed their sins and the iniquities of their ancestors" (Neh 9:2). In other words, only Yahweh, the God of Israel, may be worshiped in the land of Israel; worship by Jews of any foreign gods, is proscribed. A number of laws differentiate Jews from non-Jews: Gentiles are forbidden to eat the Passover offering (Exod 12:43), and Israelites are permitted to lend money with interest to Gentiles but not to other Israelites (Deut 23:20–21). In the presence of Gentiles, Jews retain not only circumcision as a mark of difference but also practices such as Sabbath observance, and synagogue building and associated practices. The book of Daniel even outlines the possibility that a Gentile king could venerate God and even be prepared to "become a Jew," according to Terence Donaldson.[12]

At the same time, the Israelites are to remind themselves that they once lived as aliens and that the Law requires care for the resident alien, who must not be oppressed (Exod 22:20–21; 23:9). Some laws apply both to Israelites and Gentiles living in the land, including the necessity

8. "Kiss of Heaven," 4.

9. "Gentile" in Ryken, *Dictionary of Biblical Imagery*, 324. *Gai jin* literally means "outside person."

10. See Isa 1:7; 62:8; Jer 5:19; Lam 5:2; Hos 7:9; 8:7; Obad 11.

11. See Isa 2:6; Jer 2:25; 3:13; Ezek 16:3; 44:7.

12. Donaldson, *Judaism and the Gentiles*, 30.

of material support (Num 15:15–16). Gentiles were vulnerable and their status in the land was insecure; nonetheless, "the sojourner is repeatedly pictured in the OT as the special recipient of God's favor, protection and benevolent concern. We find this in OT civil laws."[13]

In the Second Temple Era, new Jewish-Gentile encounters in the land of Israel itself led to diverse reactions. Texts from the intertestamental Pseudepigrapha display somewhat mixed attitudes towards Gentiles.[14] In the Jewish homeland, the need to adopt a stand toward other religions was one of the causes in the 160s BCE of the Maccabean uprising against a priestly regime eager to bring Judaism closer to the mainstream of Gentile (especially Hellenistic) cultural and religious practices and institutions (1 Macc 1:11–15).[15] Some Jews welcomed the changes but supporters of the revolt violently resisted the clearly intended removal of most barriers to assimilation with Gentiles. The new Hasmonean leaders established the principle that Judaism must resist imitation of other religions; they destroyed Gentile shrines (Josephus, *Ant.* 12:344), and required the conversion of resident Gentiles.

In the centuries immediately before Christ, some Jewish writers, in the words of Goldenberg, "sought opportunities to attack their neighbors' religions as stupid and corrupt beyond repair: 'the worship of idols not to be named is the beginning and cause and end of every evil'" (Wis 14:27). But Goldenberg also notes a more accommodating approach in other writings in the same period which explained "the best features of pagan religions as ultimately derived from the same source as the teachings of Moses, though of course the true Mosaic teaching

---

13. "Foreigner" in Ryken, *Dictionary of Biblical Imagery*, 300.

14. Apocalyptic literature (for example, *1 Enoch, Sibylline Oracles, Psalms of Solomon, 2 Baruch*) come mostly within the category of what Donaldson calls the "eschatological participation" of Gentiles, whereas apologetic works tend to display what he calls "sympathization, conversion, and ethical monotheism" (for example, *Letter of Aristeas, Joseph and Aseneth*). See also Donaldson, *Judaism and the Gentiles*, chs. 3 and 4.

15. There are a number of interpretive challenges in 1 and 2 Maccabees to an understanding of the precise distinctions between Judaism and Hellenism; there may a difference in attitude between 1 and 2 Maccabees with only 2 Maccabees maintaining a strong contrast between Judaism and a Hellenism that is not wholly bad. For a helpful discussion, see Wills, *Not God's People*, ch. 4.

as preserved by Israel was free of the many defects to be found in these other versions."[16] Nonetheless, the dominant attitudes are derived from deeply felt issues of self-understanding as Jewish identity is defined over against Gentile otherness. There are what Philip Esler calls "fundamental notions of differentiation between Israelite and non-Israelite which it was the whole purpose of the Mosaic law to preserve."[17]

A Certain Ambivalence toward Gentile Religious Practices?

However, even within the biblical text it seems that attitudes toward Gentile religious practices vary widely.[18] In the Torah, there is the apparently clear statement that within their own lands Gentiles are not only allowed but in fact are expected by God to worship their own gods (the heavenly bodies) if they wish (Deut 4:19). But other currents of thought (mostly from the exilic period and later, and prompted by an understanding that Yahweh was the one, true God) mock Gentiles for their worship of idols (notably Isa 44:6-20). From these two apparently divergent currents of thought, Goldenberg concludes that it is not clear whether other nations may be left alone to maintain their own religious traditions, even though it "is taken for granted that no Israelite may take part in the religious practices of outsiders; on this point the Scriptures are fiercely unanimous."[19]

In the Second Temple Period this ambivalent attitude continued. On the one hand there is an abundant literature that ridicules and condemns Gentile worship as vain and foolish idolatry and asserts that Gentile religious beliefs also display themselves in "perverse acts, including murder, theft, licentiousness, infanticide, and cannibalism. . . . Gentiles display ignorance of God, are prone to violent and licentious behavior, and pose a physical danger to Jews."[20] An example is found

---

16. Goldenberg, "Pagan Religions," 1015. Wisdom is usually dated in the first century BCE.

17. Esler, "Jesus and the Reduction," 341.

18. "The Scriptures of ancient Israel express a variety of opinions with respect to the religious traditions of other peoples" (Goldenberg, "Pagan Religions," 1015).

19. Ibid.

20. Gilbert, "Gentiles," 671.

in Jubilees: ". . . keep the commandments of Abraham, your father. Separate yourself from the gentiles, and do not eat with them . . . because their deeds are defiled, and all their ways are contaminated, and despicable, and abominable" (Jub 2:16). But, on the other hand, there are also more tolerant Jewish texts that acknowledge both that some individual Gentiles can be recognized as righteous and worthy of respect and also that a certain legitimacy can be attached to Gentile worship. This is especially true of diaspora Judaism where the LXX translates Exod 22:27 (LXX: 22:28), whose meaning in Hebrew is an injunction against blasphemy, as "Do not speak ill of gods," translating the Hebrew *elohim* ("gods") as a plural that forbids criticism of Gentile deities. Within Palestine itself, Josephus is found acknowledging the permissibility of Gentiles worshiping their own gods (*Ant.* 4.207; *Ag. Ap.* 2.237).

Gentiles and Ritual Purity

Another way of describing the Jew/Gentile (or Israelite/alien) dyad is in terms of purity/impurity. As Christine Hayes puts it in an important study, "in ancient Jewish culture, the paired terms 'pure' and 'impure' were employed in various ways not only to describe but also to inscribe sociocultural boundaries between Jews and Gentiles."[21] However, the traditional conclusion (that ancient Jews considered Gentiles to be impure and that Gentiles imparted impurity to all people and objects that they were in contact with) has been modified in the past decade or so by Jonathan Klawans[22] and Hayes herself. Hayes, for example, begins her volume with a close analysis of the relevant biblical material and from it concludes that three distinct modes of impurity existed.[23] The first is ritual impurity (removable by cultic procedures but *not* applicable to Gentiles except for corpse impurity). The second is moral impurity; although not contagious it is applicable to Gentiles (and is rectifiable by behavioral reformation). The third is genealogical impurity: the idea that Gentiles are intrinsically profane by comparison with the stringent

21. Hayes, *Gentile Impurities*, 3.
22. See his *Impurity and Sin*.
23. See the discussion of "Gentiles and the three modes of impurity" in Hayes, *Gentile Impurities*, 19–34.

portrayal by Ezra (see, especially, Ezra 9) and Nehemiah of Israel as a holy seed; such impurity is impermeable. Hayes and Klawans draw a distinction between ritual impurity and moral impurity (dealt with, respectively, in Leviticus 12–15 and 18–26) and it is only moral impurity which cannot be transferred by contact that could be ascribed to Gentiles—with the exception of corpse impurity (Num 19:10) and the eating of animal carcasses (Lev 17:15–16). In other words, with the possible exception of the Essenes / Qumran community, Gentiles are not thought to be ritually impure in the Biblical and Second Temple Eras; claims to the contrary are liable to be but "a volley in the internal cultural wars of first-century Judaism."[24]

Nonetheless, what Hayes calls "cultural wars"—or what others see as embedded traditional practice—does help to explain the range of Jewish attitudes to Gentiles. Genealogical impurity is particularly profound; it is an impurity intrinsic to a nationality and cannot be cleansed through conversion or assimilation. This idea is maintained and further developed at Qumran (see 4QMMT) and in Jubilees; its proponents, according to Hayes, prohibit and polemicize against intermarriage and are intolerant of any form of conversion. Such an attitude helps explain Jewish concerns about the conversion of Gentiles and social relations with them—as we shall now see.

Proselytes and Conversion

Some Gentiles can and do become members of Israel. Rahab the prostitute (Josh 2:8–13),[25] and the inhabitants of Gibeon who want to avoid the fate of Jericho and Ai (Joshua 9), join Israel. Ruth the Moabite comes to live in Israel, and Uriah the Hittite fights in David's army and follows Jewish purity laws while maintaining his non-Israelite ethnic identity (2 Sam 11:6–13). All these appear to become full members of the people of Israel. In the later Diaspora, some individuals are attracted to aspects of Jewish life and join local Jewish communities.[26] "It appears that such

24. Hayes, *Gentile Impuritiess*, 196.

25. For an interesting discussion of Rahab as an "Israelite theologian," see Gillmayr-Bucher, "'She Came to Test Him,'" 146–48.

26. And perhaps in Israel if the centurion whose servant is healed by Jesus is a proselyte or "God-fearer."

proselytes were numerous; Jewish writings make frequent reference to them, and Roman authors of the first two centuries CE deplore their widespread presence with equal frequency."[27] Gilbert adds: "Jews by and large held a positive attitude towards Gentiles who wished to join the Jewish people as converts. . . . Jews also welcomed Gentiles who engaged Judaism and Jewish communities through less formal relationships. Often designated as God-fearers, such persons might participate in synagogue or festival activities and were honored for their contributions to the Jewish community."[28]

A recent study by Michael Bird concludes that Second Temple Judaism did attract proselytes and did facilitate the conversion of Gentiles who wanted to convert to Judaism, much to the irritation and contempt of some Greek and Latin authors. Nonetheless, this possibility ought not to be described in missional terms since the role of Israel, the Torah, and the synagogue was never directed unequivocally towards Gentile recruitment.[29] Terence Donaldson's extensive survey also concludes that there is little evidence of an active mission of Jews to create an interest in Israel's God among Gentiles; Jewish initiative in Gentile conversions was "a response to a prior interest in Judaism on the part of the Gentiles."[30]

Interactions between Jews and Gentiles

Alongside their distinctive religious beliefs and practices, Jews in the Second Temple Era remain an *ethnos* with a range of everyday social relationships with Gentile neighbors—relationships that often include tolerance, respect, and cooperation. "Jews were educated in the gymnasium, attended performances in theater, relaxed in bath houses, engaged in business transactions with Gentiles, and worked in shops alongside them."[31] Nonetheless, as Goldberg points out, somewhat later rabbinic

27. Goldenberg, "Pagan Religions," 1016.
28. Gilbert, "Gentiles," 672.
29. Bird, *Crossing over Sea and Land*.
30. Donaldson, *Judaism and the Gentiles*, 492. Cf. Schnabel, "Israel, the People of God," 38.
31. Gilbert, "Gentiles," 671, though this attitude is more prominently found in the Diaspora and the Hellenized regions of Palestine.

law "contains many restrictions on Jewish use of Gentile foodstuffs but also acknowledges that the real aim of such rules was to prevent excessive contact with Gentile women."[32] This is because one major concern in relations with Gentiles is marriage. The Torah forbids marriage with certain specified peoples because of concern that idolatry would follow (Exod 34:16) and, at the beginning of the Second Temple Period, Ezra advocates a general prohibition against marriage with Gentiles (Ezra 9–10). The later Second Temple Era generally consolidates and expands the principle of *amixia* (separation from non-Jews), including the refusal to eat with Gentiles.[33] This principle of separation is a partial reason for the tensions of later centuries.[34]

Given the range of attitudes to purity already noted, it is not surprising to find such attitudes to conversion and marriage. It follows that, as Hayes also demonstrates, Second Temple Era Jews exhibited widely varying attitudes towards intermarriage and conversion—the two processes by which group boundaries might be crossed. These diverse views of the permeability of the Jewish–Gentile boundary through intermarriage or conversion, deriving in turn from diverse conceptions of Gentile impurity and Jewish identity, contribute to the rise of sectarianism in Second Temple Judaism, and to the separation of the early church from what would later become rabbinic Judaism.[35]

Rabbinic Perspectives

Concerning the relationship of later rabbinic teaching to the first-century CE era, Goldenberg warns that "rabbinic opinions cannot

---

32. Goldenberg, "Pagan Religions," 1016.

33. See the examples and references cited by Gilbert, "Gentiles," 671–72.

34. "Terrible explosions of violence in the first and second centuries CE led to the obliteration of Alexandrian Jewry, once the jewel of the Hellenistic Diaspora. In Judea, two huge uprisings against the Roman Empire, in 66–70 CE and 132–135 CE, left the Jerusalem Temple in ruins and the country devastated" (Goldenberg, "Pagan Religions," 1016). For a study from the perspective of historical sociology that concludes that relations between Jews and Gentiles showed a remarkable but not very positive structural durability (with occasional genuine symbiosis but more usually conflict and hostility) see Cahnman, *Jews and Gentiles*.

35. From an abstract of Hayes, *Gentile Impurities*.

simply be projected onto the Second Temple period" but he also adds that "in all likelihood they do represent a crystallization of earlier attitudes." To the principled rejection of Gentile religious practices by the later prophets and the Maccabees, later rabbinic thinking adds the pragmatic conclusion that nothing of value could be drawn from Gentile religions whose ubiquitous idolatry separates Gentiles from Jews. Although some rabbinic texts affirm that some Gentiles are honest and even admirable there is, nonetheless, what Goldenberg calls "much hostile polemic, stressing the absurdity and the uselessness of idol-worship. One striking passage takes for granted that Gentiles overall, since they live without effective religious restraint, are prone to violence and depravity..."[36]

Gentiles in Eschatological Perspective

Many biblical texts (especially from the prophets) envisage a future universal recognition of Yahweh that includes the Gentile nations as well as the chosen people.[37] At times there is the additional promise that "*then they will know that I am the Lord*" (see Ezekiel especially; quote from 47:22). One key role given to the Servant of the Lord is that he will be a light for the Gentiles and bring justice and salvation to the nations.[38] The prophets also see a pilgrimage of the Gentile nations to Mount Zion, "the mountain of the Lord,"[39] as they come to present themselves at the temple in Jerusalem.[40] Gary Gilbert sums up Second Temple Era texts that build on this eschatological perspective as follows: "The attitude persists throughout the Second Temple period (Tobit 14:6; Sirach 36; *T. Levi* 14:4; *Ps. Sol.* 17:34). As Jews developed more grandiose eschatological scenarios, the status of Gentiles becomes more of an issue. On the one hand, *Jubilees* expresses the idea that salvation belongs only to the Jews, whereas the *Testament of Abraham* emphasizes that ethi-

---

36. Goldenberg, "Pagan Religions," 1016.
37. See, for example, Isa 2:2–4; 66:18–20; Joel 2:28–32.
38. See Isa 42:1, 6; 49:6; 51:4–5; 52:10; 61:1–2.
39. See, for example: Isa 2:2–4; 25:6–8; 66:20; Jer 3:17; Mic 4:1–3; Zech 8:3, 20–23; 14:16–19.
40. Isa 56:6–7; 66:23; Mic 4; Zech 14.

cal behavior rather than covenantal affiliation establishes the basis for divine judgment."[41]

Conclusions: Balancing the Particular and the Universal

The eschatological texts mentioned in the section above are a reminder that, while God's electing purposes are seen to center on Israel, the wider vision of the Hebrew Scriptures also includes the other nations of the world. This means that discussion of the Jewish appraisal of Gentiles needs to be expanded, and balanced, by this further universal dimension. Alongside Israel's usual claims of Abraham as its exclusive ancestor is the statement that Abraham will be a "father of many nations" (Gen 17:4–6), and God intends him to be a blessing to "all nations on earth," and not to Israel alone.[42] The universal dimension is found, to some extent at least, in the wisdom literature and among the prophets.[43] This eschatological perspective does somewhat blur the line between Jew and Gentile. Nonetheless, much of the universalism derives from assumptions of a religio-moral superiority based on the possession of the divinely revealed law. It is, argues Charles Cosgrove, a "universalism tinctured with religio-ethnocentrism: Jews are the superior people who possess the superior law and thus become guardians of the truth for the world and benefactors to humankind." Other Jews, however, expect some blessing for the nations as a result of Israel's final vindication and exaltation by God; they express themselves "in universalistic terms that were simultaneously ethnocentric."[44]

Three fairly recent studies have made aspects of this particular-universal dynamic clearer. Frank Spina's *The Faith of the Outsider: Exclusion and Inclusion in the Biblical Story* discusses stories in the biblical narrative that show how God's apparently exclusive election of Israel intends an inclusive purpose for others. He shows that, at times,

41. Gilbert, "Gentiles," 672.
42. Gen 12:3; 18:18; 22:18; 26:4; 28:14.
43. See, for example, the summary and discussion by Bruce Malchow, "Wisdom's Contribution to Dialogue" and "Prophetic Contribution to Dialogue."
44. Cosgrove, "Did Paul Value Ethnicity?," 276; he offers extensive documentation for his assertion.

non-Jews have decisive roles in the divine plan of salvation. The first five chapters of *The Faith of the Outsider* contrast "outsiders," who are apparently accepted by God, with "insiders," who are rejected or criticized by God.[45] Spina's claim is that acceptance into the covenant community is dependent not on ethnic identity as an Israelite or Jew, but upon spiritual insight and faithfulness to God and God's will. The notion of election does not intend to denigrate or devalue the non-Jewish peoples of the world but intends their benefit.

Perhaps even more helpful for our overall theme is Terence Donaldson's *Judaism and the Gentiles: Jewish Patterns of Universalism* in which he reproduces and analyzes all the relevant texts from the Hellenistic period through to the end of the second Jewish rebellion (135 CE) that relate to Gentile sympathizers, proselytes, "God-fearers," and ethical monotheists. He points out that Jews are unable to tell their story without reference to the Gentile nations and this, in turn, leads to questions about the relationship between these nations and the God who had created them. Donaldson's study analyzes the development of patterns of universalism in the Second Temple Era as Gentiles are attracted to Jewish communal life, religious observance and theological beliefs. He finds that some Jews are able to envisage and even to welcome a place for such Gentiles. Donaldson follows a consensus in biblical studies correcting previous scholarship that had labeled ancient Judaism as "particularistic" in contrast to Christianity's universalism. According to Donaldson, "Judaism was in its own ways just as "universalistic" as was Christianity—indeed, in some ways even more so."[46] He defines "universalism" in the context of contemporary religious dialogue as "approaches that ascribe legitimacy to the religious 'other' without requiring conversion," while a particularist religion stipulates conversion as "the only option" (4). Concerning Gentile sympathizers toward Judaism, Donaldson argues that the available evidence suggests that Gentiles who engaged in monotheistic worship, who recognized the divine origin of Israel's law, and who adopted a Jewish way of life

---

45. Esau is contrasted with Jacob, Tamar with Judah, Rahab with Achan, Naaman with Gehazi, and Jonah with the Ninevites.

46. *Judaism and the Gentiles*, 1; further page numbers are indicated in the paragraph.

(in what areas remains undetermined) fulfilled "everything that God expected of them as Gentiles" (481).[47]

A third relevant volume is Joel Kaminsky's *Yet I Loved Jacob: Reclaiming the Biblical Concept of Election*.[48] In it, Kaminsky discusses and extends another way of looking at the Jew/Gentile binary: the categories of elect and non-elect. In chapters 7 and 8 of his volume, Kaminsky develops his distinctive understanding of election by means of three distinct categories: the elect, the non-elect, and the anti-elect. He concludes that the Hebrew Bible's doctrine of election does not construct a binary opposition between the elect and all others but a triad. According to Kaminsky, the elect are those chosen by God—God's special people, the nation of Israel (or in some late books of the Hebrew Bible and in some apocalyptic works from the Second Temple Period, the faithful remnant of Israel). "The anti-elect are those few groups who are deemed to be enemies of God and whom Israel is commanded to annihilate": the Canaanites and the Amalekites (perhaps also the Midianites).[49] The non-elect are everyone else—in fact, most of humanity. This is where the majority of non-Israelite people are to be found: those who were not chosen but who "were always considered fully part of the divine economy," those whom "Israel was to work out her destiny in relation to . . . even if in separation from them."[50]

Distinguishing between the non-elect and the anti-elect becomes the primary challenge for Kaminsky, and he seeks to demonstrate that, although there are indeed difficult passages regarding the anti-elect, their fate is not shared by all non-Israelites. The non-elect have a responsibility to God *and to the chosen*, while Israel too must work out its status in relation to the non-elect. The anti-elect do not enter the divine economy but are rare examples of people deemed enemies of

---

47. Donaldson's argument for a universalist perspective is both appealing and persuasive. Nonetheless, as a Jewish academic reviewer concedes, "the Hebrew Bible, which, although it contained the seeds of universalism, also reflected a reality in which religion was too firmly embedded in family, clan, or nation to allow for much universalistic movement" (Schwartz, review of *Judaism and the Gentiles*).

48. Parts of what follow draw on reviews of the volume to be found in *Review of Biblical Literature*, March 2008.

49. *Yet I Loved Jacob*, 109, 112.

50. Ibid., 109.

God—those doomed for destruction. Many non-elect characters (and, on rare occasions, nations) of the Hebrew Bible feature positively, or seem to know Israel's God intimately, responding appropriately to him (e.g., King Abimelech, Rahab, perhaps Balaam, the people of Nineveh). Some critics reject the biblical notion of election as particularistic and ethnocentric, and they contrast it to the universal, inclusivist streams of biblical thought. But Kaminsky argues that the universalist tendency is consistently the product of the same biblical authors who celebrate particularism. In fact, the inclusive tendencies are consequences of the very doctrine of election these authors articulate.

These three discussions are a reminder that the boundary between supposed particular and universal outlooks among Jews is somewhat blurred, or porous.[51] Jewish opinion concerning Gentiles is, by the end of the Second Temple Era, usually cautious and often negative, although it is sometimes affirmative, either when an eschatological perspective is added, or as the result of accommodating cultural or theological tendencies. How this range of attitudes translates into what is found in the Galilee of the time of Jesus is the issue to which discussion now turns.

Herodian Galilee: Hellenized and Romanized?

"You can take the Gospel out of Galilee, but you cannot take Galilee out of the Gospel."[52]

The remainder of this chapter is an attempt to provide a contextual framework to help understand the Galilean context of Jesus. That context might be seen as historically determined. But it is also geographical in origin—which adds a theological reason given that God created the material world that, in turn, partly defines this regional Galilean context of the Jesus of history. "The more accurately we understand the historical setting of 1st-century Palestine, the more precise and faithful will be our understanding of what [Jesus] taught, did, and suffered."[53]

---

51. A fourth volume could also have been considered: Lohr, *Chosen and Unchosen*.
52. Bockmuehl, review of *Jesus, a Jewish Galilean*, 531.
53. Hays, "Reading the Bible," 12. Francis Watson (along with many others) argues that in "all four Gospels, Jesus' story unfolds within a consistent set of geographical

Jesus and the Religions

Some eighty percent of the Synoptic Gospel narratives about Jesus are situated in Galilee.[54] The canonical Gospels are the oldest and most detailed sources about Jesus and, for all their undoubted theological and apologetic interests and motivation, they clearly intend to embed the life and ministry of Jesus in a specific geographical and cultural milieu.

One reason for the fairly detailed discussion of Galilee that follows is the longstanding recognition that geographical references within Scripture often have much greater significance than their utility in marking places and events. References to mountains, plains, seas, and deserts convey symbolic meaning as well. Jerusalem, for example, is more than an urban center of commerce and habitation, and Galilee is more than a region. The symbolic and theological significance of such places has been underscored in twentieth-century NT studies. One recent example is Paul Hertig, whose volume *Matthew's Narrative Use of Galilee in the Multicultural and Missiological Journeys of Jesus* draws particular attention to the significance of Galilee. Matthew's Gospel, with its canonically significant first place in the NT, opens the ministry of Jesus in Galilee (4:14–16 where he cites Isa 9:1–2 the dawning of light [meaning salvation] on Galilee), and ends with the Great Commission on a mountain in Galilee (28:16–20). In other words, Hertig recognizes that Galilee is not merely a geographical marker for the region in which much of Jesus' ministry took place; "Galilee" has a much deeper symbolic and theological meaning.[55] This setting is "not a secondary 'framework' that can be ignored, but part of the 'historicizing tendency' of the first stories told by Jesus."[56] The setting is "Herodian" Galilee, by which is meant the region of Galilee during the reign of Herod the Great (37–4 BCE) over both Judaea and Galilee and his son Antipas' (simply called "Herod" in the Gospels) rule over Galilee, until 39 CE. Occasional refer-

---

and historical coordinates," including places such as Galilee and figures such as Herod Antipas. He concludes that "research has shown that beyond doubt coordinates such as these anchor the story of Jesus in empirical reality" (*"Veritas Christi,"* 108).

54. The Fourth Gospel does, of course, know of and refer to Galilee, but its focus (presumably for theological reasons), is on Jerusalem/Judea.

55. Not, of course, that understanding symbolically presented issues is easy; see the warnings sounded by N. T. Wright in ch. 9 ("Symbol and Controversy") of his *Jesus and the Victory of God*.

56. Schröter, "Jesus of Galilee," in Charlesworth and Pokorný, *Jesus Research*, 40.

ence will be made to "early Roman" Galilee to refer to the period up to but not beyond the first revolt (66–70 CE). The studies surveyed usually use either of these descriptors or something like "Galilee in the time of Jesus."

The notable scholar of Galilean studies Seán Freyne contends that Jesus scholars have attended too much to Jesus' history (his time) and not enough to his place. From a methodological point of view he stresses the importance of Jesus' Jewish context—especially Jesus as a "Jewish Galilean."[57] According to Freyne, "Jesus' actual career in Galilee informed the early Christian proclamation about him to a far greater extent than is often recognized in modern efforts to separate him from the earliest memories that the gospel writers have given us."[58] Most of the encounters of Jesus with Gentiles take place near or in the region of Galilee and his comments about them are made from a Galilean setting. So, before looking at what the Gospels themselves say about Jesus (and his relationship with Gentiles), it is important to ask, "What do we know about Galilee and its ethos?" The past few decades have seen a rich proliferation of studies of the region and these studies, ranging across fields as diverse as archaeology, political and social-science studies, socioeconomics and historical sociology, have contributed greatly to a more substantial understanding of the religio-cultural milieu of Galilee than has been possible on the basis of the literary sources alone. The "quest for the historical Galilee"—which has at times been strongly polarized[59]—has centered on two major debates: the extent to which Herodian Galilee was Hellenized (and Romanized) and the kind of Judaism found there.[60] To frame the discussion in terms of two questions: What was the extent of Jesus' encounter with Gentiles? And what was the kind of Judaism that might have framed Jesus' reaction to such

57. *Jesus, a Jewish Galilean*, ch. 1, esp. pp. 7–9. Elsewhere, Freyne describes Jesus' Galilean ministry as "an integral part" of the Christian proclamation (Freyne, "Jesus in Context," 17).

58. "Jesus in Context," 18.

59. Paula Fredriksen describes "the quest for the historical Galilee" as "fraught" and "contentious" (*Jesus of Nazareth*, 156).

60. For a more comprehensive summary and analysis of these studies see Robinson, "A 'Fifth Gospel' Less Torn and More Legible?: On Recent Attempts to Retrieve Herodian Galilee," in Church and Walker, *Gospel and the Land*, 86–102.

encounters?[61] The results of this research is discussed and followed by an attempt to draw out some implications from this research for the study of Jesus and the canonical reports about Gentiles and Samaritans from Galilee and surrounding regions that Jesus is reported as meeting and speaking about.

How Hellenized (and Romanized) Was Herodian Galilee?

How widespread was Gentile presence and influence, especially Greek and Roman, in the Galilee of Jesus' time? During the middle decades of the twentieth century (and in some notable earlier examples) there was speculation that Galilee was both ethnically diverse and significantly Hellenized and partly Romanized as the result of successive waves of Gentile influence, both Greek (following Alexander's conquest) and Roman (following the conquest by Pompey of Jerusalem in 63 BCE), eventually leading to the proxy rule of Palestine by the Romans through the Herodian client kings. These influences supposedly rendered Galilee only marginally Jewish or even, in the description of Funk, "semi-pagan."[62] In 1988 and 1993, Burton Mack could confidently describe Galilee as "complex in cultural mixture" and with an "open" attitude towards cultural exchange between traditional Jewish villagers and more recent arrivals of Hellenized Jews; the belief of most Galileans was not Jewish in ethos but a rather vague monotheism.[63] Daniel Sperber can confidently assert that "Roman-period cities in the Land of Israel were pagan both in spirit and population." While "the residents of these cities

---

61. Discussion in chapters 4 and 5 below will ask the same questions of his encounter with and comments on Samaritans.

62. Funk, *Honest to Jesus*, 58; repeated at p. 189 as "a largely pagan environment." Batey, in *Jesus and the Forgotten City*, also argues for the extensive Hellenization of Galilee that spread from Sepphoris in particular. (See also his "Sepphoris and the Jesus Movement.") For a summary of these assertions of a Gentile Galilee, see Chancey, *Myth of a Gentile Galilee*, ch. 1, "Images of Galilee's Population in Biblical Scholarship" (especially pp. 11–16, "Before the Digs"). Seán Freyne also criticizes such "distorted approaches" with their reductionist and sometimes anti-Semitic biases; see the summary in his "Jesus in Context," 18–22.

63. Mack, *Myth of Innocence*, 62–63; *Lost Gospel*, 53. Chancey summarizes Mack's portrait as one in which "Galilee has only the thinnest of Jewish veneers" (*Myth of a Gentile Galilee*, 3).

may have basically derived from Semitic stock, . . . the 'official' religious milieu was certainly Hellenistic-Roman."[64] The notable NT scholar Martin Hengel believes that by the first century CE, "[m]any areas of Palestine had heavy concentrations of pagans." After a detailed survey, he concludes that from the middle of the third century BC, "all Judaism must really be designated 'Hellenistic Judaism' in the strict sense."[65] Gregory Riley claims that the Greco-Roman culture had a "pervasive" influence on Judaism and was "fundamental to the life and teachings of Jesus."[66] An evangelical writer in 2002 considers "the evidence for a considerable pagan population in Palestine continuously from the time of the Assyrian conquest onwards, and for Jewish assimilation of Hellenism in many forms, is overwhelming"—despite what he goes on to call "the refusal of Christian scholars for so many years to perceive the pervasive nature of Hellenistic influence in Judaism."[67] And, as recently as 2007, Arnal could write simply that "'Galilee of the Gentiles' supported a multiethnic populace with multiple social and cultural ties to a diverse range of urban centers."[68]

Typical of the supposed influence of Hellenism were centers such as Sepphoris, Tiberias, and Hippos (on a prominent hill on the eastern edge of the Sea of Galilee, and currently under excavation).[69] The renovated Sepphoris, a city with an estimated eight thousand to twelve thousand inhabitants, was set out on a typically Hellenistic grid with prominent civic markers and contained a spread of Greek features: aqueducts and baths, open spaces, basilicas, an acropolis, and the probable first phase of a sizeable theater. It became a very significant city: Sepphoris is mentioned more times in premodern Jewish literature

---

64. Sperber, *City in Roman Palestine*, 190. See also Arnal, "Galilee, Galileans," 517; Batey, "Sepphoris and the Jesus Movement."

65. See Hengel, *Judaism and Hellenism*, 14–37, 43–47, 86–88; quotes from 51, 104. Cf. the survey by Tcherikover of some thirty Hellenistic towns within Palestine that leads him to conclude that the cultural influence of Hellenism was pervasive (Tcherikover, *Hellenistic Civilization*, 90–116).

66. Riley, *One Jesus*, 64, 29.

67. Smillie, "'Even the Dogs,'" 79–80.

68. Arnal, "Galilee, Galileans," 517.

69. On Hippos, see the comments of Schuler, "Recent Archaeology of Galilee," 111–13.

than any other city apart from Jerusalem, and the Mishnah was codified there at the end of the second century.[70] Tiberias was newly built in 19 CE on the shores of Sea of Galilee; it had some six thousand to twelve thousand inhabitants and included a stadium. Such an understanding of Galilee greatly increases the likelihood of Jesus encountering Gentiles especially if, for example, he (and Joseph) were employed in the role of *tektōn* (skilled builder) in Sepphoris or Hippos or in other Gentile-related sites. These are the kinds of possibilities that lead an evangelical missiologist to write that "There is every possibility that Jesus was in frequent contact with non-Jews. . . . In Jerusalem, Judea, and the countryside surrounding the Sea of Galilee, it would be almost impossible for him to avoid them."[71]

However, it has more recently become clear that considerable caution should be exercised in such evaluations. Jonathan Reed laments what he calls "scholarly excesses." He is critical of descriptions of Sepphoris and Tiberias as highly urbane with "ridiculously high population sizes," a large proportion of Gentiles (including some cynic-styled philosophers), alongside a "parasitic role in ravishing the Galilean countryside."[72] A number of factors count against the thesis of a Hellenized Galilee populated with Gentiles and Jews who were less observant than those living further south in Judea. Even if the cultural impact of cities such as Sepphoris and Tiberias as a Hellenizing force is acknowledged, critics point out that Graeco-Roman style urbanization was only in its infancy under Antipas.[73] In his *Greco-Roman Culture and the Galilee of Jesus*, Mark Chancey employs standard archaeological criteria to demonstrate a clear contrast between the limited urbanization seen in a few urban centers and the continuing rural character of Galilean culture: "Hellenistic culture was the culture of cities, not villages, and Galilee as yet had no major cities . . ."[74]

---

70. In the time of Jesus, these population estimates, and a number of the urban features mentioned, had not yet been realized.

71. Glasser, *Announcing the Kingdom*, 217.

72. Reed, review of Jensen, *Herod Antipas in Galilee*, 403.

73. A balanced account of the actual influence of the two centers is found in Horsley, *Galilee*, 174–81.

74. Chancey, *Greco-Roman Culture*, 33.

Finally, mention must be made of the phrase "Galilee of the Gentiles" found in Matt 4:15. The description in Isa 8:23 of *galil ha-goyim* ("Galilee of the Gentiles/nations"[75])—cf. the LXX designation *Galilaia allophulōn* ("Galilee of the aliens," Joel 4:4; 1 Macc 5:15)—raises a number of issues and a variety of interpretive options.[76] Chancey in a chapter title refers to "Galilee and the Circle of Nations" and goes on to speak of Galilee as among the "district" of the nations.[77] Theissen and Merz describe Galilee as "a Jewish enclave" given the way in which it was surrounded by "Hellenistic city republics": Sidon, Tyre, and Ptolemais to the west and north, the ten-city state of the Dekapolis to the east, while to the south there lay Samaria whose center, Sebaste, "was a city with a Hellenistic stamp."[78] For some scholars, however, the phrase has been a factor in their religio-cultural definition of Galilee: what Freyne sums up as the view that the phrase has "an ethno-centric connotation that sees other ethnic groups as hostile, even perverted, from an Israelite perspective."[79] This includes the assertion that Galilee was only marginally Jewish (in effect, "Galilee containing a number of Gentiles").[80] However, the most satisfactory explanation seems to be that the phrase replicates the early experiences of the first settlers of the region, for whom the name Galilee denotes a potentially hostile or alien encirclement by Gentiles.[81]

---

75. Found as Isa 9:1 in English translations.

76. For example, it is unclear whether the phrase in 1 Macc is "an ethnic description or a polemical assertion" by the author (Freyne, "Galilee as Laboratory," 150). And then there is the question of whether it is intended to suggest some delimitation of the ministry of Jesus, or the opposite (corresponding to the universal extension of the gospel, which comes to clearest expression in the Great Commission of Matt 28:18-20; a reading favored by those who contend that the First Gospel should be read from the end to the beginning).

77. Chancey, *Myth of a Gentile Galilee*, ch. 4; quote from p. 170.

78. *Historical Jesus*, 170.

79. "Jesus in Context," 20.

80. See discussion in Freyne, "Galilean Jesus," 291.

81. See Freyne, *Galilee, Jesus*, 143–44; Reed, *Archaeology and the Galilean Jesus*, 51–52. In other words, this writer agrees with the growing consensus that most Galileans were descended from Jews who migrated north and settled in Galilee during the time of the Hasmonean expansion.

It seems reasonable to conclude, then, that Herodian Galilee was predominantly Jewish. Argument for a pagan Galilee is poorly supported by the literary evidence "and receives no confirmation from the archaeological explorations."[82] Some ambiguities and variations in the density, as it were, of the Jewishness of Galilee do remain. Nonetheless, the conclusion of scholars such as Chancey, Freyne and Reed is unanimous: Herodian Galilee was predominantly—perhaps even overwhelmingly—Jewish.[83]

Some Conclusions

A number of conclusions might be drawn from these recent attempts to retrieve Herodian Galilee. A fairly widespread consensus has emerged that interdisciplinary approaches—for example, a combination of archaeology and social scientific perspectives alongside the literary sources—have provided an enhanced methodology for the retrieval of Herodian and early Roman Galilee. As well as references in the Gospels, Josephus names forty-five Galilean villages and the Talmud refers to some sixty-three villages in Galilee. But subsequently, as Crossan puts it, "from Jewish literary texts, then, across almost one thousand five hundred years, nothing"[84]—meaning nothing new, that is, until the critical retrieval of Galilee from a range of material alongside literary sources offered new sources of information and new perspectives on older sources.

In particular, it is archaeology that has contributed substantially to a more objective reading of the cultural milieu of Galilee than has been possible on the basis of the literary sources alone. The archaeologi-

---

82. Freyne, "Galilee and Judaea," 41; in more detail: Freyne, *Galilee from Alexander*, 101–45; see also the discussion by Chancey, *Myth of a Gentile Galilee*, 118–19.

83. The evidence does seem to support the conclusion of Seán Freyne that a depiction of Herodian Galilee as only marginally Jewish can be "exposed for what it was and still is today, namely, the product of a nineteenth-century overemphasis on the Hellenized and therefore enlightened, it is claimed, ethos of the region, and the devaluing of Galilee's Jewishness . . ." (Freyne, "Galilean Jesus," 291). A similar conclusion is reached by Mark Chancey, "How Jewish Was Jesus' Galilee?" (and in his pointedly entitled *The Myth of a Gentile Galilee*).

84. Crossan, *Historical Jesus*, 15.

cal retrieval of Herodian Galilee increasingly confirms the picture by Josephus of it as essentially rural and village-centered in character; only a small proportion of the population lived in Sepphoris and Tiberias or other centers that might be called "urban" (and Hellenized to some extent).[85] The retrieval has strongly empirical foundations, is generally cumulative in its conclusions, and begins with questions generated by the material culture of Roman Galilee itself rather than starting with questions that arise from textual traditions. These recent studies offer the possibility of what might be called an "intertextual" hermeneutic as archaeology enhances what literary sources disclose in order to broaden interpretative horizons concerning Herodian Galilee.

Freyne offers a good example of this methodology. Although he concedes that drawing up "a coherent and plausible account of the overall ethos of the region is a . . . difficult and tentative exercise,"[86] he is also clear that the intensive archaeological investigation of Hellenistic and Roman Galilee has substantially verified and clarified understanding of the Jewish ethos of that period. Freyne writes that "[t]oo often still our historical investigations are based on ancient documents only, ignoring the alternative 'text' from below, which modern processual archaeology is able to offer us through its engagement with the social sciences." He goes on to add that "[l]istening to the alternative stories 'from below' that archaeology can tell us is one way of broadening further our interpretative horizons."[87]

Nonetheless, the provisionality of archaeological and historical findings should also be noted. Although Chancey is critical of analyses that overestimate or exaggerate the extent of Greco-Roman culture in Galilee, he also concedes that, like all studies based on archaeological data, the conclusions are provisional given "the haphazard nature of archaeological discovery, the randomness of survival, and the obliteration of earlier buildings by later construction."[88] Jens Schröter acknowledges

---

85. In the words of Horsley, "the Galilee is best understood as a traditional agrarian society with peasants living in relatively autonomous villages" (Horsley, *Galilee*, 189).

86. Freyne, "Galilee, Jesus," 581.

87. Freyne, "Galilee as Laboratory," 149, 164.

88. Chancey, *Greco-Roman Culture*, 224.

the importance of research into Galilee including the role of a growing mass of archaeological findings about the region. But he also adds a warning about the provisionality of conclusions drawn from the data. "Methodologically . . . this expansion of the source basis does not thereby entail overcoming the provisional and changing nature of historical reconstruction, leading to a supposedly more definite knowledge of the facts." Rather, "because the study of the past always takes place from the perspective of the present and leads to a better understanding of the present, it is something that always changes."[89] Nonetheless, he also points out that even if historical research does not lead to "unchanging certainties," it does allow for "probabilities that are oriented towards the source material and open to modification. Historical portrayals of Jesus, therefore, are also hypotheses about how things *could have been*. . . . The sources have a corrective function or . . . a 'right of veto.' They prohibit certain interpretations and can protect us from making mistakes, but they do not tell us what a story sketched out on a critical basis should look like."[90]

One further reason for the provisionality of archaeological and historical findings is that there is still no agreement over the precise definition of a number of key terms in the discussion—terms such as "ethnicity," "Jew," "Judean *Ioudaios*," "pagan," "Gentile," "village," and "city." There is, for example, no "clear theoretical idea (beyond population) about what constitutes a village or about the relation of local assemblages to elite material culture"—and this means that debates often remain at the level of unhelpful abstraction.[91] In fact, even the term "Galilee" is somewhat problematic. A survey by Ruth Vale of "Views of Galilee in the Literary Sources"[92] is able to illustrate the way in which the descriptions of "Galilee" in the intertestamental literature, in Josephus, and then in the Gospels and the rabbinic literature typically and primarily emphasize Galilee as "other." She concludes that, "in archaeological terms, it might be said then that the documents are of

89. Schröter, "Jesus of Galilee," in Charlesworth and Pokorný, *Jesus Research*, 36–37.
90. Ibid., 37–38, 40; original emphasis and quoting Reinhart Koselleck.
91. Oakman, review of Horsley, *Archaeology, History*, 568.
92. Section heading in Vale, "Literary Sources," 211–16.

no great help to us, since they provide only indirect data well screened through foreign, and sometimes polemicized narrative frameworks."[93]

Regional variations within Galilee itself, and complex interactions between Galilee and its neighbors, are reasons why debates continue about understanding and integrating the research findings into an integrated and plausible picture of the Galilean ethos. Upper Galilee (the Golan), for example, had begun what were to become strong trading and other commercial links with Tyre and Syria[94]—but not to the detriment of a strongly Jewish ethos, especially in its villages. The ambiguous nature of the religio-cultural status of a border town such as Bethsaida (both Gentile and Jewish it seems) has long been recognized.[95] Lower Galilee, partly because of the influence of its urban areas, displayed a rather greater cultural diversity but also remained distinctively Jewish in ethos. Most of our discussion has centered on Lower Galilee because that is where Jesus is mostly found in the Gospel narratives. Nonetheless, it is difficult to conceive of radical changes to the general portrait presented by Freyne, Chancey, and others. Without a substantial material change in the current pattern of archaeological findings, it seems reasonable to suppose that the picture will remain one in which the Jewish contours of Herodian Galilee are clearer than ever—even if they do remain somewhat blurred in places. The Galilee of Renan's often-cited description as "a fifth gospel, torn, but still legible"[96] might now be said to be somewhat less torn and rather more legible.

Herodian Galilee: The Jewish Religious Milieu

Given the way in which the narrative of the Gospels so firmly ties Jesus to Galilee, is its cultural milieu best described in religious categories? If so, how might this religious milieu be best described? The first of

---

93. Vale, "Literary Sources," 216. The problem derives, she argues, from "the manner in which the literature itself has shaped our interpretation" of the archaeological data (209).

94. See the evidence cited in Vale, "Literary Sources," 224–25.

95. Given the importance of Bethsaida in the Gospels, discussion will return to the town in chapter 3 below.

96. Renan, *Life of Jesus*, 31.

these two questions raises the question of possible religious bias in the academic retrieval and assessment of Galilee.[97] It is true that some approaches to the retrieval and evaluation of the past—whether the past of Galilee or some other place—have at times served religious and theological agendas in inappropriate or tendentious ways.[98] But the possibility of bias certainly exists if Freyne's assertion is accurate: that for some social-scientific models, "politics, economic, and class struggle [are] deemed more important than religion" in evaluating the dynamics of Herodian Galilee.[99] The reductionist tendencies of explanatory models drawn from the social sciences are one reason for such an attitude. Another is that often the social science method appears to be driven deductively by social science models instead of being led inductively by the data itself.[100] However, as Freyne points out, the two major revolts that took place in first century Palestine both had strongly religious dimensions as well as social, economic, and political components.[101]

A helpful starting point is found in the material culture described above. One feature of the discussion of this culture is the division between archaeology concerned with public space and activities and the archaeology of private spaces. In terms of public space there is a growing consensus that, while the presence of Greek architecture and culture in Herodian Galilee need not be denied or even doubted, this presence

97. On the bias that can lead historians to fail to acknowledge (or simply to deny) the importance of religious beliefs and values among the people and subjects they explore, see Chapman, Coffey, and Gregory, *Seeing Things Their Way*.

98. See the reminders in Crossley, *Why Christianity Happened*, and his "Social-Sciences, Ideology and Christian Origins."

99. Freyne, "Archaeology and the Historical Jesus," 68; he actually has the "Lenski-Kautsky model" as well as "Jesus and his message" in mind. An example of this tendency is found in Bruce Malina who argues that access to the social world of the NT world is blocked by "widespread belief that Jesus and his program were about religion" (Malina, *Social Gospel of Jesus*, 10), and a failure to realize that religion in the NT era "was embedded in politics and kinship, as was economics" (11).

100. The danger is acknowledged by a leader within the "Context Group." See the introduction by Neyrey in Neyrey and Stewart, *Social World of the New Testament*, xxi–xxiv. A preference for a social science approach is sometimes said to be needed because the literary sources are supposedly replete with difficulties.

101. Freyne, "Galilee and Judaea," 41; Levine makes the same point, and with greater emphasis ("Theory, Apologetic, History," 59–60).

is well described as a "veneer" over a culture that remained distinctively Jewish.[102] Further confirmation of the Jewishness of Galilean ethnicity and religion is found in the material culture of private spaces. Jonathan Reed points out that "[p]ublic architecture and visible inscriptions along with coins and statues were built either by political rulers or by local elites. Instead of looking to such public and visible space, there are artifacts found inside domestic space or controlled by private initiative that provide better evidence for the populace's identity..."[103] A number of scholars (Reed himself, Freyne, Chancey, Jensen, and others) have drawn attention to the finding that domestic space in both urban and rural dwellings in Galilee disclose a material culture associated with distinctive Jewish religious identity. These artifacts are: stone (or chalk) vessels that, unlike ceramic vessels, were believed to be impervious to ritual impurity; stepped, plastered or stone immersion pools (*miqva'ot*), sometimes shared by several dwellings; secondary burial with ossuaries in loculi tombs; and bone profiles that completely lack pig bones. In particular, the presence of stone vessels is widespread; they are found "in every single house in well excavated sites like both Capernaum and Sepphoris, that they point to widespread purity concerns among the population who wished to live in such a way that acknowledged God." These *miqva'ot* and stone jars are "sparse along the coast and in Samaria and Transjordan,"[104] lending support to the conclusion that Galilee was overwhelmingly Jewish and had never been as Hellenized as the coastal cities of Palestine or the Dekapolis. This kind of archaeological evidence offers apparent confirmation of a widespread "common Judaism" as re-

---

102. Reed, "Archeological Contributions," 49. Freyne points out that "Sepphoris, even after its later expansion, which presumably meant the introduction of non-Jewish population, continued to be a major center of Jewish learning for several centuries" (Freyne, "Galilee, Jesus," 578). Reed also emphasizes the Jewishness of Sepphoris (see his *Archaeology and the Galilean Jesus*, 100–38). Even "the oriental cities of the Decapolis and other gentile cities should not be viewed solely as purveyors of Greco-Roman culture but rather as eastern cities with a Hellenistic overlay that often facilitated the expression of aspects of Semitic religion and practice, including Judaism" (and extending, for example, to Jewish musical culture; Myers, "Jesus and His Galilean Context," 62.)

103. Reed, "Archeological Contributions," 51–52.

104. Ibid., 52.

constructed by E.P. Sanders.[105] In other words, it seems reasonable to conclude that Herodian Galilee was predominantly or even thoroughly Jewish.

The portrayal just outlined does, however, serve to qualify any picture that completely *excludes* the presence of Hellenism from Herodian Galilee. It appears that there was no rigid dichotomy between Hellenization and Judaism; they existed in a kind of tension. One reason is that, as Chancey puts it, Hellenization was not uniform or homogeneous across the ancient Mediterranean. "We scholars have been quicker to recognize the diversity in the *Judaism* of Hellenistic Judaism than in the *Hellenism* of Hellenistic Judaism."[106] Some of this diversity relates to conflict and resistance between Galilean Jewish particularity and a variety of intra-Jewish accommodating attitudes (most typically seen in a degree of acceptance of Hellenization). Freyne is not untypical; after a survey of the extent of Hellenization in Galilee (one of many stretching over several decades), Freyne concludes that contemporary reconstructions of a pagan Galilee are essentially misleading if they lead to conclusions that Galilean Judaism was non-observant or even hostile to traditional faith and practice. Jewish Galileans remained conservative in religious beliefs and practices "even when day-to-day contacts with non-Jews were frequent and necessary."[107]

---

105. For example Sanders, *Judaism*; Grabbe, *Judaic Religion* (see his ch. 15, ("Judaism in the Second Temple Period: A Holistic Perspective") adds to Sanders' description the emergence of a body of sacred Scripture (*Judaic Religion*, 318). On the link with Galilean material culture see, for example, two essays in a recent symposium (Udoh, *Redefining First-Century Jewish and Christian Identities*). In one, Eric Meyers uses archaeological findings (baths, ossuaries, stone vessels, food remains) in an examination of "'Common Judaism' and the Common Judaism of Material Culture" (153–74) and concludes that Jewish practice in key areas of daily Jewish life accords well with Sanders' thesis. In a second essay, Jürgen Zangenberg also analyzes the apparent correspondence between these retrieved elements of Jewish material culture and Sanders' thesis of a common Judaism; see his "'Common Judaism' and the Common Judaism of Material Culture" (175–93).

106. Chancey, *Greco-Roman Culture*, 229.

107. Freyne, "Galilee as Laboratory," 156.

Judaism and Gentiles: Jesus, Galilee, and Gospels

Some Unresolved Issues

There are still some unresolved questions about the religious ethos and culture of Galilee. One question concerns the kind of late Second Temple Era Judaism found in Galilee in the first century CE. Was it the religion of recent converts to Judaism who were perceived to be lax in their observance of the Law?[108] Or was it the Judaism of militant nationalism, hostile towards Gentile and Samaritan neighbors?[109] Were there significant regional variations within Galilee itself (such as Bethsaida)? One question that might be asked about the methodology of Chancey (especially in his *The Myth of a Gentile Galilee*) is whether Galilee was a homogenous region—to be studied as such—or whether it is better described as several subregions (Upper and Lower Galilee, and the area around the lake). Does the lake district, for example, imply a distinct economic, commercial and demographic profile, as Freyne, Reed, and others conclude?[110] The question of regional variation is also raised by the role of *miqva'ot*. Jonathan Lawrence's detailed discussion concludes that the archaeological evidence for *miqva'ot* shows uneven distribution.[111] This is, of course, an example of the continuing provisionality of archaeological findings. And, as Reed concedes, such material culture as the presence of *miqva'ot* reveals little or nothing of how people *interpreted* the practices involved especially if, as Reed also points out, such evidence might suggest that the inhabitants were perhaps mostly

---

108. Geza Vermes cites the reported conclusion of the Pharisee who had spent eighteen fruitless years in the region: "Galilee, Galilee, you hate the Torah!" (Vermes, *Jesus the Jew*, 53).

109. For a survey of the issue see Freyne, "Galilee as Laboratory," 154–56.

110. See, for example, Freyne, *Jesus, a Jewish Galilean*, 50–53; Reed, *Archaeology and the Galilean Jesus*, ch. 5.

111. "*Miqva'ot* first appear in the second century B.C.E. at sites connected to the Hasmonean rule of Judea. For the rest of the Second Temple period, they are concentrated in Jerusalem and surrounding Judea, with *only a few* in the Galilee and Transjordan." (Lawrence, *Washing in Water*, 190; emphasis added); the comparative rarity of *miqva'ot* in the countryside is also noted by Downing, "In Quest of First-Century C.E. Galilee," 80.)

transplants from the region of Judea.[112] In this case the evidence might not enable safe conclusions to be drawn about *Galilean* piety.

Nonetheless, Seán Freyne remains confident that assertions about a "Hellenised Galilee are neither wholly appropriate nor helpful, especially when it is meant to imply a hostile Galilee or a non-observant Jewish one."[113] Demographic analysis by Reed leads him to conclude that, while Herodian Galileans had a different social, economic, and political matrix to that of the Jews of Judea (as revealed by a different archaeological profile), they shared a common ethnic and religious identity with them.[114] In other words, the Galilean world largely retained the central values of late Second Temple Judaism(s): land, temple, and the election of Israel, with these distinctives reinforced by a range of purity laws. Departure from the general thrust of the great tradition would have been viewed as disloyal and unacceptable. Josephus affirms that Jerusalem seems largely (perhaps completely) to have retained Galilean loyalty despite taxation and other economic pressures, and regardless of whether these pressures were exerted by an ethnically mixed Herodian court, the Romans or fellow Jews.[115] The temple functioned as a source of unity between Galilee and Judea with no evidence yet uncovered of any serious alternatives to it as the cultic centre for the religious life of Galilee. Freyne concludes that Galilean commitment to the Jerusalem temple was both longstanding and unwavering.[116] The temple served as "the focal point" for Galilean loyalties and "the symbol of their identity," which enabled the Galileans to remain faithful to traditional Judaism even in the presence of Hellenizing and other Gentile influences.[117] There is, then, widespread agreement concerning the following essential constituents of Jewish self-understanding during the Second Temple Era: worship of the one God, keeping the Sabbath, circumcision, purity observances, support of the temple, sacred Scripture. There was also di-

---

112. Reed, *Archaeology and the Galilean Jesus*, 55, 44–49; see also Chancey, *Myth of a Gentile Galilee*, 79–80.

113. Freyne, "Galilee as Laboratory," 153.

114. Reed, *Archaeology and the Galilean Jesus*, ch. 2.

115. The evidence is presented and discussed in Freyne, "Galilee-Jerusalem Relations," and in his *Galilee, Jesus*, 179–90.

116. Freyne, *Galilee from Alexander*, 273, 275.

117. Ibid., 287, 292; cf. 275.

versity (especially in matters of lifestyle and practice outside Palestine, and occasional examples of heterodoxy such that the term "Judaisms" is appropriate), but this commonality and unity is clearly substantiated as the heart of Jewish identity. Such diversity as was found in Galilee need not be seen as threatening an overarching common Judaism.

Jesus, Galilee and Gentiles

Jesus as a Galilean

As we have seen, Herodian Galilee emerges from recent study as quite strongly Jewish in ethos but with a veneer of Gentile influence—confined mainly to public space—because of Hellenistic and Roman presence. What, then, are the implications of this recent study of Herodian Galilee for an understanding of the historical Jesus—especially his possible or likely attitude to Gentiles? According to a notable German NT scholar, "Jesus' openness to non-Jews . . . probably has some connection with the Galilean context of his ministry."[118] How, exactly, might that context have contributed to an "openness to non-Jews"?

A scholarly consensus is emerging that recent retrieval of Galilee reinforces the way in which the generally Jewish and regional Galilean ethos provide the essential context for understanding Jesus and the Gospel accounts concerning him.[119] Not all scholars are persuaded: "[t]o assume that Jesus and his first followers in Galilee were unaffected by or out of communication with Hellenistic culture is historically untenable."[120] Nonetheless, the consensus is that there is no reason to doubt the distinctly Jewish character of Jesus' Galilean context.[121] Both literary and material sources help locate the ministry of Jesus in a fairly well-delineated social, cultural and political milieu. As Jens Schröter points out, the Gospels, in "preserving the memory of the places, peo-

---

118. Schnelle, *Theology of the New Testament*, 138.

119. See, for example, Osiek, "Jesus and Galilee"; Freyne, *Galilean*; Freyne, "Jesus and Archaeology"; Sawicki, *Crossing Galilee*; Race, "Galilee's Influence"; Schuler, "Recent Archaeology of Galilee."

120. Kee, "Early Christianity in the Galilee," 15.

121. See also Dunn, "Did Jesus Attend the Synagogue?," in Charlesworth, *Jesus and Archaeology*, 207–12.

ple, and social and religious background connected with Jesus' ministry . . . represent it as being set in a particular time and place."[122] Such a perspective is in harmony with the widely accepted viewpoint that to understand ancient texts requires knowledge of the writers' (and readers') culture and relationships.

One advantage of reading the Gospel texts in the light of archaeology is described by Seán Freyne. He writes that by "adopting what may be loosely described as an inter-textual approach, I have attempted to bypass the *cul de sac* of deciding on suitable criteria for distinguishing between authentic and inauthentic fragments of Jesus-traditions."[123] Freyne is here building on the work done by Gerd Theissen and others since the 1990s which has seen these criteria shift from dissimilarity to contextual plausibility; as archaeology reveals more about the context, so has the plausibility of the Gospel accounts, generally speaking, been enhanced.

Archaeological retrieval of the material culture of Herodian Galilee has extended understanding of the region in a number of ways. For example, Jesus' public ministry to and teaching about the poor has a realistic tone to it given the Galilean context of poverty exacerbated by economic exploitation, forced labor and contractual debt disclosed by recent research.[124] A number of these conclusions are derived from social-scientific analysis and models and their evaluation will depend upon judgments about the conflict models that undergird many of them.[125] But it also seems clear that an understanding of more than the material and social culture of Galilee is needed in order to understand Jesus and his message; causal factors may well be located among prevailing social, political and economic conditions but are by no means

---

122. Schröter, "Jesus of Galilee," in Charlesworth and Pokorný, *Jesus Research*, 51. He adds: "It is not detached from these specifics and offered as a timeless teaching, as in the *Gospel of Thomas*."

123. Freyne, "Galilee as Laboratory," 157.

124. Reed, *Archaeology and the Galilean Jesus*, 77–89; Reed, "Archaeological Contributions," 50; Freyne, *Galilee and Gospel*, 190–96; Freyne, "Galilee and Judaea," 47–48.

125. See the comments—mainly critical but extensively annotated—concerning the employment of social science models in Robinson, "'Fifth Gospel' Less Torn?," 90–94.

limited to them. Economic deprivation and social conflict do not appear to be the central or only determinants of the message of Jesus; the elaboration of context certainly does not exclude religious and theological factors as also causative. Even James Crossley, while advocating a wide-ranging employment of social science methodology, also documents the way in which a number of the originators of social-scientific approaches have emphasized that their approaches did not exclude some role for theological ideas.[126]

In other words, a religious and theological dimension must remain central if the Jewish context is to be given an appropriately central place in understanding Jesus within his Galilean context. Schröter notes that, for example, "[i]n the Gospels it is never Antipas or the Romans who are mentioned as the opponents of the kingdom of God, but Satan and the demons."[127] The often-discussed absence of reference to Sepphoris or Tiberias in the Gospels may well have a theological reason: "Jesus came proclaiming the coming of a kingdom that would eclipse that of Herod and his sons."[128] According to Rapinchuk, "the silence may have been a means of suggesting that the cities and what they stood for were irrelevant to 'true Israel.'"[129] A theological reason need not, of course, exclude other reasons. Freyne suggests that the avoidance is because

---

126. See Crossley, *Why Christianity Happened*, ch. 1. He can also write that "I still do think that Jesus, theology and ideas played some role in the grand scheme of things, even if I am not convinced by the massive overemphasis in scholarship" (Crossley, "Social-Sciences," 23).

127. Schröter, "Jesus of Galilee," in Charlesworth and Pokorný, *Jesus Research*, 47. "The more archaeology demonstrates the significance of Sepphoris, the more eloquent is the silence of the Jesus tradition about this city: Jesus must have known it" (Theissen and Merz, *Historical Jesus*, 166).

128. Hoppe, "Capernaum and Its Synagogue," 255. Hoppe is making the point that Jesus' choice of Capernaum as the base for his Galilean ministry might be seen as a contrast with that of the politically and economically more important and strategic Sepphoris located only four miles away.

129. Rapinchuk, "Galilee and Jesus," 218. The central chapters of Mark disclose ministry by Jesus within the vicinity of urban Gentile centers ("the country of the Gerasenes," 5:1; "the region of Tyre," 7:24; "in the region of the Dekapolis," 7:31; "the villages of [or "around"] Caesarea Philippi," 8:27), but the wording seems clearly to avoid any suggestion of ministry *within* any of the urban areas mentioned; cf. Freyne, *Jesus, a Jewish Galilean*, 40, 55–57, 76–77.

Jesus was "reluctant to become directly embroiled in the politics of urbanization and the damage that was being wrought to the fabric of village life..."[130]—what Freyne elsewhere calls the avoidance of "a confrontation with Herodian power."[131] Urban areas were associated with Herod Antipas, whom Jesus disliked (Luke 13:32),[132] probably because Antipas had John the Baptist executed (Matt 14:10; Mark 6.27). In his (apparent) refusal to acknowledge the significance of the Herodian cities, Jesus "is laying claim to a different source of authority than that to which the elite urbanites subscribed. His activity, no less than his teaching, was likely to have been perceived as a serious threat to the power structures on which the wealthy depended."[133] As with Josephus, the only city of true significance is Jerusalem; "rather than a matter of social or political conflict, Jesus' ministry is directed towards Jerusalem as the *religious* center of Israel."[134]

Given the overwhelmingly Jewish ethos of Galilee, it seems highly plausible that Jesus advocated some kind of continuity with the hopes and expectations of the Jewish religious tradition inherited by him and his followers. Depictions of Jesus' thought as essentially in continuity with Jewish tradition do not exclude a regional ethos. Craig Keener, for example, draws attention to the presence of distinctively Galilean imagery—some of it derived from or substantiated by archaeology—in the telling of parables that was a central part of Jesus' teaching methods. He concludes that the parables display considerable "insight... from a storyteller genuinely in touch with the Galilean countryside."[135] And Freyne, in his *Jesus, a Jewish Galilean*, argues that the Galilean landscape and religious ethos particular to Galilee played decisive roles in the formation of the mission of Jesus. There is nothing unexpected

---

130. Freyne, *Jesus, a Jewish Galilean*, 57.

131. Freyne, *Galilee, Jesus*, 140.

132. The reference in Luke 7:24–27/Matt 7:1–10 to those who are "dressed in fine garments and dwell in royal palaces" is plausibly an allusion to Herod and his royal residence in Tiberias.

133. Freyne, "Galilee as Laboratory," 159.

134. Schröter, "Jesus of Galilee," in Charlesworth and Pokorný, *Jesus Research*, 50; original emphasis.

135. Keener, *Historical Jesus of the Gospels*, 193–94; quote from 194.

about this conclusion. The sections above outline the contribution of archaeology to the retrieval of the Galilean ethos. In a similar way it has also contributed to knowledge of the historical Jesus.[136]

Jesus and Gentiles

The precise frequency and contours of Jesus' contact with Gentiles remains unclear even though there are occasional glimpses in the Gospels. For example, during the third (or possibly second) year of his ministry, Jesus left Galilee and entered the Gentile region of Tyre (Mark 7:24, 31). Reasons are given and even in this Gentile region Jesus is portrayed as mainly meeting Jews. Nonetheless, as we shall see, Jesus is also reported as meeting some Gentiles who exhibit faith and who receive healing for needy dependents as a result; they are the object of comment (both positive and negative) in a number of places in his teaching as well. There seems no good reason to doubt the general authenticity of the accounts. N. T. Wright observes that "Jesus' meetings with Gentiles are few and cryptic, and thus all the more likely to be authentic."[137] Even if the narratives of journeys into Gentile territory are colored by post-Easter language, they are "not without a basis in the life of the historical Jesus."[138] If, with Howard Kee, one is persuaded by "the evidence from archeological and literary sources for the common and inescapable interchange between Jews and residents of Hellenistic background and culture in the Galilee and adjoining regions, there is no reason to dismiss out of hand these gospel accounts of Jesus' initiative in reaching people from Hellenistic centers adjacent to the Galilee as later additions to the Jesus tradition, written after the Church had begun to undertake a conscious mission to gentiles."[139]

---

136. As James Charlesworth concludes: "We are learning to raise questions and correct an earlier text-based myopic reconstruction of Jesus' life and social environment" ("Jesus Research and Archaeology," in Charlesworth, *Jesus and Archaeology*, 58).

137. Wright, *Jesus and the Victory of God*, 431.

138. Theissen and Merz, *Historical Jesus*, 171.

139. Kee, "Early Christianity in the Galilee," 18-19.

Jesus and the Religions

One of the most extensive surveys of the Gentile ethos of Galilee has been provided by Mark Chancey. He acknowledges that contact with Gentiles did occur in Herodian Galilee, especially in the border regions, but concludes that "nothing in the literary or archaeological record suggests that such contact was especially frequent."[140] The fairly recent excavation by Douglas Edwards of a Galilean village "indicates that villages were not isolated economically or culturally from the urban centers nor from one another. Nor is there evidence of strict cultural isolation from surrounding non-Jewish territories . . ."[141] Despite his own conclusions about the small number of gentiles in Galilee, Chancey nonetheless concludes that the few stories in the Gospels about an encounter between Jesus and Gentiles are "historically plausible . . . given what we know of social conditions in Galilee," though he also adds that the Galilean context for the ministry of Jesus "should not prompt scholarly speculation that frequent contact with gentiles was formative in the development of his ministry."[142] In fact, confidence in the historicity of the encounters may well be increased on the grounds that the reported encounters are so sparse. The paucity of references can be taken as evidence that the Gospel writers resist the temptation to make Jesus offer commentary on the controversial issues that were to puzzle the first generation of Christians. As Craig Keener points out, "The gospel tradition nowhere address the later-burning issue (attested in Acts and Paul's letters) of whether Gentiles must be circumcised to join God's people."[143]

We have already noted above that the material retrieval of Galilee seems to increase the likelihood of Jesus encountering Gentiles in Galilee. This would have been unavoidable if, for example, he had

---

140. Chancey, *Myth of a Gentile Galilee*, 166.

141. Edwards, "Recent Work in Galilee."

142. Chancey, *Myth of a Gentile Galilee*, 174, 179.

143. Keener, *Historical Jesus of the Gospels*, 144. In other words, the historical plausibility of Jesus' contact with Gentiles is enhanced by the now commonplace assumption in much NT scholarship that references to events or sayings in the gospels do seem plausibly to cohere with what is known of a Jewish Galilean context (although able to subvert it at times), while the same events or sayings can also often help to explain later developments in early Christianity (without being replicated there).

been employed on any of the numerous Gentile-controlled construction sites in Galilee. More specifically, a tentative case can be made for Jesus as familiar with a Gentile environment such as that to be found in Sepphoris—geographically close to Nazareth (even if there are no references to it in the Gospels). The suggestion of a degree of familiarity need not imply that Jesus participated in the town's displays of Greco-Roman culture; but Jesus' familiarity with some aspects of Gentile culture could be argued for in several ways.[144]

In the first place, the canonical Gospels imply that Jesus seems remarkably at ease with both Gentiles and Samaritans. His reported immediate response to the Roman centurion's request at Matt 8:7 is, "I will come [to your home] and heal him" seems at odds with contemporary Jewish attitudes towards entry into non-*kosher* settings.[145] Such scenes as Matt 9:10–11; 11:19 (//Luke 7:34); and Luke 15:1–2, where Jesus and his disciples have table fellowship with toll collectors and "sinners" imply a degree of ease with the marginalized. If he did have contact with Sepphoris (only a few miles from Nazareth)—especially if he, or he and Joseph, had worked there[146]—then this degree of comfort with Gentiles would be understandable. And there are the equally remarkable reports of John 4 where Jesus not only receives water from a Samaritan hand but in verse 40, "[w]hen the Samaritans came to him, they urged him to stay with them, and he stayed two days." These are remarkable, given that contemporary Jewish opinion about Samaritans esteemed them no more highly than Gentiles (as we shall see in chapter 4 below).

Secondly, it might be asked whether there was an intended connection (even if not an identity) between "sinners" and "Gentiles." Jesus gives special attention to "the poor" and this concern clearly echoes the prophetic tradition. But it is less easy to determine a referent for "sinners." Dunn offers an extensive discussion.[147] We have already noted the

---

144. The three points that follow draw initially on Smillie, "'Even the Dogs,'" 83.

145. As noted in the opening section of this chapter.

146. Given that Jesus as known in his adult life as "the *tektōn*" ("the carpenter/stonemason"; see Mark 6:3), and given the proximity of Nazareth to Sepphoris, it is not surprising to find speculation that Jesus might have found work there for some period of his working life. See the discussion in, for example, Batey, *Jesus and the Forgotten City*, 70; Dunn, *Jesus Remembered*, 319.

147. Dunn, *Jesus Remembered*, esp. 526–34.

way in which "sinners" in the intertestamental literature can and sometimes explicitly does include Gentiles.[148] "If Jesus referred to Gentiles as 'sinners' (Lk 6.34; cf. Matt 5.47) he would simply be reflecting characteristic usage of the time."[149] At the same time, OT and intertestamental literature by no means confines "sinner" to Gentiles. There is a strong antithesis drawn between the "righteous" and "sinners" in, for example, the intertestamental *Psalms of Solomon* and 1 Maccabees,[150] and in the Gospels in passages such as Matt 9:11–13//Mark 2:16–17//Luke 5:30–32. Luke's conclusion to the parable of lost sheep (15:7) and the parable of the Pharisee and the toll collector (18:9, 14) draw the same contrast. In a detailed study, Dwayne Adams—having surveyed "Hellenistic and Jewish concepts of the 'sinner'"[151]—concludes that that "the call to repentance was not new, but the call to the 'sinner' was" and also adds that Lukan usage includes a new significant dimension of meaning: the use of "sinner" to include reference to Gentiles[152] (for example, in Luke 24:7, "the Son of Man must be handed over to sinners, and be crucified . . ."). And, thirdly, there is the report by Josephus in his *Antiquities* that Jesus "won over many Jews and many of the Greeks" (*Ant.* 18.3.3, Whiston translation). While there are good grounds for doubting the authenticity of much of the rest of the paragraph (much of which appears to be a later Christian interpolation), a strong case can be made for the authenticity of these comments about the inclusion of Gentiles.[153]

The emphasis on Galilee in the Gospels may also have missional and not merely geographical significance. Mention has already been made of Paul Hertig's *Matthew's Narrative Use of Galilee in the Multicultural*

148. And Smillie notes the conjunction in *1 Enoch* and *Jubilees* (Smillie, "'Even the Dogs,'" 83).

149. Dunn, *Jesus Remembered*, 538 n. 239.

150. See, for example, ibid., 282–85, 530; and further: Dunn, "Pharisees, Sinners."

151. The title of ch. 2 of Adams, *Sinner in Luke*.

152. Ibid., 67 (citing Neale); this designation follows some OT precedents in which "sinners" can include Gentiles. Carey, *Sinners*, offers an initial definition of "sinner" in the Gospels as "one who habitually lives outside of Israel's covenant with its God" (11). In ch. 3 he considers the ritually impure, including Gentiles.

153. This position is defended in some detail in Paget, "Some Observations" (see esp. 603–6). For a more detailed historical survey of the text, see Wheatley, *Josephus on Jesus*.

and Missiological Journeys of Jesus with its emphasis on Galilee as not simply a geographical reference but as a place loaded with symbolic meaning. Hertig also argues that the very word "Galilee" is an indicator of a missional theme running through the Gospel of Matthew in the person of Jesus. "Galilee of the Gentiles" becomes the place where the meaning of Israel is widened to include Gentiles. The ministry of Jesus in Galilee recenters the presence and mission of God from Jerusalem to Galilee. One implication of Hertig's thesis is that mission begins (or often begins) from and is to be found at the margins—in peripheral places of which bilingual and ethnically diverse Galilee might be seen as an example in the divine outreach to the nations.

One final issue related to Jesus' contact with Gentiles is the question, "Did Jesus speak Greek?" A potential answer depends upon conclusions drawn about the frequency of his contact with Gentiles. There has been some speculation that, given the extent of Hellenistic influence in Galilee, he probably did. For Howard Kee, the multiethnic (and therefore multilingual) cultural milieu of Galilee means that "for Jesus to have conversed with inhabitants of cities in . . . Galilee, and especially of cities in the Decapolis and the Phoenician region, he would have had to have known Greek, certainly at the conversational level."[154] Martin Hengel argues that it is inappropriate to distinguish between "Judean-Hellenistic" literature of the Diaspora and "genuine Judean" literature of Palestine. There were connections in both directions and a constant interchange, usually in Greek.[155] And Stanley Porter concludes: "[t]hat Greek was used not only in the Diaspora but also in Palestine, even for composition by Jews of distinctly Jewish literature including much religious literature, indicates that Greek was an important and widely used language by a sizable portion of the Palestinian Jewish population."[156] Further evidence may be found in the distribution of Greek names among the Jewish population: two high priests in the Herodian period (Boethus and Theophilus) had Greek names, as did two members of

---

154. Kee, "Early Christianity in the Galilee," 21; see also Meyers and Strange, *Archaeology*, 62–91.

155. Hengel, *"Hellenization" of Judaea*, 25–26.

156. Porter, "Jesus and the Use of Greek," 142.

the inner circle of the Jesus movement (Andrew and Philip).[157] The Gospels seem to assume that Jesus could speak in Greek to the centurion in Capernaum, the Syro-Phoenician mother (identified as "Greek" [*Hellēnis*]; Mark 7:26) and to Pilate.[158]

Others, as we have seen, emphasize the limited extent of Hellenistic influence; as Chancey points out about Herodian Galilee, "Hellenistic culture was the culture of cities, not villages, and Galilee as yet had no major cities."[159] The evidence for Greek being frequently spoken in Galilee does not appear until about 120 CE, when a Roman legion made its first permanent base there.[160] How much Greek Jesus knew will never be clear, notes Chancey, "but he most likely would not have needed it to be a carpenter, to teach the Galilean crowds, to travel around the lake, or to venture into the villages associated with Tyre, Caesarea Philippi, and the Decapolis cities."[161] On the other hand, Smillie considers it probable that Jesus did have contact with Sepphoris which would imply regular dealing "with Gentiles as a matter of course throughout his adolescence and early adulthood. He could have even grown up speaking Greek, and maybe even some Latin, along with his maternal Aramaic."[162]

The question of whether Jesus spoke Greek is an issue that has received rather little scholarly attention—with one exception: the

157. See Hengel, *"Hellenization" of Judaea*, 9.

158. Ibid., 17; cf. Porter, "Jesus and the Use of Greek," 148–53.

159. Chancey, *Greco-Roman Culture*, 33; see the whole of his ch. 5, "The Use of Greek in Jesus' Galilee."

160. It is for this kind of reason that Chancey and Meyers conclude: "As we analyze the archaeological data, we find that the real question is not whether Jesus spoke Greek, but whether, and to what extent, we can use later evidence to understand conditions in first-century Galilee.... Rather than assuming that many first-century Galileans knew some Greek, it is safer to say that by looking at first-century Galilee, we can already see the initial stages of later linguistic trends" ("Did Jesus Speak Greek?"; see also Fitzmyer, "Did Jesus Speak Greek?").

161. Chancey, *Greco-Roman Culture*, 141, 163.

162. Smillie, "'Even the Dogs,'" 82. Smillie goes on to invite comparison of his scenario (that Jesus took up the undoubted opportunities for work in Sepphoris) with alternative possibilities. "The possibility that Joseph, and then Jesus, supported Mary and the household of at least six children by steadily finding work for twenty years exclusively in the sleepy hamlet of Nazareth demands a high level of credulity." He concludes that working in Sepphoris "seems far more likely" (Smillie, "'Even the Dogs,'" 83).

forcefully argued" case made by Stanley Porter that the Gospels do, in places, preserve dialogues involving Jesus that were originally spoken in Greek.¹⁶³ The response to Porter has been disappointingly thin and often of an *ad hominem* nature, but with one exception: a fairly lengthy reply by Michael Bird. Because Porter's is a "cumulative weight of probability" kind of argument, it is worth citing his own summary of the factors that he believes have a cumulative effect:

> The first is the fact that Greek was a language in widespread use among not only the general Mediterranean world of the first century, but the Jewish people of the time, including those in Palestine and especially the Galilean region.... Greek was part and parcel of Jewish identity of the first century, including in Galilee. On this basis, one must recognize that Jesus could have spoken Greek. In fact, many scholars are willing to admit this fact, even if they do not pursue the argument further to establish whether Jesus did speak Greek on a given occasion. However, this criterion tries to establish that we can have some degree of confidence that on particular occasions Jesus may have spoken Greek.¹⁶⁴

By way of a response, Bird concedes that "[v]ery few scholars would doubt that Jesus probably knew some Greek and he might have conversed in Greek on occasion. The problem lies in demonstrating that it did happen" and that the words of Jesus "are now retrievable from the Gospel manuscripts as they are. In contrast, ... the character of the Jesus tradition and the literary intention of the Evangelists render this

---

163. See Porter, *Criteria for Authenticity*, 126–80; "Luke 17.11–19"; and "Criterion of Greek Language."

164. Porter, "Criterion of Greek Language," 70–71. He continues: "Such occasions are those that fulfill the following: the probability of the participants speaking Greek, the particular context and the theme being plausibly discussed in Greek, and the likely determination that the words recorded might have been spoken. At each level of the accumulating argument, there is ground for refutation of the hypothesis, so that the probability is definable. I determined that a small number of episodes might well record the words of Jesus in Greek, and determined the level of their probability as either: reasonably high probability, reasonable probability or some probability."

task impossible from the outset."¹⁶⁵ The question of whether Jesus spoke Greek cannot be answered with any degree of certainty; however, there is some likelihood that he did.

Some Chapter Conclusions

This chapter has attempted to do a number of things. It has demonstrated the range of Jewish attitudes towards Gentiles during Second Temple Judaism and has underlined a tension between particularity and universality in Jewish thought of the period. It has drawn attention to the significance of Galilee for the ministry and teaching of Jesus—and attempted to assess the extent of Gentile influence upon the region. It has also sought to describe the kind of Judaism found in Herodian Galilee, and to describe and assess the role of the archaeology in the material and religio-cultural retrieval of Galilee. And it has outlined some of the implications of these findings for the construction of a contextual framework for the encounter of Jesus with the Gentiles he is recorded as having met and spoken about. It is to some of these reported encounters that discussion now turns.

---

165. Bird, "Criterion of Greek Language," 60. Bird also offers a summary of "recent studies which reinforce the Jewishness of Galilee [such] that Porter's assertion about the widespread usage of Greek in Galilee is somewhat overstated" (62).

2

Some Key Encounters with Gentiles

ATTENTION NOW TURNS TO two encounters that are central to one of the key points that this volume attempts to make—that the example of Jesus in his encounter with Gentiles offers insight for contemporary readers in a religiously plural world.

Introduction: Issues Regarding Historicity and Parallel Accounts

Before discussing the actual passages, a comment should be made about several aspects of the material considered. Although a theological reading prefers not to begin with issues raised by historical-critical method, questions do sometimes arise about the meaning of a given incident or didactic passage when parallel accounts are found in the canonical text (e.g., John 4:46–54 as a possible variant of the centurion story of Matt 8:5–12//Luke 7:1–10; or the chronologically diverse accounts of the "temple action"). Of the many discussions of such diversity, the general explanation offered by Richard Bauckham in his *Jesus and the Eyewitnesses* seems the most satisfactory to this writer. Bauckham outlines five factors that seem to account for these sorts of variations. The first three account for what he considers to be the less significant variations: differences that arise from varying versions of his sayings that Jesus himself used on different occasions; variant translations from Aramaic to Greek; the variability normal in oral performances of a tradition, especially narrative. But more significant is a certain amount of redactional activity by the Gospel writers themselves: "deliberate alterations or additions, by which [an authorized] tradent sought to explain or to adapt the teaching when the post-Easter situation seemed to require this." As well, there are redactional changes by the Evangelists "in order to integrate the traditions into the connected narrative of their Gospels."[1] This writer is comfortable with such explanations of the diversity found in Gospel accounts of a given story.

Although detailed discussion of issues of historicity is not included in what follows, there is a place for some brief explanatory comment (in addition to the remarks in chapter 1 above about the general contextual plausibility of the accounts of Jesus' encounters with Gentiles as established, in part, by the material retrieval of Galilee). Graham Twelftree's acclaimed study of the miracle stories of Jesus concludes that the incidents considered in this chapter (the exorcism of the Syrophoenician woman's daughter, the healing of the centurion's servant, the healing of the official's son) to be stories that "can be judged with high confidence to reflect an event or events most likely in the life of the historical Jesus."[2] Moreover, they are stories told with restraint by comparison with the extravagance of implausible detail to be found in the apocryphal "Gospels."[3] One concern sometimes heard is that miracle stories (among others) were written in the service of the theological, missional, and catechetical interests and concerns of the early church—issues such as the Gentile mission or Jewish-Gentile fellowship. However, a persuasive argument against such creativity by the evangelists is found in the

---

1. Bauckham, *Jesus and the Eyewitnesses*, 286. Elsewhere Bauckham writes: "The Gospel writers exercised the freedom that all writers of historical narrative in the ancient world took to shape the material they gathered, even when (as ideally) this was from eyewitnesses" ("Eyewitnesses and Critical History," 230). For a carefully constructed argument that behind the written Gospels there stands a conserving process that preserves both the voice and deeds of Jesus (as delivered through the interpretive grid of the Evangelists); see Bird, "Purpose and Preservation."

2. Twelftree, *Jesus the Miracle Worker*, 328.

3. For example, in the Lukan account of the healing of the centurion's servant, "the healing itself is presented almost as an addendum" (Bovon, *Luke 1*, 258a). He later adds about the account: "The main character is the officer, and his faith forms the center of the story, with the healing of his servant rather on the fringe" (264b).

Pauline writings and Acts where there is a distinct absence of appeal to Jesus traditions in the service of such supposed interests and concerns. Moreover, there are also what Michael Bird calls "substantial grounds" for advocating the authenticity of these major encounters of Jesus and Gentiles. Bird lists six such grounds, ranging from the sheer paucity of the material and the way in which these are Gentile initiatives, to potentially embarrassing content and the fact that none of the Gentiles converts, or is even invited to become a disciple (showing, he argues, that the stories are not parables or examples of the success of the later mission to Gentiles). Bird acknowledges the redactional activity of the evangelists but concludes that "wholesale creation and inventiveness does not seem to be the case."[4] Moreover, a theological approach to the biblical material usually gives preference to a "synchronic" reading: it attends to the reading of texts as found in their present canonical form (as opposed to a "diachronic" reading with its discussion of possible stages of composition). A synchronic reading is what John Ashton calls a "smooth" approach: "reading the text as it has been transmitted, without delving into its prehistory"[5]—and it is the approach taken in this study.

The Centurion Whose Servant Is Healed in Capernaum

We now consider the story of a centurion whose servant (perhaps son) is healed by Jesus (Matt 8:5–13//Luke 7:1–10[6]) in the border town of Capernaum. After some explanatory and summary comments, attention will turn, later in the chapter, to implications for the interreligious encounter. As with each of the encounters considered, there is only space for limited comment on redactional issues (e.g., the reasons behind the differences between Matthew and Luke).[7] Or, the differences may derive

---

4. Bird's list is found in his *Jesus and the Origins*, 122–23; quote from 123. For some further general discussion of the historicity of the material, see Nolland, "Gospels and the Historical Jesus," in his *Gospel of Matthew*, 12–14.

5. Ashton, "John and the Johannine Literature," 260.

6. The possible variant (or echoes) of the story in John 4:46–54 are considered later in this chapter.

7. In fact, for the purposes of our discussion, it matters little whether, as France

from the way in which the story is one that Matthew and Luke appear to know quite independently of Mark (and which they both place in the same part of the unfolding narrative about Jesus and in the context of the healing of other individuals).[8] As already mentioned, there are good reasons for maintaining the authenticity of the encounters of Jesus with Gentiles, to which might be added, in this case: its multiple attestation, its plausible links with Capernaum (known to be a center for Jesus' ministry[9] and, as a frontier town, a center for Herodian officials), the presence of multiple semiticisms in Matthew's account, and the potentially embarrassing features of Jesus' astonishment and his initial refusal to heal.[10] Although our discussion begins with Mathew's account, some issues of interest are commented on in the relevant portions of Luke's treatment that follows below.[11]

However, three introductory questions have engaged scholarly attention and, although there is space here to offer only summary conclusions before moving on to the themes that our own study most wants to pursue, they should be mentioned. The questions are:

---

puts it (*Gospel of Matthew*, 310), this is "a story of a good and humble man whose extraordinary request was granted" (Luke's account) or a story written as a paradigm for the extension of the gospel to outsiders (Matthew). A conservative scholar, Gene Smillie, considers the differences to be "striking" ("'Even the Dogs,'" 91) although this may simply be an indication of his unwillingness to recognize differing redactional intentions in the first and third Gospels.

8. See Matt 8:1–4 (a leper); 8:14–17 (multiple healings including Peter's mother-in-law); Luke 7:11–17 (the widow in Nain).

9. Capernaum is established in Matthew as Jesus' home base in 4:13 (cf. 11:23; 17:24). For a summary discussion of the prominence of Capernaum in the Gospels, see Theissen and Merz, *Historical Jesus*, 166–67. The region of Galilee is also associated with healing sites and the presence of medical practitioners (cf. the proverb assumed to be known to the audience in the Capernaum: "Physician heal yourself" (Luke 4:23). These health care concerns of elites and the places that they frequented may shed some light on Jesus' move to the region of the Lake in view of the healing aspects of his ministry (Freyne, "Galilee as Laboratory," 159).

10. See further in Bird, *Jesus and the Origins*, 118, with substantial annotation.

11. As with other discussion of passages in the Gospels, readers are referred to commentaries and specialist studies for exegetical detail that is not repeated here. A helpful summary of resources is found in ibid., 116 n. 143.

Is the Event in John 4 the Same Healing That Is Found in Matthew 8 and Luke 7?

There appear to be sufficient reasons for answering in the affirmative "in light of the similarities seeming to be greater than the differences between the stories and most of the differences being open to logical explanations."[12] James Dunn writes of eleven points of overlapping detail between the three accounts, and concludes that the Johannine story is indeed "another version (more distant echo?)"[13] of the story in Matthew 8 and Luke 7. Bird concludes that "it is an interlocking independent tradition of the same story."[14] Both Bovon and Bird conclude that the Synoptic and Johannine stories derive from the same incident because of a number of elements in common: the sick person lives in Capernaum; the distinguished official is in the service of Herod Antipas; the sick person is part of the official's household; the official takes the initiative to ask Jesus for healing for another; his faith plays a highly significant role; the servant is at the point of death (Luke and John); healing is performed at a distance; the hour of healing is indicated (Matthew and John); and there are a number of close verbal similarities.[15] (Despite the probability that these are accounts of the same healing that takes place at the beginning of Jesus' public ministry in Galilee, the somewhat differently worded story in John 4 is discussed separately below.)

Is the Individual Whose Son Is Healed a Political or Military Official?

Even if it is accepted that the accounts from Matthew/Luke and John are recalling the same event, the role in society or precise occupation of the seeker is somewhat unclear. The term "centurion" (*hekatontarchos*) is used in Matthew 8 and Luke 7 and ordinarily refers to a Roman soldier commanding eighty or one hundred men.[16] Michael Bird points out

---

12. Twelftree, *Jesus the Miracle Worker*, 296.
13. Dunn, *Jesus Remembered*, 215.
14. Bird, *Jesus and the Origins*, 117.
15. Bovon, *Luke 1*, 259a; and Bird, *Jesus and the Origins*, 117.
16. Bird, *Jesus and the Origins*, 118. Because Herod's army was modeled along

that, on the one hand, this term is also used to denote civil functions (a "centurion" could be "employed as a building project manager, a tax-collector, policeman or diplomat") but also that "royal official" (*basilikos*), the term used in John 4, can designate either a person of royal blood or a servant to the king and probably speaks of someone "employed in Herod Antipas' bureaucracy."[17] Schlatter points out that Josephus uses the term to describe all the relatives and officials of the Herods, and their troops.[18] Because Capernaum was a border town there were likely to have been many administrative officials in residence there. Moreover, *basilikos* often refers to an officer of the military forces of Roman or Herodian rulers.[19] If John 4:46–54 records the same incident as that in Matt 8:5–13//Luke 7:1–10, we may view the official as an officer in the army of Herod Agrippa or perhaps even of Rome.[20] In other words, the semantic range of "centurion" appears to be sufficiently wide to cover the somewhat different roles that appear in the three accounts.

Is He a Gentile?

The ethnicity or nationality of this person is also uncertain. The official in John 4 is not explicitly identified as a Gentile and some commentators argue along the lines that "John has a theological purpose in making the man a Jew."[21] However, Francis Moloney offers a more persuasive alter-

---

Roman lines, it is also possible that the reference is to a Herodian officer. Cotter points out that, by the first century CE, the number commanded by a centurion was eighty (*Christ of the Miracle Stories*, 111).

17. Bird, *Jesus and the Origins*, 119; cf. Keener, *Bible Background Commentary*, 275. This is despite the fact that Herod's official title was tetrarch rather than king. Keener also suggests that the "man who comes to Jesus would be a wealthy aristocrat, probably much influence by Greco-Roman culture and not very religious by general Palestinian Jewish standards" (275). See also Keener, *Commentary on Matthew*, 267; cf. 258.

18. Beasley-Murray, *John*, 69 n. a (referring to Schlatter).

19. Bird, *Jesus and the Origins*, 119.

20. Cf. Beasley-Murray, *John*, 69 n. a. Some suggest he cannot have been a Roman soldier but was a Herodian officer or a Syrian recruit; see, for example, the discussion in Chancey, *Greco-Roman Culture*, ch. 2, "The Roman Army in Palestine."

21. Bird, *Jesus and the Origins*, 119.

native as he points out that "[a]ll the other characters in [John] 4:1–54 are Samaritans, people from the world outside Judaism. It is most likely that this particular *basilikos* is understood and presented to the reader by the author as a final example of the reception of the word of Jesus from the non-Jewish world."[22] The centurion in Matthew and Luke appears even more clearly to be portrayed as a Gentile. The setting of the story in Capernaum is also illuminating given the evidence of a Jewish element in the population which potentially had considerable contact with Gentiles. Although some commentators argue for the presence of Roman soldiers in Capernaum, it is perhaps more likely that, as Bird puts it, "the official was in Antipas' governmental apparatus which included non-Jews recruited into his service and, therefore, probably Syrian." In light of all this, Bird concludes that "a Gentile person is more probable"[23] although others, such as Spina, remain uncertain. "He might have been Roman, but he could just as likely have been a Jewish administrative officer."[24] The term *hekatontarchos* was also used within Herod's army, potentially making him a Jew.[25] Even so, as Whitacre points out, "for many Jews a [Jewish] servant at Herod's court would be little better than a Gentile."[26] It remains most likely that the man is a Gentile; there may be some uncertainty in Matthew, and more in John, but his Gentile status is clear to Luke.[27] Imperial centurions were very rarely Jewish[28]

22. Moloney, *Gospel of John*, 153. Nonetheless, Moloney later argues that it is "impossible to determine the ethnic origins of the *basilikos*" even though John's literary context does incline him towards the Gentile option (160–61).

23. Bird, *Jesus and the Origins*, 119–20.

24. Spina, *Faith of the Outsider*, 142. He adds: "Given the ambiguity, there is no warrant for seeing this as an outsider story pure and simple."

25. Bird, *Jesus and the Origins*, 118. According to Josephus, Herod Antipas, like his father (Herod the Great), primarily used non-Jewish soldiers (*Ant.* 17.198; 18.113–14).

26. *John*, 115. The same point is made by Keener who calls the official "an aristocratic partisan of Rome or Herod" (*Commentary on Matthew*, 267; cf. 258)—which leaves open the question of whether he is Jew or Gentile, but certainly confirms his "outsider" status, at least to Jews.

27. He was "most likely a Gentile commander" according to Luz, *Matthew 8–20*, 9.

28. But some were; see Schnabel, *Early Christian Mission*, 1:333, and the evidence he cites.

and Matthew's readers would not have assumed anything other than that the centurion was a Gentile. Cotter's careful analysis leads her to call him "this Gentile of Gentiles."[29]

Whatever precise conclusions are reached about these three questions, from the viewpoint of this present book's overall theme—implications derived from the encounter between Jesus and "outsiders"—it matters little.

Matthew 8:5–13

In Matthew's account, the centurion comes directly and by himself to Jesus. Jesus' first response is an immediate affirmation: "I will come and heal" the servant. This response is met with humility and faith on the part of the Gentile soldier who goes on to express his belief that Jesus could simply speak authoritatively from where he stands and that the healing would be brought about without Jesus needing to travel. The encounter takes place in the administratively important border-crossing town of Capernaum in which, alongside the town's Jewish population, there was "potentially . . . much Gentile contact due to its location near the Golan and the Decapolis"[30]—perhaps a factor in the unbelief (cf. Matt 11:23) that will stand in contrast with the centurion's faith. The dialogue, as presented by Matthew, raises questions about the language spoken in the encounter. Morna Hooker is certain that "unless the centurion were a Syrian recruit, Jesus undoubtedly speaks with him in Greek, the common language of the eastern Mediterranean."[31]

As noted above, the ethnicity of the *hekatontarchos* is disputed. If he was indeed Roman, a number of characteristics of the centurion are probably relevant. There is a generally positive portrayal of centurions in the NT—and this story is no exception; it does nothing to negate the generally accepted portrait of (military) centurions as reliable, and cautious yet courageous.[32] The precise nature of the man's formal religious

29. Cotter, *Christ of the Miracle Stories*, 107.

30. Bird, *Jesus and the Origins*, 119.

31. Cited by Keener, *Commentary on Matthew*, 268 n. 21. (This is an issue that has been discussed in chapter 1 above.)

32. See the helpful discussion of the functions and character of Roman centurions

faith remains unknown. As Eugene Boring points out, "we do not even know whether he was a theist, not to speak of monotheism."³³ He was obliged to swear what, to Jewish ears, would have been distinctly pagan oaths of allegiance. Typical army religious practice was simple, plain "and focused on the task of being an obedient soldier."³⁴ The centurion is certainly an imperial agent and enforcer and so, in both religious and political terms, he is doubly an outsider—and this will make his faith, and Jesus' commendation of it, all the more remarkable. A fine summary of the Matthean account is provided by Warren Carter: "This bold, subversive, and witty scene brings together two empires (Rome's and God's), two ethnicities (Gentile and Jew), and two people with different social roles (centurion and Jesus), yet two people who for different reasons occupy the margins (foreigner, prophet)."³⁵

This, then, is an officer (or official) of some kind who has heard of the reputation of Jesus as a healer and brings to Jesus his servant's acute need (v. 6). The word usually translated "servant" (*pais*) can mean son or child—but probably means "servant" (as it does for Luke)³⁶ and perhaps, as France suggests, "a soldier detailed to act as a personal aide to the commanding officer."³⁷ He is clearly someone the centurion loves; if a servant, the person may have been the equivalent of his whole family. The centurion addresses Jesus as "Sir" (*kyrie* in Greek; "Lord" in Christian discourse),³⁸ and Jesus answers the centurion's request with an astonished reply, given that, as a Jew, he cannot enter a Gentile's house (v. 7). Both the syntax and the flow of the dialogue suggest that the wording (either a question or a statement in Greek) be understood as a question, which France translates as "You want *me* to come and heal

in Cotter, *Christ of the Miracle Stories*, 111–17.

33. Boring, "Matthew," 227.
34. Cotter, *Christ of the Miracle Stories*, 119; see her description on 117–19.
35. *Matthew and the Margins*, 200.
36. On the possible translation of *pais* as "son" or "boy" or "child," see: *BAGD*, 604–5; Luz, *Matthew 8–20*, 10 (who opts for "son" (n. 17); as does Hagner, *Matthew 1–13*, 204. For further discussion see Nolland, *Gospel of Matthew*, 354.
37. France, *Gospel of Matthew*, 312. Whether *pais* means "servant" or "boy," the person is clearly a member of the centurion's household and may even be the centurion's entire "family."
38. This form of address is discussed below in commenting on Luke 7:6.

him?"³⁹ Perhaps it is something of a snub to the Gentile.⁴⁰ On the other hand, if it is a statement, it would signal the readiness of Jesus to cross an important cultural boundary given that observant Jews were highly reluctant to enter Gentile houses and generally considered contact with Gentiles to be contaminating.⁴¹

The centurion acknowledges his unworthiness: "Lord, I am not worthy" (v. 8). His self-deprecating expression is not unlike that of the Canaanite woman's humble acceptance of the label "dog" by the Jewish healer with whom she is talking (15:27; on which, see further below). The centurion, apparently sensitive to Jewish scruples about entering Gentile houses, concedes Jesus' special mission to Israel (cf. 15:27). At the same time he expresses great faith for, as Craig Keener puts it, "Jewish people considered long-distance miracles especially difficult and rare, the domain of only the most powerful holy men."⁴² The centurion also understands the principle of the "authority" exercised by Jesus (v. 9); Roman soldiers were disciplined examples of obedience to authority.

Matthew rarely attributes emotions to Jesus but does so here with the recollection that Jesus "marveled" (or "was amazed" or "was astonished") at this display of faith.⁴³ Keener rightly comments that "so palpably quantifiable a nonverbal expression would have had to have made a profound impression on the earliest disciples from whom the tradition stems."⁴⁴ Jesus' commendation of the centurion's faith is introduced with the solemn "truly" as he affirms that in no one in Israel

39. France, *Gospel of Matthew*, 312-13 (original emphasis); perhaps there is a wider contextual understanding of Jesus as hesitant to interact with Gentiles; cf. 15:26. Some commentators read the words as a statement because of the immediate context of grace and point to Jesus' affirmation of the centurion and his willingness to help.

40. Keener, *Historical Jesus*, 144.

41. See the discussion in the first part of chapter 1 above; and the attitudes on display in Acts 10:27-29. According to (later) rabbinic teaching, to enter the house of a Gentile would be to defile oneself (*m. Ohol* 18:7).

42. Keener, *Commentary on Matthew*, 267.

43. The verb used appears only twice in the Gospels: here in response to a Gentile's faith and in Mark 6:6 at the unbelief of Jesus' hometown.

44. *Commentary on Matthew*, 268 n. 22. Meier appeals to the criterion of embarrassment to endorse the probability that the narrative is authentic: Meier, *Marginal Jew*, 2:725 (see also his wider discussion, 2:718-26).

has he found such faith as this Gentile displays. The remarks are directed to those following, and within the hearing of the centurion; this is "striking" according to Nolland: "Jesus is not saying that he has failed to find faith in Israel, but he is saying that he has not found faith on the level of the centurion's (this will apply as much to the disciples as to the others)."[45]

Verses 11 and 12 (in which many will come to the eschatological banquet from east and west while the apparent heirs of the kingdom are rejected) have attracted considerable interest in scholarly discussions of mission and eschatology in the Synoptic Gospels. The authenticity of the verses has been widely defended, notably by Joachim Jeremias who finds strong evidence in the form of semiticisms and other background material that supports authenticity.[46] The use of the meal imagery ("eat") is significant for the establishing of God's reign and draws on the Jewish image of the coming eschatological banquet with the great patriarchs, Abraham, Isaac and Jacob. Although the Hebrew Scriptures declare that it is to be a meal for all peoples (Isa 25:6; cf. 56:3–8), there was quite widespread agreement in Second Temple Era Judaism that it could not include Gentiles, with whom table fellowship was not possible for Jews. The verses sound a distinctive note of affirmation by Jesus of Gentile faith. Jesus foreshadows an alternative community drawn from the marginalized as a foretaste of the messianic banquet. The entry of these "others," these aliens, is not simply predicted of the eschatological future; it has already begun. Moreover, the clear implication is that the centurion is among the many who "will come from east and west" to celebrate the eschatological feast.

Bruner cites Chrysostom to the affect that the centurion came seeking healing but also received heaven.[47] And John Calvin remarks that "before Christ healed his servant, he himself [the centurion] had been healed by the Lord."[48] It is true that Jesus could have been refer-

---

45. *Gospel of Matthew*, 356.

46. *Jesus' Promise*, 55–62.

47. Bruner, *Matthew*, 1:382.

48. Calvin, *Matthew, Mark and Luke*, 247. Calvin is also impressed by what he sees as a further miraculous dimension: "that a military man, who had crossed the sea in armed force to subdue the Jews into accepting the yoke of Roman tyranny,

ring to *diaspora* or "unprivileged" Jews as those who would come "from the east and the west" but the context—with its sharp and surprising contrasts, and the fact that the inclusion in the eschatological banquet of *diaspora* Jews was not in question—means that "Jesus very probably meant Gentiles" and Matthew certainly means Gentiles, not gathered Jews (given that Rome is the great power to the west and Gentiles have already come from the east: the magi of Matt 2:1–12).[49]

A "long-distance" healing follows (13). This sort of healing was rare, both in the Jewish scriptures and in the ancient world generally; as already noted, it was seen as a sign of extraordinary power. A healing was generally thought to possess greater credibility if the prophet or magician was present in person. In the Gospels, the only reported long-distance healings are with two Gentiles (here and at 15:28) and with the royal official of John 4:49–53 (if that is a different individual).

Luke 7:1–10[50]

The officer's status as a Gentile is made clear in v. 5 (the contrast with "our people") and is certainly implied in other parts of the account. It also seems likely that this particular Gentile belongs to the sociological category of "God-fearers."[51] The centurion's standing and sincerity are such that the community's elders appear to want to make an exception to the rule that a Jew (in this case a Jewish healer) could not be expected to go into the home of a Gentile (v. 3).

In both Luke 7:6 and Matt 8:8 the centurion addresses Jesus as "Sir" (*kyrie* in Greek; "Lord" in Christian discourse). The term is common

---

should submit himself to the God of Israel of his own accord, and devote himself to His obedience" (247–48).

49. *Commentary on Matthew*, 270; France also rejects the reading that some Jews are in mind here (*Gospel of Matthew*, 317–18).

50. Much of the discussion above of the Matthean account of the story is relevant to the account in Luke and so is not repeated here.

51. These are described by one commentator as those who, although "attracted to Judaism, its monotheism, and its ethical teachings, . . . avoided the final step of circumcision, to avoid betraying their race and homeland. They did, however, attend Jewish liturgical services, knew the Law, and kept its major commands" (Bovon, *Luke 1*, 260b).

in personal dialogue and does not necessarily imply any recognition of transcendent status—though, for Christians, a greater significance would be discerned in the centurion's language. Moreover, even as a term expressing politeness, it certainly is "remarkable as addressed by an officer of the occupying forces to a socially insignificant member of the subject race."[52] Howard Marshall argues that *kyrios* is "the Greek equivalent for 'Rabbi.'"[53] A detailed discussion of this employment of *kyrie* is provided by Kavin Rowe who offers a careful exegesis of all the passages in the Gospel of Luke that use *kyrios* for Jesus in order to trace the complex and deliberate development in Luke's narrative of Jesus' identity as Lord. A number of commentators see only a mundane reference in the vocative *kyrie* ("Lord" or "Sir" when addressing another) and, as Rowe points out, the word "undoubtedly was an important way a Gentile centurion in the ancient Mediterranean world could greet a person to whom he would pay respect." But at the end of his study, Rowe concludes that "excellent scholars have regrettably missed Luke's literary technique as they have endeavored to treat the vocative within an either/or framework (either christological or mundane).... As elsewhere, Luke here exploits the semantic range and ambiguity of the vocative such that within the same word readers can hear both 'sir/master' and 'Lord' simultaneously. Thus is the possibility excluded that *kyrie* in 7:6 is to be read only as 'Sir' or only as 'Lord.'"[54] The healing is accomplished—and, significantly (as already noted), at a distance (10).[55]

---

52. France, *Gospel of Matthew*, 312; cf. Carter, *Matthew and the Margins*, 201: "Surprisingly, he subordinates himself to one who, as a Jew, is under his authority."

53. *Luke*, 281.

54. Rowe, *Early Narrative Christology*, 114–17 (quotes from 115–16). John Nolland also feels that the word's meaning is much more than mundane, partly because of the centurion's highly deferential tone (*Luke*, 1:317).

55. Bovon makes the additional point that the actual words of healing are "purposely not recounted, so that the readers ascribe the healing, above all, to the centurion's faith" (Bovon, *Luke 1*, 263b). This is, presumably, to avoid any suggestion that some 'magical formula' is used or is available for repetition by others.

Jesus Heals a Royal Official's Son (John 4:46–54)

The narrative in chapter 4 of the Fourth Gospel records Jesus as moving from the Samaritan village in Samaria back to Galilee. The reason for revisiting Cana (v. 46) is not given. The story of healing that unfolds centers on faith. In it, "the faith of the Samaritans, which has just been described, is contrasted with the lack of faith among the Galileans. Yet we meet a royal official who is an amazing example of one who has the characteristics of true discipleship."[56] As we have seen, it is probable that the official is a Gentile. If so, the three persons with whom Jesus has dialogue in this early ministry as portrayed in John's Gospel represent Jews, Samaritans, and Gentiles—in short, the world he has came to save. The Fourth Gospel, though it mainly records the ministry of Jesus in Jerusalem, has a much wider horizon than that of geography alone. The references to Galilee that surround the story (vv. 43–47, 54), and the (admittedly puzzling) reference to rejection (v. 44), may well be making the same point.[57]

The report that Jesus has healed people in Jerusalem reaches the official. Learning that Jesus has returned to Galilee, the man immediately seeks Jesus out and urges him to heal his son who is dangerously ill. His request is recounted in the imperfect tense and implies repeated or persistent action; the request is insistent and might well be translated "begged." The reply from Jesus is unexpected: "unless you see signs and wonders you will not believe" (v. 48)[58] The verbs in the reply are plural in Greek; so, while the rebuke is spoken to the official, it is directed also to all those present ("you people" might be an accurate paraphrase of the Greek) and to the readers of the Gospel as well. The official is, it seems, addressed as representative of Galilean Jews, "who would not

---

56. Whitacre, *John*, 114.

57. This could follow from what Thomas Brodie calls the Fourth Gospel's "space-based structure" in which "'Galilee' is not just a geographic term; it symbolizes acceptance. . . . Jesus' Judaic compatriots showed him no honor; but the Galileans—intimating the reaction of the Gentiles—welcomed him" (*Gospel according to John*, 228–29).

58. The answer of Jesus is treated as an exclamation in most translations but as a question in the New English Bible (even as most recent exegesis sees Matt 8:7 as a question, implying an objection).

think too highly of a servant of Herod. They need to see signs and wonders performed for such a despised person before they will understand that God loves him also and is willing to freely grant life to his son."[59]

The reply of Jesus seems like a heartless rejection and appears to imply that the official, like the rest of the Galileans, was only giving an excuse for eliciting a miracle from Jesus. On the other hand, Jesus' words may express his hope more than his exasperation. He looks for a belief characterized by sincerity rather than amazement, and the second half of the episode shows that his aim is to inculcate a genuine commitment rather than merely to perform a cure. If so, it is a test of faith to which the official responds by means of his patience and perseverance.[60] The genuine distress of the father is heard in his words: "Sir, come down at once before my little boy dies!" (v. 49). Jesus' response ("Go; your son will live") still seems somewhat impersonal and casual but the official "believed the word Jesus spoke to him" (50) and as he was "going down" to Capernaum from Cana (a descent of some 20 miles)[61] the news of the healing is brought to him (51). After the father considers the timing and details of his meeting with Jesus, and the good news concerning his son's recovery that coincided with Jesus' word to him (52–53), "he and his household believed" (53b).[62]

The Syrophoenician/Canaanite Mother

Before the two accounts (Mark 7:24–30//Matt 15:21–28) are discussed, there are some important background issues to consider.[63] The context

---

59. Whitacre, *John*, 115. Note also the connection with the preceding transitional passage; the Galileans had observed Jesus' signs at the Passover in Jerusalem—by way of contrast with the Samaritans who believe without miracles.

60. Such a possible test of faith might be of the kind implied in John 2:4; Mark 7:27; Matt 8:7.

61. Note the familiarity with Palestinian geography.

62. Note the contrast with Westernized understandings of salvation in individualistic terms. The verse is reminiscent of the household conversions in Acts (10:2; 11:14; 16:15, 31–34; 18:8).

63. Limitations of space mean that a number of historical-critical and hermeneutical issues (as discussed in commentaries and specialist studies) are bypassed in what follows. Of the specialist studies, particular attention might be made of the very

in the Gospels of Mark and Matthew seems highly significant. In Mark there is a central "Gentile section" (7:1–8:10) that covers Jesus' reinterpretation of dietary laws (an impediment to Jewish-Gentile contact); this encounter with the Syrophoenician mother; ministry by Jesus in the Dekapolis; and the feeding of the four thousand on the Gentile side of the Sea of Galilee.[64] In Matthew, too, the encounter also follows a lengthy discussion of purity issues and is followed by the feeding of the four thousand. Matthew's description of the woman as a "Canaanite" reinforces the Gentile context of the meeting. The authenticity of the passage seems well-established in terms of the criteria mentioned at the start of this chapter.[65] The embarrassment factor (what Bird describes as "the discourteous and derogatory nature of Jesus' response to the Gentile woman" and the probable reason for its omission by Luke) adds to the likelihood of its authenticity.[66] The plausibility of a journey to Tyre is also affirmed by Bird and others.[67]

---

detailed discussion (including an account of the passage's reception history) by Pablo Alonso, *The Woman Who Changed Jesus*—even though this writer dissents from several of Alonso's major conclusions. Some of Alonso's findings are included in the chapter by him, "Woman Who Changed Jesus," in another publication.

64. This central "Gentile section" within Mark is further discussed below in chapter 3.

65. There are those who doubt its authenticity and who see the narrative as a later creation related to an emerging Gentile mission; see, for example, Meier, *Marginal Jew*, 2:660–61. Freyne, however, defends the authenticity of the passage on the grounds of "the realist character of both the situation and the actors in the context of our knowledge of Tyre/Galilee relations and ethnic tensions . . . ("Jesus in Context," 25). Alonso also defends the story on the grounds that it "violates cultural norms for both purity codes and gender roles, together with its critical view of Jesus" ("Woman Who Changed Jesus," 126).

66. See the discussion, with extensive annotation, by Bird, *Jesus and the Origins*, 113–15 (quote from 113); Bird also quotes Klausner as writing that the statement is "so brusque and chauvinistic that if any other Jewish teacher of the time had said such a thing Christians would never have forgiven Judaism for it" (113).

67. Bird, *Jesus and the Origins*, 113–14, again with extensive annotation.

Mark 7:24–30

The story is highly significant for the overall theme of our volume. Mark is very precise in his identification of the woman: a "Greek, Syrophoenician by ethnicity." No other person in the second Gospel is identified so clearly, nor so precisely as a Gentile. The setting of the story is certainly noteworthy. "The region of Tyre" refers generally to the area under the jurisdiction of the wealthy coastal city of Tyre to the north of Galilee. As Robert Guelich points out, "Tyre, often linked with Sidon in Scripture (Isa 23:1–12; Jer 47:4; Joel 3:4–8; Zech 9:2; cf. 7:31), was a gentile area, whose inhabitants Josephus describes as 'notoriously our bitterest enemies' (*Ag. Ap.*, 1.13)."[68] It appears that Jesus is simply seeking privacy from the public and most commentators exclude any missional interest in Gentiles from the encounter.[69] Yet, even in this Gentile territory, Jesus cannot escape public notice (v. 24); his reputation has spread beyond Galilee.[70] "Non-Israelites were known to seek help from Israelite holy men (folk healers and exorcists)."[71]

By placing the story about the Syrophoenician woman within this territory of Tyre which was synonymous with non-Jews, and within the context of a broader discussion of defilement (7:1–21), Mark underscores "the force of Jesus' ministry in removing all barriers between Jews and Gentiles."[72] Not only has Jesus entered Gentile territory, but he is shown to have contact with a specific Gentile woman whose daughter has an "unclean" spirit (v. 25). The mention of this "unclean spirit" also reinforces the "unclean" setting for Jesus and offers a connection with the preceding Markan discussion of defilement. With this in mind, a Japanese commentator notes that "the woman might be herself socially ostracized because of the unclean spirit in her child."[73]

---

68. Guelich, *Mark 1—8:26*, 384.

69. However, as noted above, a somewhat different note—strongly suggestive of some kind of mission to Gentiles—is maintained by some scholars. This perspective is discussed in chapter 3 below.

70. Mark 3:8 has already informed the reader that Jesus' fame had spread throughout the area.

71. Malina and Rohrbaugh, *Social Science Commentary*, 177.

72. Guelich, *Mark 1—8:26*, 388.

73. Hisako Kinukawa, "Mark," in Patte, *Global Bible Commentary*, 373a.

The woman "bowed down at his feet" (25)—the only other occurrence of the expression in Mark's Gospel is in reference to Jairus (5:22); as president of the synagogue he stands in sharp contrast with the Gentile woman. Verse 26 identifies her as a Greek[74] and she is also described as Syrophoenician—a further underscoring of the Gentile setting of the story and of the woman as a Gentile. Her approach certainly acknowledges his power to help her. The heart of Jesus' response ("Let the children be fed first," 27) maintains the distinction between the Jews and Gentiles by drawing attention to Israel's prerogative: as God's "children" they have a claim on the "bread," that is, God's blessing through Jesus. As with the centurion, the woman's address of Jesus as *kyrie* suggests more than a polite "Sir" from a Gentile. As the context implies, the woman acknowledges, in accordance with the address typical of Gentile Christianity, that Jesus is "Lord."

Jesus draws attention to the woman's response (29) and identifies it as the reason he has heard her request. The unclean spirit leaves the daughter, although without mention of any direct act or word of healing offered by Jesus. As with the centurion's story, no tangible healing act is portrayed. And it is also possible (as many commentators also note) that the healing of Gentiles at a distance may relate directly or indirectly to issues of purity-related separation between Jew and Gentile. The miracle is confirmed when the woman returns home and finds that the demon has, in fact, left her daughter (30).

Matthew 15:21–28

Although Matthew's parallel account is also about healing from a distance, he focuses not on the healing itself but on the faith of the Gentile woman who makes the request.[75] As with Mark, the context in Matthew

---

74. The designation might well imply that the conversation between her and Jesus would have been held in Greek.

75. By comparison with the Gospel of Mark, and in terms of redaction activity, "Matthew . . . abbreviates Mark in this pericope but more importantly reformulates the story so as to put great emphasis on the exclusivity of Jesus' mission to the Jews and yet at the same time to recognize the reality of the faith of a Gentile. . . . Matthew's literary artistry is . . . at work in the construction of this pericope" (Hagner, *Matthew 14–28*, 440; Hagner lists other redactional details and compares the two accounts on

is significant. The preceding statements about true purity (15:10–20) receive an implied implementation as Jesus encounters an "unclean" Gentile. The geographical setting is also important. For Matthew, Tyre and Sidon are outside the symbolic boundaries of Israel. The reference could be to the actual Gentile towns along the Syrophoenician coast (cf. Matt 11:21–22 and also Mark 3:8) or to the larger territories known by those names that extended far to the east of the towns, in which case the population could still have been largely Jewish (and this Jewish presence may partly explain why Jesus was known there). Upper Galilee (the Golan) had already initiated what were to become strong trading and other commercial links with Tyre and Syria[76]—but not to the detriment of a strongly Jewish ethos, especially in its villages. Most, or all, of Matthew's readers would know that Jezebel, who helped Ahab introduce Baal worship into Israel, came from Sidon. The dog metaphor "presupposes a Gentile setting, since Jews did not typically have dogs as household pets."[77]

One feature of Matthew's account is that he describes the woman as a "Canaanite" (the only use of the word in the NT) "from those regions" rather than Mark's "Greek" ("Gentile") and "Syrophoenician." The term "Canaanite" has inevitable OT associations with the pagan inhabitants of Palestine displaced by the Jews and it thereby contrasts the woman all the more with the covenantal people of God. (The term is also used for non-Jews in later rabbinic literature.) Of the many reasons suggested for Matthew's change of Mark's "Syrophoenician" into "Canaanite," the most plausible is that Matthew has in mind the OT associations that the word will evoke: distrust and even fear of Gentiles "which in turn allows one to see in Jesus the overcoming of such fear and revulsion."[78] Matthew's identification of the woman as "Canaanite" would lead most of his Jewish readers to think of "the traditional arch-enemies of Israel

---

439–40). The encounter is not mentioned in Luke and Matthew's incorporation of new material is, presumably, for his rather different audience.

76. See the evidence cited in Vale, "Literary Sources," 224–25; in summary: "The numismatic evidence points to Tyre as the commercial focus for Upper Galilee, and further suggests that the nucleus of its cultural life may lie to the north and east rather than south to Lower Galilee and Jerusalem" (226).

77. Boring, "Matthew," 336.

78. Davies and Allison, *Gospel according to Matthew*, 2:547.

in the biblical saga and the chasm between the pagan world and that of Israel."[79] Or, to suggest a complementary dimension, "Canaanite" is a person native to Palestine—the object of Jewish "ethnic cleansing" with some Canaanites left as an enslaved remnant.[80] The woman is both Hellenized and yet acquainted with Judaism as well. Her opening words are distinctly Jewish: "have mercy on me, Lord, Son of David," given that "Son of David" is a Jewish title for the Messiah.

The woman is described as "crying out" (*ekrazen*)—a verb whose imperfect tense suggests that she needs to labor to get the attention of Jesus who is probably sheltered by his disciples. She consistently addresses Jesus as *kyrie*, "Lord" (22, 25, 27). At first, Jesus completely ignores her pleading (23; the Greek literally states Jesus "did not answer a word"). The disciples' request for Jesus to send her away is also in the imperfect tense, indicating that they make it repeatedly in response to the woman's crying out. After his initially silent response to the woman's request, and after her persistent appeals, Jesus merely offers the apparently absolute "I was sent only to the lost sheep of the house of Israel" (24). The woman is not discouraged by this implicit rejection; she admits the priority of Israel in salvation-history but perseveres in the request on behalf of her afflicted daughter. Her persistence prevails and her faith is strongly praised by Jesus; the apparent exclusivism of his reply is immediately tempered in this very narrative by the healing (and discussion below will also suggest that the account is worded in strongly ironic terms).

The dilemmas regarding Jesus' restrictive missional intent (sent *only* to Israel to the exclusion of Gentiles and Samaritans) are best resolved in terms of a restoration theology. As Michael Bird explains (commenting on the restrictive texts of Matt 10:6 and 15:24): "[t]he positive actions of Jesus towards Gentiles show how the restoration of

---

79. Senior, *Matthew*, 181.

80. It is possible to read the use of the anachronistic "Canaanite" as intentional in order to allow Jesus to deconstruct the violent OT conquest narrative with the suggestion that the kingdom of God has a radically different approach to "the other." This is a theme picked up by Brian McLaren, who writes that, "in this encounter, instead of a Jew violently and mercilessly conquering a Canaanite in harmony with the old stories of Exodus and Joshua, the Canaanite wins and conquers the Jew so that he responds to her request for mercy" (McLaren, *Everything Must Change*, 157).

Israel that he is announcing and performing impacts Gentiles in the present. There is no need to wait for the eschaton, but as the tide of restoration rises, more and more Gentiles get to experience its liberating power."[81]

Despite Jesus' reply in terms of being sent only to Israel, the woman is not rebuffed into silence. In fact, she "began to worship him." As Donald Hagner adds, "[d]riven by a mother's love for her child, she again made her plea: . . . 'Lord, help me,' a re-expression of the request in v. 22 but in more idiomatic Greek."[82] In the remarkable exchange that follows (26–27), the Jewish view of the salvation-historical primacy of Israel continues to be assumed by Jesus and accepted without challenge by the woman, but with the reminder that Israel's blessings can, even in limited ways, extend to Gentiles. Blakley draws a poignant conclusion to the story as a whole. "In the end, the woman's conviction as to the sufficiency of the crumbs is vindicated for her daughter's salvation is as complete and miraculous as anything experienced by Jews thus far, despite the fact that Jesus issues no command, never touches the girl, and, in fact, is not even in her presence."[83]

Is There a Rejection of the Woman by Jesus?

One feature of the story draws frequent comment: Jesus' apparent rejection of the woman, especially by means of his disparaging equation of Gentiles with "dogs." Because this has obvious implications for the exemplary Christology to which this volume draws attention, it is important to consider the issue. Considerable concern has been expressed over the centuries about the apparently demeaning attitude of Jesus towards the woman. Because of its tone, some commentators consider harsh dimension to have been overlaid on the narrative. For example, John Meier writes that this is a story in which Jesus speaks to a "sincere petitioner" with "harsh, insulting language" created to exemplify (and thus justify) the missionary theology and practice of conserva-

---

81. Bird, *Jesus and the Origins*, 123.
82. Hagner, *Matthew 14–28*, 442.
83. Blakley, "Incomprehension or Resistance?," 253 n. 153.

tive Jewish Christians who opposed the Gentile mission.[84] But Meier's assessment is unnecessary; in fact, his conclusion fails his own test of (non-inventable) embarrassment. The story has many widely accepted marks of authenticity, including a strong contrast with the Jewish tone of the Gospels as a whole, and it reflects a widely attested hostility between Galileans and Syrophoenicians—as our comments will make clear. If, as this volume suggests, the example of Jesus in his encounter with Gentiles and Samaritans is worthy of imitation, then discussion is certainly needed.

When, in another context, Jesus says "Do not give what is holy to dogs" (Matt 7:6), he does quite likely have Gentiles in view. It is true that "dogs"—meaning scavenging dogs—was, in Craig Keener's words, "a title recognized as an insult throughout the ancient Mediterranean world." But Keener also adds that "[c]ommentators who suggest that Jewish people regularly called Gentiles 'dogs' . . . might make too much of relatively scant references . . ."[85] Nonetheless, even if it is the case that "it is by no means true that Jews used the epithet 'dog' primarily with reference to Gentiles,"[86] a clear and unflattering analogy is drawn. Jesus' explanation that he is sent "only to the lost sheep of Israel" (Matt 15:24) seems excessively and inappropriately ethnocentric in a situation of pressing human need. It is an explanation that is made worse by the apparent ethnocentric slur of calling the woman and her daughter "dogs." There have been a number of attempted explanations, of which the following are the most common.

The (Jewish) Humanity of Jesus

Does the story tell of an initial refusal by Jesus who then changes his mind because of the mother's witty reply? Some commentators argue that the (Jewish) prejudices of Jesus are overcome as he receives illumi-

---

84. *Marginal Jew*, 2:660–62. However, in the same volume, Meier apparently defends the story: the church preserves the story rather than yielding to a "convenient amnesia" about it (168–70).

85. Keener, *Historical Jesus*, 144, 471 n. 76.

86. Hare, *Matthew*, 176.

nation from this Gentile woman.⁸⁷ For Frances Gench, the Canaanite woman is a paradigmatic example of human initiative and persistence over prejudice. She calls Jesus' identification of the woman with "the dogs" a "participat[ion] in human prejudice."⁸⁸ Spina writes of "Jesus' harsh posture and demeaning rhetoric."⁸⁹ Theissen and Merz argue that "Mark 7.24–30 is the only apophthegm in the NT in which Jesus does not dominate the argument but allows himself to be convinced."⁹⁰ The problem with such assertions is that they appeal to what Michael Bird calls "some kind of psychologizing of Jesus."⁹¹ N.T. Wright is highly critical of "a fashionable theory concerning Jesus' innate prejudices and his willingness to receive rebuke and illumination from a foreign woman."⁹² Moreover, as Blakley points out,

> it is fundamentally at odds with the narrative's ideological and evaluative viewpoints of Jesus. It implies that Jesus' attitudes towards Gentiles are inadequate, mistaken, and in need of correction; yet, from the narrator's perspective, Jesus—who has been anointed by God's Spirit, has God's unqualified approval—is the one character who *always* thinks and does the things of God. Jesus is never in need of correction; thus, interpreting his initial response as a refusal to heal cuts against the grain of the narrative's rhetoric and the implied reader's expectations.⁹³

---

87. See, for example, Rhoads, "Jesus and the Syrophoenician Woman," 361–63; Cotter, *Christ of the Miracle Stories*, 157–59; McLaren, *Everything Must Change*, 157; Alonso, *Woman Who Changed Jesus*, 295–99, 328–32; idem, "Woman Who Changed Jesus," 125–26.

88. Gench, *Back to the Well*, 23.

89. Spina, *Faith of the Outsider*, 138.

90. Theissen and Merz, *Historical Jesus*, 222.

91. He goes on to quote Morna Hooker to the effect that we lack the kind of evidence that might enable the discernment of such a development (Bird, *Jesus and the Origins*, 115); contemporary exegetes simply do not have enough insight into what he goes on to call such "enigmatic mind games" (118 n. 150).

92. Wright, *Jesus and the Victory of God*, 309 n. 244.

93. Blakley, "Incomprehension or Resistance?," 249; Blakley has the Markan passage in mind.

Nonetheless, Jesus is quite capable of speaking sharply, and in a way that offends contemporary sensitivities. And, as Garland comments, "possibly our modern sensitivities are mistaken. We assume that Jesus is obligated to respond to every request and to heal everyone. We tend to dejudaize Jesus and are offended by the particularity of God's election. During the ministry of Jesus the boundary between Jews and gentiles is very real."[94] There is no denying the Jewish humanity of Jesus; but this, in itself, does not explain (or excuse) what appears to be insulting language. And Jesus does move, quickly and decisively, to heal the daughter.

The Priority of Israel

It is clear from the Gospels[95] that the natural and prior concern of Jesus is for his Jewish compatriots. It is Matthew's Gospel alone that has the explanation "only to the lost sheep of Israel" (15:24). The metaphor of food—both as the children's food and the foretold messianic banquet—seems clearly to allude to the privilege of Jewish covenant relationship with God and the priority of Israel. The eschatological setting of 8:11, and the place of Israel as asserted here in 15:26–27, does not diminish this priority, and the voice of Jesus in this passage "makes it abundantly clear that the biblical doctrine of Israel's election must be taken seriously."[96] Mark (7:27) adds the qualification "first" in his reply: "Let the children be fed first." This is not inconsistent with the notion of a (later) mission to Gentiles; such a mission does not replace the prior mission to Israel but expands it. Craig Keener considers that in both Mark and Matthew, "Jesus probably refers to the children's pet dogs; well-to-do Greeks, unlike most Jews, could raise dogs as pets and not view them as merely troublesome rodents." If the domestic setting is emphasized then the image becomes one in which children's needs take timely precedence. But such an admission, however, "hardly transforms the image into a compliment"[97] and the overtones of initial rejection

---

94. Garland, *Reading Matthew*, 165.
95. And beyond; see Rom 1:16.
96. Davies and Allison, *Gospel according to Matthew*, 2:557.
97. Keener, *Commentary on Matthew*, 416.

by Jesus remain. Perhaps Jesus' language is not really couched in ethnic terms at all. Frances Gench (drawing on Jon Sobrino) suggests that Jesus' words "give expression to the urgency that impels him" in the face of the perilous position ("harassed and helpless"—Matt 9:36) of his own Jewish people. "Thus, those human beings he perceives as the neediest are identified as the primary focus of his mission."[98] In other words, missional explanations in terms of priority, ethnicity, or need perhaps soften the apparent harshness.

Explanations in Social Science Categories

According to a detailed and, in part at least, often persuasive socio-psychological analysis by Gerd Theissen,[99] the narrative reveals the bitter relations that existed between Jews and Gentiles in the border regions between Tyre and Galilee (65). Tyre was a wealthy island city and the articulate woman seems clearly to be a relatively wealthy Hellenized Phoenician who approaches the visiting prophet in rural territory that belongs to Tyre (70–71). Tyre was dependent on food imports that resulted in a struggle for resources in which rural Jews "usually got the short end of things" (75) by comparison with the relatively wealthy inhabitants of Tyre. The woman belongs to the Hellenized upper social class, which despises and exploits Galilean Jews. If this is the case, then different power relationships than normally assumed are at work in what begins as a confrontation between Jesus and the woman. The sharp reply of Jesus to the woman's request for healing reflects the typical anger of the rural Jewish poor whom Jesus believes ought to be fed instead of having to provide for rich urban Gentiles (74–75, 79). Theissen also speaks of "aggressive prejudices, supported by economic dependency and legitimated by religious traditions" (78–79). Galileans also resented the way in which Syrian provincial leaders discriminated against them in financial and other ways and gave them only "crumbs." Jesus, as a Galilean, is testing the woman to discern how she will react when the power relationship is reversed. However, despite the appeal

---

98. Gench, *Back to the Well*, 7–8.
99. *Gospels in Context*, 61–80; page numbers from Theissen indicated in the text.

of Theissen's argument, it must be said that Matthew hints at no such dynamic as the reason for the language employed by Jesus.

A Wittily Exchanged Domestic Parable of Children and Dogs

A more plausible explanation is found in the suggestion by Martin Hengel that the woman understands Jesus' reply to her request for healing ("Let the children be satisfied first, for it is not good to take the loaf off the children and throw it to the dogs"—7:27) as a parable.[100] The woman instantly comprehends the parable—in sharp contrast with the disciples who do not (cf. Mark 4:13; 7:18). As a domestic parable, the passage may even contain an intentional softening by the deliberate employment of the diminutive *kunarion* with the implied and even somewhat affectionate acknowledgement of the woman's daughter as a domestic pet, a small puppy.[101] The woman offers the shrewd response that "even dogs eat the crumbs of children" which not only acknowledges the priority of Israel in Jesus' mission but also implies that Israel's blessings can, albeit in limited ways, extend to Gentiles in the present. David Rhoads nicely paraphrases the woman's response: "*Even now* I and my daughter at the margins (should) benefit from just one exorcism from among the many benefits for the Jews."[102] Senior considers the response to be "an artful blend of deference . . . and a clever retort."[103] Whatever the *intention* of the imagery, the woman is "seemingly unresentful of the analogy."[104] Perhaps, as Theissen suggests, "[b]ehind the sharp refusal, she can hear a positive attitude to children expressed in the image. And when she acts on behalf of a child, she is only putting into practice what

---

100. Hengel, *Studies in Mark*, 97–98.

101. Green translates, "Is it fair to take the children's bread and give it to the pups?" which he calls a "half-derogatory, half-affectionate" description (*Message of Matthew*, 172–73). Nonetheless, there is no such diminutive in Aramaic (according to Hare, *Matthew*, 176) and, although the conversation may have taken place in Greek, Guelich points out that "the passage has several diminutives without significant force" (Guelich, *Mark 1—8:26*, 386; he lists four).

102. Rhoads, "Jesus and the Syrophoenician Woman," 357; original emphasis.

103. Senior, *Matthew*, 182.

104. Boring, "Matthew," 336.

is praised in the image within the saying."[105] Although talk of tone of voice introduces a novelistic explanation that is not in the text itself, Gene Smillie is probably correct when he writes that the woman, "with more clarity than many readers of the story, has seen through the mask of Jewish exclusivism in his conventional speech and knows what he can—and, she correctly believes, will—do for her. She has faith that, even acknowledging some kind of Jewish priority in the ordered social system of the people of God, mercy and help are to be hoped for from this Master, not on the basis of her status, but of his."[106]

Ted Blakley also draws attention to the parabolic nature of the exchange. He explains that "the *children* denote the Jewish people, the *dogs* Gentiles, and *the loaf* the blessings of God's kingdom." On this understanding Jesus takes the mother's plea for the healing of her daughter as a plea to share in the "benefits that belong to God's chosen people." The parable acknowledges "the Jews' privileged priority . . . but stops short of denying these to Gentiles." It concedes that not to allow this priority "would amount to taking bread away from children and feeding it to scavenging dogs."[107] In other words, the woman's reply takes up the parable and, significantly, she

> neither objects to Jesus' designation of Gentiles as 'dogs' nor challenges their secondary status. She accepts the appellation but modifies its semantic frame so that it evokes a different connotation. Being repositioned under the table the 'dogs' no longer denote the unclean, scavenging dogs of Jewish culture but the domesticated, household pets of Greek culture. She accepts the priority of the Jews in the economy of God's salvation even while offering an alternative timetable that more closely aligns with the actual realities, for the dogs *are eating* from the children's crumbs. In other words, she maintains that Gentiles have

---

105. Theissen, *Gospels in Context*, 81.

106. Smillie, "'Even the Dogs,'" 93.

107. Blakley, "Incomprehension or Resistance?," 250 (original emphasis); see also Rhoads, who considers that Jesus' response takes the form of a parable, "an allegorical riddle" ("Jesus and the Syrophoenician Woman," 355). Wahlen also reads the dialogue as the elaboration of a parable (*Jesus and the Impurity of Spirits*, 107).

already begun to participate in Israel's blessings (e.g., 3:8; 5:1–20).[108]

In fact, the mother's reply actually "extends Jesus' riddle. She does not oppose what Jesus has said. Rather, she develops the scenario of Jesus' allegory so that she and her daughter have a place in it."[109] Or, as Gene Smillie puts it, readers throughout the centuries have been disturbed, even appalled, by these words; but the Canaanite woman apparently is not.[110] Blakley's own conclusion is that she "understands the surplus of God's salvation and its implications for Gentiles . . ."[111] And she also understands, either explicitly or implicitly, something of the profound significance of the one who offers healing.

The Exchange as Intentionally Ironic

Perhaps the most satisfactory explanation is to see the exchange as both parabolic and intentionally *ironic*—which is how Blakley understands it. He points out that the Syrophoenician woman exhibits the very qualities of faith and understanding that the disciples lack.[112] Those who

---

108. Blakley, "Incomprehension or Resistance?," 250.

109. Rhoads, "Jesus and the Syrophoenician Woman," 357.

110. Smillie, "'Even the Dogs,'" 93.

111. Blakley, "Incomprehension or Resistance?," 252. Hagner's explanation is along similar lines: "Many [Jews] expected that the overflow of the abundant eschatological blessing of God would be made available to "righteous" Gentiles (i.e., by keeping the Noachic laws [Gen 9:1–17]). The woman seems to know of this widespread idea and thus that as a Gentile, though she had no right to the eschatological banquet itself, she might well be allowed to enjoy something of the overflow, here described in the image of "the crumbs" . . . that fall from the table (cf. Luke 16:21) to the "house dogs." . . . The disarming response of the woman . . . "true, Lord," reflects an acceptance of her position, but also a constancy of faith that impresses Jesus" (Hagner, *Matthew 14-28*, 442).

112. Blakley writes that "the woman's witty rejoinder demonstrates her understanding of what the disciples have so far failed to understand . . ." In Mark 5:21–43, the two minor characters, Jairus and the hemorrhaging woman, exhibit the faith and courage that the disciples lacked. The rhetorical strategy Mark uses to contrast the minor characters in 5:21–43 with the disciples in terms of faith establishes a precedence for the contrast between the Syrophoenician woman in 7:24–30 and the disciples, although this time, in terms of understanding. According to Blakley, this

interpret Jesus' initial response to the woman as a refusal to heal miss its obvious irony.

In summary, because of some negative features of the pericope, it does seem that commentators too quickly assume that Jesus initially rejects the woman's request. Mark has already made clear (3:7–12; 5:1–20) the willingness of Jesus to heal and bless Gentiles; it seems odd that he would refuse on ethnic grounds here. Mark's readers also know that before this encounter Jesus has not once refused a request for healing (1:40; 2:5; 5:23) nor does he subsequent to this episode (7:32; 8:22; 9:22; 10:47–48, 51). Moreover, a refusal at this point in Mark's narrative would disrupt the growing significance of the central chapters of his Gospel in which each story seems clearly to reaffirm the extension of the Kingdom to Gentiles (evidence for which we will discuss in chapter 3 below). Michael Bird also sees Jesus' remarks about Israel and Gentiles as ironic; they concern the "focus of Israel in his mission" as he "deliberately attempts to elicit a shrewd comeback" from the woman.[113] Despite the insistence of the disciples, Jesus does not dismiss the woman; in fact, the conclusion of the story is a display of compassionate praxis. Put differently, Jesus' reply (in "standard" Jewish nationalistic terms, understood as such by the woman) is intended to test the sincerity and persistence of the woman's faith—which he does by means of the extended parabolic dialogue with its wit and irony—in order to elicit a response from her.[114]

Some Implications for a Religiously Plural World

Attention now turns to some possible implications of the encounters with Gentiles for contemporary readers in settings of religious plurality. Questions about interreligious meeting are not abstract or speculative in Scripture; in the Gospels they are raised by these actual encounters

---

is intentional, especially the verbal parallels shared exclusively by these two episodes. These are the parallels that contribute to the ironic quality of the way that the episode is reported (see Blakley, "Incomprehension or Resistance?," 253–55; quote from 255).

113. Bird, *Jesus and the Origins*, 115, with significant annotation (n. 140).

114. For an exegesis along these lines, see France, *Gospel of Matthew*, 590–91, 595; Talbert, *Matthew*, 190–91.

between Jesus and Gentiles. As in the Introduction, we ask: What might a theological reading of these two encounters suggest for those who experience or reflect on interfaith encounters in the contemporary world? A number of the same themes recur and can usefully serve as points of introduction in our reflections.[115] In keeping with the approach suggested by a theological reading of Luke 4 (the emergence of "fresh readings" and "fresh meanings" as discussed in chapter one above), a number of helpful perspectives seem apparent.

An Extension of the Boundaries of Israel

In terms of relevance for a contemporary setting, this theme of "expanded Israel" introduces the notes of surprise and reversal that are found in the encounters. There are certainly warnings to the first hearers and readers of the Gospels (both Jewish and Christian) about the dangers of religious presumption, especially the presumption of assured religious privilege. Clinton Wahlen draws attention to Jesus as an exorcist in the Gospels. He points out that demon possession "looks the same for both Jews and Gentiles; so does the deliverance. Beginning with the Gerasene demoniac, 'Gentile' regions are reclaimed and brought back within the orbit of a pure Israel . . . . This virtual extension of the geographic boundaries of Israel suggest also an extension of the definition of Israel itself. . . . [B]oth Jews and Gentiles can belong to a greater Israel, the precise geographic boundaries of which are left deliberately vague." Wahlen sees this principle illustrated by the Syrophoenician mother, "who is the first character in Mark to grasp the possibilities found in a parable of Jesus. By accepting the lowest place in the messianic 'house'" she receives healing for her daughter.[116] It is worth repeating David Rhoads' paraphrase of the woman's response: "*Even now* I and my daughter at the margins (should) benefit from just one exorcism from among the many benefits for the Jews."[117] And we have already emphasized the

---

115. These implications relate only to the two encounters; there will be a more complete discussion (bringing together the whole range of material from the Gospels, including the encounter with Samaritans) in the final chapter below.

116. Wahlen, *Jesus and the Impurity of Spirits*, 107.

117. Rhoads, "Jesus and the Syrophoenician Woman," 357; original emphasis.

considerable importance of Matt 8:11–12 with its assurance that many will come from East and West to join the patriarchs at the eschatological banquet at the end of the age. If Jesus can so strongly affirm the faith of a (Roman) centurion and a pagan woman, and contrast such faith with both the faith of his fellow Jews, and his own disciples, as he implicitly redraws the boundaries of Israel, there is surely an implication that contemporary disciples ought also to affirm such faith when they encounter it.

From "the Margins of Scripture . . . to Center Stage"

What we have seen in these encounters also illustrates the ways in which certain themes in Scripture, once regarded as marginal, can and sometimes do move to a more central significance. Our reading of Luke 4:16–30 (in the Introduction above) drew on the insight of Charles Scalise that "parts of Scripture [that] might formerly have been perceived as being on the margins of Scripture . . . move to center stage to address the new issues of later centuries . . ."[118] The encounter of Jesus with Gentiles (and Samaritans) provides an example of a "marginal" issue that assumes a more significant role in Scripture as a whole. The attitude towards Gentiles in the OT is predominantly negative, but now these same Gentiles become visible signs of the inaugurated Rule of God. This is seen in a number of ways.

The Example of Faith and Humility in "Outsiders"[119]

The dynamics of faith and humility that Jesus affirms in the Nazareth pericope (Luke 4:16–30) are encountered by him in person in the stories considered. Faith and humility are seen, firstly, in the attitude of the centurion. The centurion calls Jesus "Lord" and addresses him with unlimited confidence in his authority. This is a "display of exemplary

---

118. As suggested by Scalise, "Hermeneutical Circle," 224.

119. There is, of course, negative material about Gentiles in the Gospels—some of it found on the lips of Jesus himself—just as there is about Jews. See, for example: Matt 5:47; 6:7; 7:6; 18:17; Matt 6:32//Luke 12:30; Mark 10:42–43. It is probably significant that most of these passages are found in Matthew.

faith by a complete outsider"[120] that serves as a model of faith for Israel. As Warren Carter puts it, with the centurion in mind, *faith* "not ethnicity . . . , status . . . , birth, wealth, or gender, constitutes the identity and lifestyle of the community of disciples."[121] Concerning the centurion, François Bovon writes: "[f]aith means trust, and more concretely, to trust without having seen . . . ."[122] Half of Matthew's uses of "faith" are found in this section of his Gospel (8:10; 9:2, 22, 29) and the account of the healing of the centurion's servant has the NT's first explicit mention of faith. Jesus says that in no one in Israel has he found such faith as this Gentile displays (Matt 8:10).[123]

While Jesus, in Matthew, is amazed at the Gentile centurion's faith, the expression "little faith" is used of the disciples (6:30; 8:26; 14:31; 16:8; 17:20). The centurion's request is granted "because someone outside the covenant community has had the audacity to reach in and grasp for what rightly belongs to Israel."[124] One other significant point is that Jesus' word of praise for the centurion's faith is not spoken to the centurion, but "to those who followed him,"[125] an implicit indication that Matthew wants the readers of his Gospel to notice both the words of praise and the clear warning.[126] Moreover, "[t]he officer loves not only the alien people of Israel but also his neighbor. . . . His high estimation of his servant shows that he considers him not only in his function but also as a person. Jesus' love . . . responds to this double affection. Faith and love achieve an exemplary unity in the centurion."[127] Humility is

120. Garland, *Reading Matthew*, 94.

121. Carter, *Matthew and the Margins*, 203.

122. Bovon, *Luke 1*, 265b.

123. It is only to recent Western minds that the miracle is the awkward element in the story, whereas the first hearers and readers may well have been more interested in—and even amazed by—a Gentile's display of faith. And Twelftree also adds a comment (with contemporary skepticism in mind) that "[w]e cannot dismiss a story because the method of healing is not to the liking of the twentieth or twenty-first century" (*Jesus the Miracle Worker*, 296).

124. Bird, *Jesus and the Origins*, 120.

125. Matt 8:10, that is, to disciples—see Matt 9:9.

126. "The Gentile's recognition of Jesus' power and its source in God provides a model for all believers" (Harrington, *Gospel of Matthew*, 114).

127. Bovon, *Luke 1*, 261a.

another notable feature of the story. As Bovon nicely puts it, "the man becomes worthy by believing that he is not."[128] The centurion knows that, while he is powerless in this situation, "Jesus' power can cross any political and ethnic boundary."[129] The centurion becomes the first member of the Gentile church; for Gentile Christians he is the oldest ancestor in faith.[130]

In the parallel story of the official in John 4:46–54 we find that, by dismissing him with the statement that his son was alive, Jesus creates a dilemma of faith. If the father refuses to return to Capernaum without taking Jesus with him, he would show that he does not believe Jesus' word and would consequently receive no benefit because of his distrust. On the other hand, if he follows Jesus' order, he would be returning to the dying boy with no outward assurance of recovery. He is forced to make the difficult choice between insisting on evidence and thus showing disbelief and of exercising faith without any tangible proof to encourage him. The official chooses the second; he believes the word Jesus speaks to him (v. 50). His faith is confirmed and deepened when he learns his son has recovered. In fact, by the end of the story it is simply said that he *believed*, with no qualification.[131] The official's faith, which seems to have begun with an acknowledgement of Jesus' ability to heal, becomes deeper and more comprehensive. "The healing is presented by John . . . as a sign, resulting in the man placing his faith in the person of Jesus. . . . The healing is not the central focus of the narrative. Rather, it is the centrality of faith that must receive prime attention."[132] A further

---

128. Ibid.

129. Carter, *Matthew and the Margins*, 202.

130. Conservative theological concern for the importance of salvation (shared by this writer) rarely pauses to consider the centurion as an example of an *actual recipient of salvation*, given that Jesus appears clearly to seat him at the eschatological banquet. Surprise might be an appropriate response—as it was for the early church to hear that "God has given even to the Gentiles the repentance that leads to life" (Acts 11:18b); the centurion's "repentance" is, at best, only implicit in the Gospel narrative.

131. This form of expression is usually used by John in reference to a person who has insight into Jesus' identity and accepts him. There may even be a *progression* in the official's faith apparent in verses 48, 50, 53—although Moloney finds difficulty in the suggestion (*Gospel of John*, 154–55).

132. Warrington, *Jesus the Healer*, 126.

dimension is also apparent in the story: the man's humility. As a *basilikos* he is either a person of royal birth or, at least, someone of rank and privilege—and yet he is willing humbly to ask, in front of others, for help from an itinerant healer-teacher.[133]

We turn now to the faith displayed by the Syrophoenician mother. Even the syntax of Matthew's Greek accentuates the woman's faith. When Jesus is reported as saying to the woman, "Great is your faith. Let it be done for you as you wish" (15:28), not only are "great" and "your" emphasized, but the repeated "you" is also significant. The woman's final request "is amazing in both humility and insight."[134] She demonstrates faith that is "extravagant" and "warm and wholehearted";[135] her faith is "tenacious" and she displays "unshakable confidence in Jesus."[136] The woman displays "unconditional confidence" and "unconditional trust."[137] Gench writes of the woman's "dogged persistence" and "the boldness of her approach."[138] She is a "Gentile who astonishes Jesus with the tenacity of her faith, even in the face of Jesus' reminder of the gulf that separates Jews from Gentiles."[139] Importantly, "[i]t should not be lost that the example of such victorious faith is a Gentile woman, doubly an outsider."[140] She is certainly one of the "poor in spirit" affirmed by Jesus in the Beatitudes. And her behavior breaks with gender conventions as she in enters the public domain to speak with non-kin males—and in a loud and insistent manner. What determines God's

---

133. In the words of Malina and Rohrbaugh, "whether a royal retainer or a royal aristocrat, the man . . . would be very high on the social scale in a town like Capernaum. He is certainly not the type who would normally seek the patronage of a villager from Nazareth" (*Social Science Commentary on John*, 107).

134. Turner, *Matthew*, 386.

135. Green, *Message of Matthew*, 173.

136. Garland, *Reading Matthew*, 164.

137. Luz, *Matthew 8–20*, 341.

138. Gench, *Back to the Well*, 18.

139. Wright, *Mission of God*, 508.

140. Boring, "Matthew," 337. As Pablo Alonso points out, the gap between Jesus and the woman is reinforced by a range of identity markers: "male and female, Galilean and Syrophoenician, Jew and pagan, itinerant preacher and upper-class woman, man of God and mother of a possessed girl. All of these provide cultural, religious, social, and economic reasons for distance" ("Woman Who Changed Jesus," 123).

blessing, it seems, is neither Jewishness nor conventionally appropriate behavior but receptive faith. Matthew does not tell the story as he tells other miracle stories. He directs his narrative towards the concluding sentence ("Woman, great is your faith; be it for you as you wish"), "which has a majestic note about it." In Mark the mother simply returns home to find her child healed. "In Matthew only the fact and power of faith are expressed."[141]

Alongside the attitude of faith that is commended by Jesus, it may also be helpful to consider whether there is *content* in both of the examples of faith. When Jesus assures the centurion of healing for his servant, his promise to him contains the statement "as you have believed" (Matt 8:13)—wording that closely corresponds to the *content* of the centurion's initial request.[142] When Jesus tells the *basilikos* that his son will live, the official "believed the *word* that Jesus spoke to him" (John 4:50). When he hears the time of his son's recovery, the father *knows* that was the hour when Jesus had spoken to him (4:53). As Francis Moloney comments, the man "had believed in the word of Jesus, and now he "knows" the saving authority of that word. Like that of the Samaritans (cf. 4:41–42), his faith in the word of Jesus produces not only a miracle, but knowledge (v. 53ab)."[143] In other words, Jesus seems to draw attention not only to the role of the man's incipient faith but also to its content.

The presence of content seems even clearer in the Syrophoenician mother's faith—at least in the Markan account. She addresses Jesus as "Son of David," an indication that she is "turning to the Messiah of Israel who has already healed many among his suffering people. Thus she knows that Jesus is sent to Israel; and her faith is seen precisely in the fact that she nevertheless cries out to him."[144] Blakley points out that, while the woman can be praised as an exemplar of faith, "it is her

---

141. See Held, "Matthew as Interpreters," quotes from 199.

142. See the discussion in Kingsbury, "Observations on the 'Miracle Chapters,'" 571.

143. *Gospel of John*, 154.

144. Luz, *Matthew 8-20*, 339. Lawrence even considers that in the story "a Gentile pleads for mercy and justice, the core virtues of the Hebrew covenant relationship" (*Ethnography of Matthew*, 272).

insight that Jesus finds commendable, which is why he cites her *word* (Mark 7:29) and not her faith."[145] There is, then, some apparent connection between the *understanding* of these Gentiles—limited though it undoubtedly was—and the faith that Jesus commends. The faith appears to include more than heart-felt hope or desperate concern for the well-being of another.

It is also instructive to note that Matthew uses the verb *proskuneō* to describes the woman's actions. This verb means not only "to kneel" but "to worship"—as Matthew makes clear by his repeated use of the word to describe Jesus as the one entirely worthy of worship.[146] Here the attitude of worship is found in an outsider, even if this outsider does not (or cannot *yet*) become a disciple. Michael Bird writes of the Syrophoenician woman: "the story elicits no call to discipleship, no command to mission, and no request to join Jesus' entourage."[147] As noted, the woman does use the language of prayer and faith as recognizable to Jews and to Christians (she addresses Jesus as "Lord, Son of David"). But she also models the trusting affirmation that is the essence of a faith that "is not a quality which takes its support from what can be perceived.... Its essential character must consist, therefore, in a trusting despite the evidence of eye and ear."[148]

Only two people are affirmed in Matthew for their "great faith"— and both are Gentiles: the centurion (8:10) and the Canaanite woman (15:28). Robert Guelich points to the woman as an illustration of the way in which faith discloses the heart. Her "reply to Jesus demonstrates that the response of one's heart ultimately qualifies one's relationship to God (cf. 7:15-23). This message becomes clear when the woman's posture toward Jesus negates her being a Syrophoenician, a Greek, from the territory of Tyre, one of the 'dogs' who have no claim on the 'child-

---

145. In particular, "the word she speaks, which Jesus commends, concerns the children's *loaf* and its *crumbs*. Implicit in [Mark's] narrative, then, is Jesus commending the Syrophoenician woman *for understanding about the loaves*, which places her in marked contrast to the disciples who thus far do not (6:52; 7:18)" (Blakley, "Incomprehension or Resistance?," 251-52; original emphases).

146. See Matt 2:2, 8, 11; 8:2; 9:18; 14:33; 15:25; 28:9, 17.

147. Bird, *Jesus and the Origins*, 120.

148. Harrisville, "Woman of Canaan," 285.

rens' bread.'"[149] At the same time there is also a strongly implied contrast between the woman, and the Jews and disciples. Guelich concludes that "one cannot avoid the contrast the woman offers not only to the 'Jews' who reject Jesus in the previous narratives (cf. 7:1–13) but also to the disciples whose misunderstanding Mark has accented in the surrounding stories."[150]

What, then, might this affirming attitude of Jesus say to contemporary readers about the examples of faith and humility that we might, and do, find in people of other faiths? How much *content* need there be in the expression of such faith and humility? The question is not easily answered—but neither is it often asked. When it is asked, discussion, especially among theologically conservative Christians, often moves quickly to the soteriological question: could a person be *saved* by such faith and humility especially when *not* prompted, as it were, by a personal encounter with Jesus? It is obvious that the faith of the widow of Zarephath, and that displayed by Naaman, were not prompted by an encounter with Jesus. We know nothing of the "formal" religious faith of either the centurion or the Syrophoenician mother[151] and yet there is something about the content and insight of their statements that—limited though it undoubtedly is—is both affirmed and also commended by Jesus. So, beyond such biblical stories, might it be said that such commended faith, humility, and insight are prompted by the Holy Spirit of God, given that faith "is the gift of God" (Eph 2:8)? Is it really the case that, as the Anglican evangelist Michael Green writes about the Syrophoenician, "[l]ike the centurion . . . , this Gentile woman exhibits the kind of faith that God honours wherever he finds it"[152]? Are they examples of "Gentiles who . . . do instinctively what the law requires . . . . They show that what the law requires is written on their hearts" (Rom 2:14–15)? Might examples of faith, humility, and insight (parallel to those of the Syrophoenician mother and the centurion), wherever they are found in the contemporary world, be affirmed by disciples to-

---

149. Guelich, *Mark 1—8:26*, 389.

150. Ibid.; he refers to Mark 6:52; 7:18; and 8:14–21.

151. For a discussion of the possibility that she may belong to the category "God-fearer," see Alonso, *Woman Who Changed Jesus*, 179–82.

152. Green, *Message of Matthew*, 173.

day—even when they contrast less than favorably with their own? These are questions that deserve detailed attention, even if possible answers lie beyond the intended scope of this book.[153]

A Great Reversal

We have already drawn attention to the reversal signaled by a coming inclusion of Gentiles and the exclusion of at least some Jews (Matt 8:11–12). If there is an allusion to Gentiles making a pilgrimage to their places in the eschatological banquet, and to worship the God of Israel in Zion, then it certainly suggests a reversal of many of the expectations current in Second Temple Judaism; in fact, reversal is a dominant theme of the entire encounter.[154] The affirmation in Matt 8:11–12 implies a reversal not unlike the reversal so clearly seen in Luke 4:16–30. It is important to note that the inclusion of *some* Gentiles does not assume or require the inclusion of all. Nor does the text imply the exclusion of all Jews. Jesus envisages the eschatological restoration of Israel that will include both Jews and righteous Gentiles: "Judgment upon the 'heirs of the kingdom' does not imply the displacement of Jews by Gentiles but is similar to the parable of the wheat and the weeds (13:24–30), in which the 'sons of the kingdom' are the righteous (both Jew and Gentile) who will enter God's reign, while the 'sons of the evil one' are those evildoers (again, both Jew and Gentile) who will be cast outside."[155]

Turning to the centurion/official, we noted above that he was both an imperial agent and enforcer and yet, over against Israel's elite, he "occupies the margin as a foreigner and as a model of faith."[156] The passage demonstrates "Jesus' willingness to heal a Gentile who evidences the type of faith that Israel was meant to express in the face of restoration."[157] Jesus' contrast of the centurion's faith with the lack of response in Israel parallels the judgment on the Galilean cities (Matt 11:20–24) and the

---

153. This writer intends to write a complementary volume to this one in which these and related questions will be pursued.

154. This is well brought out in Witherington, *Matthew*, 181.

155. Senior, "Between Two Worlds," 12.

156. Carter, *Matthew and the Margins*, 200–201; quote from 201.

157. Bird, *Jesus and the Origins*, 120.

sayings about Nineveh and the Queen of Shebah (Matt 12:38–42).[158] This theme of reversal is also found in the story of the Syrophoenician woman in which Jesus' affirmation of her great faith contrasts sharply with Jesus' rebuke of Peter's little faith in Matt 14:31 (cf. 16:8), not to mention the unbelief of Israel (e.g., Matt 13:58).

The promise of eschatological reversal sounds a note of warning. Jesus may well be attacking *Jewish* exclusiveness[159] but the meaning extends to Christians as well. Craig Keener comments that judgment upon "those who thought themselves destined for the kingdom sounded a sober warning to nationalist Jews of Matthew's day, just as it would sound a warning to complacent Christians today."[160] Likewise, Garland can conclude that "[t]here is no gloating in Matthew over the doom of those who have not responded to God's reign. . . . The Gospel of Matthew contains ample warnings that disciples may be the ones who are cast out."[161] In other words, there seem to be clear warnings about *Christian* presumption as well; as Bruner puts it, "Jesus is attacking . . . that possessiveness, that sense of exclusiveness which disfigures every religious community too sure of itself."[162]

Once again there are transferable implications for Christians (and others) in our contemporary multireligious world. "Outsiders" who display faith and humility are declared to be included; "insiders" who presume upon their privilege find themselves excluded. The application of this principle is not, of course, an easy one! The same Jesus who announces it also warns, repeatedly, against the dangers of "judging." Nor is there the assumption that *all* Gentiles are somehow included (or *all* Jews—or others—excluded). And it is not altogether clear whether the faith and humility that Jesus affirms is provoked by *his* physical presence (and hence not repeatable in his absence) or whether it must include of a degree of religious insight as well (as seen, for example, in the "word" of the Syrophoenician woman that Jesus draws attention to as a decisive element in the healing of her daughter, at least in the Gospel of Mark).

158. Discussion will return to these texts in chapter 3 below.
159. See, for example, Bruner, *Matthew*, 1:382.
160. Keener, *Commentary on Matthew*, 269.
161. Garland, *Reading Matthew*, 96.
162. Bruner, *Matthew*, 1:382.

Jesus and the Religions

The Exclusion of Vengeance and the Sounding of a Note of Universality

Mention has already been made of the apparent exclusion of eschatological vengeance in Jesus' synagogue address and its aftermath in Luke 4:16–30. Such an exclusion, together with the call to love one's enemies, is widely acknowledged to be a central component of the Rule of God as announced by Jesus. This announcement sounds a note of universality and the structure of Matthew's Gospel amplifies it—at least in chapters 8 and 9 with their succession of miraculous healing encounters with a diverse range of people.[163] These miracles are not merely ends in themselves; "miracles performed for Gentiles . . . bear witness to the inclusion within the people of YHWH of those who had formerly been outside."[164] Moreover, these encounters follow the Sermon on the Mount (Matthew 5–7). As Gene Smillie points out, after listening to Jesus' description of Kingdom life, would-be disciples might question their ability to follow Jesus fully. They might consider that

> only the perfect, those whose righteousness exceeds that of the Pharisees, can hope to receive benefits from this King. The requirements he verbalizes are too demanding for most people to fulfill. But then chapters 8 and 9 show us a different picture. One after another, nearly a dozen characters who normally would be considered outside the realm of kingdom/covenant benefits approach Jesus in faith. To the reader's surprise, Jesus responds to them warmly, granting their requests and ministering kingdom mercies to people ostensibly outside consideration: the unclean by reason of disease, a Gentile occupying soldier, social pariahs and sinners, the demon-oppressed.[165]

---

163. The centurion story comes in a section in which "nearly a dozen characters who normally would be considered outside the realm of kingdom/covenant benefits approach Jesus in faith" (Smillie, "'Even the Dogs,'" 91). See also Evans, "Historical Jesus," 144; and Kingsbury, "Observations on the 'Miracle Chapters.'"

164. Wright, *Jesus and the Victory of God*, 192.

165. Smillie, "'Even the Dogs,'" 91.

The same universal implications are heard in the story of the *basilikos* in John 4. As Rodney Whitacre puts it, "Jesus' acceptance of a member of Herod's court would perhaps be the best possible example of God's scandalous, gracious love, whether or not this official is a Gentile."[166] What Cummins calls a "startling scenario" (he means Jesus' dialogue with the Samaritan woman in John 4 that "includes all faithful worshippers within the divine design") is "extended even further in Jesus' ensuing encounter with a believing Gentile official."[167] Galilee also features in Jesus' encounter with the *basilikos* (admittedly in a partly enigmatic way in the light of the puzzling 4:44). Raymond Brown sees the official as representative of the Galileans mentioned in vv. 44–45.[168] Thomas Brodie develops this possibility in an even more universal way as he summarizes the movement of John 2–4: Jesus withdraws from an unbelieving and even hostile Judaism (2:23, 4:1–3, 44) as he becomes oriented towards Samaritans and Gentiles (the "all" of 3:26, the betrothal imagery with the Samaritans) "and, finally, from a border town, the coming of the royal official and his whole household." There is, according to Brodie, "considerable evidence . . . for regarding the journey to the welcoming Galileans as indeed reflecting a journey to the Gentiles."[169]

As already suggested in chapter 1 above, the link between Galilee ("of the Gentiles") and the emergence of a greater-than-Israel perspective in the example of Jesus also seems likely. Seán Freyne finds it plausible that Jesus adapted Isaiah's universalizing vision of the Zion-centered restoration of Israel that includes an attitude of openness to Gentile involvement in Zion. For Jesus, an Isaian perspective in particular seems to be definitive and implies an opening towards Gentiles (seen here in passages like Matt 8:11 as interpreted in the context of Isa 25:6–8; 56:1–8).[170] Moreover, if Bird is correct in his assertion that Jesus' healing of the centurion's servant is an example of love of enemy, then it is also an example of a refusal to see Gentiles as objects only of God's

166. Whitacre, *John*, 115.
167. S. A. Cummins, "John," in Vanhoozer, *Theological Interpretation*, 67.
168. Brown, *Gospel according to John*, 191.
169. Brodie, *Gospel according to John*, 233.
170. See Freyne, *Jesus, a Jewish Galilean*, 97–108.

vengeance. The employment of the meal imagery with the centurion (Matt 8:11), foreshadows an eschatological banquet that also includes (and does not exclude) Gentiles and Samaritans. The provision of such a meal has considerable missional significance as a visible and concrete sign of the divine hospitality that extends across otherwise uncrossable boundaries. This writer is reminded of some Christian groups in India and elsewhere who use the shared meal imagery of the Last Supper as a means of an unconditional invitation of "outsiders" into an inclusive community.

Freyne adds another dimension to this universalizing theme by pointing to a Wisdom thread in the teaching of Jesus: the way in which the care of the Creator transcends ethnic boundaries—along the lines of Jesus' remarks that "He makes his sun to shine on the bad and the good and rains on the just and the unjust alike" (Matt 5:45; Luke 6:35). Freyne comments: "Jesus' understanding of God as creator underpins his whole life's work and his ethical teaching, so much so in fact that it seems to universalize his distinctively Jewish experience of God as the Yahweh of the Exodus. Thus, he can contemplate many people coming from the four cardinal points of the compass to join Abraham, Isaac, and Jacob at the great eschatological banquet foretold by Isaiah."[171] The universal contours of such a message offer hope to many. It is not surprising that the story of the Syrophoenician woman, for example, continues to speak to hearers who are marginalized, impoverished, or oppressed in other ways.[172]

Christological Implications—both Narrative and Eschatological

Narrative is a major genre in the Gospels and it is these storied portions that display the distinctive attitude of Jesus to Gentiles (and Samaritans). *Surprise* has already been noted as a feature of a narrative appraisal of material in the Gospels. With both the centurion and the Syrophoenician the "point of surprise . . . comes from the expression

---

171. Freyne, "Galilean Jesus," 295.

172. Pablo Alonso offers a number of examples in ch. 5 ("Synchronic and Contextual Reading of Mk 7,24–30") of his *The Woman Who Changed Jesus*.

of faith and hope that a Gentile character places in Jesus."[173] No less surprising is the amazement that Jesus expresses at their faith. At least some readers—past and perhaps present—would be surprised at the lack of vengeance implied by Jesus' affirming responses and compassionate attitudes towards Gentiles and Samaritans.

Jesus' attitude to authority and symbols of authority. As we saw in the previous chapter, Seán Freyne and others note the apparent indifference of Jesus to the cities of Sepphoris and Tiberias—cities that might be considered to be symbols of Gentile or Hellenizing authority. Freyne concludes that Jesus

> is laying claim to a different source of authority than that to which the elite urbanites subscribed. His activity, no less than his teaching, was likely to have been perceived as a serious threat to the power structures on which the wealthy depended: "Those who are dressed in fine garments live in royal palaces" (Luke 7.25; Matt 11.8), is indicative of Jesus' distance from such places and his attitude to them. It was in the context of a healing action by Jesus that, in Matthew's account, the Roman centurion acknowledged that reality: They were both operating under different systems of authority, he under Rome, and Jesus under the reign of God (Matt 8.8–9).[174]

Christology: the identity and authority of Jesus. With the Syrophoenician mother, Jesus' authority is displayed in his ability to effect an exorcism at a distance—without touch and without any words. Jesus' divine identity is also alluded to as the woman addresses him as *kyrie*, "Lord." As noted, this is an ambiguous term that can be used as a polite form of address ("Sir"); but it also functions as a christological title ("Lord") that early Christians used to link Jesus with Yahweh whose Hebrew name was translated *kurios* in the LXX. Although many commentators interpret the woman's address as merely a sign of respect, in Mark *kurios* "normally connotes divine authority and identity, making

---

173. Bird, *Jesus and the Origins*, 120.
174. Freyne, "Galilee as Laboratory," 159.

it more likely that the reader is expected to see in the Syrophoenician woman's address . . . a recognition of Jesus' divine identity."[175]

An eschatological reading of the encounters is also required. In fact, it seems necessary to read both Jesus and the Gospels in eschatological categories. Yarbro Collins, in her magisterial commentary, concludes that the genre of the Gospel of Mark is best described as an "eschatological historical monograph."[176] Kevin Vanhoozer makes the same point: the Bible "announces events that partake of the 'fullness' of time, events that are the result of divine as well as human agency, events in which the future breaks in, as it were, from above."[177] The encounter of Jesus with Gentiles (and Samaritans) has elements of this eschatological dimension: the arrival of the imminent Rule of God. It is clear, for example, that the centurion "expresses the eschatological faith that Israel was meant to have in God's eschatological salvation and, consequently, the centurion and his servant are beneficiaries in the present of the future saving power of the kingdom."[178]

This Jesus also sounds a clear message of reconciliation that has obvious and important implications for a religiously-divided world. If Michael Bird is correct, the encounter between Jesus and the centurion has a dimension that is usually missed. Jesus performs an act of compassionate healing "for someone who was potentially his enemy." The official was "part of the domination system of the Herodian rulers" whose "security apparatus . . . had a particular interest or concern about Jesus." This dimension transforms the story into "a living parable of loving

---

175. Blakley, "Incomprehension or Resistance?," 255. If this particular address was merely a sign of respect, it would be the only time *kurios* functions in this way in Mark. And he also adds that on at least two occasions, *kurios* associates Jesus with YHWH (Mark 1:3; 5:19–20). According to Blakley, the Syrophoenician woman is able to recognize Jesus' divine identity and authority because she understands the meaning and significance of the leftover loaves, presumably because her heart is not hardened in the ways that the disciples' hearts are (256).

176. Yarbro Collins, *Mark*, 42.

177. Vanhoozer, *Theological Interpretation*, 17. He believes that "it is likely that modern critics are working with an overly 'thin' conception of history, as a self-enclosed, linear set of temporal events whose causal explanation is to be found in the relation of earlier to later events in the same horizontal space-time spectrum" (16–17).

178. Bird, *Jesus and the Origins*, 120.

one's enemies,"[179] and reinforces Jesus' refusal to speak of Gentiles only in negative terms (although that dimension is not absent). To illustrate from the Gospel of Mark, the participation of Gentiles in the Kingdom of God becomes possible, as Robert Guelich puts it, "because of the ultimate thrust of Jesus' redemptive ministry that removed the social/ritual boundaries between Jew and Greek, clean and unclean."[180] The removal of social and ritual boundaries between peoples would transform more than one community in the contemporary world. And, to continue the eschatological theme, what Amos Yong calls Jesus' "redemptive hospitality" and his inauguration of the eschatological banquet are highly relevant.[181]

This chapter has drawn attention to a set of attitudes displayed by Jesus in his encounters with two Gentiles: a centurion/official and a Syrophoenician mother. When read in the context of religious plurality, the stories offer some surprising affirmations and present some discomforting challenges to contemporary hearers. These affirmations and challenges are reinforced by a number of other passages in the Gospels in which Jesus interacts with or speaks about or acts in such a way that Gentiles appear to be in mind—as we shall see in the coming chapter.

---

179. Ibid., 120–21.
180. Guelich, *Mark 1—8:26*, 387. He cites 1:40–45; 5:1–20, 21–43; 7:1–23, 24–30.
181. See the discussion by Yong in his *Hospitality and the Other*, 101–3.

3

Elsewhere in the Gospels: Purity, Temple, Parables

THIS CHAPTER OFFERS A theological reading of some other passages in the Gospels besides those already considered, that relate to Gentiles. In particular, it considers examples of the teaching, preaching and actions of Jesus that seems to relate to Gentiles. In fact, there appears to be a canonical link between the encounters already considered and such teaching. The Gospel of Matthew places story of the Roman Centurion (8:5–13) soon after the Sermon on the Mount (chs. 5–7). Jesus meets the Canaanite woman (15:21–28) immediately after the passage on purity (15:1–20). A similar pattern is found in Mark, and to a lesser degree in Luke. However, for the sake of convenience, this chapter will gather and consider a number of examples spread through the Gospels: Jesus' teaching about purity; the temple (including his "temple action"); several parables that seem to include reference to Gentiles and other "outsiders"; implications for a Gentile mission from the language and narrative structuring of the central chapters of Mark; and assorted other passages in which Jesus meets Gentiles. As with the Introduction and chapter 2, a synchronic reading of the passages will keep in mind our contemporary multireligious context, and will give rather little attention to historical-critical issues.

Elsewhere in the Gospels: Purity, Temple, Parables

Jesus' Teaching about Purity (Including Mark 7:1-23//Matt 15:1-20//Luke 11:37-41)

In this section, analysis will center on Jesus' discussion of defilement and tradition and, in particular, on his apparent overturning of OT food laws—and the implication of this for the encounter with Gentiles. We have already noted (in chapter 1) the importance of the paired terms "pure" and "impure" both to describe and to inscribe sociocultural boundaries between Jews and Gentiles. By the time of Second Temple Judaism(s) there are extensive prohibitions and polemic against intermarriage and conversion. Further evidence of purity concerns is found in late OT and intertestamental literature in which, as James Dunn notes, the heroes and heroines of popular Jewish piety "were portrayed as prospering precisely because of their loyalty to the food laws and refusal to eat the food of Gentiles."[1] In the Second Temple Era, "issues of cult and purity engaged and divided Jews more . . . than at any other time in antiquity."[2] Hannah Harrington's study of purity texts in the Second Temple Era leads her to define purity as "a status, achieved by both moral integrity and ritual purification, which is required of Israel in order for God's holiness to reside among and protect them."[3] In other words, "purity was a widespread concern in Second Temple Judaism, not only among minor groups, but also to an increasing degree with the Jewish population in general."[4]

---

1. Dunn, *Jesus Remembered*, 275; he cites as evidence (n. 97): Dan 1:3-16; 10:3; Tob 1:10-13; Jdt 12:2, 6-9, 19; Add Esth 14:17; 1 Macc 1:62-63; *Jos. Asen.* 7:1; 8:5.

2. Harrington, *Purity Texts*, 7.

3. Ibid., 8. Chapter 1 of Harrington's volume concludes with reflections on the rationale for purity regulations in the Hebrew Bible and at Qumran; the former is concerned to distinguish Israel from its idolatrous neighbors, whereas the importance of purity was magnified at Qumran where purity was deemed essential for success in the eschatological conflict with evil, for moral purity, and for reception of revelation. Hand-washing, for example, was unknown among the Qumran sectarians, who fully immersed before every meal, and it seems that they would have rejected the practice of handwashing.

4. Kazen, "Good Samaritan and," 135; he also refers to his volume *Jesus and Purity Halakhah*, 67-198, as offering a more extensive comment. In her summary of purity scholarship in the Dead Sea Scrolls, Harrington concludes that these "purity laws provide a strong piece of evidence corroborating literary and archaeological findings

Jesus and Purity (and Mark 7:1–23//Matt 15:1–20//Luke 11:37–41)

Attention now turns to Jesus' discussion of defilement and tradition and, in particular, to his apparent overturning of OT food laws. In Mark chapter 7, the Pharisees and scribes cross-examine Jesus, accusing his disciples of breaking the tradition of the elders by eating with unclean hands: hands that are "defiled" (vv. 1–5).[5] Jesus responds that this tradition is not from God (6–9, 13) but actually represents "human commandments" that contravene "the commandment of God" (7:8–9, 13). He continues with a parable about what does and does not defile a person (14–15), which he goes on to explain to his disciples (17–23). In his explanation, Jesus argues that purity and impurity are internal matters of the heart, unrelated to the external issue of what and how one eats. The implication, according to the narrator, is that Jesus has thereby "cleansed all foods" (19c)—usually understood along the lines of "rendered all foods clean."[6] Matthew's account (Matt 15:1–20) is a somewhat conservative redaction of Mark[7] and, although Matthew "softens the

---

that purity was especially important in Second Temple Judaism" ("Purity and the Dead Sea Scrolls," 419).

5. "With defiled hands": literally "common" hands in the biblical sense of "ritually unclean" along the lines of Acts 10:14, 28; 11:8; Rev 21:27. Booth concludes, after an extensive survey of the Jewish law and its development, that traditional law as such did not, in fact, demand washing before eating (*Jesus and the Laws of Purity*, 155–87). But strong evidence indicates that these rules for hand washing did apply among certain of the "Pharisees," the *haberim* who voluntarily undertook obligations especially regarding tithes and purity not required by general law. The "tradition of the elders" (cf. Gal 1:14) refers to the oral tradition that the Pharisees, in particular, held to be as binding as the written Law. Booth rephrases the Pharisees' question as: "Why do your disciples not wash their hands before they eat and observe the same standard of purity as we pietists do?" (189–203; quote from 202). A Jewish scholar arrives at a similar conclusion; see Furstenberg, "Defilement Penetrating the Body."

6. Leaving to one side the minority view that the narrator is, as Guelich summarizes it, simply "drawing an obvious, if sarcastic, conclusion"—perhaps suggested by the somewhat unclear "participial construction [that] hangs awkwardly without obvious syntactical connection"—that the digestive process "cleanses all foods" (Guelich, *Mark 1–8:26*, 378)—even though this is not Guelich's own conclusion.

7. He changes "there is nothing outside of a person which entering is able to defile that person" (Mark 7:15) to "it is not what goes into the mouth which defiles a person." (15:11). His avoidance of "nothing" and "is able to" (with the same omission in 15:17) makes the passage more acceptable to Jewish Christians who no doubt con-

radical teaching of Jesus found in Mark, he does not do away with it altogether."[8] In other words, Jesus calls for a more radical understanding of purity rooted in one's innermost person (the "heart") and in conduct congruent with the divine will (as defined by a relationship with God), and not necessarily as defined by the Law or by the traditions derived from the Torah. As Craig Keener puts it, "Jesus' ultimate challenge goes beyond ritual purity practices to the point he illustrates: the heart comes first (Mk 7:18–23)."[9]

Jesus' response to the challenge about eating with "unclean hands" in particular, and notions of Levitical impurity in general, corresponds generally with the Synoptic Gospels' portrait of him in "impure" settings in which he deliberately violates purity boundaries.[10] This discussion raises the complex and much-debated issue of Jesus and the Law.[11] A notable NT theologian, Udo Schnelle, can state simply that "Jesus expresses only minimal interest in his people's legal system."[12] But there does seem to be considerable merit in a rather more complex summary that sees Jesus' attitude toward OT law as made up of three comple-

---

tinue to observe Torah-based food restrictions.

8. Hagner, *Matthew 14–28*, 429. He later adds, "Matthew . . . probably minimizes the implicit revolutionary significance of v. 11a because he is writing to Jewish Christians (Mark, on the other hand, writing to gentile Christians, maximizes the point and makes it quite explicit with the editorial comment: 'Thus he declared all foods clean' [Mark 7:19])" (433).

9. Keener, *Historical Jesus*, 234.

10. For example, Jesus does not hesitate, at times, to eat in settings where it might be doubted that the food served is kosher and with individuals who might well convey impurity to him in other ways (e.g. Mark 2:15–16 where Jesus "sat at dinner" with many "tax collectors and sinners"—with this marginal grouping described in this way three times in two verses). Guelich also notes that "Mark has three miracles in which Jesus finds himself in a defiling situation. He touches the leper in 1:41 and the corpse of Jairus' daughter in 5:41 and is touched by the hemorrhaging woman in 5:27–29" (Guelich, *Mark 1–8:26*, 376). For a detailed summary see Holmén, *Jesus and Jewish Covenant Thinking*, 221–51, esp. 233–37.

11. Of the many available discussions, see especially section 14.5 of Dunn, *Jesus Remembered*, in which he emphasizes the preeminent and unprecedented place given by Jesus to Lev 19:18 (love of neighbor). For a detailed analysis and discussion, see Loader, *Jesus' Attitude*, and from a rather wider perspective, Crossley, *New Testament and Jewish Law*.

12. Schnelle, *Theology of the New Testament*, 146.

mentary components. These are summarized by Christian Stettler: firstly, "Jesus *establishes priorities* within the law," as in his distinction between the weightier and less significant matters of the law (Matt 23:23). Secondly, "Jesus *intensifies* commandments of the Torah," as in the Sermon on the Mount where he broadens definitions of "killing" and "adultery" (Matt 5:21–30). Thirdly, "Jesus *repeals* commandments of the Torah when they stand in the way of . . . unrestricted obedience to God." Stettler concludes that Jesus' purity parable and explanation in Mark 7 and in Matthew 15 fit this pattern of Jesus' attitude towards the Law, especially the third category.[13] Given these three ways in which Jesus' attitude toward the law is expressed in the Gospels—prioritization, intensification, and repeal (perhaps to be summed up as a radical *fulfillment* in line with Matt 5:17)—his abrogation of OT dietary laws implies that they hinder obedience to God. So, Jesus' purity parable in both Mark 7 and in Matthew 15 is to be read as Jesus' repeal of received dietary laws.[14]

Jesus does continue to share at least some purity concerns (implied by Mark 1:44 with the offering to be made by the healed leper) and by his "temple action." Nonetheless, as James Dunn concludes, Jesus "sat loose to the purity *halakhoth* regarding clean and unclean and table-fellowship, which suggests that Jesus did not regard such concerns as central to the definition of Israel and its practice."[15] Seán Freyne links Jesus' attitude to issues of both Galilean and Jewish identity. He concludes that "for whatever reason, purity and its maintenance as an ethnic marker appears to have been less important to him than a more expansive view of Jewish ethnicity that brought him to the margins of both Galilean and Judean life, and on occasions even dared to transgress the outer boundary walls that separated Jew from non-Jew."[16] Sawicki offers a somewhat different perspective: Jesus has been socialized into

---

13. Stettler, "Purity," 485; original emphasis. For a somewhat contrary position (that Jesus was likely to have maintained ritual purity), see Fiensy, *Jesus the Galilean*, 147–86.

14. For further helpful discussion, see Hellerman, *Jesus and the People of God*, ch. 7, "Jesus and Sacred Food."

15. Dunn, "Jesus and Purity," article abstract.

16. Freyne, "Archaeology and the Historical Jesus," 77.

(non-kosher) banquets in the Hellenistic style and thus even gains a degree of entry into Herodian social circles.[17] This is a view for which Freyne seems to offer a degree of support when he comments that in such a depiction, "Jesus seems to have abandoned his Judean heritage in favor of an older Israelite one that is not encumbered with the strategies of maintaining Israelite purity devised by the Hasmoneans."[18]

Jesus, Purity, and Gentiles

So, given Jesus' apparent overturning of OT food laws, what might this imply about his attitude towards Gentiles? From Mark's Gospel, especially the middle section of Mark (including 7:1–13), Blakley concludes that "Jesus abolishes the God-given kosher regulations because they no longer serve God's purposes. . . . The kosher laws thus served as a sort of sacrament, an outward and visible sign of Israel's election, identity and vocation, a practice that established, protected, and maintained the very distinctions that it symbolized. Consequently, by abrogating these regulations, Jesus eliminates a defining quality of Jewish ethnic, religious, and social identity, which separated Jews from Gentiles, thereby opening the door for Gentile inclusion in God's kingdom."[19] In other words, the radical principle of elevating the intentions of the heart over the cleanliness of the hands "had the potential of abolishing the entire ritual law of the Old Testament. . . . Of course, if all foods are clean, then

---

17. Sawicki, *Crossing Galilee*, 182, 194.

18. He concludes that "gospel evidence of conflicts with the Pharisees over issues of Sabbath observance, purity and dietary regulations [are] all topics to do with the maintenance of Jewish ethnic separation" (Freyne, "Archaeology and the Historical Jesus," 83). Sanders is skeptical of dating these conflicts to the ministry of Jesus (see his *Jesus and Judaism*, 264–67) but Freyne argues convincingly for their authenticity (in his *Galilee, Jesus*, 247–68).

19. Blakley, "Incomprehension or Resistance?," 246. It is true that the statement "nothing entering into a person from outside can defile" (Mark 7:18) lacks a clear referent and some have suggested it may not have been "*any* food" given the protracted debate in the early church over clean and unclean food (e.g., Acts 10:14–15; 15:28–29; Rom 14:14; Gal 2:11–14; Col 2:20–22) when the tradition seems to offer such a clear word from Jesus. Perhaps the meaning was "any *Torah-allowed* food" but that does not seem to be the intended meaning (given the forceful nature of the discussion)— which leaves unresolved the related tensions in the early church.

ritual handwashing is unnecessary and the major barrier to fellowship with the Gentiles is lifted."[20] So, as Christopher Wright points out, "the clean-unclean distinction in Israel was fundamentally symbolic of the distinction between Israel and the nations. Accordingly, if Jesus abolished the distinction in relation to food (the symbol), then he simultaneously abolished the distinction in relation to Jews and Gentiles (the reality that the symbol pointed to)."[21] In Matthew there is a connective *kai* ("and") at the beginning of 15:21 that clearly links the controversy with the story of the Canaanite woman that follows. Having addressed the issue of clean and unclean—a central issue in Jewish and Gentile relations—will he now practice what he preaches in one of his rare encounters with a Gentile woman?[22] Because he does heal her child, the answer is an implicit "yes."

Given Jesus' apparent overturning of OT food laws, what are the implication of this for the encounter with Gentiles? In considering an answer, it is helpful to note some implications of the contextual setting in Mark. It is surely significant that Mark locates the defilement pericope, with its removal of boundaries that had separated people on the basis of "impurity," immediately before Jesus' ministry to Gentiles in 7:24–37 in which he travels into Gentile territory where he meets with both the Syrophoenician mother and a deaf mute in the Decapolis. Robert Guelich concludes from this that, by "confronting the purity laws that set 'the Jews' apart (illustrated by 7:2–4 and 7:19b) as focusing on externals rather than what is from within, Jesus can move freely into the gentile area and among Gentiles." Guelich appeals to the conclusion of Gnilka to the effect that a spiritual break precedes a geographical break in Jesus' ministry with Israel. So, as Guelich goes on to point out, although Jesus does not actually eat with the Syrophoenician woman, "the allusion to 'bread' in that pericope and Jesus' contact with and help for her and the deaf mute in 7:31–37 directly relates to the theme of clean and unclean."[23] In other words, we note the significance of the

20. Blomberg, *Jesus and the Gospels*, 319.

21. Wright, *Mission of God*, 508.

22. Cf. Gench, *Back to the Well*, 5.

23. Guelich, *Mark 1—8:26*, 362, 374. Blakley and others helpfully expand this link with "bread." In asking about a possible link with Gentiles, the mention of bread,

placement of the encounter and its canonical link with the two or three miracles for Gentiles that follow in both Matthew and Mark. As Greg Carey concludes, "Jesus' transgression of the purity laws anticipates the inclusion of Gentiles—the most impure people in the world."[24] Jesus' concerns are often directed towards "sinners," a category that extends to Gentiles; his meetings with them signal a willingness to cross ethnic boundaries, especially when he encounters faith. "In a cultural system defined by holiness, sacred space, purity and defilement, Jesus' interaction with Gentiles undercuts the traditional Jew-Gentile barriers."[25]

Although Jesus' "cleansing of all foods" has a considerable number of implications for relations with Gentiles, it does not, in itself, imply a wholesale assimilation of Jewish values with the values of Gentiles. Jesus, both here and in his teaching elsewhere concerning the commandments about the Sabbath, tithing, and sacrifice, does seem to display what Theissen and Merz describe only as a "*relaxation* of norms in the Jesus tradition."[26] According to them, the ethics of the teaching of Jesus intensified the universal aspects of Torah but downplayed the ritual dimensions that separated Jews from Gentiles. However, the advocacy of these "universalistic commandments by no means points towards assimilation." The Jewish followers of Jesus are to "surpass the 'nations.'" They are still to distinguish themselves from sinners and Gentiles by loving their enemies, by being free from care and first seeking the Kingdom of God—and by being "the salt of the earth" and "the light of the world." After a discussion of what they see as a relaxation of

---

loaves and eating may well be significant. The discussion at the beginning of Mark 7 has the complaint about Jesus' disciples eating *the loaves* (7:2; *the loaf* in 7:5) with unclean hands. Why does Mark include the unnecessary *artos* in 7:2 and 7:5 when it is avoidable? One possibility is that he alludes to "the loaves" of 6:41, 43-44. If so, it links this scene in Mark 7 to that of "the loaves" which the disciples did not understand in 6:52 (cf. 7:17–18a) and will not understand after the feeding in 8:1–9 (see 8:14–21). See the detailed discussion in Blakley, "Incomprehension or Resistance?," 200–211.

24. Greg Carey, *Sinners*, 37.

25. Bird, "Jesus and the Gentiles after Jeremias," 101 (he refers to Ps 9:17; 1 Macc 2:44, 48; Pss Sol 1:1; 2:1–2; Gal 2:15). Bird also notes hesitations on the part of Jesus: cf. Matt 8:7; Mark 7:27.

26. Section heading in Theissen and Merz, *Historical Jesus*, 364–70; emphasis added.

norms, Theissen and Merz conclude: "By renouncing the status of those who want to be first, they are to offer a contrasting posture to the life of the Gentiles (Mark 10.42–44).... The universal ethical will of God is to be realized by the followers of Jesus in such a way that the identity of Jews as opposed to Gentiles can become visible precisely here."[27]

Nonetheless, Jesus' teaching does seem to point to some kind of break with Jewish ethnocentrism. His "relaxation of norms" concerning food laws, Sabbath, marriage customs, kinship duties, circumcision, and the sanctity of the temple clearly threatens the underlying identity that they signify, given that "keeping the distinctive codes was *the* means of marking Israel out from her pagan neighbours."[28] Andrew Kirk concludes that "by relativising the importance of these symbols or declaring them to be redundant... Jesus was making a major statement about the nature of belonging to a particular ethnic group." In the new community, constituted by loyalty to Jesus, "allegiance to kinship and ethnic groups was not the main source of a person's identity."[29] In the first century CE, food and purity laws were at the very center of the Jewish understanding of the Law. Udo Schnelle points out that, over against such an understanding, "the kind of table fellowship practiced by Jesus constituted an attack on the very foundations of the biblical distinction between 'clean' and 'unclean.'"[30] In the Cornelius story in Acts 10–11, the key point in the story is that Peter's vision was interpreted not in terms of eating unclean food but in terms of an openness to "unclean" people (Acts 10:28)—a decisive factor in the development of the Gentile mission.

The Galilean context may also be significant and may also suggest a middle way in some of the debates. The Gospel narratives do not mention the supposedly Hellenized centers Sepphoris, Tiberias, and Hippos; perhaps parallel to this omission is the absence of Gamla and Jotapata, both of which were substantial and conservatively *Jewish* centers in Galilee. In interesting and independent ways, the archaeological

---

27. Ibid., *Historical Jesus*, 371; cf. the whole of the section on 359–72.

28. Wright, *Jesus and the Victory of God*, 385. (This is part of a valuable discussion by Wright of "Symbols of Israel's Identity.")

29. Kirk, *What Is Mission?*, 47.

30. Schnelle, *Theology of the New Testament*, 106.

record from Gamla and Jotapata points to changing trends with regard to Jewish observance in Galilee. Freyne summarizes the archaeological evidence from these two places (especially coinage and culinary practices) that points to an increasingly Jewish-observant and even anti-Roman trend in Galilee in the two centuries before Jesus. He concludes that disputes between Jesus and these more observant coreligionists can plausibly be seen as representing insider disagreements about the essentials of Jewish observance in a changing situation, not later sectarian differences. Nor do they indicate the abandonment by Jesus of all boundaries between Jew and non-Jew in an allegedly Gentile Galilee.[31] In his discussion of Jesus and purity, Jonathan Reed concludes (from both Q and Mark) that Jesus does not censure any of the practices associated with the well-known materially retrieved indicators of Jewish religious identity that have been found in both Galilean and Judean domestic space.[32] Such conclusions lead James Charlesworth to ask: "Did Jesus choose Capernaum, a modest fishing village without evidence of conservative Judaism, and avoid Gamla, a conservative religious Jewish city, because his Jewishness was challengingly "liberal"? Such new questions are aroused by a study of Galilean archaeology, since first-century Jews in Capernaum apparently had no *mikvaot*, while Jews in Gamla frequented an impressive synagogue with a contiguous *mikveh*."[33]

What we have seen then, appears to indicate that Jesus endorses neither a complete break with Judaism nor an assimilation with Gentiles. But he does exhibit what seems to be an extraordinary openness to the "unclean." Schnelle even goes so far as to state that "Jesus paid no attention to ritual laws of any sort in his contacts with people. The unbounded love of God for all people, including especially those who have been religiously excluded, at least points in the direction of declaring such laws, which in Israel were upheld in the name of God,

31. Freyne, "Galilee as Laboratory," 161. Cf. Kazen, *Jesus and Purity Halakah*, 263–99, regarding the possible tensions felt in Galilee concerning the issue of purity in the pre-70 period, and locating Jesus' response within that setting.

32. Reed, *Archaeology and the Galilean Jesus*, 44–49, and the whole of his ch. 2. The indicators are chalk (stone) vessels; stepped, plastered pools (*miqva'ot*); secondary burial with ossuaries in loculi tombs; and bone profiles that lack pork.

33. Charlesworth, "Jesus Research and Archaeology: A New Perspective," in Charlesworth, *Jesus and Archaeology*, 57.

to be obsolete."³⁴ Some far-reaching implications of this openness for interreligious relations will be discussed in chapter 6 below.

Jesus and the Temple (Including His "Temple Action": Mark 11:15–19//)

There is no doubt about the central importance of the Jerusalem temple for Jewish self-understanding at the time of Jesus.³⁵ The size of the temple was certainly impressive and the revenue it generated was of considerable benefit—although not to the city, but to what Josephus makes clear were the aristocratic priestly families.³⁶ Nor is there doubt about the authenticity of Jesus' "temple action" even if its meaning, and Jesus' attitude in general to the temple, is much debated.

The temple action by Jesus was much more than a "cleansing." Jesus' view of the temple is seen by some as proof that he set Torah aside by dismissing the temple (or at least its cult) since the temple cult is a major theme of Torah. According to N. T. Wright, the action is a prophetic sign symbolic of the imminent destruction of the temple itself; its importance to a large extent lies in its explicit anti-sacrificial and pro-Gentile intention.³⁷ Seán Freyne in his magisterial *Jesus, a Jewish Galilean*, sees Jesus' action as a symbolic destruction of the temple that derives from his expectation that God would soon establish a new, eschatological temple.³⁸ Jesus assimilates from Isaiah the depiction of a

---

34. Schnelle, *Theology of the New Testament*, 139. Schnelle adds the comment that "God's love, which Jesus proclaims in the advent of the kingdom of God, surpasses the love previously given to Israel in the gift of the Torah."

35. For one of many summaries, see Wright, *Jesus and the Victory of God*, 406–12.

36. See *Ant.* 15.247–48. For a useful discussion see Freyne, "Galilee and Judaea," 49–50.

37. Wright, *Jesus and the Victory of God*, 417–28. The final chapter of Fiensy's *Jesus the Galilean* (187–227) introduces the Apocrypha and Pseudepigrapha in discussing Jesus' attitude to the temple. Fiensy suggests that Jesus predicts its destruction, but that the temple incident should be read apart from this. Having reviewed a number of scholarly interpretations, he concludes that the temple action is a zealous and Pharisaic protest against the improper use of the temple court, analogous to other contemporary incidents, rather than a prophetic symbolic action.

38. See Freyne, *Jesus, a Jewish Galilean*, ch. 6, especially pp. 152–63. There is not

suffering servant. He rejects "Zionization" (the popular notion of an idealized Zion that would someday be the center of the world) and this rejection undergirds his temple action (152–63); it is a reaction to the realities of the temple in contrast to the ideals of the eschatological temple of Isaiah and *1 Enoch*, especially Enoch's revelatory experiences recorded in the Book of the Watchers (*1 En.* 12–14). Freyne sees the temple action as an attack on the sacrificial system itself, motivated by a concern for Gentiles,[39] and as the key factor in provoking the authorities to act against Jesus;[40] in fact, it becomes critical among the reasons for his execution.

Discussion about the role of the temple in the ministry and teaching of Jesus has more recently been advanced by Nicholas Perrin in his *Jesus the Temple*. Scholarly discussion has often maintained that it was the early Christians who proposed the notion that the temple had been re-established in both the person of Jesus and in the church. Perrin, however, argues persuasively that the idea of Jesus as temple dates back to Jesus who sees himself and his movement as those who both anticipate and embody Yahweh's coming kingdom. In effect, they are a new temple movement, the social and confessional boundaries of which are marked off by allegiance to him. In fact, Perrin offers substantial evidence for understanding Jesus' mission in terms of a counter-temple movement.[41] Another persuasive reading is that of Timothy Gray, who

---

space to consider the opposite conclusion (expressed, for example, by Karen Wenell) that "Jesus meant that the temple was to end without an alternative to replace it" even as "Jesus does not propose . . . a replacement priesthood". Instead, the kingdom in his vision was not centered on a physical temple. See Wenell, *Jesus and Land*, ch. 2 ("The Temple as Contested Space"); quotes from pp. 50 and 57.

39. Freyne, *Jesus, a Jewish Galilean*, 157–58.

40. This, in turn, links with Jesus' journey to Caesarea Philippi and his belief that there would be no sacrifice in the eschatological temple, just as he "had already distanced himself from . . . sin-offerings and Yom-Kippur rituals" (Freyne, *Jesus, a Jewish Galilean*, 162). Freyne argues that both the suffering-servant expectation and the community wisdom motifs could be found as major themes in the Galilee of Jesus (ibid., 174).

41. See especially ch. 3 of *Jesus the Temple*, in which Perrin focuses on interpretations and implications of Jesus' temple action; chs. 4–6, which explore the distinctive economic, social, and spiritual aspects of Jesus' temple movement over against the failed temple ministry of his opponents; and chs. 7 and 8 in which Perrin examines

reads Mark's apocalyptic chapter 13 as referring not generally to the end of the world but precisely to the temple's demise.[42]

Seán Freyne, with Jesus' Galilean context in mind, offers what appears to be a balanced view of Jesus as both affirming the importance of the temple while challenging aspects of the privileged position it had come to claim. He writes: "Jesus did not abandon this central belief of his tradition, that Yahweh resided among his people in the Jerusalem temple. Yet his emphasis on the creator God's presence in the everyday lives of the Galilean peasants meant that access to Israel's God no longer had to be mediated by an official representative of the people. God was accessible to all, because his creation was meant to be shared alike and equally by all." Jesus' visit to the temple becomes a direct challenge to the priestly aristocracy who both collaborate with the Roman occupiers and deprive the rural populace of their share of the Creator's bounty. At the same time, "it is equally true that in Jesus' theological view the temple as sole symbol of God's presence to Israel was already under judgment as a result of his Galilean ministry that offered God's forgiveness to the just and unjust alike. The historical action in the temple merely confirmed that theological reality."[43]

Freyne's reference to the universal divine forgiveness could plausibly, given what we have seen of Jesus' actions and teaching, be seen as extending to Gentile, Samaritan, and Jewish poor alike. The new eschatological temple becomes a symbol for the reconciliation of all peoples before the God of Israel. Michael Bird points out that the word for "robber" used in "den of robbers" (Mark 11:17; Matt 21:13; Luke 19:46) is the word that regularly meant "bandit" rather than "thief." "Thus, Jesus censures the Temple for failing to draw the nations to Zion, and instead, it had become an icon for Jewish nationalism. . . . If Israel would not be a 'light to the nations' and if the Temple would not be 'a house of prayer for nations', then Jesus and his followers would appropriate for themselves these roles through the eschatological activity breaking in

---

Jesus' eschatological discourses (Mark 12–13), and his last supper with the disciples where he affirms his unique status as high priest of the temple movement.

42. See Gray, *Temple in the Gospel of Mark*, ch. 3, "Prophetic Eschatology and Mark 13."

43. Freyne, "Galilean Jesus," 296.

at the present time."⁴⁴ The temple action is, then, a symbolic action of judgment against an apostate and obsolete institution. What was meant to be "a house of prayer for all the nations" (quoting from Isa 56:7) had in fact become "a den of bandits." There is a notable contrast between the intended use of the "court of the *Gentiles*" and its *de facto* Jewish usage as a "nationalist stronghold."⁴⁵ The citation from Isaiah 56 does two things. It points to the universal scope of the Rule of God as Yahweh gathers outcasts and admits foreigners and eunuchs into his temple. The citation also points to an eschatological understanding of the event; as Schnabel puts it, the actions of Jesus in the temple are "the announcement of the 'hour of judgment' of the temple and its leaders, and the announcement of 'the hour of salvation for the nations' who henceforth independently of the temple, will worship the God of Israel."⁴⁶

Second Temple Era Judaisms had a lively expectation of an eschatological realization of the Rule of God. And, as Michael Wolter points out, one dimension of "the final theophany of God" that accompanies or even introduces that Rule "will naturally occur nowhere else than in Zion-Jerusalem, more specifically in the temple. From here God will exercise sovereign rule over the whole world." But Wolter also goes on to point out how Jesus' understanding of the rule diverges significantly from the received understanding because it is Jesus' own ministry in Israel that inaugurates the reality of God's rule.⁴⁷ Once again, Jesus' radical reformulation of a central symbol of Jewish self-identity (in this case dramatically acted out), has far-reaching implications for an expanded understanding of the people of God—as we shall see later in this chapter.

---

44. Bird, "Jesus and the Gentiles," 101–2, referring especially to Wright, *Jesus and the Victory of God*, 329, 419–21, 444.

45. Blomberg, *Jesus and the Gospels*, 318. There is a certain ambiguity about the "court of the Gentiles" because of its Herodian and Gentile connections; see the helpful discussion by McCane, "Simply Irresistible" 732.

46. Schnabel, *Early Christian Mission* vol. 1, *Jesus and the Twelve*, 342. Moreover, as we shall see in chapter 4 below, Jesus' discussion with the Samaritan woman signals the advent of a new transcendent means of worship that certainly relativizes and even displaces temple-dependent worship.

47. Wolter, "Jesus as Teller of Parables," in Charlesworth and Pokorný, *Jesus Research*, 137.

Jesus and the Religions

Several Parables That Seem to Include Reference to Gentiles and Other "Outsiders"

The telling of parables was a distinctive means by which Jesus communicated his message about the sovereign Rule of God. The parables are to be understood in the light of the general theme of the Gospels that Jesus' words and deeds—both "ordinary" and "mighty"—are revelatory for those who are sympathetic to his mission and aims. For those fundamentally at odds with Jesus' mission, his words and deeds reveal nothing of who he is; these are the outsiders for whom everything, words *and* deeds, happens in parables (Mark 4:11). "The phrase 'everything happens in parables' (rather than 'is spoken in parables') suggests that it is not only Jesus' teaching that is in view but his whole ministry".[48] Perhaps this includes his encounters with Gentiles and others, and perhaps some of his symbolic actions might allude to Gentiles as well.

Several parables appear to include references to Gentiles and other "outsiders" coming to a restored or reconstituted Israel. One example is the parable of the compassionate Samaritan (Luke 10:25–37) that will be discussed in the next chapter. There are also other parables in which Jesus seems to refer even more directly to participation by non-Jews in the Rule of God. There is a cluster of parables agreed by most commentators to be specifically about Israel and included in them are two parables (the great banquet/marriage feast; the vineyard and murderous tenants) that seem to contain implicit reference to Gentiles as the "new" people over against a "failed" people. There is also the parable of the mustard seed. Discussion of each of these parables follows.[49]

---

48. Blakley, "Incomprehension or Resistance?," 305–6, citing R. T. France.

49. Mention might also be made of another parable not found among those to be considered in what follows. David Bosch considers that "Gentiles are perhaps prefigured . . . in the parable of the prodigal son, which Jesus tells precisely because the Pharisees are upset when he welcomes tax-collectors and sinners and eats with them" (*Transforming Mission*, 30).

The Great Banquet (Luke 14:15-24) / The Marriage Feast (Matt 22:1-14; *Gospel of Thomas* 64)

This parable, especially in its Matthean version, presents a broad salvation history of God's dealings with Israel and the wider Gentile world. In particular, the parable "answers the question, 'Why has the Gospel, the invitation to the Kingdom of God, passed from the Jews, the chosen people, to the Gentiles?' The answer is, 'They were not worthy of it, they have proved this by their rejection of the Gospel of salvation. It is not God's fault. Like the kind and courtly host, he has done everything that was possible.'"[50] The king's messengers (the prophets, John the Baptist, and the beloved son) have been rejected and killed. Lyle Story further explains that the "rejection by the *invited guests,* and their *replacement by others,* are coupled with the purpose *that my house may be filled,* suggesting the movement of God from the narrow boundaries of some to the all-embracing call of God which reaches beyond the confines of Israel to the Gentiles and those who are dispossessed."[51]

So, as the parable of the vineyard puts it, God takes the kingdom from "you" and transfers it to a people whose fruitfulness is assured (Matt 21:43). The parable, it is true, does not specifically mention Gentiles as the alternative guests invited to the banquet. But their probable inclusion, among a wider circle of those normally excluded, does cohere with what we have already seen of eschatological reversal and banqueting in the teaching of Jesus.

Vineyard and Murderous Tenants (Mark 12:1-12; Matt 21:33-46; Luke 20:9-17; *Gospel of Thomas* 65-66)

The parable is, despite some variations in detail, essentially the same in all three Synoptic Gospels, and found in the same context in each of

---

50. Eta Linnemann, as cited by Story, "All Is Now Ready," 73-74.

51. Story, "All Is Now Ready," 77; original emphasis. Story links his explanation with Paul's affirmation, "To the Jew first, and also to the Greek" (Rom 1:16; 2:9-10). And he quotes T. W. Manson: "The whole parable might be regarded as a *midrash* on Is. 49:6" (Isa 49:6: "It is too small a thing for you to be my servant to restore the tribes of Jacob and bring back those of Israel I have kept. I will also make you a light for the Gentiles, that you may bring my salvation to the ends of the earth").

them. The key verse, in terms of a possible allusion to Gentiles, is Mark 12:9 where, after the tenants have killed the vineyard owner's son, "the owner of the vineyard . . . will come and destroy the tenants and give the vineyard to others." Are these *others* to be understood as Gentiles, or as a group of "tenants" that includes Gentiles? Given that the parable is clearly allegorical,[52] how far are the details to be pressed? The keys to allegory are plot and the way the analogy works to establish the intention(s) of the story. Snodgrass is adamant that the central point is that "[w]hat is being taken from the tenants is the privilege of being engaged with the purposes of God." And, to the question of whether the parable teaches that "God has rejected Israel by giving the kingdom to Gentiles," Snodgrass is equally sure that the answer is "No!" and that these "others" are not specified. "The passage is quite vague."[53]

However, other commentators are less certain about the non-specific nature of these "others."[54] The notion of replacement is not explicit; instead there is the less explicit "given to." A few commentators assert that Jesus and his disciples are meant. Others are confident that Gentiles are at least included among the "others." In Matthew, one theme in the parables is that those in a position of privilege have failed to live up to their calling by God. They are variously portrayed as the disobedient son (Matt 21:28–32), the murderous vineyard tenants (21:33–44), and those who contemptuously ignore their banquet invitations (22:1–10). So, who is the new "people that produces the fruits of the kingdom" (21:43)? In the opinion of R. T. France, "it is not a simple matter of 'Jews out; Gentiles in.' Rather, we are to think of a reconstitution of the true people of God which is no longer on the basis of racial ancestry, but, as

---

52. "[T]his parable is allegorical. There are obvious correspondences that make it work. No Jew would need to be told that a story of an owner and his vineyard in some way had to do with God and his people" (Snodgrass, *Stories with Intent*, 292).

53. Snodgrass, *Stories with Intent*, 293, 296–97. But it must also be said that Snodgrass's main emphasis is upon the non-rejection of Israel; the parable is "a prophetic indictment of the leaders" and "is not anti-Semitic" (297). A number of other commentators are also sure that the "other" people to whom the vineyard is given is not another or a different *ethnos* but restored Israel.

54. A good survey of the suggested meaning of "the other tenants" is found in Stein, *Mark*, 537.

symbolized by the Gentile centurion, on the basis of faith in Jesus."[55] The parable of the vineyard tenants is clearly intended to recount the story of Israel. But, unlike the Jewish expectation embedded in the metaphor of Israel as Yahweh's vineyard in Psalm 80 (see vv. 8-19), the vineyard is not threatened by external enemies whom Yahweh will destroy. Rather, the enemy is the Jewish leadership who will lose their ownership even as it is entrusted to "a people that produces the fruits of the kingdom." (21:43).

Perhaps the best explanation is that a "new" (i.e., reconstituted) Israel is implied—in which case Gentiles could certainly be part of the "others." The "others" in Mark become a singular "people" in Matthew (21:43: "given to a people that produces the fruits of the kingdom"). A case can certainly be made that the Gentiles and Samaritans encountered and spoken about by Jesus do display at least some of these "fruits of the kingdom." The change leads Robert Stein to conclude that this "suggests that the new covenant would involve a community whose ethnicity would consist of both Jew and Greek."[56] A phrase such as "new leadership within the kingdom" might be an appropriate summary. In one way or another, there is a clear echo of two of the recurring themes already seen in the teaching of Jesus about Gentiles and Samaritans: the beginnings of a "great reversal," and an expanded vision of the people of God.

The Workers in the Vineyard (Matt 20:1-16)

In the parable of the workers in the vineyard those who are hired last (vv. 8, 12, 14) are "made . . . equal" to those who have worked from the beginning in the vineyard that is also clearly an allegory of Israel. The commentators rightly emphasize that the parable is primarily about themes of justice, mercy, equality, and the abundance of divine grace. But might these "last" ones perhaps be seen as Gentiles? According to Donald Hagner, "Matthew's church possibly identified those who worked the whole day with Israel and those who came last with the Gentiles" (in order to signal the equality of Gentile and Jewish

55. France, *Gospel of Matthew*, 319.
56. Stein, *Mark*, 537.

Jesus and the Religions

Christians).[57] Although not explicitly affirmed, they may well point to "latecomers such the sinners and Gentiles gathered by Jesus."[58] Other commentators are less sure.[59] Nonetheless, the principle of reversal clear stated in the concluding verse, "[s]o the last will be first, and the first last" (16), is reminiscent of the "great reversal" dynamic that Jesus sees as fundamental to the workings of the incipient Rule of God—and that he sees as present in some Gentiles.

The Mustard Seed (Mark 4:30–32; Matt 13:31–32; Luke 13:18–19; Gospel of Thomas 20)

Most of the parables have plot options and invite listeners to take part in the story. Other parables, such as the parable of the mustard seed (Mark 4:30–32), are different: they reiterate the knowledge and experience of the listeners without inviting them to take part. Moreover, the knowledge and experience to which such parables appeal is the insight that "the Rule of God . . . has a *universal* dimension, but Israel is central to it."[60] Certain of Jesus' parables make this contrast between local and universal explicit, and appear to raise the possibility of Gentiles joining a renewed and restored Israel. They clarify the way in which ultimate endings also have a beginning, with both ending and beginning inextricably connected, while providing a contrast between large and small. These parables (such as the seed growing by itself (Mark 4:26–29), the four different kinds of soil (Mark 4:3–8), the mustard seed with its "birds" (Mark 4:30–32//), and the yeast (Luke 13:20–21//Matt 13:33) explain Jesus' seemingly insignificant ministry as being an integral element of the establishment of the eschatological, universal sovereign Rule of God.[61]

57. *Matthew 14–28*, 573.

58. Senior, *Matthew*, 223.

59. Their suggestions include a contrast between the Twelve and later disciples, or deathbed converts. See, for example, the discussion by France, *Gospel of Matthew*, 751.

60. Wolter, "Jesus as Teller of Parables," in Charlesworth and Pokorný, *Jesus Research*, 137; original emphasis.

61. According to Wolter, it is precisely in this latter group of parables that the ministry of Jesus is a hermeneutical key: the prevalent image of the eschatological

In the parable of the mustard seed, when the tree matures, "birds of the air can nest under its shade." It seems clear that the tree represents either Israel or the Rule of God. There is considerable debate about the "birds" (cf. Ezek 17:22–24; *1 En.* 90:30; *4 Ezra* 5:26). However, Joachim Jeremias argues that since the word *kataskanoun* (to "nest" or "roost") is used in Zeph 2:11 (2:14 in English translations), and in an intertestamental text, to refer to the incorporation of the Gentiles, the word is, in fact, "a technical term for the incorporation of the Gentiles into the people of God."[62] Since the kingdom, and perhaps even the restoration of Israel, is in some sense already present (Mark 1:15; Luke 11:20), then a possible meaning that incorporates Gentile inclusion becomes tenable.[63] It remains the case both that these are parables and not allegories, and that the central point of the parables in Mark 4 is that the reality of the Rule of God is not obscured by its mundane appearance. Nonetheless, as Michael Bird puts it, there is good reason to consider the "possibility that Gentiles are envisaged as participating in the restored Israel on the grounds that in Jewish literature 'birds' more readily symbolize Gentiles than Jews."[64] This possibility seems entirely congruent with what seems to be the place of such outsiders in the estimation of Jesus.

Rule of God was a well-known idea in Judaism. It had a universal dimension, and Israel would be central to it. There was a dissonance between this collective perspective and Jesus' own ministry but this particular group of parables clarifies how Jesus' own ministry might be understood as an integral part of God's universal eschatological work of salvation. These parables contain an implicit but distinctive Christology. Wolter, "Jesus as Teller of Parables," 123–39.

62. Jeremias, *Parables of Jesus*, 147.

63. Bird also adds that "[t]he authenticity of the unit seems probable since 'birds' was not a term used to refer to Gentiles in the early church and the parable would contain a deliberately ambiguous protest against Jewish nationalism" (Bird, "Jesus and the Gentiles," 99–100).

64. Ibid.," 100.

Implications for a Gentile Mission from the Narrative Structuring and Content of the Central Chapters of Mark

We have already mentioned Jesus' reported journeys into Gentile areas.[65] Attention now turns to a more detailed discussion of such a report in Mark's Gospel: the contributions of Jeffrey Gibson, Kelly Iverson, and Ted Blakley, each of whom discusses implications for a Gentile mission from the narrative structuring and content of the central chapters of Mark. We begin with Blakley whose work plausibly draws upon and develops some earlier insights of Gibson and Iverson. In his doctoral dissertation, Blakley argues for two theses. The first is that "in Mark 4:1–8:26, the disciples are characterized as resistant to Jesus' Gentile mission and to their participation in that mission, the chief consequence being that they are rendered incapable of recognizing Jesus' vocational identity as Israel's Messiah." A secondary thesis develops the christological implication: namely "that in Mark 8:27–30, Peter's recognition of Jesus' messianic identity indicates that the disciples have finally come to accept Jesus' Gentile mission and their participation in it." Prior to this acceptance is Jesus' harsh rebuke of the disciples in Mark 8:14–21—a rebuke "occasioned not by the disciples' lack of faith or incomprehension but by their active resistance to his Gentile mission . . ." This conclusion is reached after an analysis of the structure of Mark's Gospel that seeks to demonstrate that "Mark 4:1–8:30 comprises a single, unified, narrative movement, whose action and plot is oriented to the Sea of Galilee and whose most distinctive feature is the network of sea crossings that transport Jesus and his disciples back and forth between Jewish and Gentile geopolitical spaces."[66]

65. See the latter part of chapter 1 above.

66. Blakley, "Incomprehension or Resistance?," quotes from dissertation abstract. He explains his claim about sea crossings as follows: "Mark records six sea crossings, three of which are episodic, that is, three in which an event is narrated during the crossing itself. The episodic sea crossings (ESCs) are 4:35–41, 6:45–52, and 8:13–21. . . . By plotting their intended itineraries, I discovered that of the six sea crossings, the three ESCs—*all* three ESCs and *only* the three ESCs—were ones that set out from Jewish territory and were destined for Gentile territory. That the three ESCs were *exclusively* oriented toward Gentile space seemed more than coincidental. This discovery raised the possibility that what transpires during an ESC is integrally related to its Gentile trajectory" (3; original emphasis).

It has often been observed that Mark has an ambiguous view of Gentiles; sometimes they are portrayed in a negative way, sometimes more positively. This ambiguity (and the point just made about crossing between Jewish and Gentile geopolitical spaces) is well illustrated by the status of Bethsaida. The ambiguous nature of the evidence for the cultural status of Bethsaida (Gentile or Jewish) has long been recognized. In the texts of the Gospels, Matthew, Luke and John clearly assert the Jewishness of Bethsaida.[67] But Mark seems to regard Bethsaida as Gentile; as Blakley points out, "The claim that Bethsaida represents Gentile space in Mark is not new, but one shared by a number of commentators."[68] Blakley's own contribution to the discussion centers on the evidence he presents for "a dichotomy between the *Jewish* west side of the sea and the *Gentile* east side of the sea." Bethsaida is twice mentioned in the narrative and on both occasions is clearly marked in the text as being *on the other side (eis to peran)* of the sea from Jewish Galilee (6:45; 8:13, 22)."[69] Other indicators of the Gentile character of Bethsaida seem even more significant. Historically, it underwent significant growth under the Herodians,[70] and successive seasons of archaeological excavation at et-Tell (identified as ancient Bethsaida) since 1988 have found considerable material that can be called Hellenistic,

---

67. The evidence is summarized in Blakley, "Incomprehension or Resistance?," 151.

68. Ibid., 149; the not inconsiderable evidence is summarized in n. 106 of Blakley's dissertation to which add: Heinz-Wolfgang Kuhn, "Bethsaida in the Gospel of Mark," in Arav and Freund, *Bethsaida*, 3:115-31. For Blakley this notion of Bethsaida as Gentile reinforces his thesis that the disciples' resistance to participating in the Gentile mission is an important theme in the central section of the Second Gospel— which is why, "when Jesus *forces* (Mark 6:45) his disciples to embark for Bethsaida, he is sending them on a mission among and to Gentiles" (147).

69. "Incomprehension or Resistance?," 148 (quoting Svartvik, *Mark and Mission*; original emphasis). Bethsaida was situated on the northeastern shore of the Sea of Galilee and, as Blakley points out in a footnote, there is "geological evidence that, in the first-century, Bethsaida was separated from Galilee by a deep gorge cut by the Jordan river. This would have made fording nearly impossible so that travel between Bethsaida and cities like Capernaum, which were only a few miles away, would have been by boat and would have contributed to the sense that Bethsaida was on the other side of the sea" (148 n. 105, citing Strickert, *Bethsaida: Home of the Apostles*).

70. There is a helpful summary in Chancey, *Greco-Roman Culture*, 92.

but very little that appears to be Jewish.[71] There is, for example, a small temple of the imperial cult and other clearly non-Jewish cultic material.[72] This leads Markus Bockmuehl to comment that both "the literary and archaeological evidence points to the fact that Bethsaida's culture in the first century was under strongly Hellenistic influence.... If there were any Jews at et-Tell, then unlike other parts of the Gaulanitis they appear to have left no signs of a way of life that distinguished them from their Gentile neighbors.... But whether a Jewish religious presence can be documented or not, there is little doubt about the greater marginality of Jewish culture and religion in this area."[73]

In the light of recent scholarly discussion, Blakley's conclusion is appropriate: "Bethsaida appears to have had an ethnically-diverse population, one in which a Jewish minority culture existed alongside a dominant Hellenistic culture. Bethsaida might well have been regarded by some as Jewish and by others as Gentile."[74] In other words, the evidence from this corner of Galilee appears to be at odds with claims about the overwhelmingly Jewish nature of Galilee.

Part of Blakley's thesis is that what transpires during the journeys to and from Gentile territory helps resolve the ambiguity. In particular, it is the insight that the harshness of Jesus' rebuke of his disciples[75] relates not merely to their lack of faith or incomprehension but to their active resistance to (some form of) his Gentile mission.[76] Blakley discerns a theme of growing resistance in the central chapters of Mark such that three detailed investigations of Mark 8 (by Gibson, Iverson, and Blakley himself) can and do "characterize the disciples' resistance

---

71. For archaeological and geological reports (through to 2006), see Arav and Freund, *Bethsaida*, vol. 4.

72. See Rami Arav, "Bethsaida," in Charlesworth, *Jesus and Archaeology*, 161.

73. Markus Bockmuehl, "Simon Peter and Bethsaida," in Chilton and Evans, *Missions of James*, 81–82.

74. Blakley, "Incomprehension or Resistance?," 150. He adds: "Thus, the other gospels' characterization of Bethsaida as Jewish presents no obstacle to the claim that Mark characterizes it as Gentile."

75. See Mark 8:13–21, and especially his comments about their hardness of heart and lack of understanding—17b–18, 21.

76. Here Blakley is building on Gibson, "Rebuke of the Disciples"; and Iverson, *Gentiles in Mark*, 40, 82, 91–97.

Elsewhere in the Gospels: Purity, Temple, Parables

in terms of *purposeful* resistance or *willful* opposition, which is to be attributed to . . . the disciples' *neglecting* to take several loaves in 8:14 as a deliberate attempt to thwart additional outpourings of salvific favors upon Gentiles."[77] Blakley himself believes he has accumulated evidence "leading to the conclusion that, *within the Sea Crossing movement, the Markan disciples manifest resistance to Jesus' Gentile mission and to their participation in it.*"[78]

Despite the plausible nature of many of Blakley's arguments, it must also be noted that the present academic consensus is not (or not yet—his work is not yet widely known) supportive of this thesis of the disciples' supposed active resistance to a Gentile mission embraced, in some form, by Jesus. There is some wider support for the notion of some kind of incipient Gentile mission on the part of Jesus. Howard Marshall, for example, points out that some of the stories in Mark 5–8 "take place outside Judea and Galilee in territory inhabited overwhelmingly by non-Jews, and they give the impression that the coming of Jesus was not solely for the benefit of the Jews."[79] Udo Schnelle, in writing about the Gospel of Mark, believes that the evangelist's view is expressed programmatically in 7:1–23, "for Jesus's work among Gentiles begins by declaring that the Jewish ritual laws are no longer in force." Schnelle then refers to the healings of the Syrophoenician woman (7:24–30), and a person with hearing and speech impediment (7:31–37), and to the feeding of the four thousand (8:1–10). He concludes that these "must be understood as illustrations of the abolition of the fundamental distinction 'clean/unclean.' The acclamation in 7:37, 'He has done everything well,' in its Markan context refers to Jesus's ministry among Gentiles."[80] Michael Bird concedes that the Gospel writers "arguably interpret Jesus' encounters with Gentiles as embryonic indications of the coming

---

77. Blakley, "Incomprehension or Resistance?," 292 n. 1; original emphasis. He concludes: "The disciples do not *absentmindedly forget* to bring extra loaves but *purposefully neglect* to do so in an attempt to prevent Jesus from performing another feeding among Gentiles" (3, original emphasis). He adds: "The reader is left wondering, will the disciples come to understand about the loaves, or will their hearts remain resistant to Jesus' Gentile mission and their participation in it?" (297).

78. Blakley, "Incomprehension or Resistance?," 292; original emphasis.

79. Marshall, *New Testament Theology*, 65.

80. Schnelle, *Theology of the New Testament*, 422.

Gentile mission."[81] And, if the theses of Blakley, Gibson, and Iverson can be sustained, even in part, a more positive set of conclusions about Jesus' missional intentions towards Gentiles can be drawn—especially in Mark's account. Moreover, given the usual understanding of the chronological priority of Mark among the Synoptic Gospels, it might also be argued that his account more clearly reflects the intention of Jesus towards Gentiles than the more intensively redacted accounts of Matthew and Luke.[82]

Other Gospel Passages and Secondary Material about Gentiles

Before drawing some final conclusions about Jesus' encounters with, and teaching about, Gentiles and Samaritans, there is some further incidental or secondary material in the Gospels that directly connects Jesus with these "outsiders."[83] There is space only for a brief mention of it.

Gentiles Are among the Crowds

In Mark 3:7–12, the crowds that come to Jesus "in great numbers" arrive from a number of places including "Idumea, beyond the Jordan, and the region around Tyre and Sidon." The mention of Tyre and Sidon is significant. These Philistine cities were notoriously antagonistic to

---

81. Bird, *Jesus and the Origins*, 103. Bird attributes this to "their redactional and narrative aims rather than being directly attributable to Jesus." However, it must also be added that Bird does not interact with the arguments of Gibson and Iverson (and his *Jesus and the Origins of the Gentile Mission* was published before Blakley's thesis became available).

82. This tentative conclusion—that Jesus does initiate some kind of intentional mission towards Gentiles (and Samaritans, it might be added)—must be tested against much wider and long-standing debates concerning Jesus and the origins of mission to Gentiles. However, there is insufficient space in our current book to enter the discussion but a complementary volume is planned and this topic will be included in it.

83. This material is in addition to the discussion in chapter 1 above, which includes mention of Jesus and "sinners"—and the likelihood that this category includes Gentiles and thereby establishes the probability that Jesus was open to accepting Gentiles into table fellowship.

Israel and a number of texts dwell on the judgment awaiting them.[84] Jesus himself singles them out for somewhat favorable comparison in Luke 10:13-14//Matt 11:21-22 and the description in Mark chapter 3 certainly implies that it is Gentiles, even from highly unlikely areas, as well as Jews who are attracted to his healing.[85]

The Demon-Possessed Man in Gadara (Mark 5:1-20//Matt 8:28-34//Luke 8:26-39)

All three Synoptic Gospels record an incident in which Jesus sets free a demon-possessed man on the eastern shore of the Sea of Galilee.[86] The man is not specifically identified as a Gentile but it is clear that Jesus and the disciples have crossed over to the Gentile side of the lake and the possessed man is certainly a polytheist of some sort—and non-Jewish, given the description of a setting among the tombs of the dead and the repeated references to pigs in the narrative.[87] There are a number of factors that point to the authenticity of the story.[88] As described above, Blakley and others argue that this first sea crossing is the beginning of some kind of Gentile mission. Jesus himself initiates the decision to cross the sea of Galilee into Gentile territory.[89] Thus, in the

---

84. See, for example, Isa 23:1-18; Ezek 26-28; Amos 1:9-10; Zech 9:2-4; 1 Macc 5:15.

85. For a discussion of this Gentile component of these crowds (not actually mentioned in the other Gospels), see Iverson, *Gentiles in Mark*, 37-38, 49, 79.

86. The precise name of the place is not clear (it seems as if "Gerasene" or "Gergesene" was a later addition to or amendment of the text). A setting in "Gergasa" is plausibly argued by Gundry (see his *Mark*, 255-57). As for the authenticity of the account, there are a number of factors that point persuasively to it; see the summaries in, for example: Twelftree, *Jesus the Miracle Worker*, 287-89; and Wright, *Jesus and the Victory*, 195-96.

87. "For a Jew, the description of the area and of the man would connote Gentile uncleanness" (Wahlen, *Jesus and the Impurity of Spirits*, 96; Wahlen gives reasons for this statement.)

88. See the summaries of the arguments for authenticity in Twelftree and Wright as cited in n. 95 above.

89. Cf. Iverson: "The reader has been well prepared for the launching of the Gentile mission by Mark's carefully arranged story. Jesus' concern for all people, his penchant for crossing boundaries, and the characteristics of the kingdom described

absence of "*any other unambiguous markers of ethnicity in the narrative*, our best argument remains that the author intends the reader to derive the demoniac's ethnicity from the fact that he is encountered in Gentile territory, which is consistent with the function of geopolitical space in the Markan narrative."[90] If so, then the fierce storm they encounter on the way may well take on added significance: as Blakley himself points out, the storm "suggests that the opposing forces of wind and sea are not simply a threat to human life but a threat to the inclusion of Gentiles under God's apocalyptic reign"—with the storm itself described in demonic terms.[91]

Jesus Heals a Deaf Mute (Mark 7:31–37) and Then a Blind Man (Mark 8:22–26)

These two healing accounts are unique to Mark's Gospel and might be considered together, given the Gentile context of each.[92] Ted Blakley, in pursuit of his thesis about the disciples' resistance to the Gentile mission of Jesus, points out that these two miracles "are the only healings of organs of perception within the first half of the gospel. It is, therefore, more than coincidental that they essentially frame [the third episodic sea crossing], the only episode in the gospel in which the disciples are explicitly accused of blindness and deafness (8:18), making it likely that these three episodes intersect and interact on the rhetorical plane of

---

in the parables foreshadow an expansion in Jesus' ministry that finds its fulfillment in a Gentile mission" (*Gentiles in Mark*, 39).

90. Blakley, "Incomprehension or Resistance?," 170 n. 165; original emphasis. Note too that when they cross back over the lake, they are unambiguously in Jewish territory as Jesus immediately encounters Jairus, identified as a leader within the synagogue—a clear identifying mark of Jewish identity and location.

91. Ibid., 170. Blakley goes on to explain the storm's "demonic characterization. When Jesus stills the wind and calms the sea with his authoritative command, we encounter the same vocabulary employed in his exorcisms (1:25; 3:12; 9:25). In fact, the language and structure of Jesus' response to the wind and the sea clearly parallels ... Jesus' exorcism in the Capernaum synagogue (1:21–28)." In both cases Jesus rebukes, commands silence, and is met with immediate obedience. Blakley concludes: "It is not the created order that stands opposed to the advance of God's kingdom but the demonic forces that have subjugated it" (171).

92. Assuming a predominantly Gentile ethos for Bethsaida—at least in Mark.

the narrative."⁹³ The two who are healed are minor characters in the sense that they "are not offered as models of spiritual virtue for they say and do nothing" but since they do underline the spiritual deafness and blindness of the disciples, then Jesus' ability to heal these deficiencies "would seem to point to his ability to overcome the disciples' spiritual maladies. More particularly, given that the deaf mute and the blind man are both Gentiles, their healing might produce the expectation that Jesus can and will overcome his disciples' resistance to Gentile mission" (even if "subsequent to Jesus' healing of the deaf mute, the disciples still manifest resistance to Gentile mission on at least two occasions [8:4, 14]").⁹⁴

A Second Feeding of the Crowds (Mark 8:1–10//Matt 15:32–39)

This is the second feeding miracle in Mark and, although it has a number of similarities to the miracle on the Jewish side of the lake that is recorded in Mark 6, the setting (as made clear by the Second Evangelist), is on the eastern, Gentile shore. Mark places Jesus outside Galilee; this is the implication of 8:10 and, given that this event forms part of the withdrawal by Jesus from Galilee, the implication is that Jesus is repeating in mainly Gentile or mixed territory the kind of miracle previously performed by him in Jewish settings.⁹⁵ The Gentile setting is reinforced "by the reference to the people having come from afar (*apo makrothen*), a phrase used in the LXX for Gentile lands.... The point of the narrative would be, then, that Jesus is gathering together all who respond to his teaching, both Jew and Gentile."⁹⁶ The incident comes after Jesus' exor-

---

93. "Incomprehension or Resistance?," 299.

94. Ibid., 299-300.

95. All of the events in Mark 7:24–8:10 take place in Gentile territory. The story of the Syrophoenician woman introduces a clear Gentile element, as do Gentile place names—not to mention the absence of the Jewish names and Jewish places that are found in Galilee.

96. Wahlen, *Jesus and the Impurity of Spirits*, 99. Blakley ("Incomprehension or Resistanc?," 233 n. 98) quotes Boring: "The Old Testament repeatedly describes Gentiles as those who are 'far off' (e.g., Deut 28:49; 29:22; 1 Kgs 8:41; Isa 39:3; 60:4; cf. Eph 2:13, 17; Acts 2:39)" and van Iersel: "'From afar' is, both in rabbinic writings and in some places in the Second Testament (Acts 2:39 and Ephesians 2:11-22), a term

cism that follows the Syrophoenician woman's reply to Jesus that "even the dogs under the table [i.e., Gentiles] eat from the children's crumbs" (7:28)—and in this story even the "crumbs" point to an extravagant note of abundance as some four thousand people miraculously eat and are filled, with seven baskets full of leftovers gathered.[97] Mark seems deliberately to sound a note of Gentile inclusion as he shapes his narrative to evoke the earlier Jewish feeding, which leads Michael Bird to add that "[i]f the shape of the narrative is to function as a symbolic anticipation of the messianic banquet, it could be inferred that Jews and Gentiles are said to participate and Jesus' miraculous action is a foretaste of that inclusion."[98]

"Whoever Is Not against You Is for You" (Luke 9:50)

The enigmatic saying that "whoever is not against you is for you" is immediately followed in Luke by Jesus' rebuke of the disciples who want to punish unwelcoming Samaritans (Luke 9:50 and 9:51–56). In Mark the parallel passage ("whoever is not against us is for us"—9:40) occurs in the context of "unauthorized" exorcism/miracle-working and draws from Richard Drummond the comment that "in the context of consideration of contemporary rival religious parties and groups, Jesus emphasized the importance of quality of attitude or intent as compared with formal allegiance."[99] In other words, Jesus does appear in this saying, and its parallel passage, to display both the openness to "others" and impatience with religious insularity that underlies his welcome of Gentiles and Samaritans.

---

applied to the Gentiles generally" to similar effect.

97. The feeding stories are replete with possible symbolism. For example, do the twelve baskets of leftovers following the feeding in Mark 6 represent the twelve tribes of Israel? And do the seven baskets in the Gentile feeding represent the nations? Many of the specialist commentaries and studies explore these possibilities.

98. *Jesus and the Origins*, 111.

99. Drummond, *Toward a New Age*, 17–18. Drummond also goes on to point out that in the parable of the sheep and the goats, "final separation is made not on the basis of ethnic or cultural affiliation or even of religious faith, but as a consequence of the presence or lack of ethical, in particular of compassionate conduct (Matt 25.31–46)."

Sodom and Gomorrah, Tyre and Sidon

Even Sodom, Gomorrah, Tyre, and Sidon are compared favorably with the present faithlessness of Israel in a complex of passages: Luke 10:12// Matt 10:15 and Luke 10:13-15//Matt 11:20-24.[100] Jesus' reproach of the Israelite towns of Chorazin and Bethsaida includes a comparison with these Gentile towns which, he states, would have long repented in the face of his mighty works. This "sharp contrast of infamous Gentile cities with the obduracy of the Galilean towns"[101] clearly has its primary focus on Israel/Galilee rather than Gentiles who would have recognized God's agent. Mention has been made above of Tyre and Sidon; Sodom and Gomorrah were regarded with even greater distaste as notorious models of Gentile sinfulness.[102] But even such Gentiles would have responded to the signs done by Jesus. This is, of course, only a partial compliment, and not a wide-ranging affirmation of Gentile virtue—it is more like a lesser judgment—but, in the context of the generally pessimistic Second Temple Era estimates of the Gentile world, it is both surprising and notable.

The Queen of the South, the Ninevites and the "Sign of Jonah"[103]

In Matt 12:39-41; 16:4; and Luke 11:29-32, Jesus identifies himself with the "sign of Jonah." It is not clear exactly what this "sign" might be (though it does appear to threaten judgment), nor is it entirely clear why Jesus self-identifies in this way with the curious figure of Jonah.[104] The

---

100. The "probable authenticity" of the passages is defended in some detail in Bird, *Jesus and the Origin*, 62.

101. Bird, *Jesus and the Origins of the Gentile Mission*, 62.

102. Not only is their deplorable status made clear in Gen 18-19, but also in other OT passages (eg. Isa 1:9-10 (cf. Rom 9:29); Lam 4:6-16; Ezek 16:46-56; Amos 4:11 (cf. Jude 7); and numerous texts in the interTestamental literature.

103. For a discussion of reasons for the authenticity of the passage (and reasons against—though these are not favored by Bird), together with a discussion of possible redactional history, see Bird, *Jesus and the Origins*, 59-60.

104. Cary calls Jonah a comedic figure who fails with an astonishing persistence; he is "a ridiculous excuse for a prophet" (*Jonah*, 17).

context is the unbelief (or the seeking for a "sign")[105] that Jesus encounters. Jesus announces an expectation that Ninevites and the "Queen of the South" will come to condemn "this generation" of unbelieving Jews at the final judgment (Matt 12:41–42//Luke 11:31–32). Nineveh, despite its repentance under Jonah, was judged by God because of its sinfulness (Nah 1–3; Zeph 2:13). And the queen (of Egypt and Ethiopia according to Josephus), who is also an ambivalent figure, will also be an agent of the eschatological reversal that we have noted a number of times in the teaching of Jesus.

Given all that we have seen about Jesus' attitude to Gentiles, his appeal to Jonah may not be unrelated to the way in which God brings blessing to the Gentiles whom Jonah encounters. Jonah is a story about the standing of Jew and Gentile before God. Against his own aims and best efforts, Jonah becomes a blessing to his Gentile travelling companions, and then his proclamation to the inhabitants of Nineveh saves them from God's wrath—even if these Gentiles "do not know the name of the Lord or even whether they are saved," as Phillip Cary puts it.[106] But several dimensions of Jesus' appeal to Jonah are plausibly elaborated by Jonathan Reed who offers a detailed analysis of the "sign of Jonah" saying within a Galilean setting. He suggests reasons why a comparison between Jonah and Jesus would have been particularly fitting in Galilee, the homeland of both prophets, and concludes that "there are tantalizing hints that in Galilee the comparison with Jonah included both a component of openness to Gentiles and a critical edge toward Jerusalem, both important themes in Q's theology."[107] Whatever the precise nature of the sign, the appeal to Jonah and the Ninevites, and to the Southern Queen, continues a theme already noted: some Gentiles display humility, faith and even repentance, the (surprising) manifestation of which shames Israel. They certainly participate in the future kingdom (in some instrumental way as God's agents). They are contrasted with "this gen-

---

105. For a summary of what "sign" potentially conveyed under Mosaic law, and what it might have meant to Herod, Judaism and the "sign prophets," see Bird, *Jesus and the Origins*, 59 n. 1.

106. *Jonah*, 20.

107. See ch. 7 of his *Archaeology and the Galilean Jesus*; quote from 211. Reed includes a summary of what he means by Q's openness to Gentiles.

eration" of Jewish unbelief. And Jesus clearly likens himself to Solomon (to whom the queen came) and Jonah—both of whom are "known for their interaction with Gentiles."[108] And, as Seán Freyne observes about the passage, it points to the "universal scope" of the Jewish scriptural tradition: "Wisdom is available to all and repentance is a possibility for non-Jews. Insiders who espouse an ethno-phobic point of view involving total separation cannot share in the eschatological banquet which Jesus envisages."[109]

"Other sheep" and "Scattered Children" (John 10:16 and 11:52)

The Fourth Gospel has few explicit references to Gentiles. But there are, for example, intriguing references to "other sheep" and to the "scattered children of God." In commenting on Jesus the good shepherd who states that he has "other sheep that are not of this sheep pen" (10:16), Gary Burge concludes that "if they come from a different fold, they come from outside of Judaism, which no doubt refers to Gentiles."[110] There is also a reference (attributed to the intention of the high priest Caiaphas) to "the scattered children of God" who are contrasted (in 11:52) with "the Jewish nation." The meaning is not entirely clear: perhaps the author of the Gospel intends diaspora Jews, or Gentile Christians—or, perhaps Gentiles. Burge and most commentators are clear that "here John is no doubt referring to Gentiles."[111]

"Greeks" Approaching Jesus (John 12:20-26)

Apart from his encounter with the Samaritan woman and her fellow Samaritans (4:4-42), and his healing of the official's son (4:46-54), the

---

108. Bird, *Jesus and the Origins*, 61.

109. Freyne, *Jesus, a Jewish Galilean*, 119-20.

110. "If they come from a different fold, they come from outside of Judaism, which no doubt refers to Gentiles" (Burge, *John*, 292)—"most likely, the Gentiles" (304). An intentional reference to Gentiles is accepted by most commentators (for example, Brodie, *Gospel according to John*, 370-71. For a detailed discussion see Köstenberger, "Jesus the Good Shepherd." For arguments against a Gentile reference, see Ridderbos, *Gospel according to John*, 364-65.

111. Burge, *John*, 321. See also Köstenberger, *John*, 353.

Johannine Jesus' only other meeting with non-Jews—apart from the coming interrogation by Pontius Pilate—is with these Greeks who wish to meet him. Although these Greeks are clearly Gentile,[112] it is not clear at a first reading how, or even whether, his reply is directed towards them, or where we are to understand it finishing (v. 26 or v. 36?). However, the passage does provide an example of what a theological reading might disclose to a reader. Many commentators simply state that there is no development of the supposed Gentile context in the discourse that follows the arrival of these Greeks who disappear immediately from view as John reverts to a favorite theme: impending glorification. But there is much more than this theme in the passage, important though it is.

For example, a strongly christological note is sounded, and in eschatological terms. "Jesus will be 'lifted up' and draw 'all people' to himself. . . . Thus 12:32 can be taken as an indirect answer to the Greeks' question in 12:21. Paradoxically, it is through his *exaltation* that Jesus will become accessible to the Greeks."[113] Or, as Köstenberger puts it elsewhere, "[t]he salvation-historical turn of events is marked . . . by the coming of the Greeks to Jesus in 12:20, resulting in Jesus' pronouncement that, once exalted, he will 'draw all people' to himself—'all people' being all *kinds of* people, Gentiles as well as Jews—in the post-Pentecost period through the church's Spirit-empowered witness."[114] And Köstenberger also comments that "Jesus' gentle yet evasive response means that the Gentiles may "see" him, but only subsequent to his cross-death. Once lifted up from the earth, he will draw all (kinds

---

112. The term *Hellēnes* (used here) means anyone not Jewish; that is, from a Jewish viewpoint, those who are Gentiles and not converts. Perhaps they are "God-fearers" (cf. Luke 7:5; Acts 10:2, 22; 13:16, 26). They will have come from the Gentile Decapolis, or Galilean cities such as Sepphoris, to take up the standing invitation to attend the great feasts from within the confines of the Court of the Gentiles. (For more details, see: Kossen, "Who Were the Greeks?") As Greeks, their approach to Jesus is facilitated by Philip and Andrew who have both Greek name and links with the mainly Gentile Bethsaida (cf. John 1:44-46; 6:5-7). The way in which the Greeks contact a disciple rather than Jesus directly may reflect uncertainty as to whether Jesus would, in fact, receive Gentiles (especially in a temple setting).

113. Köstenberger, *Theology of John's Gospel*, 506.

114. Ibid., 463; original emphasis.

Elsewhere in the Gospels: Purity, Temple, Parables

of) people to himself."[115] All this begins to happen "now" (12:31) even as the presence of Jesus with the Samaritan woman signals the "now" when worshipers can worship the Father in spirit and in truth (4:23).

John himself clearly sees these Gentiles as important. The mention of "some Greeks" may also "invoke the Isaianic notion of Gentiles flocking to God in the end times (Isa 42:4; 49:6 . . .)."[116] And in the Gospel narrative, the announcement of the long-awaited "hour" is introduced by the arrival of the Gentiles. The conjunction and placement of the arrival and the request of the Greeks is highly significant. "It is clear . . . that the Greeks' request marks the definitive turning point in Jesus' public activity in Israel and by implication in his interaction with the crowd. . . . All at once, with the coming of the Greeks, everything seems to take a redemptive-historical turn."[117] Immediately after the entry into Jerusalem that will lead to the cross and resurrection, these Gentiles want to "see" Jesus—a verb with typically double meaning in John. They want, of course, to meet Jesus but the verbs for seeing occur some eighty-four times in the Fourth Gospel and the phrase to "come and see" is virtually synonymous with an invitation to discipleship. Their arrival activates the time for his glorification of which John has frequently spoken: "The hour has come for the Son of man to be glorified" (12:23). By comparison with the times when Jesus announces that the hour has not yet arrived (for example, 2:4, 7:30, 8:20), "something has changed; the Greeks signal the closing of a chapter for Jesus. His ministry in Judaism is finished and he now belongs to the wider world."[118]

This wider world is brought to mind by the arrival of these enquiring Gentiles. In fact, the world now begins to come to him; the arrival shows that the preceding words of the Pharisees are true: "Look, the world has gone after him" (12:19). Gentile salvation is also signaled by the explanation that Jesus goes on to give as he elaborates the meaning of this "hour" in terms of his death: just as a grain of wheat must "die" in order to bring life, so must the Son of Man die. Moreover, something about the faith of these Gentiles is indicated as well. "These Greeks' 'de-

---

115. Ibid., 375.
116. Ibid., 377.
117. Ridderbos, *Gospel according to John*, 427.
118. Burge, *John*, 343.

sire' to see Jesus . . . is not explicitly granted in this text, but the results are clear in light of the whole of John's Gospel; those who 'want' to do God's will ultimately recognize the truth of Jesus' teachings (7:17), and no one who comes to Jesus will be cast out (6:37)."[119] There are missional implications too. "If we do not understand the radical mandate of Jesus or his willingness to take the social risk of being with Greeks *in the Jerusalem temple*, we do not comprehend Jesus' extreme love for the world."[120]

The Centurion at the Cross

In the Gospel of Mark, the first and only human to confess Jesus as God's Son after the crucifixion[121] is a Gentile centurion—an archetypal "outsider." For Mark, the Gospel of Jesus Christ, God's Son, is not and cannot be understood until Jesus is comprehended as the crucified Messiah who, through that humiliation, brings salvation to all humanity. It is, significantly, a Gentile who first bears witness to this.

There are, then, a number of passages that further link Gentiles with the ministry and comments of Jesus. None of these is reported with the detail and affirmation found in the accounts of the encounters with the centurion/official and the Syrophoenician mother. Nonetheless, there are a number of these minor characters, and even those among "the crowds," who approach Jesus, or comment on him, or are fed or healed by him, or are the subject of favorable comment by him, who are identified—implicitly or explicitly—as Gentiles. His reactions, and theirs, are generally positive in tone.

Some Conclusions from the Chapter

As with other chapters, a range of conclusions might be drawn, beginning with an assessment of the identity of Jesus himself. Some christological implications are clearly apparent in what we have considered.

119. Keener, *Gospel of John*, 2:872.
120. Burge, *John*, 359; original emphasis.
121. Mark 15:39: "Truly this man was the Son of God."

For Blakley, the stance taken by Jesus concerning purity issues is highly significant. Writing about Mark 7, Blakley comments on the authority of Jesus disclosed in it:

> The absoluteness of the purity parable speaks of an authority outstripping that of Moses and the Torah and thus comparable to that of Israel's God. Jesus' authoritative pronouncements on what does and does not defile is reminiscent of his earlier pronouncements as the authoritative Son of Man (2:10; 2:27–28), especially about the sabbath, (2:27–28).... In both, Jesus is questioned ostensibly about his disciples' eating practices but in reality about his prerogative in allowing such blatant disregard for Torah and the tradition of the elders.... Jesus' attitude toward the Torah is unattested and unprecedented in his day; it can only be explained on the basis of "his awareness of his own authority and his awareness of a new epoch in redemptive history."[122]

Our discussion of Jesus and the temple (especially his "temple action") also raises christological issues. To accept that Jesus' action amounts to the symbolic destruction of the temple is to make an assertion about his prophetic status. If we also accept the conclusion reached by Nicholas Perrin in his *Jesus the Temple*, with its persuasive argument that Jesus saw himself and his movement as those who both anticipate and embody Yahweh's coming rule, then "Jesus of Nazareth's most distinctive activities, healings/exorcisms, and meals were public signs that he had reconstituted time, space, and a people around himself, the new convergence of heaven and earth, the new temple."[123] In effect, there *is already* a new temple; it centers on Jesus who embodies all that the

---

122. Blakley, "Incomprehension or Resistance?," 246; quote from Stettler, "Purity of Heart." Blakley adds: "It is Jesus' understanding of the nature and purposes of the kingdom of God and of his own role in inaugurating that kingdom that gives him the freedom to approach God's law as he does. According to Mark, then, Jesus abolishes the OT food laws because they restrict the disciples' unrestricted obedience to God, by inhibiting them from fulfilling their divine calling to become fishers of people, a calling which includes casting their nets into Gentile waters. With the advent of the eschatological reign of God, fresh wineskins are needed (2:22)."

123. Perrin, *Jesus the Temple*, 179.

temple intended—including provision for Gentiles and other "outsiders" to come into fellowship with the living God. Such a claim is but one example within a wider set of assertions that might be summed up, as we noted in the words of Michael Wolter, as "Jesus' claim that the reality of salvation of the Rule of God was present as a *local phenomenon* wherever he was at work, and the expectation that its *universal* establishment was still to come."[124] Even the "small" beginnings in certain parables (about seed, soil, yeast) are metaphorical allusions to the inauguration, growth and certain arrival of the universal Rule of God that centers on Jesus himself. This arrival reinforces the original basic theme of the parables: what Michael Wolter describes as "the self-interpretation of Jesus as the revelation of God's eschatological plan of salvation for the whole human race."[125] Other parables seem to embrace the themes of the great reversal and the expansion of Israel seen elsewhere in the teaching of Jesus. This universal note certainly has implications for the way Christians might assess interreligious encounters today.

There are soteriological implications as well. In his essay "A Contagious Purity: Jesus' Inverse Strategy for Eschatological Cleanliness," Tom Holmén observes that the impurities of the unclean do not transfer to Jesus; instead, Jesus' purity transfers to the unclean. From now on, through him, this eschatological purity begins to triumph over impurity and even the ritually unclean can become part of God's growing kingdom.[126] Jesus' encounter with the demon-possessed man in Gadara (Mark 5:1–20//Matt 8:28–34//Luke 8:26–39) embodies a triple impurity: a large herd of pigs is nearly; the man he encounters is possessed by a "legion" of unclean spirits; the demoniac lives among the dead. However, as Christopher Wright points out, Jesus transforms such "Gentile pollution" and, unusually, tells the healed individual to spread the word—which he does with enthusiasm. The healed demoniac "is in fact the first Gentile missionary to Gentiles, commissioned by Christ

---

124. Wolter, "Jesus as Teller of Parables," in Charlesworth and Pokorný, *Jesus Research*, 137–38; original emphasis.

125. Ibid., 125.

126. Essay found in Charlesworth and Pokorný, *Jesus Research*, 199–219.

himself."¹²⁷ The transformation is initiated by one who possesses unusual authority.

An equally substantial christological claim is embedded in the woes pronounced on Israelite towns (Luke 10:13-15//Matt 11:21-23). What Ben Witherington calls "the note of eschatological judgment even on the people of God" and the appeal for repentance, are clearly linked by Jesus with his miracles; they are evidence of the inbreaking of the Rule of God—with even Gentiles able rightly to assess their eschatological significance. "Jesus, then, is the one who will bring the final decisive action of God upon God's people. How one responds will determine one's final status with God."¹²⁸

One distinctive feature of Jesus' ministry is his exorcisms. In Mark's Gospel, the phrase "unclean spirit" (*pneuma akatharton*) surfaces more frequently (eleven times) than in Matthew (twice) or Luke (six times). Wahlen's research leads to the conclusion that the Second Evangelist is particularly sensitive to matters of purity and therefore is very conscious of his use of terms pertinent to this theme. He concludes that Mark's use of "unclean spirit" is informed by underlying tradition. He further believes that Mark's account of Jesus exorcising unclean spirits from both Jew and Gentile shows that both groups can belong to the people of God.¹²⁹ Once again, the boundaries of Israel are widened to include the previously excluded.

An eschatological note is also sounded in a number of ways. For example, Dick France relates the apparent repeal of food laws to the "many from the east and the west" (Matt 8:11; Luke 13:29) who will come to eat at the messianic banquet while "reclining at the same table as the Hebrew patriarchs who, we are to assume, do not fear ritual defilement by eating with those who do not share Israel's purity." The Gentiles are accepted "on equal terms with the patriarchs"—a situation that is "shocking to a traditional Jewish theology".¹³⁰ The same presence of unexpected guests at the eschatological banquet is also sounded in several of the parables discussed. Following the Lukan versions of the

---

127. Wright, *Mission of God*, 508.
128. Witherington, *Christology of Jesus*, 166-67.
129. See ch. 3 of his *Jesus and the Impurity of Spirits*; quote from 106.
130. France, *Gospel of Matthew*, 319.

parables of the seed and the yeast (Luke 13:18–21), Jesus answers the question, "Lord, will only a few be saved?" with a warning that includes a reference to "weeping and gnashing of teeth when you see Abraham, Isaac and Jacob and all the prophets in the Kingdom of God, but you yourselves thrown out. People will come from east and west, from north and south, and will eat at the feast in the Kingdom of God" (vv. 23, 28–29). The reference to those who come from the four compass points to the eschatological banquet is a clear echo of Jesus' words to the Gentile centurion in Matt 8:11. Moreover, this Lukan passage concludes (or is immediately followed by) the assurance of the working of a "great reversal": "Indeed, there are those who are last who will be first, and first who will be last" (30). Once again, Jesus tells a narrative of judgment and reversal in which Gentiles are the implied beneficiaries.

Perhaps even more startling are the references to the Southern Queen and the Ninevites who will "rise up at the judgment" in condemnation of "this [unbelieving] generation" (Matt 12:41–42//Luke 11:31–32).[131] This seems to signal their salvation at the general resurrection; Michael Bird believes the language is evidence for the view that "Jesus anticipated the salvation of *some* Gentiles."[132] These eschatological themes are further evidence of the "great reversal" dynamic that seems to be central to Jesus' understanding of the Rule of God as inaugurated by his presence and ministry and as illustrated by Gentiles (and Samaritans) participating in it—surprising as this was to most Jewish opinion.

Some Implications for Interreligious Relations

There are also a number of consequences for contemporary interfaith relations from what we have seen in this chapter. One implication of Jesus rendering all foods clean is that his followers are no longer to make a distinction between clean and unclean foods. Thus there is no longer any symbolic rationale or praxis for classifying Gentiles as unclean and therefore beyond God's salvific intentions. The kingdom is accessible by Gentiles; they are, potentially, no longer "outsiders." On a practical

131. Translation as either "stand up" or "rise up" at the judgment is also possible.
132. Bird, *Jesus and the Origins*, 63; original emphasis.

level, if all foods are now clean, Jesus' disciples can, in good conscience, accept the hospitality of Gentiles to whom they are sent on apostolic mission, both then and now. (It is also possible that Jesus' missionary instruction in Luke 10:8, "Eat what is set before you," intends to address this same concern.) And there is an even more specific soteriological consequence to be drawn from the conclusion of Holmén—already noted—that the impurities of the unclean do not transfer to Jesus; instead, Jesus' purity transfers to them. This has implications of liberation for those religious traditions that accept (or are troubled by) the notion of an inexorable *karma* at work in the lives of people.

An exemplary Christology emerges, at least implicitly, from the passages discussed. Jesus also taught as much by his example and symbolic actions as by his verbal teaching. His "temple action" begins the transformation of the temple into a universally-accessible place for an encounter with the living God and is a further indication that Jesus sees the people of God in much broader terms than those determined by the contingencies of ethnicity and land. We have already indicated substantial agreement with the Gibson/Iverson/Blakley thesis that the disciples are reproached by Jesus in the central chapters of Mark's Gospel because they demonstrate resistance to his offering of salvation to those not officially recognized as belonging to Israel. As Blakley summarizes one key episode (Mark 8:14–21): "When it comes to crossing religious, social, and cultural barriers separating Israelite society from the rest of the world, the boundaries distinguishing Jews from Gentiles, the disciples draw the line and begin to manifest all manner of resistance."[133] The way in which Jesus displays at least some missional intent towards Gentiles (at least in these central chapters in Mark), and rebukes his disciples for their failure to share his mission, certainly implies that contemporary disciples ought to display a similar concern for—and certainly not resistance towards—those beyond their own communities. Since, for Jesus, "everything happens in parables" (Mark 4:11), far-reaching implications also flow from a consideration of parables in which Jesus seems

---

133. Blakley, "Incomprehension or Resistance?," 307. He goes on to quote Gibson to the effect that Markan disciples are more akin to Jesus' religious opponents for they too are opposed to Jesus' offering of salvation "to those not officially recognized as belonging to Israel."

directly to refer to participation by non-Jews in the Rule of God. We have discussed a cluster of parables that (even allowing for allegorical and metaphorical dimensions) implies that Gentiles are—or are at least included in—the "new" people over against a "failed" people. There is a universal dynamic within the purposes of God that reaches beyond the confines of Israel to the Gentiles (and Samaritans). To imitate the example of Jesus will include an attitude of expectation towards these contemporary "Greeks," "sinners," and outsiders, whose openness to Jesus parallels the openness displayed by Gentiles and Samaritans as they are attracted to one who offers both healing and a place within the universal and re-constituted people of God. A number of these implications for the interreligious encounter will be explored in more detail in chapter 6 below.

4

Samaritans and Jesus

IN THIS CHAPTER WE will consider four topics: the history, beliefs, and practices of the Samaritans; general material in the Gospels on the Samaritans; the encounter between Jesus and the Samaritan woman (John 4:4–42); and the parable of the compassionate Samaritan (Luke 10:25–37). Some general implications for interreligious relations and Christian mission are indicated in passing; more specific implications, especially for Christian-Muslim relations, will be discussed in the next chapter.

The History, Beliefs, and Practices of the Samaritans

Before a discussion of Jesus and the Samaritans he met or spoke about, it is necessary to consider some background issues.

Terminology

The word "Samaritan" certainly requires attention. It varies in meaning according to whether it is defined *geographically*, in terms of physical descent and ethnic makeup, or in terms of *religion*.[1] "Samaritans"

---

1. Meier, "Historical Jesus," 204–5. The confusion and lack of precision over the term "Samaritan" is because of a complex overlap between the geographical, ethnographic and subsequent religious dimensions of the word with the anti-Samaritan religious and political polemic of Second Temple Judaism related to this semantic

are mentioned only in 2 Kgs 17:29 in English language versions of the Jewish Scriptures, a passage which describes the syncretistic religion of those peoples whom the king of Assyria transported to the northern kingdom of Israel to replace the exiled native population after the fall of Samaria (722/721 BCE). However, several reasons argue strongly against the identification, favored by Josephus and many others since, of this group with the Samaritans as they are more widely known from the NT,[2] some of whose descendants survive to the present day.[3] In fact, most scholars writing about Samaritan history agree that there are no references to them in the text of the OT.[4] It is also important to distinguish "Samaritan" from "Samarian."[5] The term "Samarian" is used of the inhabitants of the region of Samaria.[6] "Samaritan" is limited to the group of interest to this study, and is typically defined in religious terms.[7] The Samaritans were "Samarians" too since they lived in the re-

---

range. At least some of the political polemic was directed at the Roman and Hellenistic sympathies (both real and alleged) of the Samaritans. For a historical survey and summary, see Haacker, "Samaritan, Samaria," 449–53.

2. Matt 10:5; Luke 9:52; 10:33; 17:16; John 4:9, 39–40; 8:48; Acts 8:25.

3. Williamson summarizes the reasons as follows: (a) the Hebrew word used seems merely to mean "inhabitants of (the city or province of) Samaria," and this fits the context of 2 Kings 17 best; (b) there is no evidence that the later Samaritans inhabited Samaria. The earliest certain references to them, by contrast, all point clearly to their residence at Shechem (Ecclus 50:26; 2 Macc 5:22–23.; 6:2; cf. John 4:5–6, 20), while one of Josephus' sources refers to them as "Shechemites" (cf. *Ant.* 11.340–347; 12. 10); (c) nothing whatever that is known of later Samaritan religion and practice suggests the pagan influence of 2 Kings 17 or Ezra 4 (Williamson, "Samaritans," in Marshall, *New Bible Dictionary*, 1052).

4. Meier, "Historical Jesus," 209–10.

5. Meier cautions that "[p]erhaps the greatest lesson to be drawn from all these frustrating attempts to sketch the origins of Samaritanism is that one must carefully and consistently distinguish 'Samarians', the inhabitants and rulers of the city and territory known as Samaria, from 'Samaritans', the adherents of an Israelite religious group centered around Mt. Gerizim/Shechem (ibid., 212).

6. This includes the capital city that once bore the same name, but was renamed Sebaste (the Greek equivalent of Augustus) in the first century BCE in honor of Augustus Caesar.

7. Di Segni points out some problems with this terminology, not least that that there is no terminological distinction between Samaritan and Samarian in ancient sources ("Early Christian Authors," 245). Nonetheless, it seems sensible to maintain

gion of Samaria.[8] For their part, the Samaritans derive their name from the Hebrew word *shōmerīm* meaning "those who keep/obey," referring to their self-identification as "keepers of the covenant."[9]

History[10]

There is what Meier calls an "obscure and tangled history."[11] The traditional Jewish understanding of Samaritan history was heavily influenced by 2 Kings 17, a passage Josephus uses to identify the Samaritans of his day with the descendants of the pagans that the Assyrians settled in the northern kingdom.[12] The Samaritans did, of course, have their own account of their origins, which Meier rejects as "glorious anachronism."[13] It seems that the Samaritans were descended, in some way, from a number of the northern tribes of Israel (most likely Ephraim and Manasseh) and developed as a form of the ancient religion, derived from but eventually parallel to "mainstream" Judaism.[14] By the time of the second temple (and certainly from the second century BCE) their existence as a distinctive group is much clearer. Contemporary scholarship rejects the traditional view that the Samaritans originated in a single schism

---

the distinction (as most scholars do).

8. That is, the region to the west of the Jordon River, located south of Galilee and north of Judea. There does not appear to be any particular association between the Samaritans and the city of Samaria. Rather, the Samaritans are associated with the city of Shechem and the adjacent Mt. Gerizim.

9. Meier, "Historical Jesus," 207 n. 10.

10. For good overviews of the history and associated problems see, for example, Meier, "Historical Jesus"; Williamson and Evans, "Samaritans." For a considerably more detailed discussion, see Anderson and Giles, *Keepers*.

11. Meier, "Historical Jesus," 216.

12. Josephus' highly pejorative use of this passage appears to constitute what Meier calls "anti-Samaritan propaganda" (Meier, "Historical Jesus," 208).

13. They maintain that at the time of Eli a schism occurred because he moved from Mt. Gerizim to Shiloh, gathering around himself apostates from the true Israelites. Pummer, "Samaritanism," in Collins and Harlow, *Eerdmans Dictionary*, 1186. For a brief summary of the Samaritan view of their own origins and Jewish views of Samaritan origins see Williamson and Evans, "Samaritans," 1057–59.

14. Pummer considers that, in fact, the OT regards the inhabitants of Samaria as genuine Israelites, not semi-pagans (Pummer, "Samaritanism," 1187).

from Israel, or even in a series of schisms, in favor of a progressive period of growing division, with occasional periods of greater animosity.[15] Perhaps, then, a better way of describing the situation at the time of the Gospels is to understand that both Samaritanism and Judaism are forms of the ancient religion of Israel, a Palestinian religion that worships Yahweh as the unique God of Israel according to the prescriptions found in the five books of Moses.[16] This core religion of Israel had experienced various traumas, transformations, and developments under the assaults and influences of the Assyrian, Babylonian, Persian, and Hellenistic empires. John Meier summarizes the outcome:

> During the last centuries before the turn of the era—though at different times and in different ways—Samaritanism and Judaism emerged from the crucible of all this historical turmoil as two major expressions of the ancient religion of Israel. Neither religion was immediately derived from the other and neither broke away from the other. There was no one, definitive moment of schism. Indeed, in a real sense, there was no schism at all. This helps explain the strange symbiosis of these two . . . forms of ancient Israelite religion, at times in fierce opposition to each other, at times in uneasy rapprochement.[17]

Samaritan Religion

Again, there are problems of definition. It seems evident, from extrabiblical sources from the second century BCE onwards, that the Samaritans had come—by the end of the Second Temple Era—to be viewed as a group distinct from Jews. They are referred to as *allogenēs*,

---

15. This shift in scholarly perspective can be traced to Richard Coggins' volume *Samaritans and Jews* (published 1979).

16. Over the centuries, this religion had developed distinctive practices such as circumcision of infants, the prohibition of eating pork, the observance of the Sabbath, an emphasis on the need for one central sanctuary, and annual celebrations of special feasts of pilgrimage to this central sanctuary (e.g., Passover, Pentecost, Tabernacles).

17. Meier, "Historical Jesus," 216–17.

"foreigners," in Luke 17:18.[18] However, problems of understanding and definition persist and difficulties remain in attempts to draw up political and *religious* profiles and much of what is concluded is supplied by Samaritan literature from later in the Common Era. We may assume that Samaritans would have fallen within the category of non-Israelite in the first century CE, even though they were circumcised in accordance with the Law of Moses. Williamson identifies a number of problems facing any attempted reconstruction of Samaritan religion during the NT period, noting that all Samaritan sources (apart from the Samaritan Pentateuch) are dated considerably later than the NT and are only known from more recent manuscripts. Moreover, the Samaritan community continued to develop internally while remaining subject to external influences—thus complicating the reliability of these sources.[19]

It is also increasingly evident that there was no monolithic Samaritanism. The evidence suggests Samaritanism took several forms.[20] Meier concludes that "we might almost count it a blessing that so few passages in the NT mention the Samaritans in relation to Jesus, since our ignorance of first-century Samaritanism would leave us ill-equipped to exegete a large body of Gospel material on the subject."[21] Nonetheless, while acknowledging some difficulties in the gathering of information, it appears that the following combination of elements make up the essential core of Samaritan religion belief and practice towards the end of the Second Temple Era:[22]

18. Esler, "Jesus and the Reduction," 336.

19. Williamson and Evans, "Samaritans," 1056. "Scholars thus disagree, often quite widely, over the extent to which these sources can help in reconstructing early Samaritan history and belief."

20. There was a group called the "Dositheans"; and Isser has made a case for the existence of a synagogue-based lay movement that existed alongside the priestly Samaritanism centered on Shechem. See Williamson and Evans, "Samaritans," 1059; Williamson goes on to conclude that "[s]uch distinctions need to be borne in mind when evaluating references to contacts between the Samaritans and Jesus or the first Christians as well as between Jews and Samaritans, for the degrees of affinity between different groups across the divide may have varied far more than our severely fragmented knowledge allows us to recognize."

21. Meier, "Historical Jesus," 205–6.

22. The list that follows is mainly derived from: Anderson and Giles, *Keepers*; Pummer, "Samaritanism"; Meier, "Historical Jesus," 205–6; Williamson and Evans,

Samaritans are those Semites who (1) believe in and worship the one God, Yahweh, and who (2) revere Mt. Gerizim (near ancient Shechem in Samaria) instead of Mt. Zion in Jerusalem as the one divinely validated place to build an altar for sacrifice, or a temple, for the public worship of Yahweh. (3) They maintain that their line of Levitical priests functioning on Mt. Gerizim are the legitimate priests of the Mosaic dispensation, as opposed to the priests functioning in the Jerusalem temple. (4) They accept only the five books of Moses (in the form of the "Samaritan Pentateuch," exegeted in a somewhat distinctive manner) as authoritative Scripture, to the exclusion of the Prophets and the Writings as also accepted in mainstream Judaism.[23] This truncated canon led to (5) the Samaritan rejection of the significance of David and Jerusalem and, with the other features, led to Samaritan self-awareness as a distinctive religious group to be differentiated from Jerusalem-centered Israelite religion. (6) Even after the destruction of their temple, the Samaritans continue to offer a yearly animal sacrifice during Passover (along the lines of Exodus 12) and they generally celebrate the feasts commanded in the Pentateuch. (7) The role of the patriarch Jacob, known to the Samaritans from both biblical and non-biblical traditions, is also important. As well, there is some evidence that (8) a cluster of eschatological beliefs may have already been accepted (at least in embryonic form): a certain day of judgment and recompense, the return of Moses as *Taheb* (a non-Davidic messianic figure),[24] and the denial of resurrection.

"Samaritans." For an earlier discussion, see MacDonald, *Theology of the Samaritans*.

23. Although it is traditionally held that there are six thousand differences, the Samaritan Pentateuch is essentially the same as that of the Masoretic Text. However, there are some notable differences, many relating to Mt. Gerizim. For a discussion of the Samaritan Pentateuch, see Pummer, "Samaritan Pentateuch," in Collins and Harlow, *Eerdmans Dictionary*, 1189–90.

24. The "restorer" or "returning one"—the "prophet like Moses." From the text-type of the Pentateuch, which they elected to adopt for themselves, it is probable that already the passage in Deut 18:18–22 about a future "prophet like Moses" had been

From this summary, the differences with mainstream Judaisms are apparent. The divinely approved place for the temple (or defining altar) is one immediate example. In the fourth or fifth century BCE the Samaritans built their own shrine on Mt. Gerizim as a rival to the temple in Jerusalem. According to many Samaritan sources the temple was a stone podium with a movable tent.[25] The tenth commandment in the Samaritan Pentateuch identifies Gerizim as the place where an altar should be built (presumably based on the instruction in Deuteronomy 27 to build an altar on Gerizim).[26] Samaritans also claimed the mountain as the place where Jacob[27] received his vision of ascending and descending angels. Having received his vision, Jacob states, "This is none other than the house of God and the gate of heaven" (Gen 28:16-18).[28] At some stage a Samaritan temple (or sacrificial altar) is said to have been built in the north, although it is uncertain when,[29] or even where, given that there is still no undisputed archaeological evidence for it.

---

joined to the Exodus version of the Sinai account (following Exod 20:21; Williamson and Evans, "Samaritans," 1059).

25. See Hjelm, "What Do Samaritans?," 16. Hjelm offers considerable documentation and discussion of recent archaeological work (see 19–20 and her conclusions on 29–30); she indicates the retrieval of some 450 dedicatory inscriptions and burned bones of year-old animals that indicate the existence of a Yahwistic holy center on Mt. Gerizim for a period of more than 400 years, until its destruction around 111 BCE. A summary by Yitzhak Magen of his 25 years of excavation on Mt. Gerizim indicates the presence of a sacred compound that, along with various artifacts, points to a Samaritan temple built about the time of Nehemiah (mid-fifth century BCE); see Magen, "Bells, Pendants."

26. For a discussion that includes an appraisal of archaeological findings, see Knoppers, "Mt. Gerizim and Mt. Zion." For a more general comment on Samaritan opposition to the Jerusalem temple, see Wright, *Jesus and the Victory*, 185.

27. Affirmed by the Samaritan woman in John 4:12 as "our father Jacob."

28. See further in MacDonald, *Theology of the Samaritans*, 327–33; Josephus, *Ant.* 18:85-87.

29. In *Ant.* 13:256 Josephus dates it to between 335 and 330 BCE, while 388 BCE is another possibility.

The Reasons for Bitterness between Jews and Samaritans[30]

One key issue is the era of Hasmonean expansion in the second century BCE. When John Hyrcanus captured Shechem and destroyed the sanctuary on Mt. Gerizim in 112-111 BCE this caused not only resentment but a period of self-definition in which the Samaritan Pentateuch is launched into its own history separate from the mainstream Jerusalem version.[31] Judean dislike of the Samaritans from around the mid second century BCE is found in Ben Sira [Ecclesiasticus] 50:25-26 which denies them status as a people since the author says he hates a nation (*ethnos*) that is "not a nation at all," namely, "the foolish people that live in Shechem."[32] Later events illustrate the extent of the tension. Josephus records that in 8 CE some Samaritans scattered bones in the Jerusalem temple during Passover[33] and that later, in 52 CE, Samaritans killed one or several Galilean pilgrims on the Samaria-Galilee border—an action that provoked not only violent Jewish retaliation but bloody Roman intervention as well. And there is evidence of rabbinic teaching that Samaritan women bear the humiliation of being stereotyped as perpetually unclean.[34] (This is equivalent to the sentiment that is well

---

30. See further on Jewish-Samaritan relations in Wright, *Jesus and the Victory*, 127 n. 7 (and the literature cited there). It should be noted that the considerable variety within Samaritanism (as well as the variety within Judaism) means there is no single, unvarying attitude of Jews towards Samaritans and vice versa. There appear to have been changes over time, as well as different attitudes from person to person.

31. Pummer considers this the "decisive event" which alienated the Samaritans ("Samaritanism," 1188). Williamson concludes that although from this time "one should certainly continue to regard Samaritanism as a form of Judaism . . . it became crystallized as by far the most distinct by virtue of its wholesale rejection of the Jerusalem-centered *Heilsgeschichte*, something which cannot be said of any other variety of Judaism in antiquity" (Williamson and Evans, "Samaritans," 1059).

32. In the LXX the latter portion is translated: "those living on the mountain of Samaria" (Ecclus 50:25-26). See also the discussion in Meier, *Marginal Jew*, 535-40.

33. Esler comments: "This attempt to disrupt the temple cult by scattering objects of gross impurity around the temple, obviously a dangerous activity for the Samaritan perpetrators, looks like pure mischief of the type we would expect to find in a context of extreme group antipathy" (Esler, "Jesus and the Reduction," 331).

34. The sentiment was later codified in the Mishnah (*Niddah* 4:1) as "the daughters of the Samaritans are menstruants from their cradle" and impure, therefore, according to Lev. 15:19 and consequently a permanent source of impurity for their

captured in a later Rabbinic text (*m. Šeb* 8:10): "He that eats the bread of the Samaritans is like one that eats the flesh of swine.")

Secondary Material in the Gospels on the Samaritans

Before a discussion of the two major passages in the Gospels related to Samaritans (the encounter with the Samaritan woman and the parable of the compassionate Samaritan), mention must be made of some other passages. While the Gospel of Mark has no references to Samaritans or Samaria, and Matthew only mentions the prohibition against entering any Samaritan town (10:5), John and Luke have several references. In John 8:48, when Jesus is asked, "Are we not right in saying that you are a Samaritan and possessed by a demon?," this is an example of the highly negative Jewish attitudes to Samaritans discussed above.[35]

The Gospel of Luke mentions Samaritans more often than the other three Gospels combined. Luke's references to them are found in the central section of his Gospel (9:51—19:40), which is generally agreed to be his presentation of the unfolding of the divine plan for Jesus' transition from Galilee to Jerusalem. The fact that such an unfolding begins with a narrative in which Jesus and the disciples encounter Samaritans may well heighten the significance to be attached to it. It follows the enigmatic saying that "whoever is not against you is for you" and consists (in Luke) of Jesus' rebuke of the disciples who want to call down punishment on an inhospitable Samaritan village (Luke 9:50 and 9:51–56). Having set his face toward Jerusalem, Jesus sends messengers ahead of him who go into a Samaritan village to make preparations to stay but the villagers will not receive these travelers to Jerusalem. As a result, Jesus' own disciples call for vengeance. Philip Esler comments: "Given the aversion Judeans and Samaritans had for one another, and the enthusiasm of his disciples for their role, nothing could be less surprising than their response to this rejection: . . . 'Lord, do you want us to call down fire from heaven to burn them up?' And nothing could

---

community. See Daube, "Jesus and the Samaritan Woman," and the more recent discussion in Okure, *Johannine Approach*, 96.

35. Discussion will return to this question; the encounter between Jesus and the Samaritan woman is considered in the next section of this chapter.

Jesus and the Religions

be more surprising than Jesus' brief and forceful reaction: 'He turned and rebuked them.'"[36] This indication of his impatience with what Esler goes on to call "extreme forms of group differentiation" and his refusal to contemplate a vengeful response, are significant for what will unfold in the following chapter of Luke (the parable of the compassionate Samaritan). The reason for the rejection by the Samaritans is that Jesus' "face was set towards Jerusalem" (Luke 9:53). Because of the bitter antagonism between Jews and Samaritans, a Jewish reader would (according to David Bosch) "fully understand the attitude of James and John, not however the reaction of Jesus." Bosch is sure that the context in Luke makes clear that "Jesus' conduct reflects an explicit and active denial of the law of retaliation . . . and is, precisely as such, also a pointer toward a mission beyond Israel."[37] And the attitudes displayed by Jesus also have significant implications for contemporary interreligious relations with the continuing temptation to assert such "extreme forms of group differentiation" even to the point of vengeance.

Luke also recounts an incident in which ten leprosy sufferers are healed by Jesus but only one (a Samaritan) returns to give thanks to him (17:11–19). There appears to be no question in Jesus' mind about a prior religious or racial test for those who approach him for healing, but Jesus does point out that it is "foreigner"—a Samaritan—who is the only leper among the ten who is "found to return and give praise to God" (18). Jesus' words "your faith has cured/saved [*sesōken*] you" (19) "are another clear pointer to the fact that salvation has also come to this despised people."[38] Luke's attention to Samaritans seems significant for the overall design of his two volumes; in fact, the Samaritan mission may even be the beginning of the Gentile mission and part of the divine plan.[39] As Luke's Gospel unfolds, "God's chosen ones will include the poor, the blind, the lame, the Samaritan, the Gentile, the tax collector, the sinner, and the outcast."[40]

36. Esler, "Jesus and the Reduction," 332.
37. Bosch, *Transforming Mission*, 90.
38. Ibid., 91.
39. In Luke's second volume we find Philip leading a mission to Samaria only some years after the resurrection (Acts 8:4–25).
40. Prior, *Jesus the Liberator*, 148.

Jesus and the Samaritan Woman (John 4:4-42)

Introduction

By far the largest narrative in the NT concerning Samaritans is this well-known story. It warrants attention for many reasons, especially the way in which it embodies a number of distinctive features that enhance its relevance for today's religiously plural world. As with the Gospel encounters discussed in the last chapter, most of the issues typically debated in commentaries and specialist studies are not raised here.[41] Nonetheless, it is worth noting that, whoever the first implied readers might be, the assumption of the Fourth Gospel seems to be that they "could nevertheless find in Jesus' ministry to the Samaritan woman appropriate models for their own ministry to outsiders of various kinds."[42] Our discussion is intentionally restricted to certain issues and, on the whole, it attempts a theological reading of the passage; there is not space for other often-fruitful approaches.

Questions are sometimes raised about the historicity of the narrative. The distinctly Johannine theology, vocabulary, and literary devices of John 4:4-42 make a number of exegetes wary of claiming much beyond what Raymond Brown summarizes as "echoes of a historical tradition of an incident in Jesus' ministry" or a "substratum of traditional material" at the core of the narrative. [43] There are some features that incline Brown himself to acknowledge the story's "intrinsic claim to plausibility" such that "[e]ither we are dealing with a master of fiction, or else the stories have a basis in fact."[44] The undoubted symbolic functions of the story do not, in themselves, mean that it is devoid of historical foundations.[45] More generally, scholarly skepticism regarding

---

41. Debates about issues such as the solitary nature of the woman's trip to the well, her moral status, the literary structure of the dialogue between her and Jesus, Johannine literary style, questions about the supposed prehistory of the passage and the original Johannine audience(s), and speculation about the ecclesial standing of the intended readership, are extensively discussed in the scholarly literature and are not repeated here.

42. Keener, "Some New Testament Invitations," 196.

43. Brown, *Gospel according to John (I-XI)*, 175.

44. Ibid., 175-76.

45. For example, Hellerman's assertions about Jesus and temple space employ

historicity in the Fourth Gospel is receding somewhat.[46] Paul Anderson is one of a number of scholars who questions an equation that suggests that because John is clearly theological, it cannot be historical.[47] Discussion of the passage's historical foundations might benefit from this reconsideration.

The material retrieval of Herodian Galilee and the surrounding regions stand in a curious relationship with the Fourth Gospel where, on the face of it, archaeology seems to corroborate both specific details and the general picture of Jewish life as portrayed by John.[48] Moreover, the passage in John 4 displays considerable familiarity with Samaritan beliefs and practices. Of the eight items that characterize such Samaritanism

---

certain social-scientific insights about the symbolism of sacred space and enable him to blend statements from the encounter with the Samaritan woman with statements in the Synoptic Gospels (see Hellerman, *Jesus and the People of God*, ch. 6, "Jesus and Sacred Space").

46. In the first summary publication of the John, Jesus, and History Project of the Society of Biblical Literature (see the essays gathered in Anderson, *John, Jesus, and History*), Paul Anderson and others demonstrate how, over the past two centuries, two dynamics have been at work: the "dehistoricization" of John and the "de-Johannification" of Jesus. Most of the contributors claim that a new consensus may be emerging that is critical of those dynamics; they usually suggest that the Gospel of John is an autonomous tradition with its own sources and its own distinctive approach to history, memory and witness that merits acceptance in its own right—and not merely as the impoverished or tendentious relative of the Synoptics. Moreover, the historical status of the Fourth Gospel has also been enhanced by the discussion of John in Richard Bauckham's *Jesus and the Gospels: The Gospels as Eyewitness Testimony*. Bauckham links the process of testimony and remembering with the Gospels, including the Fourth Gospel; memory, he writes, "is also remembered and understanding grows. In what is no doubt the most reflective Gospel testimony we have, that of John, the immediacy of memory is by no means lost. Rather, the ongoing process of remembering interpretation ponders and works to yield its fullest meaning. Reflective witness is reflective *remembering* . . ." (Bauckham, *Jesus and the Eyewitnesses*, 508; original emphasis). See also Bauckham's article, "Historiographical Characteristics."

47. See the discussion in Anderson, *John, Jesus, and History*, especially Parts 1 and 2. Cf. the comment of Stephen Fowl, who, drawing on the work of Luke Timothy Johnson, which questions the priority of history over theology, argues that "it is no longer self-evident that 'history' should be treated as an autonomous realm with a privileged place when it comes to ordering and accounting for reality" (Barton, *Cambridge Companion*, ch. 5, "The Gospels and 'the Historical Jesus,'" 92).

48. See the various contributions in Charlesworth, *Jesus and Archaeology*.

(see section above) six or seven appear to be affirmed, at least in part, in the story; and nothing in the story is at odds with what is known about the Samaritans. In fact, the passage's depiction of repercussions for ritual purity, and its familiarity with Samaritan cultural and religious beliefs, and ancient non-biblical Jacob traditions, prompt John Meier to call it the NT's "most explicit and well-informed passage about the Samaritans."[49] (Although there are no explicit parallels to this encounter elsewhere in the NT, it might be noted that one emphasis within the story is the way in which Jesus emphasizes the priority of Israel—an emphasis that is, in fact, widely found throughout the Jesus tradition.[50])

Quite apart from the intrinsic appeal of the account, it is the canonical status of the passage that has ensured its continuing place in the life of the church. Instead of repeating the usual range of exegetical conclusions, attention will be given in what follows to the issues of religious hope and fulfillment, and religious tension and difference, that are features of the story. Given our concern with the possible significance of Gentiles and Samaritans it is important to note that this story "arguably contains the longest and most elaborate narrative in the entire New Testament on the outsider theme."[51] As we shall see, the Samaritan woman is an outsider who comes to grasp what insiders are unable to comprehend.

The Setting Carefully Outlined (4-6)[52]

Rejected in Judea, Jesus leaves for Galilee via Samaria, in obedience to the divine imperative of his mission. From the opening words of the story there is a theological reading of the story as a whole: it becomes "necessary" (*edei*) for him to pass through Samaria—a route avoided by

---

49. Meier, *Marginal Jew*, 548, though he also concludes that very little can be said about Jesus' own interactions with or views about a group such as the Samaritans (549).

50. It is found in Q (Luke 22:30//Matt 19:28), in Mark (7:27), in Matthew (10:5-6; 15:24), in Luke (Acts 3:25-26), in Paul (Rom 15:8), and here in John (4:20-22).

51. Spina, *Faith of the Outsider*, 142.

52. Numbers in parentheses in headings and in the text are references to verses in John 4:4-42.

most Jews.[53] As well as this suggestion of divine necessity, the story is carefully placed in its geographical setting; a theological reading does not ignore the material context of the story. The cultural contours of the story are also made clear. These opening verses carefully delineate the religio-cultural context: Jacob's well (a reminder of Samaritan descent from the patriarchs), Joseph's tomb (in the very field that his father Jacob had given him in Genesis 33), and Sychar/Shechem (former capital of the independent northern kingdom of Israel). And, within the narrative, attention will soon shift to Mt. Gerizim, the holy place of the Samaritans. The Evangelist does not want his readers to forget the longstanding significance of the actual place where Jesus and the woman have their conversation; its importance becomes a vital factor in the dialogue.

From Antagonism to Gift (7–15)

Tired by his journey, Jesus stops to rest by Jacob's well and begins a dialogue with a Samaritan woman who has come to draw water. She is astonished that he, as a Jew, would talk to her and be willing to drink from her vessels. The section begins, then, with a reminder of the painful divisions between Samaria and Jerusalem; that reality is quickly recalled by the woman as the opening of the dialogue evokes this longstanding tension. There was considerable diversity within Second Temple Judaism but "the Samaritan community would have been considered by a majority of these same Jews to be completely beyond its religious boundaries." The Samaritans are "outsiders par excellence,"[54] and yet the opening verses of the story repeatedly draw attention to the Samaritan setting and the Samaritan ethnicity of the unnamed woman. Her Samaritan origins are repeatedly affirmed in order, it seems, "to underscore the pronounced insider-outsider flavor of this exchange, leaving no doubt whatsoever about what is transpiring before our eyes."[55] According to Philip Esler, it "seems likely that the Samaritan woman in

---

53. Discussion will return in chapter 6 below to some implications of this apparent divine imperative.

54. Spina, *Faith of the Outsider*, 145.

55. Ibid., 147.

John 4 recognised that Jesus was a Judean by his clothing rather than simply deducing this from his (presumably Galilean) accent when he said 'Give me something to drink' (John 4:7–9)."[56]

Despite the undoubted barriers between them, Jesus reaches out to make personal contact with the woman. (In the Greek text, his simple request for water contains no suggestion of impoliteness.) As the dialogue develops she gradually becomes less defensive. They discuss the merits of the well, they talk about her personal life, and they discuss the continuing dispute between Samaritans and Jews concerning the divinely approved place to worship God. But Jesus then moves the discussion from her material needs to an invitation to receive God's gift. Rather than debating the issue of mutual ethnic antagonism between his people and the woman's, Jesus (as Teresa Okure puts it), "transfers the discussion from this socio-religious context of reciprocal contempt and separatism (v. 9) to the sphere of God's relationship and dealings with human beings, where the governing principle is his generous bounty or 'free gift.'"[57] Issues of gender, ethnicity, and religious distinctions fade away as the dialogue take a surprising direction. Frank Spina points out that the conversants are quickly and deeply into "a conversation that should never have started, according to the woman's own assessment of proper social conduct based on the proscriptions of gender and religious differences." The woman takes Jesus literally when he is speaking figuratively. Despite her previous surprise, she finds that "his offer of living water . . . that leads to life eternal has a shock value of a different kind."[58]

In Spirit and Truth (16–42)

Jesus explains that the Father actively seeks worshippers to worship him "in Spirit and truth" (23–24). When the woman says that she, with her

---

56. Esler, "Jesus and the Reduction," 338 n. 19; "it seems probable that Judean and non-Judean inhabitants of Palestine could be distinguished by their clothing" (337). For further discussion of Judean and non-Judean clothing of the period, see Knowles, "What Was the Victim Wearing?"

57. Okure, *Johannine Approach*, 96.

58. Spina, *Faith of the Outsider*, 149.

Jesus and the Religions

people, is waiting for the Messiah, Jesus makes an explicit revelation of who he is with the statement, "I am, the one speaking to you" (26). The disciples return and are puzzled that Jesus is speaking with such a woman. She abandons her water jar, goes to the town, and invites her people to come and encounter Jesus and to discover for themselves someone who may be the Messiah. While she is away, Jesus prepares his disciples to enter into the harvest of his work in Samaria. Many Samaritans believe and Jesus stays for several days, until many more have also believed. The Samaritans come to confess Jesus not simply as the expected Messiah, but as the "Savior of the world" (42).

Some Implications of the Encounter

The encounter embodies a number of distinctive features as Jesus intentionally breaks the boundaries of religious and cultural division as he points to a new transcendent unity in the Spirit. An analysis of the passage can usefully employ some of the categories used in earlier chapters. For example, in the Introduction above there was discussion of the claim that "Scriptural reading in each context finds fresh meaning in the text, demonstrating God's faithfulness to speak to generation after generation in its own time and place."[59] Two examples that might illustrate the claim for "fresh meaning" are found in our story: supposedly intractable divisions that are subject to a reversal, and the eschatological overcoming of alienation in worship.

There are substantial and longstanding divisions on display in this story—divisions that are to be subject to a great reversal as barriers are broken down. The divisions are embodied in what Okure calls "the rejection, prejudice, and isolation of the two main characters."[60] One way of understanding this claim is to point to four features of the woman's identity.[61]

---

59. Allen, "Divine Transcendence," 51.
60. Okure, "Jesus and the Samaritan Woman," 401.
61. The remainder of this section about the transcending of barriers draws in part on the analysis by Neyrey in his "What's Wrong with This Picture?"

1. *She is a Samaritan.* She is a foreigner "with whom Jews do not share" (4:9). She represents a mistrusted and even despised group—and yet she becomes an "insider" and Jesus stays with her and her people for several days (4:40). Moreover, the narrative reaches a climax in 4:42 when these despised Samaritans acknowledge Jesus as the "savior of the world." Then follows an episode in which Jesus bestows a gift on the official's son" (4:47–54), almost certainly a Gentile. John's Gospel goes on formally to indicate that Jesus is available to Jews, Greeks, and Romans (12:20, 32; 19:20). These particular emphases within the Fourth Gospel, although few in number, nonetheless resemble the traditions already considered in the Synoptic Gospels about the impartiality of God's blessing to all peoples and their potential inclusion in the covenant community: for example, the centurion, the Syrophoenician woman and the commission to make disciples of all nations (Matt 28:19).

2. *She is unclean, polluted.* Jesus expresses willingness to drink from the same jug as the woman, thus risking ritual uncleanness. Jesus regularly supplants the purity rules of his world by working on the Sabbath (John 5:17; 7:23; 9:16) or by using the jars containing waters for purifying hands for wine (2:6). Thus Jesus is portrayed as disregarding the purity system of his Jewish culture—as we have already seen. Sharing with the unclean was a flagrant violation of the purity code yet he is willing to drink from the Samaritan's jug.

3. *She is a sinner, an adulterer.* Parallel to Jesus' breaking of purity regulations is his studied unconcern for the "sinful" status of the woman, who appears to be either a concubine or an adulteress (the sixth man with whom she is living is *not* her husband). How culturally anomalous, then, the triple mention of the Samaritan woman's sexual past in the presence of non-kin males (John 4:16–18, 29, 39).

4. *She is female who is not his kin.* This is a world that is divided according to cultural perceptions of gender into "male" and "female" space. The implications of ascribing to females "private space" contribute to a stereotype of ideal female behavior (females are expected to dwell in private space, primarily their homes and secondarily places where fe-

male tasks are performed). This is also a culture with rigid expectations related to honor and shame, especial in female dealings with males. The gender division of space and labor requires the inevitable separation of males and females who are not kin. Strategies to separate the genders are intended to keep women not only out of the gaze of men, but out of their speech as well. And yet here is Jesus, in "public space," drawing the woman into forbidden conversation. If it is shameful for a male to talk to and about a female not of his kinship circle, it goes without saying that females should not speak to unrelated males, especially in public space. The cultural expectation of female silence in public alerts contemporary readers to the potential impropriety of the conversation between the Samaritan woman and Jesus.

All of this is in addition to gender expectations from Jesus' own Jewish culture; strictly observant Jewish males avoid food or drink vessels of any woman who might be unclean and, as already noted, some Jews appear to have regarded all Samaritan women as impure since birth. The gender issue is also raised by the woman and later in the story it is clear that the disciples of Jesus are disturbed ("astonished") that he is speaking with a woman (27). It certainly heightens the outsider issue. As Frank Spina puts it: "This is an insider-outsider interaction of a most jarring kind. Jesus is either unaware of this or doesn't care; the woman is acutely aware of it and immediately addresses the matter."[62] Her very first words discuss the encounter in terms of gender and ethnic difference; she knows that in Jewish eyes even her water vessel was considered impure and unfit for Jewish use.

What's wrong with *this picture? Almost everything!* Appreciation of the cultural expectations for females in a gender divided world helps contemporary readers to grasp the intended shock in John 4 of a noonday meeting between Jesus and the woman in public space. The details of this narrative are at odds with the expected behavior of shame-guarding females. And, as John 4:9 and 27 indicate, even the characters in the narrative are aware of these breaches of gender rules. So the readers

---

62. Spina, *Faith of the Outsider*, 147. Spina nicely juxtaposes this conversation that—culturally speaking—should not even have begun with how it should have developed in terms of accepted cultural norms; he does this to suggest both the audacity of Jesus and the openness of the woman (146–50).

and hearers are carefully reminded of the impropriety of the conversation. It is also clear from the narrative that Jesus knows and appreciates the significance of these four supposed barriers between him and the woman. In this narrative, then, John has concentrated in the person of the Samaritan woman many of the characteristics of marginal persons with whom Jesus regularly deals in the Synoptic Gospels. She is an amalgam of cultural deviance. In terms of stereotypes, she is a *non-Jew*, who is ritually *unclean*; she is a "*sinner*," a publicly recognized "*shameless*" person, even someone with whom Jesus has *commensality*. As a *shameless* woman, she embodies most of the social liabilities that would marginalize her in her society. The stereotype of gender expectations serves to portray her precisely as the quintessential deviant, the last and least person who would be expected to find favor with God (cf. 1 Cor 15:8–9).[63] As Michael Jensen describes her, "She is presented to us as a character alienated and apart, caught in a matrix of exclusions. It is not only she who is alienated, however; the 'horizons of significance' against which she is cast are problematic too. In terms of race (and so worship) and gender (and so marriage), she is an identity adrift."[64] Her status transformation is basically that of a person moving from *outsider* to *insider*: she moves from non-kin to kin; from enemy to friend. Jesus reverses long-held cultural rules. This again raises questions about his identity and the authority by which he acts in the way he does.

A second "fresh meaning" emerges from what might be called the eschatological overcoming of alienation in worship. Jesus promises the woman that there is a coming time of what he describes in eschatological categories as "worship in Spirit and in truth" (4:26) a transcendent and superior form of worship that is not construed along present cultic lines. Jensen links such worship with what the woman has disclosed about herself and concludes that the "Samaritan view is confronted here as inauthentic, just as the woman's mode of relating to it is inauthentic. The revelation of a true worship is a counterpart to the unveiling of the woman's own unsatisfactory life. There is in fact a dialectic between the two sides that needs to be recognized. . . . The story's deliberate

---

63. "In the Gospel of John, no outsider would have been more unlikely than this Samaritan woman" (Spina, *Faith of the Outsider*, 157).

64. Jensen, "'In Spirit and in Truth,'" 334.

linking of worship to the woman's desire for personal self-fulfillment is richly suggestive."[65] To the extent that human religion is such a quest for self-fulfillment, the "worship in Spirit and in truth" promised by Jesus is a highly significant challenge. The promise most certainly relativizes all human religious traditions (including Jesus' own Judaism). It is also possible to point to a wider link between peacemaking, mission and worship. Such a connection is labeled a "vital perspective" by Willard Swartley; the common worship of formerly alienated people becomes a key sign and consequence of peace-making mission given that "worship is often the first casualty in alienation arising from ethnic, gender, or racial barriers."[66] A number of contemporary situations of interreligious tension might benefit from a sympathetic reminder of this linkage.

Further application of themes suggested by these Samaritan episodes might be summed up in terms of contrasts between *particularity, discontinuity and mission* on the one hand, and *universality, continuity and dialogue* on the other.

Particularity is both affirmed and relativized. The woman's particularity as a Samaritan is repeatedly noted both by the Gospel writer and by Jesus, and by the woman herself. In fact, her reference to "our father Jacob" (12) might well be seen as an affront (whether intended or not) to Jewish belief that the Jews were privileged children of Jacob. She also points to an area of significant theological disagreement: the divinely approved location for worship of God. Jesus' initial response does not assert Jewish particularity; instead, he "says something that in effect relativizes both points of view" as he speaks of a coming time when Yahweh himself will decide the issue (21).[67] And the woman offers a similar perspective as she affirms that the coming Messiah "will explain everything to us" (25). Nonetheless, Jesus does come to declare the Jewish opinion to be the correct one: "We [Jews] worship what we know, because salvation is from the Jews" (22). And this coming Messiah is, in fact, the very one speaking to her (26).[68] The woman is a Samaritan

---

65. Ibid., 340.

66. Swartley, *Covenant of Peace*, 307.

67. Spina, *Faith of the Outsider*, 152.

68. An appeal to particularity might also be found in the discussion of the woman's "husband": her irregular alliances might, in fact, allude to false worship—along

at the beginning of the story, and she remains so at its conclusion—but with some clear differences in her life. Her Samaritanism is not obliterated by the encounter but its distinctive religious contours are no longer of central significance as she and her fellow Samaritans encounter "the savior of the world."

There is, then, religious discontinuity. In writing about the encounter between Jesus and the Samaritan woman, Michael Jensen notes "What is lacking is her knowledge ('if you knew')—of Jesus' true identity and 'the gift of God.' The two things of which she is ignorant form a hendiadys—the gift of God *is* the one speaking with her." He goes on to quote Rudolf Bultmann to the effect that the woman encapsulates the human race "which needs to recognize the riches of God's gift hidden in the poverty and tiredness of Jesus. For this recognition, a person needs to realize 'what it is that he has to receive from God, a knowledge which is at one with the realization of his own poverty.' That is to say, the 'if you knew' points to ignorance of self as well as to an ignorance of what God gives."[69] The abandoned water jar (28) may perhaps be read in a similar way, notwithstanding its presentation to the reader of a typically ambiguous Johannine symbol. It may simply be an observation about the woman's behavior as she hurries off to her village. Or, as Hendrikus Boers and others suggest, the left behind water jar signifies a dramatic abandonment of the negative values in which the woman has sought refuge throughout the dialogue: factional security (9), merely human sustenance (11–12), and partisan salvation (20).[70] If so, the left behind (perhaps even deliberately *abandoned*) jar has profound implications for the interreligious encounter: the meeting with the Christ relativizes the woman's religious past, as well as her daily and society-gendered labors.

Discontinuity is also implied by the way in which human tradition is superseded by the mission of Jesus announced in John 4.[71] Gary Burge

the lines of the OT's occasional equating of such worship with adultery.

69. Jensen, "'In Spirit and in Truth,'" 336 (quoting from Bultmann's notable commentary on John's Gospel).

70. Boers, *Neither on This Mountain*, 191.

71. This is probably symbolized by the way in which the woman leaves behind (perhaps abandons) her water jug; a sign that she now drinks from a source of "living water" that she has found.

implies affirmative answers to the following questions raised by his study of the chapter: "Do humans (Christian and non-Christian alike) have a tendency to create religious traditions as a part of the architecture of their lives? Does tradition have limited value? Are Jesus' work and the work of the Spirit at odds with such traditions?"[72] If so, such discontinuity implies that the message and mission of Jesus has a set of radical implications for the world's religious traditions—Christianity included. Discontinuity also implies, or can imply, the necessity of mission. It is Jesus who decides to wait by a well at an hour when it would normally be deserted and while the disciples are conveniently away buying food. The purpose he has in mind is to commence his testimony to the Samaritans by means of a personal encounter with this woman, rather than in a formal, traditionally religious context. Moreover, as an African commentator points out, Jesus does so as a missionary: he is outside his own territory, he is dependent upon the kindness of those he comes to serve, and he is without trappings of importance such as a large entourage of followers.[73] His mission also includes the dynamic of gathering. Jesus' use of the harvest imagery (35–38) prompts Okure to propose that "the fundamental conception of mission in the Gospel as a 'gathering in,'" a dynamic at direct odds with "the background of socio-religious separatism in which both the woman and the disciples are caught up" (9, 20, 27, and 33).[74]

Moreover, Jesus' mission is one in which divisions will be ultimately transcended. "It is of particular importance for the overall passage's interpretation as a model for cross-cultural ministry that the woman's and the townspeople's journey of faith, the disciples' lesson in ministry, and the Father's work in and through Jesus are all brought to completion in an organic unity. This models the community of true worshipers of which Jesus spoke, and points to the communion and fellowship that is the goal of all ministry."[75]

72. Burge, *John*, 158.

73. Okure, *Johannine Approach*, 86. A growing number of scholars, including Okure herself, have come to see the story of Jesus and the Samaritan woman as a Johannine variation on an OT betrothal story: mission as a kind of courtship.

74. Okure, *Johannine Approach*, 155.

75. Wyckoff, "Jesus in Samaria," 97.

By the conclusion of the story it is clear that what Jesus has proclaimed is a form of worship that overcomes the alternatives of "either this mountain or Jerusalem." In the person of Jesus, human divisions are shown as able to be transcended by the one who enables worship that is "in Spirit and in truth" (24). And, in the words of Teresa Okure, at the end of the encounter, "Jesus, the disciples, the woman, and the Samaritans enter into a communion fellowship, transcending a complex variety of socio-cultural, gender, and religious barriers that would otherwise keep them apart."[76] In a multireligious world these emphases on particularity and mission can sometimes appear to be disconcerting, even unwelcome but Christian self-understanding cannot avoid them.

However, the encounter does not only highlight issues of particularity, discontinuity and mission; it also suggests themes of universality, continuity and dialogue as well. For example, we might note the way in which patience and respect are displayed in the conversation. Jesus' initial gesture towards the woman—a request for water—initiates the discussion. Jesus does not impose himself on the woman, or launch into a monologue. A genuine dialogue and mutual exchange is initiated by him. Jesus demonstrates throughout the narrative (see, for example, 13-14) the kind of patience that is important in pluralist settings. He treats the woman, as he does women throughout the narrative of the Gospels—with non-condescending respect and patience. One result of this is that the woman gradually becomes less defensive and suspicious. In the way the story unfolds, Jesus creates an atmosphere in which the woman feels comfortable to raise "the right issues for Jesus to respond to, the fundamental need which calls for a resolution, i.e., the religious and social issues which separate Jews and Samaritans."[77]

This patience and respect are also seen in the way that the woman's concerns lead much of the dialogue. It is clear that the concepts of Jacob's well as a source of water and Jacob himself as a giver of gifts

---

76. Okure, "Jesus and the Samaritan Woman," 403. In a gender-divided world there is this pleasing reminder (suggested by the way Jesus interacts with the Samaritan woman): "African women talk about Jesus, believe in Jesus, and relate closely to Jesus who is truly a friend and companion" (Anne Nasimiyu Wasike, "Jesus: An African Perspective," in Patte, *Global Bible Commentary*, 330b).

77. Boers, *Neither on This Mountain*, 182.

are important to the woman; they are intertwined with her cultural identity as a Samaritan. According to Teresa Okure, Jesus will adopt them as natural motifs for progressively leading her to believe in him.[78] "Once he begins the dialogue, the woman takes the lead, and at each point Jesus uses her concerns (of water fetching, marital life, and the right place to worship) to reveal to her his true identity and convey to her the gift he offers."[79] Jesus' response to the woman in verses 21–24 contains elements that enable the passage as a whole to function as a model for interfaith communication. Jesus allows at least some of the woman's concerns to shape their dialogue. As Eric Wyckoff points out, Jesus explicit statement in verse 26 about his claim to messiahship "occurs only after a methodical, painstaking, dialogical process of breaking down barriers and witnessing to the truth in implicit ways which would only later be understood. Rather than setting the pace and determining the shape of this encounter himself, . . . the process [is] dictated by the existential reality of the woman's journey of faith." Wyckoff sees the passage as providing a model for contextualized mission to the Samaritans as it takes place in their territory (4–6) and employs "motifs drawn from their history and consciousness" (7–15).[80]

Moreover, the story shows the way in which outsiders may comprehend what insiders do not. The story has undoubted symbolic functions. The woman is repeatedly mentioned in terms only of her ethnic identity but remains unnamed and this suggests her role as a representative of the whole Samaritan community. She repeatedly raises the key issues that divided Samaritans from Jews. She offers a strong contrast between the inability of "the Jews" (however they are to be defined in a Johannine context[81]) to comprehend Jesus—and those outsiders such as Samaritans who do.[82] Later in the Fourth Gospel (8:48), "certain Jews viciously accuse Jesus of being a Samaritan *and* having a demon, underscoring their slanderous contention that such 'characteristics' were mu-

78. Okure, *Johannine Approach*, 91.
79. Okure, "Jesus and the Samaritan Woman," 414.
80. Wyckoff, "Jesus in Samaria," 95–96.
81. A number of scholars prefer the term "Judeans."
82. For a telling comparison of Nicodemus and the woman (especially in terms of what they do and do not comprehend), see Munro, "Pharisee and the Samaritan."

tually inclusive of the same despicable condition."[83] Jesus' sympathies towards Samaritans, and somewhat marginalized Galileans, may have led to this accusation that he was a "Samaritan" or a "Galilean" (John 7:40-52). Craig Keener notes such accusations and comments that "[s]ubsequent history no less than this narrative warns that hostile voices on both sides of ethnic barriers may regard one who crosses them as a traitor to their cause."[84] A number of commentators point out that, whereas Jesus' own people dismiss him as a "Samaritan" (John 8:48) or as a "Galilean," the Samaritan woman recognizes him as a Jew (4:9);[85] and, as the dialogue has made clear, no ordinary Jew. (The next chapter of this volume will consider some further interreligious implications of the encounter with the Samaritan woman.)

The Parable of the Compassionate Samaritan (Luke 10:25-37)

As with exegesis throughout these chapters, readers are referred to commentaries and specialist studies for findings and discussion that, on the whole, are not repeated here; neither is there discussion of a range of historical-critical issues such as speculation about the possible origins of the parable.[86]

The authenticity of the parable as coming from Jesus is widely accepted. Nolland notes possible influences on the parable (what he calls either "early church retelling or . . . Lukan artistry") but goes on to add that there is substantial evidence that the parable's "imaginative core goes back to the historical Jesus." Despite these redactional and other

83. Spina, *Faith of the Outsider*, 145.

84. Keener, "Some New Testament Invitations," 201-2.

85. Ironically, in John's Gospel only non-Jews explicitly recognize Jesus' Jewishness (4:9 and 18:33-35).

86. One exception, however, is that there will be a number of references to Philip Esler's article "Jesus and the Reduction," wherein he situates Luke 10:25-37 within a hermeneutical framework derived from social-scientific theory. His intention is to investigate the message which the passage would have communicated to its initial recipients and to indicate the relevance that a social-scientific perspective and exegetical results might have for problems of pressing contemporary significance in the area of interethnic relationships and conflict—issues of interest for our overall theme.

influences "there is still every reason for thinking that the historical Jesus is the creative source of the parable."[87] And it a theological reading of the parable offers a range of potential insights for the interreligious encounter.

The whole passage is made up of two separate but closely related pericopes each beginning with questions from an interrogating "lawyer."[88] Jesus' answer to his first question, "Teacher, what shall I do to inherit eternal life?" (25), leads to the lawyer's appeal to OT passages (Deut 6:5 and Lev 19:18: the double command to love God and neighbor).[89] The mention of love of neighbor (27) leads to a second and decisive question, "Who is my neighbor?" (29)—a question seen by Esler as open to social-scientific analysis:

> It is a boundary question of an exclusionary type. So put, it enables Judeans to determine those who fall within the obligation of the law just cited from Lev. 19:18 and those who do not. Whom does God require us to love as ourselves and whom not? Or, more specifically, what is the outer limit of the people we must treat as neighbours? A common answer at this period was that "neighbour" meant fellow Israelite. After all, Lev. 19:18 the source of the quoted statement "(You must love) your neighbour as yourself" . . . .[90]

There is an agenda behind the lawyer's question. He is, as N. T. Wright puts it, "seeking to draw the boundaries of the covenant at the appropriate place, with (of course) himself inside, and sundry other

---

87. Nolland, *Luke 9:21—18:34*, 590, 597. In the redactional activity of Luke it seems that he has probably used Mark 12:28–34 in the opening four verses of this passage.

88. Meaning a legal expert, "a professional interpreter of the Torah" (Bauckham, "Scrupulous Priest," 475).

89. These are passages used by Jesus himself in Mark 12:29–31.

90. Esler, "Jesus and the Reduction," 335. It might be significant to note that the context in the chapter of Leviticus to which appeal is made goes on to apply the neighborly principle to *any non-Israelite* in the land (19:34).

specifiable categories outside."[91] The question assumes a restricted scope for neighbor love.[92]

By way of a response, Jesus tells the familiar parable. It seems as if the precise details of the way Jesus begins are significant. The first traveler is simply "a certain man" (30). According to Esler, Jesus' failure to specify the man's ethnicity is essential to the story as it unfolds. The man was stripped of his clothing. Not only was clothing valuable but, according to Esler, two other important consequences follow: an observer had lost the chance to assess the victim's ethnicity by what he was wearing, and "the man's nakedness enabled an observer to determine whether he was circumcised or not. If uncircumcised, he was a Gentile and certainly not a neighbour; if circumcised an Israelite or a Samaritan."[93]

Potential help arrives in the person of a traveling priest (31)—a "prime representative of the religion that, in the person of the lawyer, has just agreed upon the fundamental place of love hardens his heart and passes by on the other side."[94] The reason for his failure to help is not clear in the story. Even if the man's nakedness disclosed that he was circumcised, the priest (and the Levite who follows) would have been uncertain as to whether he was Israelite and a "neighbor" to be loved or a Samaritan and therefore not a "neighbor." And there was also the possibility of the priest (and perhaps the Levite) breaking Mosaic law concerning corpse impurity.[95] The scenario seems to be that in approaching the dying man, the priest risks corpse defilement. If the man is unconscious the priest cannot tell whether he is dead or alive without coming up close.[96]

91. Wright, *Jesus and the Victory*, 306.

92. Cf. the sentiment expressed in the book of Sirach (written about 180 BCE): "If you do good, know to whom you do it. Give to the devout, but do not help the sinner" (Sir 12:1a, 4).

93. Esler, "Jesus and the Reduction," 337–38. On the significance of clothing, see also the helpful article by Knowles, "What Was the Victim Wearing?"

94. Nolland, *Luke 9:21—18:34*, 593.

95. See Lev 21:1–3; Num 5:2; 19:2–13; cf. Ezek 44:25–27. The purity issue is discussed by Bauckham in his "The Scrupulous Priest and the Good Samaritan." See also the extensive discussion in Kazen, "Good Samaritan," and the analysis by Esler in his "Jesus and the Reduction," 339–41.

96. "He cannot get close enough to tell without risking defilement from the corpse

So the problem presented by the parable is that, when the priest encounters a man lying half dead on the road, it "sets up an halakhic issue, which any first-century Jew alert to halakhic issues would readily have recognized as one. The situation is one in which two commandments might seem to apply: one forbids the priest to contract impurity by contact with a dead body, while the other requires the priest to show neighbourly love to the wounded man."[97]

The next traveler is a Samaritan (33). Given the Samaritan acceptance of the Torah, the Samaritan could have undertaken the same kind of legal analysis as the priest and Levite in order to ask, "'Is he a Samaritan—and therefore my neighbour such as to activate the obligation of Lev. 19:18—or not?' Yet the text makes it quite plain that he did no such thing."[98] Rather, when he saw the wounded man "he was moved with compassion" (*esplangchnisthē*); here "we reach the fulcrum upon which the story turns. The word translated "he was moved with compassion" is reserved until the final position in the clause to build suspense and to allow maximum impact."[99] His caring, practical actions are then described in some detail (34-35). Jesus commends the loving actions of the compassionate Samaritan whose *actions* disclose his delivering love; in fact, nine specific actions are recounted in what is a rather brief account.

The concluding exchange of the encounter (36-37) includes a call to action which echoes the call in verse 28 but with the additional and compelling insight of the second round of engagement. The parable of the compassionate Samaritan answers the lawyer's question, "Who is

---

if that is what it turns out to be. This is because, in first-century Jewish thought about such matters, corpse impurity travels vertically through the air. If any part of the priest's body were to be above any part of a corpse, he would contract impurity" (Bauckham, "Scrupulous Priest," 477).

97. Ibid. There is an alternative understanding of the passage that reads the priest's actions in literary terms: "The story's focus is on the priest's failure to help rather than on the reason that he failed to help. . . . In the story the role of the priest is to raise hopes and then to dash them" (Nolland, *Luke 9:21—18:34*, 597). Nonetheless, the reading followed here is based on the actual contrast between the behaviors of the two men.

98. Esler, "Jesus and the Reduction," 342-43.

99. Nolland, *Luke 9:21—18:34*, 594.

my neighbor?," by means of an appeal to behavior that reflects the divine character of mercy (37).

In terms of interreligious relations, a number of issues and possible implications of the parable might be mentioned.

It Is Neither Samaritans nor Samaritanism That Is Exemplary

The story does not intend to prove anything about the Samaritan, as a Samaritan, but to show who in the story acts as a true neighbor. The central point of the story is not that the Samaritan saw the afflicted man as a neighbor (he did, but that is not the significance of the parable). Although the story begins with the question, "Who is my neighbor?," it does not answer it directly but discusses *how* to be a neighbor. It is not Samaritanism as a religion or worldview as such that is commended. It is the ability and willingness of an individual who happens to be Samaritan to see, feel and act as he did. The parable "does not actually require us to assume that in real life Samaritans would ever behave in such an exemplary manner, only that if one were to do so we should have to recognize that he had been neighbor to the one in need."[100] Presumably a Samaritan storyteller could tell a similar story about a compassionate Jew. In other words, Jesus is commending actions (that he compares with the divine "mercy" with which the story ends) that might be found across religious boundaries.

The Prophetic Critique within a Provocative Parable

In his parable, Jesus commends the attitude and the actions of the "compassionate Samaritan." "The parable marks a significant, highly provocative, and novel step in the mission of Jesus. . . . Jesus' audience must have found this parable unpalatable, indeed obnoxious. . . . In terms of Jewish religion the Samaritans were enemies not only of Jews, but also of God. In the context of the narrative the Samaritan thus has a negative religious value."[101] But the parable draws precisely the opposite conclusion to that suggested by the widely held stereotype. As James Dunn puts it,

100. Ibid., 590.
101. Bosch, *Transforming Mission*, 90.

Jesus and the Religions

"in his telling the parable of the Good Samaritan Jesus must deliberately have intended to shock his hearers."[102] The hearers include the lawyer who is apparently unable even to utter the word "Samaritan" at the end of the encounter; when Jesus asks him which one was neighbor to the man who fell among thieves, he answers with a circumlocution: "the one who showed him kindness." (10:37) In terms of Philip Esler's social-scientific analysis, what Jesus is seeking to accomplish in the story is not justification for certain behavior but a refusal to group differentiate and stereotype. "In the body of the parable Jesus has refused to engage in the processes of group differentiation and stereotypification, indeed he has positively subverted them."[103] Perhaps in today's world with its surplus of religious stereotyping, some similarly forceful and prophetic language is need to draw attention to commendatory examples of the behavior commended by Jesus—across whatever boundaries it might be found.

The Universality of Love over against Notions of Ethnic or Religious Superiority

The superiority of the dynamic of universal compassion is brought out in several ways. Firstly by what Richard Bauckham calls the superiority of the love commandment. He argues that from "this particular case the tendency of the parable is towards a general halakhic principle, so far as we know novel: that the commandment to love the neighbour is a commandment of such importance that it must always override others in cases of conflict."[104] Bauckham later adds, "Since purity was one of the

---

102. Dunn, *Jesus Remembered*, 538–39.

103. Esler, "Jesus and the Reduction," 344.

104. Bauckham, "Scrupulous Priest," 489. He has earlier commented: "The notion that one commandment can override another is unremarkable, but the application of it to a commandment as general in scope as the commandment to love the neighbour seems to be unparalleled outside the Gospels" (485). Perhaps another of making the same point is to note the way in which the two love commandments here in Luke are unified by making both God and neighbor objects of the single verb "to love." In other words, "the Law itself, understood holistically, with the separate commandments to love God and to love one's neighbor brought into unity and mutual interaction, provides the path to life" (Byrne, *Hospitality of God*, 100).

dominant halakhic concerns of the time, the general principle can be presented especially pointedly by means of a case where the love commandment must override even a priest's special purity obligation."[105] Once again, a warning with contemporary application is sounded here: commendable (religious) behavior is not defined by rule keeping—however exalted the source of the rules; it is to be measured against the kind of love displayed by the religious outsider of the story.

Dialogue Is Not to Be Based on External "Markers"

According to Michael Knowles, Jesus—especially in the parable of the compassionate Samaritan—"proposes an ethic that is determined neither in relation to the shared codes of social stratification, nor in relation to membership within a particular group, but solely on the basis of an internalized ethical orientation."[106] Knowles draws attention to the role played by clothing in determining social relations among the actors in the unfolding drama and its first hearers. He describes this as follows:

> A series of passers-by, each in distinctive garb, consider their respective obligations to a man deprived of most social markers, and therefore (at least for the listener/ reader) of indeterminate social, ethnic, and economic status. But clothing—or lack of it—turns out to be a misleading social indicator, the wrong "voice" or context for evaluation. In this sense, the account of the unfortunate victim anticipates and illustrates in parabolic form the intent of Jesus' words in Luke 12:23, that "life is more than food, and the body more than clothing." Such a response would have seemed all the more pointed to the original questioner, whose own social standing and distinctive manner of dress are both well-attested in ancient sources.[107]

External "markers" such as clothing and speech ought not to impede the interreligious meeting but at times in the contemporary world such

---

105. "Scrupulous Priest," 480.
106. Knowles, "What Was the Victim Wearing?," 171.
107. Ibid., 171–72.

markers still seem to generate prejudicial attitudes. Whenever they do, perhaps the parable can offer the reminder of a different set of attitudes, even if they derive from an unlikely source.

A Condition for Positive Interreligious Relations: The "Seeing Heart"

Bernd Wannenwetsch, in a fine discussion of moral reasoning in the NT, writes of "sensory-affective perception," which he explains as the "seeing heart" and illustrates from the parable. He argues that it "demonstrates that sensory perception like 'seeing' does matter morally. . . . At stake is truthful perception that sees things as they really are instead of seeing them as we would like them to be and declaring this, and ourselves, 'aright.'"[108] All three travelers in the parable are said to have "seen" the wounded man but only the Samaritan sees a person in misery. The other two perceived something else (danger, impurity, irritating delay, or something more). "Their seeing really makes the difference; all parties in the parable are acting out of what they have perceived." In the case of the Samaritan, his "eyes were, so to speak, connected to his heart, which was 'torn open'—'compassion' is perhaps too weak a translation for what the Greek verb connotes." Each of the three travelers is described in term of a participial construction in the Greek: with the priest and the Levite, "seeing the man, they passed by," but for the Samaritan it is a matter of "seeing him, he felt compassion." The psychological process is one in which "the affections [connect] sensual perception and will-guided action." Wannenwetsch notes "the simultaneity of seeing and feeling suggested by the Greek participial construction: in seeing him he felt compassion; the heart was 'in' the eye, so to speak." From this he concludes that "when our sensual perception is oriented appropriately as a matter of a 'seeing or listening heart,' the right action can be expected to 'flow' from it by engaging our mind and

---

108. Wannenwetsch, "Fourfold Pattern," in Bockmuehl and Torrance, *Scripture's Doctrine*, 182. He adds that this is part of the prophetic tradition with its "emphasis on the signs of the messianic age in terms of the recovery of sensory perception. . . . Jesus' liberating ministry is one of creating eyes that really see" (183).

will accordingly."[109] Once again the parable offers a difficult reminder for today's world. The central difference between the Samaritan and the others is shown to be a matter not of ethnicity or religion but the condition of the "seeing heart."[110] As Jesus himself says (in a different but not unrelated context), "it is from within, from the human heart" (Mark 7:21) that human behavior is decided.

Potential for Conflict Reduction

The parable also has application to settings of interreligious tension. Philip Esler discusses various approaches in social identity theory to reducing intergroup conflict (crossed categorization, recategorization and decategorization)[111] and the latter is found to be closest to the approach taken by the Jesus in the parable. Such a conclusion suggests the relevance of the parable to contemporary efforts to eliminate intergroup conflict; in fact, Esler finds that the Samaritan "simply disregards" the question of which of the three possible categories (Gentile, Jewish, Samaritan) ought to be applied to the victim. By refusing to be bound by the expectations attached to such categories, "Jesus transforms the whole concept of 'neighbour' from the recipient of compassion to the agent of such compassion."[112] Once again the relevance to the contemporary world is both startling and obvious. In settings of intergroup conflict, the example of the Samaritan and of the Jesus who told the story (one who also proclaims "love your enemies") would have far-reaching consequences.

---

109. Ibid., 183.

110. There may also be significance in the way that the theme of revelation is linked by Jesus with seeing and not seeing (Luke 10:21-24): "Blessed are the eyes that see what you see!" (v. 23b).

111. Esler, "Jesus and the Reduction," 345-50.

112. Ibid., 348-49.

5

Some Implications for the Encounter with Islam

THIS CHAPTER FURTHER DISCUSSES Jesus' meeting with Samaritans—and his comments on them—and will suggest a number of implications from this encounter for what is, for many Christians, the most difficult of all interreligious meetings: that with the world of Islam.

Samaritans, Jesus, and the World of Islam

Thirteen Characteristics Shared by Samaritanism and Islam

One of the characteristics of the theological exegesis employed in this volume is its supposed capacity to produce new insights into well-known biblical themes. The possibility of such a "fresh reading" (as Richard Hays calls it) becomes apparent as some implications for the contemporary Christian encounter with the world of Islam are considered. In particular, a number of interesting parallels between Samaritans and Muslims emerge; in fact, some thirteen similarities between Samaritan belief and practice at the time of Jesus, and the beliefs and practices of Islam, suggest themselves. What we are undertaking is, to employ a hermeneutical term, a *synchronic* reading[1] of Samaritanism and Islam in order to

---

1. In hermeneutical terms, "synchronic" refers to the state of something at a given moment. In textual study it means "concerned with the state of something at a given moment; thus a synchronic study of a text is interested in the relationship of the parts

suggest their relationship to a contemporary reader of them. These will be outlined as a prelude to asking the question: "If Samaritanism shows a number of parallels to Islam, and if we have insight into how Jesus reacted to the Samaritans he encountered, what might his reactions suggest in terms of a contemporary Christian response to Muslims?" Such a reading begins by outlining the similarities between the three religious traditions: Judaism, Samaritanism, Islam. Some thirteen apparently shared sets of characteristics will be described.

A DISTINCT AND DISTINCTIVE AND SELF-DEFINING COMMUNITY

Each of the three religious traditions sees itself as distinct, distinctive and separate from the others, and not part of or "under" or subservient to any other—even the group or groups they derived from or have been related to historically. Each claims the right to self-define its beliefs and practices and not to be defined by others. There is a definable set of discontinuities between the three groups and these are reinforced by language and even clothing.[2] With varying degrees of intensity (and notable internal variations), each "tribe" sees itself as the "true religion"—divinely constituted—viewing the others as ignorant, misguided (innocently or culpably), heretical or worse.

RELATED TO OTHERS; YET CONSCIOUSLY "DEVIANT"

At the same time, despite being consciously distinct, each of the three groups is clearly related to the others. Both Judaism and Samaritanism are forms of the ancient religion of Israel that gradually separated and then developed independently. Neusner describes Samaritans as "part of the larger spectrum of Judaism,"[3] though it may be more accurate to

---

with each other in its present form" ("Glossary" in Barton, *Cambridge Companion*, xv).

2. Some of the distinctiveness, then and now, is made apparent by clothing. For example, Esler notes that "it seems probable that Judean and non-Judean inhabitants of Palestine could be distinguished by their clothing" (Esler, "Jesus and the Reduction," 337).

3. Neusner, "Samaritans," in *Dictionary of Judaism*, 2:548.

speak of Samaritanism as a form of Israelite religion, rather than a form of Judaism.[4] Samaritans consider themselves to be the true Israelites. Perhaps it is possible to speak of them as "deviant Jews" (with "deviant" understood in a non-pejorative sense—as the word is used in social-science terminology). Islam understands itself as the pure form of the religion of Abraham and the patriarchs, the prophets and even of Jesus himself. Muslims see themselves as faithful worshippers of the God of Abraham, and as standing in continuity with what Allah has been speaking throughout human history, while holding that the other "religions of the book" (Judaism and Christianity) have distorted the truth and have corrupted the Scripture. Thus, while being related to the others, Islam is the truest form of the Abrahamic religions (Christianity included), and "religion" (in the singular). Although Muslims insist that the Qur'an came directly to Muhammad, Jews (and Christians) usually point out the historical probability that Muhammad knew Jews (and Christians) from whom he heard details of Jewish worship, many stories from the OT, and even some rabbinic teaching. Islam certainly affirms a degree of continuity with Judaism (and Christianity) but does not regard itself as the direct derivative of Judaism/ancient Israelite religion that Samaritanism is.

FIRMLY AND UNAMBIGUOUSLY MONOTHEISTIC BELIEF

In contrast to the religions of the many polytheistic nations surrounding Israel, most varieties of Judaism are staunchly monotheistic, believing that creation is the work of one God, and that this God has remained in a dynamic relationship with it. Likewise, Samaritans worship one God and see themselves as God's true people; their beliefs and practices was based primarily upon the Pentateuch. For Muslims, *tawhid*, the oneness of Allah, is the most important Islamic belief. This monotheism is so central to Islam that the *shahadah*, the Muslim declaration of belief begins: "There is no god except Allah . . ."

---

4. Meier, "Historical Jesus," n.p., n. 32.

Some Implications for the Encounter with Islam

A SCRIPTURALLY BASED RELIGION OF REVELATION

Both Judaism and Samaritanism see themselves as scripturally based religions—even if Samaritans restrict Scripture (and hence the written revelation) to the Pentateuch.[5] Islam firmly declares itself to be *the* scripturally based religion of divine revelation. The Qur'an is seen as a confirmation of the Jewish Scriptures as well as the Gospels but Islam also believes that Christians and Jews have distorted their Scriptures and thus the Qur'an is the only truly reliable source of divine revelation. Nonetheless, all three faiths do consider themselves to be scripturally based religions of revelation.

GEOGRAPHICALLY DISTINCTIVE;
THE OTHERS AS GEOGRAPHICALLY DISLOCATED

For what might be called "mainstream" Judaism, Jerusalem became the geographic center of salvation history with the temple as the most significant religious symbol. For Samaritans the equivalent center became not Jerusalem (or its temple) but Mt. Gerizim. Samaritanism rejected and was rejected "by those aspects of Judaism that were tied specifically to the cultic observance of Jerusalem."[6] So central was Mt. Gerizim that Samaritanism reworded the tenth commandment of the Decalogue to validate this location. For Islam, Mecca and its *Ka'ba*, the "House of Allah" (a sanctuary and ancient pilgrimage site) is highly significant.[7] The pilgrimage to Mecca (the *hajj*) is a sacred obligation that is required of all Muslims if they are able to undertake it. At first, Muslims prayed in the direction of Jerusalem but later began to pray facing Mecca. In other words, as with Judaism and Samaritanism, Islam has certain distinctively and divinely sanctioned holy sites, but regards its related faith traditions (Christianity included) as geographically dislocated.

 5. As already noted, the Samaritan Pentateuch is essentially the same as the Masoretic text; it describes Mt. Gerizim as chosen by God to be the only place of legitimate sacrifice; see further below.

 6. Neusner, "Samaritans," in *Dictionary of Judaism*, 2:548.

 7. The second most holy site is Medina (the site of the first Islamic state), while the third is Jerusalem (the location to which Muhammad is said to have travelled on his "night journey").

TRUTH AND SUSPICION: OTHERS HAVE DISTORTED THE TRUTH

Both Jews and Samaritans considered themselves the keepers of the true faith while regarding the other as deviant. Despite a common heritage, each has maintained that they are the true inheritors of the sacred tradition. Samaritans regarded Jews as descended from apostates of the time of Eli. Jewish polemic towards Samaritans portrayed them as semi-pagans who were descendents of those settled in the northern kingdom by the Assyrians. Muslims, likewise, consider themselves as standing in direct continuity with the religion of Abraham while seeing Christians and Jews as having deliberately distorted that true religion—especially by means of the deliberate rewriting of parts of the sacred revelation.

A HISTORY OF MUTUAL VERBAL SLANDER AND EVEN VIOLENT CONFRONTATION

The destruction of the sanctuary of Mt. Gerizim in 122–111 BCE is considered the "decisive event that alienated the Samaritans and caused them to recognize Mt. Gerizim as the only legitimate place of worship."[8] This becomes a further point of tension between Jews and Samaritans. Although care must be taken over Josephus' testimony about the Samaritans (because of his animosity towards them), his reports of Samaritan attacks, and subsequent Jewish retaliation, are taken seriously.[9] Following Muhammad and his followers' migration to Medina, animosity developed between the Muslim community and certain Jewish tribes. Although there have been periods (some very lengthy and widespread) when Muslims and Jews have coexisted peacefully, there have been periods of violent (often localized) tensions between them, especially in relation to Israel/Palestine from 1948. The long history of Christian-Muslim mistrust is well known.

---

8. Pummer, "Samaritanism," in Collins and Harlow, *Eerdmans Dictionary*, 1188.

9. Meier notes that Josephus' account, in the estimation of most critics, is hostile to the Samaritans, though it is unclear whether the hostility derives from Josephus or from his sources (Meier, "Historical Jesus," 206). Yet, there is general agreement that, despite Josephus' bias against Samaritans, his account does have a secure foundation (Grabbe, *Judaic Religion*, 438–39; Williamson and Evans, "Samaritans," 1059–60).

Some Implications for the Encounter with Islam

A STRONGLY ASSERTED ETHNICITY-CULTURE-RELIGION LINK

For both Jews and Samaritans, there is no dichotomy between social and religious life; religion is deeply woven into the totality of life and is strongly linked with ethnic and cultural identity. To be an ethnic-cultural Jew/Samaritan *is* to be a religious Jew/Samaritan. Likewise, for the Muslim, there is typically no clear division between one's religious faith and one's culture; religious faith is not regarded as an individual choice, as has become common in the Global North.

CLEAR DISTINCTIONS BETWEEN MALE AND FEMALE SPACE AND FUNCTIONS

Cultural anthropologists have long known that in the ancient Mediterranean world there were distinctly different cultural expectations for males and females; in fact, all of reality is viewed in terms of gender division. The proper place for males is in public, engaging in public activities, while females belong in "private space"— primarily their homes and secondarily places where female tasks are performed (as our discussion of the cultural expectations of Jesus and the Samaritan woman outlined). In a similar way, Islamic law defines private and public spaces and puts a "screen" between them[10] and Islam typically does not allow (or at least discourages) the free mixing of men and women. Likewise women are typically expected to function within the private sphere or with other women in the wider world.

HONOR AND SHAME EXPECTATIONS, ESPECIALLY FOR FEMALES

Connected with expectations about male and female space is a set of social values derived from the dynamics of honor and dishonor; these are foundational to first-century Jewish and Samaritan cultural identity. All behavior relates to these dynamics of honor and shame, although the dynamics are differently understood for males and females.

---

10. Al-Muhajabah, "On Veiling," n.p. Online http://www.muhajabah.com/onveiling.htm. The Arabic word for screen is *hijab*, which is the same word for the modest dress of Muslim women.

Islamic/Middle Eastern (as well as many other non-Western) cultures are also largely oriented around honor and shame. Honor is so highly regarded within Islam that a Muslim academic can speak of today's global/Westernized culture as being a "post-honor world."[11] For the purpose of our comparison, these outlines of female space, functions, and honor/shame expectations point to the parallel between Islam and Samaritanism that we want to draw attention to.[12]

NON-SCRIPTURAL TRADITIONS (INCLUDING PURITY AND FOOD LAWS)

Judaism has a range of adopted traditions intended to clarify the Torah. Samaritans also developed their own traditions of biblical exegesis, *halakah*, worship and history in order to interpret and apply the Pentateuch. Because the Pentateuch relates to all of life, a range of Samaritan literature was "written purposely to give insight into the commandments of the Pentateuch, and to offer advice on how to live in accordance with them."[13] In a related way, a wide range of Muslim practices and beliefs are based, not upon the Qur'an, but on the *hadith* (traditional records of the actions and sayings of Muhammad and his companions). The reason the *hadith* is so valued is that Muslims desire to imitate the life of Muhammad as closely as possible, given that he is a perfect exemplar of and for humanity. Thus, Muslims have a (diverse) set of non-scriptural traditions that relate to diet, relationships, clothing and dress, prayer, and wisdom.

---

11. Ahmed, *Islam under Siege*, 56–63. "Today, notions of honor under attack remain an important discourse in political rhetoric and even behavior in much of the Muslim world. . . . Muslims everywhere [feel] deprived of honor and dignity" (59).

12. The dynamics of honor and shame are, of course, much more complex than this brief summary can describe; see, for example, the comments of Crook, "Honor, Shame."

13. Hjelm, "What Do Samaritans?," 35–36.

Some Implications for the Encounter with Islam

A ROLE FOR SACRIFICIAL RITUAL

The sacrificial foundations of the Jewish religious tradition are clearly outlined in the Torah and are a prominent feature of the temple cultus. Although the presence of a temple on Mt. Gerizim is debated among scholars, all agree that well before the Common Era there existed some kind of cult site on the mountain which included an altar for sacrifice (probably built at some time during the fourth or fifth century BCE). A line of priests, said to be the legitimate Levitical priests of the Mosaic dispensation, officiated at this altar/temple. Moreover, "even after the destruction of their temple, the Samaritans continued to offer a yearly animal sacrifice at Passover by slaughtering, roasting, and eating sheep as prescribed in Exodus 12."[14] Islam has also retained a sacrificial component within its prescribed practices. During the Muslim festival of *Idul Adha* (or the "Festival of Sacrifice"), Muslims offer congregational prayer and they sacrifice animals such as sheep, cows, goats and camels.[15] Despite differences, a place for sacrificial ritual is common to all three religious traditions.

DISTINCTIVE PROPHETIC AND ESCHATOLOGICAL EXPECTATIONS

Although there are a variety of Judaisms during the Second Temple Era, eschatological beliefs (including expectation of a coming restoration) are central to all of them. Samaritanism had its own set of developing eschatological beliefs. Not only was it awaiting a day of judgment and recompense, but it appears that an important element of Samaritan belief related to the coming of a "prophet like Moses," a belief that was later crystallized into the concept of a messianic figure, *Taheb* (the "restorer" or "returning one"). Islam also has a set of not unrelated eschatological expectations including judgment, reward and punishment. Muslims hold that the prophet Jesus will return to earth at the end of history.

---

14. Pummer, "Samaritanism," in Collins and Harlow, *Eerdmans Dictionary*, 1188.

15. For the Muslim the sacrifice has nothing to do with atoning for sins: "It is not their meat nor their blood that reaches Allah; it is your piety that reaches Him" (Qur'an 22:37).

Jesus and the Religions

There are, then, a number of interesting religio-cultural parallels between the worlds of Samaritanism and Judaism, on the one hand, and much of the worlds of Islam and Christianity, on the other. The central point we want to make concerns the *attitudes* that Jews and Samaritans had towards what was the closely related religious tradition of the other. Some (perhaps most) of these attitudes can rightly be called misrepresentation and prejudice. As Colin Chapman points out, "the prejudices which many Christians have towards Muslims are very similar to the prejudices the Jews showed towards Samaritans at the time of Jesus."[16] And there is usually rather little place for any affirmation of the other. It is to the attitude and example of Jesus, in the face of such tension, prejudice, and lack of affirmation, that we now turn.

The Example of Jesus with Samaritans and Attitudes towards Muslims

What we have seen are interesting—even if anachronistic—parallels between three related Semitic faiths. They are not always exact parallels (given the obvious geographical, historical and other differences); and they are not intended to be comparative in the sense of any implication of a *contemporary evaluation* of the faiths concerned; they simply point to parallels. (They attempt to be descriptive rather than prescriptive.) But the parallels do, nonetheless, point to real similarities between Samaritanism and Islam and provide a backdrop to the question, "What do the example of and teaching of Jesus (especially with Samaritans) imply about what ought to be Christian attitudes towards Muslims?"

Discussion can helpfully begin with the story of Jesus and the Samaritan woman in which there are substantial and longstanding divisions on parade. Some of these are minor. For example, it "seems likely that the Samaritan woman . . . recognised that Jesus was a Judean by his clothing rather than simply deducing this from his (presumably Galilean) accent when he said 'Give me something to drink' (John

---

16. Chapman, *Cross and Crescent*, 54. With the Canaanite mother in mind, Bruner also draws a parallel between Jewish attitudes towards "Canaanites" and contemporary Christian attitudes towards Muslims (Bruner, *Matthew*, 2:97).

4:7–9)."[17] But there is much more to the story than everyday cultural (and geographical) distinctives; beneath the surface are divisive issues embodied in what Okure calls "the rejection, prejudice, and isolation of the two main characters"[18]—by which she means the rejection, prejudice, and isolation that Jews and Samaritans typically displayed towards one another. A missiologist, Stuart Caldwell, also challenges Christians to consider the parallels between the obstacles Jesus faced when communicating with Samaritans and the obstacles Christians face with Muslims. He considers that Jesus' ministry in Samaria is "highly applicable" to the meeting of Christians and Muslims.[19]

We might consider, for example, the problematical question of how Samaritans, with their divergent beliefs and practices, relate to the people of God. The usual answer for Second Temple Era Judaism is framed in negative ways. However, as we have seen, the Samaritan woman comprehends what Nicodemus (the Jewish religious leader who meets Jesus in John 3) does not; she is an "outsider" who comes to see what Nicodemus as an "insider" fails to grasp. The Samaritan townspeople grasp what "the Jews" fail to understand as they articulate their faith in "the savior of the world," while Jesus' own disciples stand silent. The words that conclude the narrative affirm a universal savior and "unmistakably convey the thrust of the story: salvation is not only for Jews. The Samaritans understood this from the manner in which Jesus had made himself known to the woman . . . and had spent two days with them. They do not call him by the name which was typical for the future

---

17. Esler, "Jesus and the Reduction," 338 n. 19.

18. Okure, "Jesus and the Samaritan Woman," 401.

19. Caldwell, "Jesus in Samaria," 25, 27. He specifically notes the way in which Jesus critically adopts Samaritan terminology in the face of disputed issues surrounding the place and means of worship of the divine. With conservative Christians in mind, Caldwell makes the point that, in spite of the positive example of Jesus in Samaria, "many hesitate to do similarly in Islamic contexts. They explain that Islam is different from Samaritanism. Islam was founded by a false prophet, who may have borrowed from Biblical revelation but nevertheless ended with incomplete and inaccurate conclusions about Scripture and the Messiah." But Caldwell then adds that "this is precisely how Jesus saw Samaritans in the first century" (27).

expectation of the Jews, 'Messiah,' or by their own, Taheb, but by a name in accord with universal salvation."[20]

The Samaritan of the parable models the heart of covenant law in a way that priest and Levite do not. The Samaritan healed of leprosy is presented as a model example of praise and gratitude. Even inhospitable Samaritans are not to be treated with vengeful disdain. As with Jesus' encounters with Gentiles, the attention given to Samaritans enables us to see that the "weight" to be attached to encounters with them far exceeds the actual number of such occurrences. The significance of the Samaritans for Jesus is demonstrated by his deployment of their example as signs and affirmations of the eschatological inversion of the present/coming Rule of God. The marginalized and despised Samaritans (seen by Jewish neighbors as theologically and socially deviant) display the qualities expected of the Israel of God. As we observed about Gentiles, considerable missional and relational implications might flow if the church were to scrutinize its evaluation of the religious faith of others along the lines of this principle of "elevation from the margins" apparently embraced by Jesus himself.[21]

What might Jesus' example suggest about contemporary attitudes to Muslims among a fourth "tribe of Abraham," the Christian community?[22] Mention has already been made of the prejudices that many Christians have towards Muslims. We might reword the question posed earlier: "Given that Samaritanism shows a number of parallels to Islam, and given insight into Jesus' attitude and example towards the Samaritans he encounters, what might these reactions imply for a contemporary Christian—meaning Christ-like—response to Muslims?" The fact that some Muslims can and sometimes do entertain misleading or even false and prejudicial beliefs about Christians (and Jews) is no reason for Christians (and Jews) to do the same. The example and

---

20. Ridderbos, *Gospel of John*, 172. There are not dissimilar contemporary accounts of Muslims who encounter Christ and become his disciples but, for a number of reasons, do not or cannot take on the name "Christian" (see the examples discussed by Medearis, *Muslims, Christians*, 133–45).

21. As we saw with the Gentile examples discussed in the Introduction and chapters 2 and 3.

22. See also, Caldwell, "Jesus in Samaria."

teaching of Jesus point in a quite different direction; they imply a quite different attitude.

Undeniable Particularities

Although discussion is going to emphasize similarities and continuities between Christianity and Islam, such an emphasis does not intend to overlook or avoid the reality of the particularities and discontinuities that are also embedded in each of the traditions when considered in the light of the other so-called Abrahamic faiths. Each of the thirteen areas of similarity considered above also contains examples of divergence and difference between the Abrahamic faiths. One recent discussion (notable for its well-informed and irenic tone) that makes this point is Michael Lodahl's *Claiming Abraham: Reading the Bible and the Qur'an Side by Side*. Lodahl, who includes Christianity in the group of Abrahamic faiths, argues that "the Bible and Qur'an often construe God, humans, and the world as a whole in noticeably different ways—and in ways that make for significant differences both in theology and in practice" for Islam and Christianity. Several key topics illustrate the difference for him between these two traditions: revelation, the place and function of the Qur'an and Christ, belief in God as creator.[23] The differences are equally apparent when the other two "tribes" (Judaism and Samaritanism) are added to the comparisons. As we saw in a section above ("Religion and the interreligious encounter: particularity, discontinuity and mission") there is clear evidence of dissonance—perhaps even to the point of incommensurability—between Judaism and Samaritanism.

Nonetheless, despite the significant differences, and the somewhat negative implications concerning Samaritanism (when assessed in the light of particularity, discontinuity and missional intention), there are other notable features of what Jesus did and said regarding Samaritans. Similarities and continuities are also apparent. These are *related* faith traditions and the thirteen points of comparison are intended to show

23. See *Claiming Abraham*, chs. 2-4 (quote from p. 4). Miroslav Volf, however, mounts a plausible counterargument to this conclusion by Lodahl; see the discussion of his *Allah* below.

similarities between two of the traditions (Judaism and Samaritanism) in order to make suggestions about the relationship between two other of the Abrahamic traditions (Christianity and Islam).

Reconciliation—Even of Enemies

The tone of reconciliation, clearly implied in Jesus' dealings with Gentiles and Samaritans and other "outsider" groups, has obvious and important implications for a religiously divided world. If Michael Bird is correct, the encounter between Jesus and the centurion has a dimension that is usually missed. Jesus performs an act of compassionate healing "for someone who was potentially his enemy," given that the official was "part of the domination system of the Herodian rulers" whose "security apparatus . . . had a particular interest or concern about Jesus as attested in [the Gospels]. The story is transformed into a living parable of loving one's enemies."[24] It also notable that in the Acts of the Apostles, "When the apostles in Jerusalem heard that Samaria had accepted the word of God, they sent Peter and John to Samaria" (Acts 8:14). Chapman sees this as "an official apostolic delegation to welcome the new believers. In view of all the animosities between Jews and Samaritans in the past, some public gesture was called for to show to all the world that in the church there would be no place for any bad feelings between Jewish and Samaritan believers."[25]

From a social-scientific perspective, it can be seen that in John 4:4–42 John concentrates in the one figure of the Samaritan woman many of the characteristics of marginal persons with whom Jesus regularly deals in the Synoptic Gospels. As we saw in the analysis by Neyrey, she is an amalgam of cultural deviance, embodying most of the social liabilities that would marginalize her in Samaritan society—and yet her status moves from that of outsider to insider as the narrative develops. Moreover, the passage goes on to portray Jesus as staying with Samaritans for a number of days. All of this takes place in what Teresa Okure calls a "socio-religious context of reciprocal contempt and

24. Bird, *Jesus and the Origins*, 120–21.
25. Chapman, *Cross and Crescent*, 55.

separatism."[26] And, over against the attitude and actions of a priest and a Levite, Jesus commends the attitude and the actions of the "compassionate Samaritan" (Luke 10:29–37) a phrase that is a virtual oxymoron in the minds of his hearers. "If we wanted to capture the original impact of the parable, we would need to say that if Jesus were addressing Protestants in Northern Ireland, the good Samaritan would have been a Catholic; if he were speaking to Palestinian Arabs, the person who so unexpectedly showed kindness would have been a Jew; if he were talking to Armenians, it would have been 'the good Turk.'"[27] Or, to press the point of our comparison, the original impact of the parable would be captured in some Christian circles by suggesting a compassionate Muslim as the heroic exemplar of the story. However, as we have seen, the Samaritan is the defining actor in the story. He knows and acts out the heart of the Law better than the two Jewish religious leaders. The bitterness of the Jewish-Samaritan relationship has already been discussed in the previous chapter; the hostility is captured in the Fourth Gospel (8:48) as certain Jews viciously accuse Jesus of being a both Samaritan *and* having a demon, "underscoring their slanderous contention that such 'characteristics' were mutually inclusive of the same despicable condition."[28] Nonetheless, as we have also tried to illustrate, Jesus both advocates and models a response that rises above such well-entrenched suspicion and hostility.

The theme of reconciliation suggests a number of related issues that also have relevance for contemporary Christian-Muslim relations. The example of Jesus clearly suggests the following set of attitudes.

A Refusal to Blame or Denigrate

Jesus, along with his fellow Jews, is well aware of the reasons for the history of bitter disputation between Jews and Samaritans (the reasons as

---

26. Okure, *Johannine Approach to Mission*, 96. According to Craig Keener, this is roughly equivalent to defying segregation in the southern United States during the 1950s or apartheid in South Africa in the 1980s—shocking to the holders of power and privilege, difficult and even dangerous (*IVP Bible Background Commentary*, 274).

27. Chapman, *Cross and Crescent*, 55.

28. Spina, *Faith of the Outsider*, 145.

outlined in the previous chapter). He might have used such reasons to justify a description of Samaritans as (and the employment of somewhat anachronistic language is intentional): slanderous, suspicious, hostile, deviant, theologically ignorant, geographically and cultically confused, and (mis)led by an indefensible and mistake-riddled scripture. But his actions and teaching demonstrate an altogether different spirit—as the summary that follows below attempts to demonstrate. This is not to say that Jesus ignores or overlooks some points of disagreement between Jews and Samaritans—a number of them are clearly heard in the encounter in John 4—but both his words and actions offer a different way of thinking about Samaritans. It does not require a large imaginative leap to transpose these attitudes to a contemporary setting of Christian-Muslim relations. To put the conclusion as simply and clearly as possible, and to use a "worst-case" description that is *not* the position of this writer (but is a view held by some Christians): *even if* there might be some reason to describe some aspects of Islam, both past and present, as "slanderous, suspicious, hostile, deviant, theologically ignorant, geographically and cultically confused, and (mis)led by an indefensible and mistake-riddled scripture," the example of Jesus, in both word and deed, clearly requires that this is not to become the settled attitude of his disciples. The example of Jesus offers a firm "no" to any position of denigration and hostility. His example can be summed up in a number of ways that include the following.

A Refusal to Consider Vengeance or to Enact It

In Luke 9:51–56, immediately after the positive affirmation that "whoever is not against you is for you," and not long before Jesus will tell the story of the compassionate Samaritan, Luke recounts Jesus' rebuke of the disciples who want to call down fiery retribution on inhospitable Samaritan villagers (whose rejection is, apparently, based on religious grounds). The example of Jesus in Luke 4—in which he praises a notable military enemy of Israel—certainly implies a refusal to act from motives of vengeance or retaliation; given the story of Naaman, it might even prompt a forgiving spirit. Love for enemies becomes one of the distinctive features of Jesus' ethical teaching. Our earlier discussion also placed considerable emphasis upon Jesus' non-vengeful eschatology.[29] David Bosch, for example, concludes his survey of the portrayal of Samaritans in the Lukan material with the words, "all Luke's stories and parables about Samaritans give evidence to Jesus' refusal to embrace the vengeful sentiments of his compatriots."[30] Moreover, this notion of lack of vengeance is also found in the *inaugurated* eschatology of the Fourth Gospel.[31] In other words, non-vengeance is to be a *present* behavioral attitude, and not simply an expectation of some coming age. The implications of such a dynamic for a divided world are far-reaching (as we shall suggest in our final concluding section below).

Hospitality—a Means and Consequence of Reconciliation

In asking for water in the Samaritan encounter, Jesus is also asking for hospitality[32] and, as the stranger in the encounter, he implicitly acknowledges that acceptance or rejection of the request is entirely in the woman's hands. The careful, even reluctant, responses of the woman indicate her awareness of the barriers she will have to consider and overcome in order to provide the hospitality Jesus is asking for (John 4:9). Nonetheless, a reader finishes the story in no doubt that it is the woman's positive response and witness that leads to the wider Samaritan offer of hospitality to Jesus that follows (4:39–41). Other dimensions of hospitality are also suggested in the story. There is, for example, a link with dialogue. Pierre-François de Béthune points out that dialogue and

---

29. Especially in our discussion of Luke 4; see the Introduction above.

30. Bosch, *Transforming Mission*, 111.

31. Given the rather stark duality of the Fourth Gospel readers might expect John's Jesus to threaten divine wrath against "the world." But this is not what Jesus does. "The theme of divine judgment *is* present. Jesus spoke of God's wrath against unbelievers (3:36) and understood himself as the executioner of that judgment in the end time (5:27–29). But he stated repeatedly and emphatically that he has *not* come into the world to judge it but to save it (3:17; 12:47). . . . *He* does not actively judge, *his words and actions* judge, depending on how people respond to them (3:17–21). John does have many negative things to say about the world, but startlingly he combines them with a non-condemnatory and utterly loving attitude toward the world rather than antipathy for it" (Volf, "Johannine Dualism," 206; original emphasis).

32. Larsen, *Recognizing the Stranger*, 129–31.

Jesus and the Religions

hospitality are two forms of complementary encounter. Participants in dialogue seek to meet each other at the place of shared language. "In short, hospitality acts as an environment for dialogue."³³ Hospitality includes a willingness both to offer entry into one's "own" space and to enter the space of another. Moreover, in both John 4 and in the parable of the compassionate Samaritan, a significant place is given to food, and the giving and receiving of hospitality.³⁴ In his comments on the parable, De Béthune links the Samaritan's willingness to assist with his experience of being an *other*; this is one reason why the church fathers "saw in this Samaritan Jesus himself."³⁵ In settings of religious plurality, these two Samaritan stories model the central importance of relationship, and the receiving of people in the way that Christ did.³⁶ If Jesus holds a Samaritan as an example, contemporary Christians might well learn from Muslims with their "highly developed sense of hospitality."³⁷

Respectful, Constructive, and Practical Dialogue

In the story of the Samaritan woman we saw evidence of a careful contextual framing (by the author/editor of the text and, apparently, by Jesus himself) that affirms the religio-cultural significance of the meeting place. A patient and respectful attitude is also seen in the way that Jesus allows and perhaps even encourages the woman's concerns to lead the dialogue (at least to some extent). Moreover, as Jesus offers her the messianic salvation that comes "from the Jews," he does so "without asking her to become a Jew."³⁸ Both of those dynamics—a willingness

33. De Béthune, *By Faith and Hospitality*, 2–3; quote from 3. See further his *Interreligious Hospitality*.

34. And if the Blakley thesis (discussed in chapter 3 above) is accepted, then the opposite also holds: the intentional withholding of food by the disciples is a clear sign of an inhospitable spirit.

35. De Béthune, *By Faith and Hospitality*, 11.

36. Ibid., 43. Jesus "kept company with people normally on or beyond the borders of respectable society which . . . meant not merely social respectability but religious uprightness, proper covenant behaviour, loyalty to the traditions and hence to the aspirations of Israel" (Wright, *Jesus and the Victory*, 149).

37. Johns, "Islam as a Challenge," 21.

38. Michaels, *Gospel of John*, 252.

Some Implications for the Encounter with Islam

for extended dialogue and the display of genuine cultural respect—have implications for the interreligious encounter today (again, as we shall see in our final conclusions below). One means of ensuring such dialogue and respect will include a willingness to *listen* to what Muslims have to say, For example, are Christians able and willing to hear that many Muslim scholars do believe that a close reading of the Qur'an and Prophet Muhammad support both religious tolerance and freedom?[39]

Outsiders Comprehend What Insiders Do Not Grasp

In the Gospels of John and Luke, it is clear that Samaritans as "outsiders" comprehend what "insiders" do not grasp. The compassionate Samaritan understands and exemplifies the heart of the Law. The Samaritan woman raises the key issues that divide Samaritans from Jews (as Christians and Muslims sometimes do in their conversations with one another) but, nonetheless, she does comprehend what privileged insiders do not. This is illustrated by the sharp contrast, in adjacent chapters in the Gospel of John, between Nicodemus and the Samaritan woman—to the distinct disadvantage of the Pharisee.[40] If, in the woman (symbolic as she is of many others), "different kinds of hierarchy, of ethnicity, gender, and social caste that subordinate and exclude"[41] are moderated or even overcome, is there not the possibility, or at least the hope, that perhaps some of the Christian-Muslim divide might not also be able to be moderated or overcome by means of the openness and humility on display in the story? In the Christian-Muslim encounter are there similar issues? For example, might Christians hear from Muslims reminders of the majestic freedom and sovereignty of God? Might Muslim hear reminders from Christians of the relational tenderness of God?

---

39. See, for example, Saeed, "Islamic Case for Religious Liberty."

40. In particular, Mary Margaret Pazdan has argued that the woman "functions as a contrast figure" to the hostile Jewish response to Jesus after the episode in the temple (John 2:12–25; Pazdan, "Nicodemus and the Samaritan Woman," 145–48). Mariam Francis emphasizes the woman's low status and compares her theological questioning with that of Nicodemus ("Samaritan Woman," 147–48).

41. Munro, "Pharisee and the Samaritan," 722.

Jesus and the Religions

Contested Locations for Worship and Eschatological Answers

The disputed geographical *loci* for divinely approved worship also deserve comment. Michael Jensen perceptively calls Samaria "not exactly foreign territory but not really home soil either." It is almost as if the meeting ground in the story is a place of spiritual indeterminacy; as the Samaritan woman herself reminds Jesus, the proper venue of divine-human encounter is disputed.[42] In writing about the encounter, Jensen points out that in the passage

> Jesus' answer avoids (for the moment) the either-or with which the woman has presented him; and instead points to a future in which these local considerations will be transcended. In fact, this eschatological reality is already present (4:23). In this new age, worship will be "in spirit and in truth"). The terms *spirit* and *truth* inform each other: what is spiritual corresponds to the truth of God himself; and authentic worship is according to God's spiritual nature. Further, the (temporary) cultic practice will be surpassed, as the (temporary) earthly water was surpassed, by the presence of the authentic and lasting spiritual reality.[43]

Is it possible that both Christians and Muslims might find in this affirmation of "worship in spirit and truth" a reminder of the temporality of so much of their difference? That is, an affirmation of the *temporary* nature of all preferred worship locations?[44] The new worship will not take place "in" Mt. Gerizim and "in" Jerusalem; it is to take place "in" Spirit and truth (4:20–24). The essence of the new worship that Jesus advocates is "a conception of worship in which the religious discord between Jews and Samaritans is overcome in a new community of believers who worship in spirit and truth."[45] It is probably significant that Jesus speaks of God as "Father" to the Samaritan woman; it echoes her

---

42. Jensen, "'In Spirit and in Truth,'" 335.

43. Ibid., 338.

44. Such a wish does not ignore or deny the difficulties faced by a potential Muslim dialogue partner in accepting the proffered solution of the Fourth Gospel with its elevated Christology.

45. Boers, *Neither on This Mountain*, 180.

use of "father" to refer to Jacob (John 4:12) and other ancestors (4:20). Perhaps Jesus, by referring to the "Father," makes her appeals to "fathers" obsolete. "From the Johannine point of view, fathers with their cults belong to the past, whereas the hour has already come when the only Father is worshiped by the true worshipers."[46]

The People of God Redefined?

As we have seen a number of times in this volume, Jesus appears to redefine the boundaries of the people of God. In the story of the ten lepers who approach him to ask for healing (Luke 17:11–19), the only one who responds with gratitude and worship, is a Samaritan.[47] "With this identification, Luke has pulled the rug from under any prejudgments concerning . . . who might receive divine benefits . . . ."[48] Placing this insight alongside Jesus' words to the Samaritan woman might suggest that there will be some surprises among the final composition of those who will worship "in spirit and in truth." In the same way that many Second Temple Era Jews would have been surprised at any affirmation that Samaritans could be seen as included in the people of God, so there are a number of Christians who are quite sure that Muslims will not be included among them. Perhaps they too will be surprised.

The parable of the compassionate Samaritan clearly implies that the Samaritan (or one who acts like the Samaritan) embodies the highest ideal of the Torah, and relativizes the temple and its cultus. In other words, external "markers" do not determine a person's true worth or the validity of their ethics. Jesus, especially in the parable of the compassionate Samaritan, "proposes an ethic that is determined neither in relation to the shared codes of social stratification, nor in relation to membership within a particular group, but solely on the basis of an internalized ethical orientation."[49] Might not the application of the same

---

46. Hakola, *Identity Matters*, 100.

47. There may also be echoes here of Luke's programmatic statement in Luke 4:16–30, with its reference to the healing of Naaman the Syrian leper (4:27).

48. Green, *Gospel of Luke*, 625.

49. Knowles, "What Was the Victim Wearing?," 171. He adds that "the shock of unexpected kindness stands in contrast to the portrayal of the Samaritan in a familiar

principle begin to transform Christian and Muslim evaluations of the other in the same way? To what extent might we even say that it is *required* of Christians to consider whether the people of God will exceed traditionally expected boundaries?

An Appeal to Abraham?

The problem of particularism—the apparently exclusive claims of both Christianity and Islam—persists. Each (at least in their classical modes of understanding) unable fully to embrace or to acknowledge that the other might possess the kind of universal validity claimed for itself. But even in the face of this substantial obstacle, an appeal might be made to Abraham, the common ancestor of both religions. The significance of Abraham can perhaps be summed up by two biblical affirmations: Abraham is the "friend of God" (Isa 41:8; Jas 2:23) and the "ancestor of a multitude of nations" (Gen 17:4; cf. 12:2–3). In Islam, he is called *khalil Allah*, "friend of God" and the Qur'an (37:83–113) sees Abraham as modeling obedience to God. With these commonalities in mind, the world's two largest faiths, Christianity and Islam, together with the Judaism out of which they both developed, are often called "the Abrahamic religions" because of the way that Abraham is a foundational figure in all three.[50] Such an appeal to Abraham might be developed in several ways.

(and perhaps unpopular) social and economic role: that of travelling merchant" (171).

50. Not all Christian commentators on Christian-Muslim relations are convinced of the appropriateness of such appeals to Abraham; see, for example, Lodahl, *Claiming Abraham*, 4–5 (who mentions none of the scriptural texts cited in the paragraph). Lodahl is an American evangelical who writes with fellow evangelicals in mind and they are often suspicious of dialogue with Muslims. Nonetheless, it is best to avoid the somewhat sentimental and perhaps tendentious phrase "children of Abraham" that is sometimes used; in which case, "tribes of Abraham," or even Lodahl's more modest phrase "claiming Abraham," may better express the rather elusive nature of the appeal.

Some Implications for the Encounter with Islam

ABRAHAM AS MODEL OF AN INCLUSIVE-EXCLUSIVE DIALECTIC

As already noted (in chapter 1 above), the Torah makes clear that Abraham enjoyed a positive relationship with the various cultures and religions that he encountered on his travels. An appeal to this example of Abraham is made by an anonymous author writing for an online journal of a British college in 2007. S/he concedes that this apparently healthy relationship did not mean the absence of problems between Abraham and others, but adds that "when relationships faltered, Abraham mediated reconciliation. He modelled inclusiveness toward the *other*, while maintaining a deep devotion to God. Another way of saying this is that Abraham loved God with his whole being as well as loving his neighbours. Abraham founded and remained in a distinct community, with boundaries flexible enough to allow others to join, while remaining on good terms with other distinct communities. Moreover, Abraham defended those communities, including Sodom and Gomorrah. Abraham's love of the *other* was unconditional. This brings to mind Jesus' habit of unconditionally blessing any with needs."[51]

The author of the article believes that Abraham provides "a model of horizontal social inclusiveness and vertical divine exclusiveness" and calls this an "inclusive/exclusive dialectic."[52] The author then illustrates from the narrative of the ten lepers, of whom all but one (a Samaritan) remains ungrateful (Luke 17:12–19) and from the apparent willingness of Jesus to heal and exorcize without regard to faith commitments (Matt 4:23–24).

ABRAHAM AS A MODEL FOR MISSION

The anonymous author cited above goes on to point out the way in which some other features of Abraham's life can function as a model for mission today. The author does not directly draw attention to Christian-Muslim relations but the conclusions are highly relevant. As portrayed

---

51. "Kiss of Heaven," 4. Presumably the writer remains anonymous either because of living and working in a Muslim setting, or because of the disapproval with which their opinions might be received in a conservative Christian setting.

52. Ibid.

in the Torah, Abraham has a range of dealings with Egyptians, Hittites, Philistines and Amorites and, in most of these, he is supportive, cooperative, benevolent, and respectful of the political authority of the neighbouring nations. He does not display neither attitudes of superiority nor inclinations towards the assertion of power over them—despite the divine promises of greatness that are his.[53] Rather, Abraham's attitude is "characterised by blessing . . . and reconciliation when relationships suffer. . . . He neither demonizes nor excludes" the nations he has to deal with. Moreover,

> Abraham respects the freedom of his neighbours to make their own religious and cultural choices. There is no evidence that Abraham sought to coerce his neighbours into accepting his faith or belief system. This is a divinely rooted ethic. The God of the Bible grants all freedom of choice. Jesus' parable of the wheat and the tares illustrate this. Christians in mission follow this pattern, avoiding extremist religious behaviour that denies others the freedom to differ. Abraham lives with the tension of dual authority (cf. Matt. 22:21; Rom 13:1–2). God secures Abraham's ultimate allegiance. But Abraham respects the authority which his neighbours possess.[54]

Abraham is, in effect, subverting the universal but dangerous tendency toward "tribalism" and notions of ethnic and religious superiority. There are, of course, other dimensions to Christian mission besides Abraham-like good relations with political and other figures,[55] but the author of the article concludes that Abraham provides a model for mission as he blesses the peoples he meets. Moreover, Abraham "affirms their liberty of choice, but does not denigrate them when they do not choose God. In fact, he intercedes for blessing on their behalf. . . . Abraham's life provides an essential picture of mission, a foretaste of the

---

53. His modesty is seen, for example, in the way that he pays for Sarah's burial plot at Hebron even though Yahweh had previously promised that the land was his.

54. Ibid.

55. "Abraham does not give us the total picture of mission. In our day, we add to that the power and message of the cross, the power of the indwelling Spirit of God, and the gifts and richness of the community of Jesus" (ibid., 5).

Kingdom of God, a kiss of heaven."⁵⁶ Given the importance of Abraham for all the Semitic faiths, his example in these ways is surely significant. If the article's analysis is correct, Abraham becomes an advocate of religious freedom—itself an issue in Christian-Muslim relations.⁵⁷ A case can also be made for Jesus as one who endorsed a universal ideal in which Israel would live "peacefully, Abraham-like, with other ethnic groups in the land."⁵⁸

Some Changing Attitudes

It might once have been said, especially by those not among their number, that the very features we have endorsed—well-informed understanding and a willingness for patient dialogue—are not often found among theologically conservative Christians. But, over the last few decades, that has begun to change. Such "theologically conservative Christians" are mentioned here because they often have the activist inclinations and missional intent that makes them the most likely to encounter Muslims (for example) in the Global South, or to comment on them from the relative isolation of their enclaves in the Global North. In fact, a strong case can be made that, in terms of enabling Muslims to understand the cultural and justice traditions of the West, religious conservatives are best placed to explain such Western ideals. As Ross McCullough argues, despite the way in which Western liberals and secularists often think themselves best fitted for this interpretive task, "there is reason to think only conservatives can effectively carry it out. In particular, only committed, religious conservatives can effectively address it, because only we have the traditions and institutions at hand

---

56. Ibid. For one of many examples, see Gen 18:16–33 (where Abraham intercedes for Sodom).

57. This is a much-discussed issue; see, for example, Muck and Adeney, *Christianity Encountering World Religions*, 18–28; Volf, *Allah*, chs. 11–12.

58. Freyne, "Jesus and the 'Servant,'" 113. Freyne's argument is that Jesus, despite his journeys to the borders of the land that suggest an awareness of the vision for the reestablishment of a greater Israel as espoused by many of his contemporaries, does not harbor territorial aims. Rather, his focus on the lost sheep of the house of Israel coincides with a more universal ideal in which Israel would live peacefully, Abraham-like, with other groups.

for bringing together Western justice and an uncompromised commitment to God." McCullough continues:

> Better than anybody, we know that a committed believer will not enter the public square on the secularist's terms. The false dilemma of secularism—accept the benefits of the West and an anemic faith, or retain a robust faith and continued backwardness—is no help to the Muslim struggling to bring together the Western and Islamic traditions of justice into a system that can speak persuasively in the modern world. The secular pedant... is not a helpful interlocutor for one struggling with questions of Creation and sin, of reason and revelation, of human and divine justice. But the Muslim and I can talk together: of truth, and God, and good and evil; of the sanctity of life and the perfecting of people; of the errors in his culture and the errors in mine precisely as errors and not mere differences. . . . I do not mean to deny all the differences between my creed and the Muslim's. I mean only that we—traditional Catholics, Protestants, and Jews—are the natural interlocutors for Muslims in the West. We have the most to teach them, and we are best placed to learn from them in turn.[59]

This writer agrees. For these and related reasons the trends discussed in three recent publications are both interesting and even encouraging.[60]

One example of a constructive and theologically conservative appraisal of Islam is found in Peter Kreeft's volume, *Between Allah and Jesus*. He is concerned to do justice to the beliefs and life practices of truly devout Muslims—but in a balanced way. In the Introduction to his book he lists twelve things that "Christians should *not* learn from Muslims" (10–11: anger at Western civilization, a proneness to violence, the treatment of apostates and of women etc) but immediately follows that with a list of "what Christians *obviously* should learn from Muslims" (11–12: the absoluteness of God and moral laws and submission to them, the sacredness of family, children and hospitality, faithful-

---

59. McCullough, "Westernizing Islam," 18.

60. Page references to the three volumes are found in brackets in the paragraphs that follow; original emphasis is retained.

ness in religious practice, and so on). He contrasts (18–19) what he calls "two Islams" (one of peace and divine justice, the other aggressive and intolerant, even to fellow Muslims) and "two Christianities" (one that is faithful to the NT, the other that accommodates the contemporary world). Kreeft goes on to discuss similarities and differences between the two traditions in a way that parallels our own approach—by means of persistent, sympathetic, and well-informed dialogue. Kreeft invites his readers to reflect on questions concerning the nature of God, the nature and content of divine revelation, the character of morality (public and private), and the future of the world—all by means of a series of dialogues between a devout but curious Muslim student and a variety of Christians.

A second example is provided by Miroslav Volf in his *Allah: A Christian Response*. Volf's intention is to enquire into what he calls "the central 'ideological' question in relations between those two faiths—the identity and character of God" (16). His conclusion is that, to the extent that Christians and Muslims embrace the normative teachings of their faiths about God, and strive to love God, "they believe in a common God" and "they *worship* that same true God" (123).[61] He acknowledges and does not minimize the presence of differences and pays particular attention to what he calls the critical themes of "The one God and the Holy Trinity," "God's mercy" and "Eternal and unconditional love" (chapters 7, 8, 9).[62] For example, there are some differences between

---

61. In a little more detail, the two faiths believe (with bracketed references to the biblical and Qur'anic texts): there is only one God, the one and only divine being (Mark 12:29; Muhammad 47:19). God created everything that is not God (Gen 1:1; Al Shura 42:11). God is different from everything that is not God (1 Tim 6:6; Al An'am 6:103). God is good (1 John 4:16; Al Buruj 85:14). Both Muslims and Christians believe in adherence to what Jesus called the two greatest commandments: Love God with our whole being (Deut 6:5; Al Zimar 39:45); love neighbors as ourselves (Matt 7:12; Hadith) (*Allah*, 97–101, 104–5). That is, "Muslims and Christians agree on the following six claims about God: 1. There is only one God, the one and only divine being. 2. God created everything that is not God. 3. God is radically different from everything that is not God. 4. God is good. 5. God commands that we love God with our whole being. 6. God commands that we love our neighbors as ourselves" (*Allah*, 110).

62. Although Volf concedes the difficulties for Muslims of Christian Trinitarian belief he has, according to Sidney Griffith, failed to acknowledge the depth of the problem in that "the Qur'an does not reject only unorthodox Christian doctrines of

some of God's commands in the Bible and related commands in the Qur'an (108-9) but Volf also points out that "the differences that exist *between* Muslim and Christian understandings of God are . . . loosely analogous to the corresponding differences that exist *within* the Christian and Muslim faiths" (124). To the question of right beliefs as necessary for right worship, Volf adds right actions (119-23). And he sounds a critical note as he concludes that, within both traditions, "1. A pattern of wrong practices overshadows correct beliefs about God and exposes those who engage in them as worshippers of false gods. 2. Wrong beliefs about God do not invalidate right practices as worship required by God" (123). There are areas that Volf chooses not to discuss: "I leave the questions of salvation and eternal destiny aside" (13). And a number of his conclusions will continue to attract critical scrutiny.[63] But there are also areas that link directly with the themes of our book, especially Part IV of *Allah*, "Living under the Same Roof," which discusses the difficult issues of prejudice, proselytism, mission and religious freedom as well as the potential of partnership and the pursuit of the common good.

Finally, mention might be made of the helpful record of a far-reaching discussion between Muslims and (evangelical) Christians about many of the most difficult issues raised by the encounter between the two religious traditions. It is found in a volume edited by Abu-Nimer and Augsburger: *Peace-Building by, between and beyond*

---

the Trinity, as some have thought; by denying the divinity of Jesus, the Qur'an rejects the entire doctrine of the Trinity, root and branch. Rather than glossing over this difference, the more sound position is to admit the incommensurability of Christian and Muslim views of this radical article of the Christian creed" (Griffith, review of *Allah* by Volf, 57).

63. See, for example, the comments of Griffith who, while welcoming the book, notes that Volf's intended readership seems to be Protestant Christians. Griffith is critical of what he calls Volf's "dubious desire to convict Pope Benedict XVI of thinking that Muslims worship another God than do Christians" and what he calls Volf's neglect of "the influential thought of other major writers on Christian-Muslim relations, most notably the Catholic Louis Massignon and the Anglican Kenneth Cragg." He also points to Volf's overlooking of "what those Christians who actually lived with Muslims for centuries in the Arabic-speaking world have had to say on the subject" (Griffith, review of *Allah* by Volf, 56.)

Some Implications for the Encounter with Islam

Muslims and Evangelical Christians.[64] The discussions and conclusions are too numerous and detailed to summarize here but it is helpful to list the subject areas covered in the four sections of the volume. They are: (1) peace building, nonviolence, and conflict resolution (including forgiveness, reconciliation, war, and just peacemaking); (2) religious diversity and identity (especially theologies of pluralism and how social location influences religious identity); (3) interfaith and intrafaith dialogue (dealing not only with peaceful coexistence, and overcoming fear of interreligious encounter but also with the more difficult topics of with apostasy and proselytization); and (4) contemporary issues such as human rights, conflict transformation, and a case study of a long-term example of interfaith dialogue. The volume provides an actual example of the way that concrete and fruitful progress can be made when fully committed Christians and Muslims meet in a cordial and co-operative spirit that neither ignores particularity and difference nor advocates an unobtainable consensus and unity. Mention should also be made of some other recent notable volumes by Christian authors that display a similar mix of accurate presentation and fair-minded assessment of Muslim views, and that neither ignore nor fixate upon the undoubted differences.[65]

With all this in mind, we turn to a summary and concluding discussion in our final chapter.

---

64. The contents are the most substantial of the scholarly presentations and responses made at two consultations, in April 2005 and April 2006, convened by faculty of Fuller Theological Seminary, the Salam Institute of Peace and Justice, and the Islamic Society of North America. (Some of the book's case studies refer to highly specific and localized settings with limited transferable significance.)

65. For example (to mention a sample of recent volumes, with subtitles, across the spectrum of theologically conservative Christian views): Lodahl, *Claiming Abraham* (aspects of this work were briefly discussed above); McDermott, *Can Evangelicals Learn?*; Pinnock, *Wideness in God's Mercy*; Chapman, *Cross and Crescent.*

6

Some Conclusions about Jesus, Gentiles, and Samaritans

AMONG THE QUESTIONS WITH which this book started were: Why and how did Christianity and Judaism pull apart in the first century of the Common Era? What led to this emergence of Christian distinctiveness when the Christian movement clearly began in a thoroughly Jewish context? What we have seen suggests that the actions and attitudes of Jesus himself must be included among the answers. Concerning the *Jewishness* of which Jesus was heir, with its predominantly negative assessment of all things Gentile and Samaritan, Peter Carrell asks: "Is it possible that Jesus was Jewish . . . but also simultaneously post-Jewish in the sense of being a Jew threatening to turn all things Jewish (culture, religion, politics, economics) upside-down and even . . . beginning to turn threat to achievement?"[1] Jesus' attitude to Gentiles and Samaritans might well be one example of this dynamic, given what we have seen in the four Gospels. Although the encounters of Jesus with Gentiles and Samaritans are few in number, each of them is significant because of the way in which they usually display genuine dialogue, compassionate response and even forms of affirmation by Jesus as he stretches the received understanding of the possibility and place of Gentiles and Samaritans within the coming Rule of God; in fact, he sees their responses as signs of the inaugurated kingdom.

1. Carrell, review of *The Parting of the Ways*, 4.

Some Conclusions about Jesus, Gentiles, and Samaritans

These meetings and responses generate comments by Jesus himself; when they and other aspects of his teaching and symbolic actions are viewed through the lenses of recent hermeneutical approaches (especially reader-centered approaches), they suggest an exemplary Christology that has potentially transformative and missional implications for concrete interreligious relations in today's religiously plural world. The example of Jesus models both an appropriately sympathetic (and yet not uncritical) appraisal of religion, and the religions, and mission to them. We have suggested that this exemplary Christology can even offer a new understanding of the Christian-Muslim encounter derived from an analysis of Jewish-Samaritan hostility during the Second Temple Era—and Jesus' radically transformative attitude towards it. What the example of Jesus discloses for the interreligious encounters of our own day may be summarized under a number of related, complementary and, in places, somewhat overlapping headings.

Jesus Commends Certain Attitudes and Behaviors Shown by Some Gentiles and Samaritans

Jesus is reported as commending examples of faith, humility and praxis that he encounters in "outsiders," both Gentile and Samaritan. Some of these individuals receive healing as a result, and some are the object of comment (both positive and negative) in a number of places in his teaching as well. His negative comments, while not unexpected from the lips of a Jewish person of the time, do not cannot obscure the commendations that he also offers.[2] In the Nazareth pericope (Luke

2. The negative features may be summarized as follows: Gentiles are a closed group, greeting only one another (Matt 5:47); their prayers are repetitive, empty and ineffective (Matt 6:7); they strive for material things (Matt 6:32; Luke 12:30–31); and they provide an example of authoritative leadership to be avoided (Mark 10:42–43). Jesus appears to refer to them as "dogs" (Matt 7:6; Mark 7:27) and instructs the community that a member who is expelled by the church is to be "treated as a tax collector and a Gentile," that is, as an outsider to be shunned (Matt 18:17). According to Glasser, Jesus appears— at least in places—to describe the Gentiles as "spiritually ignorant, verbose in their formal religious activity, materialistically inclined, and hostile toward God" (*Announcing the Kingdom*, 313; he appears to restrict his comments to Matt 6:7, 32; Mark 10:33–34). There is no reason to deny or to attempt to diminish the force of these negative comments; they fairly represent aspects of Jewish opinion about Gentiles.

4:16–30), Jesus appeals to the faith of the Gentile widow of Zarephath and he also employs Naaman the Syrian as an example of humility. In both stories, Israel receives *from Gentiles* rebuke for what it was blind to—its religious and nationalist insularity. The dynamics of faith and humility that Jesus affirms in Luke 4 are also encountered by him in person in the stories of the centurion/official and the Syrophoenician mother. Faith and humility are seen in the attitude of the centurion who calls Jesus "Lord" and expresses unlimited confidence in the authority of Jesus to heal. As we saw in chapter 2 above, this "display of exemplary faith by a complete outsider" (Garland), and the healing to which it leads, reinforces the comment of Donald Baillie that we also noted: "it is plain that Jesus came to single out this faith-attitude as a very vital one and to attach unlimited importance to it." When ten leprosy sufferers are healed, they remain ungrateful except for the gratitude and praise displayed by a Samaritan (Luke 17:12–19).

The account of the healing of the centurion's servant has the NT's first explicit mention of "faith" and Jesus is willing to contrast such faith favorably what he finds "in Israel" and, by implication, with the "little faith" of his own disciples. We also noted the faith displayed by the Syrophoenician mother; her faith is full of humility and insight, it is extravagant, tenacious and displays an unconditional confidence and trust. Even in the face of Jesus' reminder of the gulf that separates Jews from Gentiles (and he reminds the Samaritan woman of a similar divide) it becomes clear in the story of both women, and the centurion/official, that what determines God's blessing is neither Jewishness, nor conventionally appropriate behavior, but receptive faith. As Wendy Cotter observes, the examples of persistent petitioners who are affirmed by Jesus demand of disciples "the abandonment of usual criteria of what is 'worthy,' to focus on the quality of faith, regardless of status or class."[3]

Our discussion of the Nazareth incident sounded a note that is heard in all four Gospels: that some Gentiles and Samaritans respond to Jesus, or display behaviors of which he approves, while the chosen people hesitate or even reject him. The encounters show the way in which "outsiders" may comprehend what insiders do not. In the Gospels of John and Luke there is an implicit warning that even Samaritans as out-

3. Cotter, *Christ of the Miracle Stories*, 7.

Some Conclusions about Jesus, Gentiles, and Samaritans

siders understand what "insiders" do not grasp. The Samaritan woman repeatedly raises the key issues that divided Samaritans from Jews—as Muslims can sometimes do with their differences with Christians—but, nonetheless, she does comprehend what privileged insiders fail to understand. Over against the attitude and actions of a priest and a Levite, Jesus commends the attitude and the actions of the compassionate Samaritan (Luke 10:29-37), an implied description that would function as a startling oxymoron in the minds of his hearers. In the parable, the Samaritan is the defining actor in the story; he knows and acts out the heart of the Law better than the two Jewish religious leaders. Nonetheless, it is neither Samaritans nor Samaritanism that is exemplary, any more than the "formal" religious faith (whatever it was) of the Syrophoenician mother or the centurion/official is commended. The contemporary church might well consider the implications of these examples of faith, humility and right behavior. They might even stand as a rebuke for some of the Christian community's attitudes towards those of other faiths, given that Jesus is seen to affirm at least some dimensions of the faith of some outsiders—difficult as it is to translate what he affirms into a contemporary context of the encounter with those of other "faith."[4] At the very least, the encounters suggest that these marginalized outsiders "actually provide a model for the virtues to be sought by followers of Jesus."[5]

Jesus and the Religions: Universality and Continuity

Questions about interreligious meeting are not abstract or speculative in Scripture; they are raised by the large number of biblical encounters that have an interreligious dimension to them and one account lists

---

4. The proposed complementary volume to this present book will look at this issue. Some clarification is found in some of the writings of Wilfred Cantwell Smith, and in Paul Tillich's *Dynamics of Faith*, and Terence Tilley's recent *Faith* (see especially 102-27 on "Assessing Faith"), even though the latter two works do not touch upon faith as commended by Jesus.

5. Cotter, *Christ of the Miracle Stories*, 254. Cotter also writes that the accounts "ask the follower to learn from these petitioners, and to emulate the adamantine character of their faith" (13).

some 239 of them.⁶ In the Gospels these questions are raised for a reader by the actual encounters between Jesus and Gentiles and Samaritans. In Scripture as a whole, there appear to be two perspectives concerning the religions. Our analysis has outlined two contrasting attitudes within the Judaisms of the Second Temple Era towards the Gentile world: a negative stream and one whose tone is more positive.⁷ A generally positive assessment of religion, religious desire and the religions can flow from this second stream; multiple points of contact, convergence, complementarity, and similarity between the religions become apparent.

The more positive assessment also includes the notion of some kind of continuity. Given the overwhelmingly Jewish ethos of Galilee, it seems highly plausible that Jesus advocated some kind of continuity with the hopes and expectations of the Jewish religious tradition inherited by him and his first followers. As well as continuity with Jewish tradition, Jesus also draws upon a regional Galilean ethos as seen, for example, in the presence of distinctively Galilean imagery in his parables. There is also a degree of continuity between the message of Jesus and the Samaritanism he encountered. These are related faith traditions and the thirteen points of comparison detailed in the previous chapter are intended to show similarities between these two so-called Abrahamic traditions (Judaism and Samaritanism) in order to make suggestions about the relationship between two other of the traditions (Christianity and Islam). As we have seen, for example from Miroslav Volf, the commonalities between Christianity and Islam can—with care—be affirmed, alongside some substantial and persistent differences. One of Volf's conclusions is that, to the extent that Christians and Muslims embrace the normative teachings of their faiths about God, and strive to love God, "they believe in a common God" and "they *worship* that same true God."⁸ (The refusal of vengeance is another feature of this universality and discussion will return to it.)

---

6. See Muck and Adeney, *Christianity Encountering World Religions*, 379–85. This writer believes the number should be set a little higher by the inclusion of Jesus' encounters with Samaritans given that, in Jewish eyes, Samaritanism is functionally equivalent to Gentile religion.

7. See the first part of chapter 1 above.

8. Volf, *Allah*, 123; original emphasis.

Some Conclusions about Jesus, Gentiles, and Samaritans

Our reading of the parable of the compassionate Samaritan has pointed in a similar direction; it is the disclosure of the compassionate heart of the Samaritan that indicates that his intention is in conformity with the divine will. Although Jesus' intention was hardly to endorse or promote Samaritanism as such, there is an implied continuity of some kind between the Samaritan's instinctive action and the divine intention of love that is the heart of covenant law. Despite reminders of the enmity between Samaritans and Jews in John 4 (some of them suggested by the Samaritan woman herself), Jesus does not denigrate Samaritanism but clearly assumes a degree of continuity; he assumes the woman understands, from her own faith, what he is claiming.

Given such continuity, it follows that Christians can and should pursue respectful, constructive and practical dialogue with people of other faiths.[9] In the story of the Samaritan woman we saw evidence of careful contextual framing (by the author / editor of the text, and apparently by Jesus himself) in order to affirm the religio-cultural significance of the meeting place. A patient and respectful attitude is also seen in the way that Jesus allows, and perhaps even encourages, the woman's concerns to lead the dialogue, at least to some extent. Both of those dynamics—a willingness for extended dialogue and the display of genuine respect—have constructive implications for the interreligious encounter today. It is Jesus' weariness, thirst and vulnerability that launches the dialogue with the Samaritan woman. It is a response to the vulnerability and distress of a traveler that leads to the Samaritan rescue. Human need is seen as a starting point in the story of the Samaritan woman and the parable of the compassionate Samaritan. Such a starting point may also have some advantages in the Christian-Muslim encounter in which religious starting points can (and often do) quickly become highly contested. Starting with human need may also give opportunity to display the divine characteristics of universal compassion and practical mercy as modeled in the parable.

Christians often want discussion to start with religion; Jesus in these examples starts with human need. They prefer religious points of contacts; Jesus (as with his parables) seems willing to begin in other

---

9. For a not uncritical defense of such dialogue (and with a mainly non-theistic religious tradition in mind), see Robinson, "Christian-Hindu Dialogue."

places. Physical proximity and a willingness to engage are required. Robert Goldenberg offers a telling comparative comment from the world of early Judaism. "Rabbinic literature is full of encounters—sometimes friendly, sometimes hostile—between rabbis and Gentile interlocutors, and many of these conversations touch on fundamental religious questions, but the rabbinic participant in these discussions is never depicted as having begun the conversation. It appears that the ancient rabbis preferred to have as little to do with non-Jews as possible."[10] In the story of the compassionate Samaritan, it is a Samaritan who implements the love requirement of the Torah in an exemplary fashion.[11] Although Jesus' intention was not any kind of endorsement or promotion of Samaritanism as such, there is an implied continuity of some kind between the Samaritan's instinctive action and the heart of covenantal law and love.

A display of both human religious desire and genuine dialogue are also features of the encounter between Jesus and the Samaritan woman. In writing about the story, Michael Jensen notes that "the overlapping levels and types of desire connect the dialogue that follows, which otherwise seems to jump rapidly from topic to topic."[12] In other words, Jesus is both alert to and connects with the religious interests and human desires of the woman. There is genuine dialogue; he treats the woman with non-condescending respect. One commentator summarizes the passage as the Samaritan woman learning that salvation does indeed come from the Jews and through Messiah Jesus, "who reaches out and includes all faithful worshippers within the divine design."[13] Both of those dynamics—a willingness for extended dialogue and the display of genuine respect—have implications for the interreligious encounter today. In the story in John 4, the Gospel writer begins his narrative with a careful delineation of the physical and cultural context. If, as we have

10. Goldenberg, "Pagan Religions," in *Eerdmans Encyclopedia of Early Judaism*, 1016.

11. The Samaritan, "who notoriously misinterpreted purity laws and thereby, in Jewish eyes, failed to obey them, illustrates the overriding importance of the love commandment in [an] . . . arresting, not to say shocking form" (Bauckham, "Scrupulous Priest," 488).

12. Jensen, "'In Spirit and in Truth,'" 336.

13. Cummins, "John," in Vanhoozer, *Theological Interpretation*, 67.

argued, the passage might serve as a model for cross-cultural ministry, then this delineation is intentional. Perhaps it is even a reminder of the principle announced in the prologue to the Gospel: that "the Word became flesh and lived among us" (1:14).

The context of the encounter plays an important role in the story. In the narrative, the reader is quickly alerted to the religio-cultural significance of the place to which Jesus has been divinely guided. A number of key markers of Samaritan identity and history are indicated: Mt. Gerizim, Jacob's well, Joseph's tomb and Shechem are all within view. Perhaps this is intended to reassure any Samaritan readers and hearers of the story, but at the same time some uncomfortable reminders might also be heard. As Eric Wyckoff points out, the Samaritans' "ancestral link to the patriarchs is being asserted here and the prejudice against them denied, though in an indirect and non-condescending way. The enmity, however, is also made physically present by the context. This narrative will unfold literally in the shadow of the once-proud city and of the ruins of the revered sanctuary that had been destroyed by an army from Jerusalem."[14] Despite such reminders (with some of them suggested by the Samaritan woman herself), Jesus does not denigrate Samaritanism.

Moreover, a theological basis for the encounter is also apparent in the narrative. The opening words of the account imply a theological reading of the story as a whole. It becomes "necessary" (*edei*) for Jesus to pass through Samaria (John 4:4; most Jews avoided Samaria even though it was the shortest route between Judea and Galilee). This is not simply a necessity of convenience or geography. As often in John, there is a second and deeper meaning—a divine imperative is made clear to the reader.[15] Most commentators see here an implication of the divine necessity of Jesus' presence among the Samaritans.[16] Such an imperative

14. Wyckoff, "Jesus in Samaria," 91.

15. Its importance in the Fourth Gospel is seen in the story's placement in John. The word used (*dei*) is the fourth and perhaps even the climax of a series of similarly constructed statements: *it is necessary* to be born from above (3:7); *it is necessary* that the Son of Man be lifted up (3:14); *it is necessary* for Jesus to increase (3:30); *it is necessary* for him to go through Samaria (4:4). See also: John 9:4; 10:16; 12:34; 20:9—and elsewhere in the present story: 4:20, 24.

16. A good example of a detailed elaboration of this point is found in Okure, *Johannine Approach to Mission*, 83–86.

suggests, in turn, not only divine approval for mission into Samaria but also for its method: humble encounter framed in contextually sensitive categories, and respectful (and yet culture-transcending) dialogue as well. The contemporary implications of such an example are obvious.

The developing argument of this volume has repeatedly drawn attention to examples in the encounters and teaching that display the (divine) characteristics of universal compassion and mercy. The encounter with the Samaritan woman contains these elements and they are especially clear in the parable of the compassionate Samaritan. As Philip Esler movingly puts it, the behavior of the Samaritan was "a compassion with few limits, as shown in the rich and loving detail which Jesus . . . supplies . . . [Luke 10:34-35]. The force of this case drives one to conclude that compassion which transcends legally sanctioned ethnic boundaries and discriminations when faced with real human need is a superior form of human behaviour than continuing to live within their limits."[17] The conclusion to the parable appeals simply and directly to behavior that reflects the divine character of mercy (Luke 10:37)—mercy that both extends across ethnic/religious boundaries and is found in the surprising example of the Samaritan. Once again, behavior is modeled that has transformative implications for all who would follow the example suggested. The closing verses of the story of the Samaritan woman also sound a universal note with their confession of Jesus as "the savior of the world." Herman Ridderbos catches well the significance of a message that clearly discloses that "salvation is not only for Jews. . . . The fact that God loved the world in [Christ] could hardly be more clearly evident than here; and this was undoubtedly the compelling reason that the Evangelist took so much care to include among the deliberately selected encounters between Jesus and people this encounter with a Samaritan woman."[18]

Jesus and the Religions: Dialogue

This volume attempts to draw upon a somewhat neglected asset for the contemporary Christian community: the example of Jesus him-

17. Esler, "Jesus and the Reduction," 343.
18. Ridderbos, *Gospel according to John*, 172.

self as a model for dialogue. Care must be taken not to exaggerate the place of dialogue as a means of communicating the Gospel in the NT. However, there is often the assumption among many Christians that proclamation—in the sense of monologue—is the only biblically based or biblically endorsed means of communicating the Christian message. This writer's previous research has found that the principled and even pragmatic reasons usually advanced for interfaith dialogue (both informal and formal) are reasons that, with care, can even be suggested to evangelical and Pentecostal Christians who usually believe there to be few or even no benefits to be gained from dialogue and interreligious cooperation.[19] Pragmatic reasons such as enhanced understanding, the avoidance of social conflict, the bridging of communal divides, and even the multiplication of the social capital that exists within and between diverse faith communities—all of these can be discussed with evangelicals and Pentecostals. The reasons offer at least some evidence of beneficial consequences that might prove to be equally persuasive for conservative Christians of a pragmatic disposition: dialogue can be shown to produce at least some good results—and without compromising Christian self-understanding or indulging in the denigration of other faiths. In a postmodern context a narrative retelling of these lived examples of fruitful and intentional encounters across religious boundaries may be helpfully reassuring—and even inspiring—to those Christians who wonder about *how* they might live interreligiously in a faithful way. One distinct advantage of the exemplary Christology advocated in this study is that it helps enable a christocentric approach in the interreligious encounter as it draws attention to the considerable openness of Jesus in his reported meeting with Gentiles and others.

Christianity has always seen itself as a contextual faith so, alongside this appeal to some biblical precedents for some kind of dialogue, the contemporary globalized context can also play a significant role in shaping Christian attitudes towards others. Traditional boundaries and identity markers are challenged and blurred in most areas of human life (economic, ethical, cultural, ethnic, intellectual and religious) as

19. See Robinson, *Christians Meeting Hindus*, chs. 2–4; and Robinson, "Christian-Hindu Dialogue." And for some constructive evangelical responses to religious pluralism see, for example, the articles in *Evangelical Interfaith Dialogue* 1/2 (Spring 2010).

global interdependence becomes increasingly apparent. As the center of gravity of Christianity shifts from the Western church to the church in the majority world, there are rich possibilities for enhancing theological reflection and praxis, especially in the context of interreligious relations, as Western churches learn from those who have long lived with the realities of religious plurality.

The global context is also one in which complaints are heard about conflicts that are said to be caused or exacerbated by interreligious tensions. This can even be a complaint born of exasperation at the failure of the religions visibly to realize the potential they possess for communal and global harmony. In a number of settings there can be pressure from governments—usually for pragmatic reasons such as the avoidance of social conflict—for religions to be less confrontational and more accommodating in their attitudes towards each another. Nonetheless, it might also be the case that, "put simply, religion is perhaps our last hope for civilized, humane cooperation among the peoples of the world."[20] And, among Christians, questions about the content and shape of a faithful and yet contextually appropriate response to a multifaith world are increasingly heard. New synergies are emerging for what the world is *becoming* and these have the potential to replace synergies related to how the world *used to be*.

Jesus and the Religions: Particularity, Discontinuity, and Mission

Alongside the positive implications for interreligious relations of universality, continuity and a willingness for dialogue that we have just noted, there are other features of the encounter with the Samaritan woman that invite comment. There is, for example, no missing the clear evidence of dissonance between Judaism and Samaritanism, even though both parties in the story of the Samaritan woman acknowledge that the well water was provided by Jacob himself, a patriarch revered by both Jews and Samaritans. The discord serves as a reminder of the differences (sometimes to the point of incommensurability) among the world's religious traditions. This includes Christianity and Islam where

20. Muck and Adeney, *Christianity Encountering World Religions*, 30.

it can also be argued (as we saw with Lodahl) that key topics illustrate significant differences between the two faiths: for example, the place and function of the Qur'an and of Christ, the understanding of revelation, God, humanity, and the world as a whole.

Given the comments that Jesus makes about the woman, and aspects of her Samaritan religion, it might be argued that both the negative dimension that surfaces in the encounter, along with some more positive affirmations (as we have seen above), offer insight into the human religious condition.[21] What Michael Jensen discerns in the passage as "problems of dissatisfaction and incompletion, and also of untruth and ignorance—we might say *inauthenticity*" in the woman's life, might be applied more widely to the human religious condition. The woman is lacking in knowledge ("if you knew") both of Jesus' true identity and of "the gift of God" (v. 10). For Jensen, "the 'if you knew' points to ignorance of self as well as to an ignorance of what God gives" (336).

Any attempted deployment of these dynamics of the exposure of humanity's ignorance and moral shortcoming, and of Jesus as the divine revealer in either an evaluative sense or a missional setting, requires extreme care—not least because their judgments will not appear to be entirely self-evident to their hearers! The application of this principle to the universal search for self-realization and a transcendent reference point would need to be handled with sensitivity, especially if a specific religious tradition is named and discussed. Christians would do well to begin any such critique with scrutiny of their own religious tradition; Jesus' prophetic critique of his own Judaism provides a bracing example here. If religion is the search for the divine, then Jesus certainly presents himself both here in the encounter with the Samaritan woman and elsewhere—especially in the Fourth Gospel—as its divinely given revelation and pathway.[22] Such christocentrism appears to be an inescapable part of Christian self-understanding. Craig Koester's analysis of

21. Some of this paragraph, and the three paragraphs that follow, draw on Jensen, "'In Spirit and in Truth,'" 334–41, with page numbers for quotes from the article indicated in parentheses, and original emphasis retained. Jensen's is a philosophical-cultural study of aspects of "inauthenticity," but parts of his analysis are entirely appropriate for a discussion of religion and the religions.

22. This is what the Fourth Gospel will later present as the way, the truth, and the life that is Jesus (14:6).

the phrase "savior of the world" (John 4:42) leads him to conclude that the language employed by John is a deliberate attempt to show that the Samaritan confession signals a move "to true worship of God, and beyond national identity . . . to become true people of God."[23] Particularity is both affirmed and relativized.

If religion is a human construct, then this dialogue suggests that it might be compared with the water that the woman herself concedes offers only a temporary quenching of thirst and necessitates repeated returns to the well (4:15). This stands in strong contrast with the "living water" that can bring an end to thirst (4:13–14). The dualism found here contrasts the transitory and inauthentic sphere of earthly things with the eternal and authentic heavenly sphere. If religion is the human search for the divine, then Jesus' dialogue with the Samaritan woman comments sharply on that quest. Jesus shows the woman that, as Jensen puts it, her "thirst for life is not just a matter of her repeated visits to the well." Her irregular marital life (however construed) "is an echo of her sequence of visits to drink the earthly water" (340). In fact, the "exposure of the woman to herself is part of the revelation that takes place in this encounter, and is necessary to it: for her to have true knowledge of God, she must understand the truth about herself, to have *a reflexive awareness of herself*. But it is also simultaneously true (in the story's terms) that knowledge of God bestows self-knowledge. The discussion of the location of authentic worship that follows is thus not tangential to the woman's own life-situation at all, but deeply intertwined with it" (338).

The encounter with Jesus, it seems, brings self-understanding of an individual's shortcomings and deepest needs. The human quest for significance and authenticity—what Jensen calls "the inescapable need for human beings to *worship* some transcendent other: we are *homo adorans*" (340)—is certainly problematical. In fact,

> the radical symbolism of John's thought-world would suggest that the problem is . . . deeply entrenched in intractable human behaviours and dispositions. In other words, human beings are kept from self-knowledge because the

---

23. Koester, "Savior of the World," 680.

> problem of self-ignorance itself is not merely intellectual but *ethical*. . . . In the story, on the other hand, we have a knowledge that is *given*, coming in the form of a divine–human encounter; and which contains within it both a revelation of the self and a revelation of the divine character. The story witnesses to the addressing of the human from the sphere of the divine. (340)

To the extent that the unnamed woman is a symbolic representation of humanity as a whole, she embodies—as the narrative begins to unfold—the absence of the two essential elements of true religion (along the lines famously summarized by John Calvin in the opening chapters of his *Institutes*): the inescapably twinned knowledge of self and of God.

There is also an apparent missional intention on the part of Jesus in the story. By entering into dialogue, and even asking for a drink from the Samaritan woman, he seems intentionally to confront Jewish prejudices concerning Samaritans, starting with the supposed risks of impurity from contact with their food and drink. Despite the two prohibition imperatives in Matthew (10:5-6—with its specific mention of Samaritans—and 15:24), Jesus does reach out to the marginalized in all four gospel traditions, often transgressing contemporary social mores and religious strictures in the process.[24] As for the parable of the compassionate Samaritan, the way in which it "follows hard on the sending out and the return of the seventy(-two) disciples further emphasizes a future mission to all nations"[25] according to one missiologist. Towards the conclusion of the encounter with the Samaritan woman, John reports Jesus as employing harvest imagery with its explicitly missional language (John 4:35-38). Although Jesus and his disciples have been engaged in such "harvesting" in the sense of baptizing and making new disciples (John 3:22; 4:1-2), the pattern in Samaria is now substantially altered. "Typically, insiders do the planting, hoping to transform outsid-

---

24. This raises the much-debated question of the *extent* of any intentional pre-Easter Gentile mission on the part of Jesus. As we have seen in chapter 3 above, there is some evidence for such an intentional mission but complex issues surround the debate.

25. Bosch, *Transforming Mission*, 90.

ers into insiders. But that process has been reversed in this instance."[26] Here it is the woman from the well who does the planting (4:29, 39). The story models missional intent, perhaps even missional obligation, for all who grasp (or are grasped by) its meaning.

The encounter with Samaritans in John 4 concludes with the remarkable public confession of faith in Jesus as "the savior of the world" (4:42). In one sense such a confession is not surprising given that in the previous chapter of John there is the claim that Jesus' mission is for "the world" (3:16); now he is recognized by the Samaritans as "savior" of "a world which therefore inevitably includes them."[27] The title ("the savior of the world") is used nowhere else in John's Gospel and only once more in the NT (1 John 4:14). It is a summary of the central issues of the Gospel: its truth, its power—and its universal scope. Many commentators draw attention to the way in which the title (in various forms) was applied to or even claimed by a string of Roman Emperors from Julius Caesar to Hadrian (and Hadrian employed precisely this form: *sōtēr tou kosmou*). Udo Schnelle points out that the "semantic field *soter/soteria/sozo* has a political-religious connotation in NT times: the Roman emperor is the benefactor and savior of the world who not only guarantees the political unity of the realm but grants its citizens prosperity, well-being, and meaning."[28] The same kind of claim is being made here; for John, Jesus Christ is the only savior, and the one who grants eternal life to those who believe. All of these christological consequences flow from a reading of the passage in term of the particularity, discontinuity and missional intention that is embedded in it. The clear implication for a contemporary reader is that, however distasteful this might be in postmodern and globalized settings, some kind of missional intent is required of all who would follow this "savior of the world."

Christology

Our enquiry into Jesus, Gentiles and Samaritans has repeatedly raised questions about the person and identity of Jesus.

26. Spina, *Faith of the Outsider*, 158–59.
27. Keener, "Some New Testament Invitations," 196.
28. Schnelle, *Theology of the New Testament*, 692.

Some Conclusions about Jesus, Gentiles, and Samaritans

The Jesus of History

Any appeal to the example of Jesus as foundational for Christian belief and practice is necessarily tied to the retrieval of what Jesus said and did. Such a retrieval is, in part, an exercise in understanding the context in which he lived. Discussion in chapter 1 above demonstrated the range of Jewish attitudes towards Gentiles during the era of Second Temple Judaism, including a notable tension between particularity and universality. A number of features emerge from the attempted retrieval of Herodian Galilee and its significance for the ministry and teaching of Jesus—including an assessment of the extent of Gentile influence on the region. The survey also sought to describe the kind of Judaism found in Herodian Galilee in particular, and to describe and assess the role of the archaeology in the material and religio-cultural retrieval of Galilee. And it outlined some of the implications of these findings for the construction of a contextual framework for the encounter of Jesus with the Gentiles he is said to have met and spoken about.

Herodian Galilee emerges from recent study as quite strongly Jewish in ethos but with a veneer of Gentile influence (confined mainly to public space). A scholarly consensus is emerging that recent retrieval of Galilee reinforces the way in which the generally Jewish and regional Galilean ethos provide the essential context for understanding Jesus and the Gospel accounts concerning him. There is no reason to doubt the distinctly Jewish character of Jesus' Galilean context. It is this very context that offers an enhanced understanding of a number of issues that appear to have been especially significant in the self-understanding of Jesus: land and people; purity and Torah; temple and Jerusalem/Zion; Messiah—with these each influenced by his Galilean context and each, in turn, significant in his understanding of and reaction to Gentiles and Samaritans.

We also noted that the material retrieval of Galilee seems to increase the likelihood of Jesus encountering Gentiles in Galilee. Such meetings would, it seems, have been unavoidable, and in keeping with the implication of the Gospels that Jesus is remarkably at ease with Gentiles (and also with Samaritans). The paucity of references might also be taken as evidence that the Gospel writers resist the temptation to construct commentary by Jesus on the controversial Gentile-related issues that were to puzzle the first generation of Christians.[29] The frequency and nature of Jesus' contact with Gentiles remains unclear even though there are occasional glimpses whose historical plausibility is enhanced by their coherence with what we know of social conditions in Galilee—as we have seen. Moreover, as we have also seen, there are reports of a degree of intentionality on Jesus' part; for example, that during the second or third year of his public ministry he left Galilee and entered the Gentile region of Tyre (Mark 7:24, 31). Galilee emerges not simply as a geographical reference but as a place loaded with symbolic meaning; "Galilee of the Gentiles" becomes the very place where the meaning of Israel is widened to include Gentiles.

Christological Claims

What we have seen of the actions (including apparently symbolic actions) of Jesus, and his reported teaching, raises complex christological claims with far-reaching implications for a multireligious world. A number of examples are found in the material we have considered from the four Gospels.

There is Jesus' attitude to authority and symbols of authority as shown by his apparent indifference to the cities of Sepphoris and Tiberias and to other symbols of Gentile, Hellenizing, imperial or Herodian authority. Jesus' healing power is displayed in his ability to effect exorcism and healing at a distance, and to do so without touch and without any words addressed directly to the afflicted person. Jesus' divine identity is suggested as the Syrophoenician mother and the centurion/official address him as *kurie*, "Lord." Jesus' stance concerning purity issues also reveals his sense of authority; in fact, his apparent repeal of food laws seems to be the reason why the Hebrew patriarchs will not need to fear ritual defilement by eating with the "many from the east and the west" who will come to the eschatological banquet. Substantial christological and eschatological claims are also embedded in the woes pronounced on Israelite towns—with even Gentiles able to assess their eschatologi-

---

29. This is not to overlook the way in which the gospels are redacted with particular audiences in mind (as our discussion has noted from time to time).

Some Conclusions about Jesus, Gentiles, and Samaritans

cal significance. Such themes are further evidence of the "great reversal" dynamic that seems to be central to Jesus' understanding of the Rule of God as inaugurated by his presence and ministry and as illustrated by Gentiles (and Samaritans) participating in it.

CHRISTOLOGY AND TORAH

A distinctly christological set of conclusions can also be drawn from the parable of the compassionate Samaritan. According to the analysis of Philip Esler, Jesus announces in the parable a general principle that *diverges* markedly from the Mosaic law and does not merely reinterpret it.[30] Christ the exegete[31] "is really formulating a new principle altogether."[32] Jesus advocates a major divergence from the Mosaic law by asserting the superiority of the love command. Richard Bauckham points out that, "by stressing the superiority of the love commandment specifically to purity laws, the parable tends to downgrade, while not necessarily invalidating, purity concerns, in rather striking contrast to the emphasis on them in much Second Temple halakhah."[33] Jesus redefines "neighbor" away from an inward-looking category to a person who acts mercifully towards another who is in need. "Jesus thus calls for a movement from a group-oriented ethic to a universal one — and at the level of principle.... [He] thus establishes a rationale for moral obligation which is independent of the Mosaic law."[34] In the story, the despised Samaritan knows the heart of the Law better than the two Jewish religious figures; the despised Samaritan *keeps* the heart of the

---

30. Esler, "Jesus and the Reduction," 344.

31. To re-employ a description by Bovon (*Luke the Theologian*, 120).

32. Esler, "Jesus and the Reduction," 345. By this Esler means that "Jesus gives a word from the Mosaic law an entirely fresh meaning, so that it henceforth functions to establish a norm governing our own behaviour to others, rather than serving to differentiate for the purpose of the satisfaction of a juridical requirement whom we must love as ourselves and whom not" (344).

33. Bauckham, "Scrupulous Priest," 489. The parable is also a useful reminder of Jesus and purity issues; Jesus breaks these corpse purity rules with the widow's son in Nain (Luke 7:11-17) and with Jairus' daughter (Mark 5:21-24, 35-43). All this in addition to what we have seen of his stance on food laws.

34. Esler, "Jesus and the Reduction," 345.

Jesus and the Religions

Law better than the two Jewish religious figures.[35] The parable's contrast between priest and Samaritan "makes emphatic the implicit assertion of the superiority of the love commandment over purity laws."[36] Jesus appears to see himself as in some sense above the law of Moses in making such an assertion.[37] His attitude toward the Torah is unattested and unprecedented in his day; it can only be explained on the basis of "his awareness of his own authority and his awareness of a new epoch in redemptive history" (as we noted in a conclusion by Christian Stettler): the advent of the eschatological reign of God in his own person. The clear implication—that the Rule of God and faithfulness to the heart of Torah—might be found *beyond* the covenant community, suggests a principle of continuing relevance: that examples of what might be called "Torah-faithful behavior of which Jesus approved" are found in unexpected places. The contemporary challenge is, of course, to provide specific examples; that might be difficult, but one thing is equally likely: examples will not be discerned without a prior *openness* to the possibility that they do exist.

THE SAMARITAN AND THE TEMPLE

Richard Bauckham also points out that, in the parable, "the Temple would loom in the background to the narrative as heard by any Jewish hearer." So, when the Samaritan traveler enters the story, he is known by the Jewish hearers to disregard or distort the Torah with regard to tem-

---

35. We have already noted the self-identification of the Samaritans as *shōmerīm*, "those who keep/obey," referring to themselves as "keepers of the covenant" (Meier, "Historical Jesus," 207 n. 10). So, as Williamson observes, the selection of a Samaritan for the positive role in the parable told in answer to the question "who is my neighbor?" is telling, and in a veiled manner anticipates the Jewish acknowledgment (recorded much later) that the Samaritans were often more punctilious in their observance of the law than the Jews (Williamson and Evans, "Samaritans," 1058).

36. Bauckham, "Scrupulous Priest," 487–88. This is the very principle stated by the apostle Paul: "the whole law is summed up in a single commandment, 'You shall love your neighbor as yourself'" (Gal 5:14; cf. Rom 13:8b, 10b).

37. This is how Jesus also appears to see himself in at least some of the 'antitheses' in Matt 5:21–48.

Some Conclusions about Jesus, Gentiles, and Samaritans

ple and purity.[38] The parable is, therefore, about "the unrestricted love of neighbor and the consequent relativization of cult and sacrifice."[39] Once again there appear to be transferable and universal implications for contemporary observers of religious plurality.

CHRISTOLOGY: THE SAMARITAN AND THE PEOPLE OF GOD

Given that the Samaritan of the parable both discerns and observes the heart of covenant law in exemplary fashion, it is understandable that N.T. Wright concludes that the story of the compassionate Samaritan "dramatically redefines the covenant boundary of Israel." Wright continues that, to the question of who would benefit when the Rule of God arrived, the story of the compassionate Samaritan offers an answer "with sharp clarity. Outsiders were coming into the kingdom, and—at least by implication—insiders were being left out." The parable explicitly shows that "there was a way of being Israel which would be truly and radically faithful to the very centre of Torah, as summed up in the *Shema*. But this way, when pursued to the limits, would involve the redrawing of Israel's boundaries, to include those normally reckoned beyond the pale."[40] We have already noted that this principle of an expanded Israel apparently includes Gentiles. The two stories embedded in the Nazareth episode in Luke 4 imply a dramatic redefinition of who Israel is. Israel is now, with the coming of Jesus, reconstituted; it now includes Gentiles and Samaritans among the chosen people of God.

This apparent likelihood, then, that Jesus inclusively redefined Israel's key markers of identity (temple, Torah, purity and people) has far reaching implications, especially for the Christian assessment of and potential relationship with people of other faiths. Such a redefinition constitutes a sizeable christological claim in terms of Jesus' self-under-

---

38. Bauckham, "Scrupulous Priest," 487. N. T. Wright also thinks that the demonizing of Jesus as a "Samaritan" in John 8:48 derives from this dispute about the temple: Jesus is thought to be opposing the Jerusalem temple, as Samaritans did (*Jesus and the Victory*, 185).

39. Wright, *Jesus and the Victory*, 305. He also writes of "the *firm* relativization of cult and sacrifice" in the parable (305; emphasis added). Some christological implications of this "relativization" are discussed below.

40. Ibid., 307.

standing, identity and authority; as we have noted, who else but Yahweh (or Yahweh's authorized agent) could redefine the people of God in this way? If this Jesus is able to redefine and reconstitute the people of God, does this not imply that the global people of God are to be defined and constituted in him? Certainly the first generation of Gentile Christians, with their affirmation that "Jesus is Lord," and their assertion that both Gentile and Jew could be found "in Christ" (an implicit form of cosmic Christology), appear to believe something like this.

CHRISTOLOGY AND CONTESTED WORSHIP

The christological claims in the above section relate to the world(s) of religion in a number of ways. One example is the implications for contested worship locations. The Gospel of John emphasizes the role of Jesus as the unique place and mediation of God's presence.[41] When Jesus states, "I am, the one speaking to you" (26; an "astonishing self-revelation unparalleled in the Gospel for its explicitness"[42]) this probably seems to the woman to be a declaration of Messiahship. But it is also the first in a series of seven "I am" sayings in the Fourth Gospel. Richard Bauckham observes that this number of "I am" statements in John exactly matches the number of times in the OT where Yahweh identifies himself as "I AM." Bauckham writes that the series of "I am" sayings "thus comprehensively identifies Jesus with the God of Israel who sums up his identity in the declaration 'I am he.' More than that, these sayings identify Jesus as the eschatological revelation of the unique identity of God . . ."[43]

The dialogue in John 4—including the stunning "I am" claim, made in the face of contested worship claims—also prepares a reader for the reality that Jesus is himself the divinely sanctioned means by which acceptable worship is possible. When the Samaritan woman raises the question of *where* worship is to be performed (v. 20), Jesus does not debate the issue but points to a time in which regionalized preferences (however sanctioned) will be transcended: a time when worship will

---

41. See, for example, the prologue (John 1:1–18).
42. Okure, *Johannine Approach*, 121.
43. *God Crucified*, 55–56; Bauckham has in mind passages from Isaiah.

Some Conclusions about Jesus, Gentiles, and Samaritans

be "in spirit and in truth" (v. 23). Such worship is *now* possible because Jesus is present. As a Catholic theologian rather forcefully concludes, "[t]hus, Jesus' presence renders the former cultic dispositions obsolete and gives eschatological significance to the destruction of the temples on Mounts Gerizim and Zion."[44] In fact, from the opening verses of the passage, with their affirmation of the divine imperative behind his actions, to the communal Samaritan conclusion that he is "the savior of the world," the narrative presents an exalted view of this Jesus in terms of both his person and his actions.

The Christ, who reveals the Samaritan's shortcomings, who offers her the water of life, and who announces himself as the *locus* of all true worship of the divine—such a one clearly stands as a challenge to all human religion. The role of this Jesus is to do the divine will and to accomplish a divine mission (John 4:34). His arrival relativizes all religious claims, beginning with those of his own Jewish faith. "If Jesus . . . can question the religious significance of Jerusalem (4:21), what else could stand in his way?"[45] The passage portrays Jesus as one who transcends religious, ethnic, cultural and gender barriers (beginning with some Jewish-Samaritan displays of such divisions). He invites not only the woman and other Samaritans but also his own wary disciples and, implicitly, all readers, to do the same. Christian discourse about the uniqueness and finality of Christ among the world's religious options is constructed upon such foundations.

Jesus' statement in the Nazareth synagogue makes prophetic claims about the arrival of the Rule of God: not only is the divine promise fulfilled, the one who accomplishes the fulfillment announces it (Luke 4:21). There are missional dimensions as well. The central component of Jesus' mission is identified as being sent: sent to proclaim good news, sent to proclaim freedom, sent to proclaim recovery of sight, sent to set free, sent to proclaim the Lord's favor. The Samaritan encounter in John chapter 4 make fairly extensive use of harvest imagery (with obvious missional intent). All of these christological claims have implications for the world of religious encounter—as we shall attempt to make clear in the concluding section of this chapter.

44. Wyckoff, "Jesus in Samaria," 94.
45. Burge, *John*, 155.

Jesus and the Religions

AN EXEMPLARY CHRISTOLOGY

The *example* of Jesus also emerges as a significant issue in the passages discussed. Jesus taught as much by his example and symbolic actions as by his verbal teaching. As noted in the Introduction above, this exemplary dimension has received rather little scholarly attention.[46] The suggestion of this volume is that disciples today, by reflecting on the Gospels, can discern something of the attitude of Jesus towards the religions he encountered or spoke about.

This "imitation of Christ" has always been the Christian way. It is certainly found in the apostle Paul ("imitate me as I imitate Christ"—1 Cor. 11:1). And it is deeply embedded in the Gospels. In fact, one reason *why* there are Gospel accounts of Jesus' encounters is to provide such an example for would-be followers of Jesus. The recent analysis by Wendy Cotter of the healing miracles of Jesus (in her *The Christ of the Miracle Stories: Portrait through Encounter*) is particularly instructive. She convincingly demonstrates that it is the compassion of Jesus that emerges as a significant (and transferable) component of the stories. Her discussion of the healing encounters with the centurion/official and the Syrophoenician mother, for example, shows the role that these encounters play in revealing of the character of Jesus as a model of behavior for his followers. Cotter begins by measuring the behavior and speech of the petitioners against her very considerable knowledge of conventional good manners as understood in the Greco-Roman world. From her comparisons she concludes that while some of the petitioners are said by Jesus to be examples of faith, they "provide a very challenging ideal to the ordinary person"[47] because the Gospel narrators seem to have chosen petitioners who are: "bold, brash, outrageous, rude" (7), "forward, pushy, and insistent" (8), "spunky, noisy, . . . and outrageous" (256) in their approaches to Jesus. She points out that the stories are

---

46. This writer has plans to publish a second volume, complementary to this one, in which a theology of the imitation of Christ will be developed.

47. Cotter, *Christ of the Miracle Stories*, 6-7; further page references to Cotter's volume are in parentheses in the text. Cotter has in mind not only the two stories we have considered but also the healing of the leper (Mark 1:40-45), the healing of the paralytic (Mark 2:1-12), the father of the demonized boy (Mark 9:14-29), and the healing of Bartimaeus (Mark 10:46-52).

Some Conclusions about Jesus, Gentiles, and Samaritans

written in such a way as to show that they are "not simply a vehicle to hurry us to the amazing miraculous action at all. Rather, ... the narrator, having caught the listener's attention with the presence of these bold petitioners, now illustrates Jesus' view of them and his response" (7). Jesus' reaction to these persons who, according to social convention deserved a strong rebuke and could hardly be considered as desirable examples of faith, is remarkable and certainly surprising. "Jesus does not seem to pay any attention to their behavior, but he rather sees past it to the desperation that brings them to him, and to the unshakeable confidence that explains their determination, a confidence that astonishes Jesus" (8). Instead of rebuke, a listener "instead sees Jesus move over to the side of the petitioner and answer not only with the miracle, but in a way that shows deep recognition of the person's need" (8–9).

In other words, the point of recounting the miracle stories is not simply to portray works of power by Jesus, but to place them in a context that shows how Jesus himself deals with the kind of demanding persons who will come to his followers. These stories of Jesus are meant not only to preserve the memory of his power "but also to inspire his followers in their own responses [by] ... modeling his great virtues for the edification and imitation by the community" (9). "The function of such stories seems to presume an audience keen on observing Jesus' manner of receiving these petitioners, who are imperfect, poor, rude, rough, and objectionable to polite society" (254).

The healing stories reveal Jesus' *philanthrōpia* (loving concern for others) and, especially when dealing with parents who petition Jesus on behalf of their demonized children, he displays the quality of *praos* (humility). Even if Jesus' initial response appears to be disapproving, he nonetheless displays "his *praos* in listening closely to each parent's response, recognizing the truth in their words, and immediately granting the miracle for which they ask" (13). Jesus also displays *epiekeia* (graciousness or clemency) that Cotter describes as "a 'sweetness,' a 'gentleness,' in his astonishment at the confidence that these petitioners have in him" (255). She concludes:

> These stories that reveal not only Jesus' power, but also his person, are meant to inspire great confidence and love for

> Jesus, but they also instigate in his followers ... a striving for emulation in the concrete examples. They challenge a community living in a very stratified society to confront the social criteria of "acceptability" and to abandon any notion of personal or religious superiority. They ask the follower to learn from these petitioners, and to emulate the adamantine character of their faith.... We may say that these stories reveal how the virtues of Jesus are profound expressions of the *agapē* enjoined on all his followers. (13)

This book attaches considerable importance to the exemplary Christology that emerges from the encounters between Jesus and Gentiles and Samaritans. Cotter makes a highly plausible case that at least some of the accounts of miracle stories serve a community *Sitz im Leben* in which disciples face encounters with a variety of people, some of whom are "rude, brusque, importunate, and insistent persons who will come to them, with a rough, and even rude, manner of request. The portrait of Jesus in the miracle story encounters calls for the abandonment of judgment, rejection, reproof, or denial on any grounds, and call the followers to look beneath the externals to the desperate need, the anxiety, the shame, the abuse, and the social rejection that explain their externals. It calls on the followers to feel compassion, understanding, and more." (9) The Syrophoenician mother provides an excellent example as Cotter draws attention to her socially marginal behavior: a woman alone in public space, loudly approaching a non-kin male and engaging in insistent bartering with him.[48]

According to Cotter, even when Jesus attaches blame to his petitioners,[49] he displays "the humility which allows him to see things in another way and grant generously what had been withheld" (256). If the followers of Jesus *then* were "to feel compassion, understanding,

---

48. This behavior is so culturally inappropriate and shameful that one analyst, working from a social-scientific viewpoint, is sure that the woman is a prostitute and that the story is included to show how Jesus' merciful mission extends to non-Israelites, even those of dubious character; see Love, *Jesus and Marginal Women*, ch. 6.

49. She has in mind the parents of the demonized children "for it is clear that Jesus holds them responsible for permitting a climate devoid of faith to allow the demon access to the child" (*Christ of the Miracle Stories*, 255; she explains in more detail on 179–80).

and more" (9) then nothing less should be expected in today's interreligious encounters which can also have their share of robust, insistent and even harsh dialogue and unfair polemic. The contemporary disciple who encounters such an atmosphere is offered, in the encounter stories, a reminder of how Jesus responded: with humility, graciousness and loving concern.[50]

Christian faith has always drawn attention to the unique and irreplaceable position occupied by Christ in Christian self-understanding, and his example in the encounters considered illustrates this centrality. With the encounters in mind it is helpful to repeat the point made near the beginning of our opening chapter: that it is the person of Jesus who, more effectively than any other aspect of Christianity, enables the Christian "word" to be apprehended across a range of religious contexts because—to repeat the helpful metaphor of Mark Heim—"people cross the membranes between different cultures more effectively than ideas or concepts do." And this Jesus, in his references to Gentiles and Samaritans, offers a generally positive assessment of their faith and humility.

Moreover, Jesus attaches eschatological significance to their responses to the prophetic word; they are exemplary confirmation of the Word that is heard *today* (Luke 4:21). They foreshadow and even illustrate aspects of a new eschatological age. As Jacques Dupuis points out, "the miracles worked by Jesus for 'foreigners' have the very same meaning that he gives to all of his other miracles. They mean that the Reign of God is already present and at work."[51] The miracles of Jesus, "performed for Gentiles, and for a Samaritan, bear witness to the inclusion within the people of YHWH of those who had formerly been outside."[52] This is particularly true of the healings: "[w]hen Jesus heals, his act has eschatological significance and is always the sign and pledge of the breaking in of the Messianic Age, an anticipatory participation in

50. In the Greco-Roman world, *philanthrōpia* was understood as "affability, courtesy, liberality, kindness, clemency, etc. The *philanthrōpos* is gracious and considerate towards all with whom he associates, he is generous towards the needy, he is also merciful and clement towards his enemies." (Hubert Martin as cited by Cotter, *Christ of the Miracle Stories*, 10.)

51. Dupuis, *Christianity and the Religions*, 24.

52. Wright, *Jesus and the Victory*, 192.

its blessings."[53] The way in which Jesus displays at least some missional intent towards Gentiles (especially in the central chapters of Mark, and elsewhere in the gospels), and his rebuke of his disciples for their failure to share his mission, certainly implies that contemporary disciples ought to display the concern shown by Jesus for those outside their own communities. And Christian responses, past and present, to supposedly harsh, unfair, and even aggressive behavior from some Muslims and Hindus (for example), have not always followed the example of Christ when he encountered similar behavior.

From "the Margins of Scripture . . . to Center Stage"

Previous chapters have noted how occasional contact with "outsiders" (Gentiles and others) assumes greater significance in the canonical fullness of Scripture. The same kind of dynamic seems to be at work in Jesus' encounter with Samaritans. In the case of the Gentiles, the principle emerges that an earlier event in the Scriptural text can assume new significance when, for example, it is reconsidered in a new context. This leads to a distinction between the "original meaning" of a text (derived from an understanding of historical setting and context) and the "full meaning" in a canonical sense; there is "new significance because of the way things turn out". [54] As Scripture unfolds, the narrative and theological significance of the encounters with "outsiders" enlarges. To repeat the helpful image used by Charles Scalise, issues can and do move from "the margins of Scripture . . . to center stage."[55] The significance of Gentiles and Samaritans is one such issue as a more universal perspective assumes greater importance in the unfolding narrative of Scripture.

One way in which the Fourth Gospel seems to signal such an enlargement is by means of the significant space devoted to the encounter with the Samaritans (not simply the woman). The encounter of Jesus with these Samaritans, and their significant place in his teaching, provides another example of a marginal issue (the significance of "outsiders" in the OT and the Gospels) that warrants elevation from a minor to

53. Jeremias, *Jesus' Promise*, 28.
54. Leithart, *Deep Exegesis*, 46.
55. Scalise, "Hermeneutical Circle," 224.

a major key in the canonical mix—with this elevation signaled by Jesus in the passages considered. In the case of the Samaritans (about whom there are no OT references), this principle might be re worded along the lines of moving an issue (the worth of Samaritans) from the margins of Jewish consciousness to a more central position. As already noted, theological exegesis also holds out the possibility of a certain kind of constructive synthesis: what Richard Hays calls "canonical coherence" as "theological exegetes . . . seek the big picture, asking how any particular text fits into the larger biblical story" so that "some sort of complex unity" is sought and articulated—rather than simply hearing a variety of biblical witnesses.[56] The inclusion of Samaritans and Gentiles within the universal people of God, and even the emergence of a biblical theology of the religions, can certainly be seen as part of this "complex unity."

A Wider Theological Trinitarian Context

A theological reading also notes that a Trinitarian perspective, or aspects of it, are suggested by some of the encounters. Our discussion of Luke chapter 4 noted Luke's "high" Christology (Jesus' status as messiah, savior, divine Son), and Jesus' close connection with the Spirit (reinforced by the citation of Isa 61:1). In the power of the Spirit, Jesus announces his coming as one sent by the Father. A theological reading could also note that a Trinitarian perspective is implied in the encounter with the Samaritan woman. In the Fourth Gospel, the symbolism of water points to the Spirit of God. The gift of living water offered by Jesus to the Samaritan woman (4:10, 13–14) seems to supersede the ritual waters of John the Baptist (1:26, 33), the water used for ceremonial purification (2:6), perhaps the baptism of proselytes (if this is the intended meaning of 3:5) and the Feast of Tabernacles (7:37–39; 9:7). The living water also appears to supersede the water of holy places, such as healing sanctuaries (5:2–8) and Jacob's well in the narrative of the Samaritan woman. The divine agency at work in John chapter 4 has, then, a triune form: it is the Father who requires the detour through Samaria; it is the Son who initiates and sustains the dialogue that results; it is the Spirit who inaugurates the promised eschatological blessing. The conclusion

56. Hays, "Reading the Bible," 13.

of Udo Schnelle is a fitting summary of what we have seen in the encounters and teaching of Jesus:

> The expression *pneuma ho theos* (John 4:24, "God is Spirit") is a climactic statement of Hellenistic religious history and of Johannine theology. Because God is Spirit and thus can only be approached in prayer that is inspired by the Spirit, the Johannine understanding of worship is universal, allowing no discrimination based on religious-national status, social class, or gender. Samaritans, Greeks, and Jews can all participate in this worship, just as can both men and women. With the appearance of Jesus in this world, there arrives the true worship of God "in Spirit and truth," without bloody sacrifices, and corresponding to the nature of God who is love. The question of "where" God can be truly worshiped is no longer valid, for Jesus Christ is himself the new locus of salvation (cf. John 2:14–22).[57]

A Trinitarian perspective has some perhaps unexpected consequences for those who see uniqueness only in exclusivist and christomonistic categories. In his *The Meeting of the Religions and the Trinity*, Part II, D'Costa goes so far as to claim that "Trinitarian exclusivism can acknowledge God's actions within other traditions, without domesticating or obliterating their alterity, such that real conversation and engagement might occur."[58] Others have elaborated the implications of pneumatology for an enhanced theological understanding of the religions.[59]

---

57. Schnelle, *Theology of the New Testament*, 668.

58. D'Costa, *Meeting of the Religions*, 47. See also, Newbigin, *Open Secret*, ch. 3, "The Mission of the Triune God"; and the essays in Vanhoozer, *Trinity in a Pluralistic Age*. For a more inclusivist perspective see Dupuis, *Toward a Christian Theology*, 220–23, 242–44, 262–68.

59. See, for example, Yong, "Turn to Pneumatology" and "'Not Knowing Where.'"

Some Conclusions about Jesus, Gentiles, and Samaritans

Implications for a Religiously Plural World[60]

The Challenge of the Person and Identity of Jesus

Traditional Christian discourse about the person and identity of Jesus begins with the narrative of the Gospels. Although this discourse might be elaborated in terms of the theological category that we called have "christocentrism," even such a prescriptive category derives from the accounts of the Gospels themselves. The notion of the "identity" of Jesus (or of anyone) is complex.[61] In the particular case of Jesus, discussion is quickly rendered even more complex by the realization that the Gospels (the source of the data from which conclusions about Jesus' identity might be sought) are themselves written with certain theological convictions about Jesus' identity apparently already established by the writers or redactors of the accounts.[62] As Robert Jenson puts it, in asking about the identity of Jesus in the Gospel records, "we are asking a question that is at once historical and dogmatic."[63] Or, to put the issue in a related manner: "There is no path to a secure portrait of Jesus independent of how he has been responded to."[64] This realization requires, then, a careful weighing of both the historical and theological elements in the Gospels.[65]

---

60. This writer, in a second book intended to complement this volume, hopes to return to and expand these conclusions, with each of them illustrated from examples gathered from a number of places around the world.

61. See, for example, the discussion by Jenson, "Identity, Jesus," 4–6; in fact, the whole of the lengthy volume, *Seeking the Identity of Jesus*, is a sustained investigation of the complex issues surrounding any quest for the identity of Jesus (see further: 60–61, 306), and is the result of a collaborative ecumenical venture, the Identity of Jesus Project, of the Center of Theological Enquiry.

62. It is clear that the Gospel writers or redactors are not innocent of christological belief. They present their material about Jesus from this side, as it were, of Easter; our discussion of the meaning of *kurie*—the mundane "Sir" or the divine "Lord"?—is one example of this.

63. "Identity, Jesus," 48.

64. Williams, "Looking for Jesus," 151. Cf. the thesis of Francis Watson: "The theologically significant Jesus (the Christ of faith) is the Jesus whose reception by his first followers is definitively articulated in the fourfold Gospel narrative" ("*Veritas Christi*," 105).

65. For an example of such a careful and judicious weighing of the two dimensions, see Watson, "*Veritas Christi*."

Jesus and the Religions

In order to anticipate the contemporary interreligious setting, some of what we have seen can be brought together now in the form of questions. From the interreligious encounters that we have looked at in the Gospels, we might ask: "Who is this one who heals, by a word, and at a distance, and who lives under the authority of the inaugurated Rule of God? Who is it who can redefine the borders of Israel to accept some of those who are assuredly excluded by his compatriots? Who is it who can re arrange priorities within the Torah as he diminishes the importance of purity rules and promotes the supremacy of the love command? Who is it who accepts address as *kurie* with its implied associations of divine authority and identity? Who is it who offers "living water" and announces, in his own person, a settlement of contested worship locations, including the obsolescence of the temple? Who is this in whom history is broken into by a future age now present, and who is recognized by those who have come from the nations?" Traditional Christian conclusions and assertions about the uniqueness, finality and universality of Christ derive from answers to such questions.[66]

Christians, and others, will rightly have misgivings about any implied "ranking" of religious authority figures. Nonetheless, most of the world's religious traditions either have founders or are indebted to (even if not dependent upon) the credentials and authority of key figures. Comparisons may be odious, but they are inevitable and can, if carefully invoked in a fair and balanced way, at least point to areas of true difference and distinctiveness.[67] The encounters of Jesus do seem to reveal him as one who is altogether different from others and whose authority adds an unprecedented and even unique dimension to the world's range of religious authority figures. There seems no escaping the way in which the Gospels "are *history-like witnesses to truths both historical and transcendent.*"[68] To mention one example from the material considered: we noted the soteriological implications of Holmén's observation

---

66. For a discussion that calls for a careful reassessment of the (often too casual) way in which theological conservatives use "unique" and "uniqueness" and that explores alternatives, see Robinson, "What Exactly Is Meant?"

67. See, for example, the debate found in Hick, "On Grading Religions"; and Griffiths and Lewis, "On Grading Religions . . . Reply to Hick."

68. Placher, "How the Gospels Mean," 27, 37; original emphasis.

Some Conclusions about Jesus, Gentiles, and Samaritans

about Jesus and purity that the impurities of those considered unclean do not transfer to Jesus; instead, Jesus' purity transfers to them. This has a missional implication for those religious traditions that accept (or are troubled by) the notion of *karma*: Hinduism, Buddhism, and a number of aspects of the "new spirituality."

A Universal Compassion

We have argued that Jesus' announcement of the restoration of Israel opens the way for Gentiles and Samaritans to join the reconstituted people of God and to experience the blessing of Israel's salvation by means of healing, exorcism and other signs. Seán Freyne discerns a universalizing dynamic as he points to a Wisdom theme in the teaching of Jesus: the way in which a bountiful creation benefits all people (as made clear in the Sermon on the Mount: Matt 5:45). In the Nazareth episode (Luke 4:16-30) it becomes clear that the living God has a compassionate concern for at least some of those who reside—geographically and spiritually—outside the borders of Israel. It is also apparent, in the two stories as briefly exegeted by Jesus, that Yahweh has the ability to direct the lives of Gentiles. The story offers the reassurance that God is able to reveal himself to people outside Israel and to guide them. This is the same divine guidance that brings Jesus to his encounter with the Samaritan woman and her fellow Samaritans. Jesus is willing to heal and exorcize, it seems, without regard to faith commitments (for example, Matt 4:23-24). At the same time, the inclusion of *some* Gentiles does not assume the inclusion of all; nonetheless, we have emphasized the considerable importance of Matt 8:11-12 with its assurance that *many* will come from East and West to join the patriarchs in the eschatological banquet at the end of the age.

The principle of universality is also demonstrated in the encounter with Samaritans. In the one figure of the Samaritan woman are found many of the characteristics of the marginal persons with whom Jesus regularly deals in the Synoptic Gospels. As we saw in the analysis by Neyrey, she is an amalgam of cultural deviance who embodies most of the social liabilities which would marginalize her in Samaritan soci-

259

ety[69]—and yet her status is transformed from that of outsider to insider because of the encounter with Jesus. The universality and centrality of the love command over against any notion of ethnic or religious superiority is asserted by Jesus—as the parable of the compassionate Samaritan makes clear. And, if Michael Bird is correct, the encounter between Jesus and the centurion has a dimension that is usually missed: Jesus performs an act of compassionate healing for someone who was a potential enemy. It makes the story a living parable of loving one's enemies. One condition for positive interreligious relations is surely the "seeing heart" of the compassionate Samaritan that is modeled in the teller of the story, Jesus himself. The parable offers a radical "relativization of cult and sacrifice."[70] What, then, might Christians conclude when Muslims (or any other "outsiders") display the principles of the love commandment that Jesus so greatly affirmed (thus keeping the religious "Law"—however that might be defined—more scrupulously than they)? Might they conclude with N.T. Wright that, as we have seen, the story of the compassionate Samaritan "dramatically redefines the covenant boundary of Israel" and explicitly shows that "there was a way of being Israel which would be truly and radically faithful to the very centre of Torah" even if it "would involve the redrawing of Israel's boundaries, to include those normally reckoned beyond the pale"[71]?

The theme of reversal is prominent in many of the passages considered and certainly provides warnings to the first hearers and readers of the Gospels (both Jewish and Christian) about the dangers of religious presumption, especially presumptions of assured privilege. This is confirmed by the encounter of Jesus with the centurion/official and the Syrophoenician mother. They, like the widow of Zarephath and Naaman the Syrian, become models of faith by comparison with recalcitrant Israel and even his own disciples. "Outsiders" who display faith and humility are declared to be included; "insiders" who presume upon their privilege find themselves excluded. If Jesus can so strongly affirm the

---

69. The Syrophoenician woman, the widow of Zarephath, and Naaman the Syrian also embody many of the same social liabilities, at least in Jewish eyes.

70. Wright, *Jesus and the Victory*, 305.

71. Ibid., 307.

Some Conclusions about Jesus, Gentiles, and Samaritans

faith of a (Roman) centurion and a Gentile woman, and contrast such faith with both the faith of his fellow Jews, and his own disciples, what are the implications for a comparative assessment today? Such a question is more easily (and less often) asked than answered as Christians (and others) look at a contemporary multireligious world. But that is no reason not to go on asking such questions as comparable examples of faith and humility do appear to be seen among neighbors near and far. The dangers of presumption about assumed religious privilege persist, including forms of Christian presumption that seem immune to challenge from the example of Jesus himself. In all such cases, the forceful challenge of Gaventa and Hays might be heard: "Wherever Jesus is invoked as the guarantor of an established order, we may rightly suspect that identity fraud is being perpetrated."[72]

One helpful and transferable aspect that emerges as significant from the healing encounters with the centurion/official and the Syrophoenician mother is the compassionate example of Jesus. As noted, Wendy Cotter plausibly elaborates the view that these (and some other) miracle stories were remembered and re told in the early Christian community in order to reveal the character of Jesus to would-be imitators of him, and to remind them of his kindness and humility. It is this dynamic of universal compassion that seems to provide the foundation for what we have repeatedly seen: that Jesus redefines Israel and extends the boundaries of the people of God. Might Christians be willing to draw a related conclusion concerning at least some Muslims, Jews and others if their visibly seen virtues of faith, humility, and praxis were to echo those commended by Jesus?

The Renunciation of Vengeance and Violence

The exclusion of vengeance is also presented as one consequence of God's universal compassion and we have placed considerable emphasis upon Jesus' non-vengeful eschatology. The two stories about Gentiles deployed by Jesus in Luke 4 are examples to Israel of a sovereign display of Yahweh's universal compassion. The message of hope in Isaiah 61, originally intended to console returned exiles, is exegeted by Jesus in

72. Gaventa and Hays, "Seeking the Identity of Jesus," 21.

Luke 4 as good news of reversal, freedom and Jubilee-release for *all* who are oppressed; it becomes a message of universal hope that excludes retribution. Jesus rejects the notion of eschatological vengeance on Israel's Gentile enemies. Instead, he will offer healing and even inclusion to them. And, if Bird is correct in his assertion that Jesus' healing of the centurion's servant is an example of love of enemy, then it is also an example of a refusal to see Gentiles as objects only of God's vengeance. In Luke 9:51–56, immediately after the positive affirmation that "whoever is not against you is for you," and not long before Jesus will tell the story of the compassionate Samaritan, Luke recounts Jesus' rebuke of his own followers. The disciples want to call down fiery retribution on inhospitable Samaritan villagers who reject them, apparently on religious grounds. The example of Jesus in Luke 4—in which he praises Naaman, a notable military enemy of Israel—also implies a refusal to act from motives of vengeance or retaliation and models the insistently forgiving spirit that becomes one of the distinctive features of Jesus' ethical teaching. The principle of the renunciation of vengeance and violence certainly relates to the Christian-Muslim encounter where retaliation, past and present, has often been an item on the agendas of the aggrieved—or projected into assurances about the eschatological future.

Reconciliation—Even of Enemies

The parable of the compassionate Samaritan has relevance for the Christian evaluation of the faith of others. The parable clearly commends judgment of the "other" based upon an internal orientation that Jesus identifies as an embodiment of the love commandment, rather than judgment based on membership of or identification with a particular group. The note of reconciliation—implicit in Jesus' dealings with Gentiles and Samaritans and other "outsider" groups—has obvious and important implications for conflict reduction in a religiously divided world. It extends even to the vexing question of contested locations for worship for which Jesus offers an eschatological answer. Is it possible that both Christian and Muslim might find in this affirmation a reminder of the *temporary* nature of all preferred worship locations?—at least by comparison with the eschatological finalities and even the appeal to

Some Conclusions about Jesus, Gentiles, and Samaritans

love of neighbor that both also affirm. A wider NT perspective makes it clear that the ultimate thrust of Jesus' redemptive ministry is to remove the social and ritual boundaries between Jew and Gentile, clean and unclean, male and female (cf. Gal 3:28). It is the person of Jesus who offers the reconciliation by which such divisions might be overcome. He is the one who has "broken down the dividing wall, that is, the hostility between [Jew and Gentile]" (Eph 2:14; cf. 2:11–19). One telling and even provocative contemporary application of the principle of reconciliation is found in the advocacy of "forgiveness as foreign policy."[73] Another writer offers a reading of the Gospel stories about Jesus and Samaritans in the light of present-day conflicts in Israel-Palestine.[74]

What might this affirming attitude of Jesus say to contemporary readers about the examples of faith, humility and commendable praxis that we might (and do) find in some people of other faiths? This too is a question that is not easily answered—but neither is it often asked. And, when it is asked, discussion (especially among theologically conservative Christians) often moves quickly to the soteriological question: could a person be *saved* by such faith, humility and behavior when these qualities are not provoked, as it were, by a personal encounter with Jesus? The Syrophoenician woman is willing (at least in the Matthean recounting of the story) to voice some distinctly Jewish affirmations but it must also be conceded that the precise nature of her formal religious faith (if any) remains elusive. Is this the reason why, as Michael Bird points out, "the story elicits no call to discipleship, no command to mission, and no request to join Jesus' entourage"?[75] The contours of the religio-political allegiance of the centurion/official are also unclear. To frame the issue another way, it is not clear from the stories whether it is the innate faith of the Gentile (or Samaritan) that is being commended to the reader, or whether this faith is simply the appropriate (perhaps even inevitable) response to the presence of Jesus; a faith that is perhaps dormant until desperate need awakens it.[76]

---

73. See Rae, "Ethics of Jesus," 47–64.
74. See Durber, "Political Reading."
75. Bird, *Jesus and the Origins*, 120.
76. Obviously the Gentile examples that Jesus quotes in the dialogue in Luke 4:25–27 do not depend upon a personal encounter with Jesus (though they are a

Recognition of Particularity

Religious distinctiveness and contrast is apparent (and not avoided or ignored) in a number of the encounter stories discussed. In the story of the meeting with the Samaritan woman, substantial and longstanding divisions are on display. Perhaps the initial silence with which Jesus responds to the Syrophoenician mother derives from a similar tension. Scripture, as a whole, has multiple examples of encounters that straddle religious boundaries (as noted earlier in this chapter). Abraham is, it seems, willing to live with this reality of multiple and different religious allegiances among those he meets and interacts with. Such undeniable particularities are also apparent in today's multireligious world. The Christian appraisal of Islam seems to require a similar willingness to acknowledge difference—and the writers mentioned in the last chapter (Volf, Kreeft, Chapman, and even Lodahl to some extent) show themselves willing and able to present a balanced account of the beliefs and life practices of devout Muslims. Any embrace of dialogue is an embrace of the listening and understanding that should leave no doubts about the deep-seated nature of the distinctive particularities of the world's religious traditions, even if there are continuities as well.

Understanding, Openness, Dialogue—and Risk

Jesus' attitude towards Samaritans displays the risks, discomfort and even danger that can be attached to Christian-Muslim and other interreligious encounters.[77] There is a theological necessity that leads Jesus to his dialogue with the Samaritan woman. Such an imperative suggests, in turn, not only divine approval for mission into Samaria but also an endorsement of its method: humble encounter framed in contextually sensitive categories and respectful, non-condescending (and yet culture-transcending) dialogue as well. The contemporary implications of such an example are obvious. Well-informed understanding and a will-

---

direct or indirect response to a prophetic encounter).

77. In the proposed complementary volume already mentioned, a number of such theological and practical implications—including a detailed discussion of interfaith dialogue—will be discussed in some detail.

Some Conclusions about Jesus, Gentiles, and Samaritans

ingness for patient dialogue almost always result in improved interreligious relations.[78] At the same time, the encounters of Jesus with Gentiles and Samaritans also show the risks, discomfort and even danger that is found in openness and dialogue. Elijah is led into the company of a pagan woman, a lowly and vulnerable widow in which his actions (in the eyes of many or most Second Temple Era Jews) are suspect: he not only associates but also eats and lodges with a woman who, nonetheless, is seen both to recognize and to accept a prophet sent by God. The way that this Gentile-favoring behavior is endorsed by Jesus is, in part, the reason for the hostile reaction after his synagogue address in Nazareth.

Reports that Gentiles have even come from Tyre and Sidon to Jesus (Luke 6:17) and the perhaps even more surprising disclosure that Jesus himself deliberately goes to "the district of Tyre and Sidon" (Matt 15:21) might well have added to the disquiet. (In fact, Blakley makes a strong case for active *resistance* by the disciples to an intentional mission to Gentiles.) The compassionate Samaritan of the parable is said to stay at least one night at the inn, doubtless to the discomfort of some or even all of the other guests. Jesus is willing to undertake a deliberate violation of cultural norms in order to bring the Samaritan woman into the equivalent of his kinship circle. He is even reported as staying for two days in Sychar with the Samaritans (John 4:40), doubtless to the discomfort of his disciples.

Assertions of any kind of continuity across religious boundaries always carry the risk of alienating those who read their own position in exclusivist terms. Perhaps this is the reason that Jesus is accused of being a Samaritan.[79] Is this simply a term of abuse, or is the accusation grounded in a real suspicion that Jesus was a Samaritan sympathizer because he identified so closely with them? Sometimes Judeans regarded

---

78. One of the features of Muck and Adeney's *Christianity Encountering World Religions* is the emphasis that they place upon the careful acquisition of knowledge of other faith and cultures, including "The Spiral of Knowledge Acquisition" (ch. 16) and "Encountering: Learning from a New Culture and Religion" (ch. 17). A similar point is made in Robinson, *Christians Meeting Hindus*, 60–61, 77–78, 82–84, 94–97.

79. "Are we not right in saying that you are a Samaritan?" (John 8:48). In the following chapter in John, Jesus is accused of being a "sinner": 9:16, 24, cf. 25, 31—which seems to be an equivalent stigma (and, from the perspective of the Synoptic Gospels, would imply a status no different from that of "Gentile").

Galileans as virtually Samaritans because of the ethnically diverse nature of Galilee but could there be something more to the accusation than simple ignorance or abuse? Is Jesus so identified with the Samaritans that his opponents could think that he might have been one? Do his prophecies about the temple or his opposition to its *cultus* lead some to think that he had Samaritan sympathies? To read or hear of Jesus' encounter with the Samaritan woman would not necessarily diminish suspicion; as Winsome Munro points out, "from the Jewish perspective with which Jesus is identified (4:9, 22), he has left the area of supreme holiness, the temple, Jerusalem, and the land of the Jews, to enter alien, profane territory, inhabited by people who have fallen away from the covenant and become unholy."[80] Gail O'Day also notes the link with the preceding material in John: Jesus "leaves the land and the people who are 'clean', to enter a land that is 'unclean.'"[81] Dialogue between people of different faiths requires conversation; conversation requires a proximity that can invite misunderstanding, risk and even danger. These can be features of the interreligious encounter today, not least in meetings between Christians and Muslims.

Despite such risks, Jesus' attitude towards Samaritans includes a refusal to respond to provocation. We have noted Jesus' brief but forceful rebuke to the disciples' request for reprisals against inhospitable Samaritans (Luke 9:51–56). The response is a revealing indication of his impatience with ethnic bias and the refusal of vengeance that characterizes his teaching about Gentiles (as we have seen in the Nazareth synagogue address) and in his call to love enemies (Matt 5:44). As Ida Glaser puts it, the Samaritans "raise issues most likely to spoil relationships with people of other faiths, the issues of prejudice and hostility." But she also adds that it is with the Samaritans that we have the best example of Jesus interacting with people of a different faith.[82]

The theme of reversal offers warning (and even reprimand) to those whose attitudes today display indifference to the faith of "outsiders," or whose self-assured confidence attempts triumphantly to exclude or denigrate others. Christian history displays sad examples of the self-

---

80. Munro, "Pharisee and the Samaritan," 712.

81. O'Day, "Surprised by Faith," 115.

82. *Bible and Other Faiths*, 162.

Some Conclusions about Jesus, Gentiles, and Samaritans

assured willingness to coerce the very categories of people ("sinners" and "outsiders") that seem to be treated by Jesus as worthy of respect, given what we have seen of his attitudes to Gentiles and Samaritans. The example of Jesus offers repeated warnings that religious appraisal of the other is not to be based on external markers such as unconventional behavior and certainly not on those of gender or ethnicity.

A Final Word

Richard Hays writes that God is involved in the biblical drama in three interwoven ways: as author of and as chief actor in the drama, but also as "actually *working through* the drama to transform the audience."[83] Theological exegesis derives its essential characteristics from the *character* of the divine author/speaker who is disclosed on the pages of Scripture. Such exegesis and interpretation has some distinctive characteristics: the author is the living God, and this author remains, by means of his Spirit, present to the reader. "The divine author of Scripture is perennially present and ubiquitously speaking."[84] The model we have advocated in this book calls for *engagement* with the religions based on the example of Jesus disclosed on the pages of Scripture—a transformative model as Scripture inspires new perspectives, fresh insights, and a willingness (perhaps even a determination) to look with new eyes at a religiously plural world.

Jesus signals the extraordinary significance of Gentiles and Samaritans by his employment of their example as signs and affirmations of the eschatological inversion of the present/coming Rule of God. In Luke 4 he employs a principle of eschatological reversal when exegeting what might seem to be two rather minor and insignificant incidents centering on Gentiles to characterize the new eschatological age being inaugurated in him. He employs a hermeneutical method that enables hearers—then and now—to see that the "weight" to be attached to his encounters with Gentiles far exceeds the actual number of their occurrences. Like the mustard seed of the parable, the kind of faith, humil-

---

83. "Can Narrative Criticism Recover,?" 201; original emphasis. Hays does go on to add the qualification that "here the metaphor starts to reach its limitations."

84. Bowald, "Character of Theological Interpretation," 168.

Jesus and the Religions

ity, and behavior displayed by some Gentiles (and some Samaritans), is elevated by Jesus to assume theological and missional significance beyond what might have been imagined. Considerable transformative, missional and relational implications might flow if the church were to scrutinize its own evaluation of the religions along the lines of this principle of "elevation from the margins" apparently embraced by Jesus himself.

At the beginning of this book we outlined a spectrum of Christian attitudes to the religions, a spectrum that ranges from indifference and sentimentality to hostility and confrontation. To consider the example of Jesus is to have these attitudes challenged. Our attempts at a contextual and theological reading of Scripture have endeavored (as Brevard Childs puts it) to model the "true expositor of the Christian scriptures . . . who awaits in anticipation toward becoming the interpreted rather than the interpreter."[85] Mention has already been made of Koskie's remark that one "theological way of reading would be to allow Scripture to change our questions and challenge us, bringing to our attention something other than the agenda we bring to it."[86] Such an agenda might be generated by an over-preoccupation with salvation (usually formulated only in individualistic categories) that can impede the recognition of God's actions outside the covenantal communities of faith, whether Jewish or Christian.

Given the continuing temptation among Christians towards triumphalism, the humanity and servant spirit of Jesus offers a better path. One finding of the recently concluded "Identity of Jesus Project" is that *"Jesus is a disturbing, destabilizing figure. . . .* And it has remained true across time that Jesus' teachings and presence have a way of unsettling things, challenging privilege . . ."[87] Disciples are still called to measure their fears, insecurities, prejudices and indifferences against the example of Jesus; our attempt to find a better way has involved looking at his example. In terms of method and a desirable outcome, we might even re word (in what follows) a claim that Karl Barth attributed to John Calvin: "Having first established what stands in the text, we have

85. Childs, *Biblical Theology*, 86.
86. Koskie, "Seeking Comment," 247.
87. Gaventa and Hays, "Seeking the Identity of Jesus," 21; original emphasis.

Some Conclusions about Jesus, Gentiles, and Samaritans

set ourselves to re-think the material about Jesus and to wrestle with it, till the walls which separate the twenty-first century from the first have become transparent. Jesus speaks and acts, and the person of the twenty-first century hears. The conversation between the original record and the reader moves round the subject-matter, until a distinction between yesterday and to-day becomes impossible."[88] To the extent that we have heard Jesus speak and act in his encounters with Gentiles and Samaritans, this making "transparent" has been our experience too. We have, in fact, heard something of what it means to "have the same attitude of mind that Christ Jesus had" (Phil 2:5), and to hear that "whoever claims to live in him must live [literally 'walk'] as Jesus did" (1 John 2:6).

---

88. Barth's original text, with the apostle Paul in mind, reads: "How energetically Calvin, having first established what stands in the text, sets himself to re-think the whole material and to wrestle with it, till the walls which separate the sixteenth century from the first become transparent! Paul speaks, and the man of the sixteenth century hears. The conversation between the original record and the reader moves round the subject-matter, until a distinction between yesterday and to-day becomes impossible" (*Epistle to the Romans*, 7).

Bibliography

Abu-Nimer, Mohammed, and David Augsburger. *Peace-Building by, between and beyond Muslims and Evangelical Christians*. Lanham, MD: Lexington, 2009.
Adams, Dwayne H. *The Sinner in Luke*. ETS Monograph Series 8. Eugene, OR: Pickwick, 2008.
Ahmed, Akbar S. *Islam under Siege: Living Dangerously in a Post-Honor World*. Cambridge, UK: Polity, 2003.
Allen, Michael. "Divine Transcendence and the Reading of Scripture." *Scottish Bulletin of Evangelical Theology* 26 (2008) 32–56.
Alonso, Pablo. *Bethsaida: A City by the North Shore of the Sea of Galilee*. Bethsaida Excavations Project 4. Kirksville, MO: Truman State University Press, 2009.
———. *The Woman Who Changed Jesus: Crossing Boundaries in Mk 7,24–30*. Biblical Tools and Studies 11. Leuven, Belgium: Peeters, 2011.
———. "The Woman Who Changed Jesus: Text and Context." In *Jesus of Galilee: Contextual Christology for the 21st Century*, edited by Robert Lassalle-Klein, 121–34. Maryknoll, NY: Orbis, 2011.
Anderson, Paul N., et al. *John, Jesus, and History*. Vol. 1, *Critical Appraisals of Critical Views*. Atlanta: Society of Biblical Literature, 2007.
Anderson, Robert T., and Terry Giles. *The Keepers: An Introduction to the History and Culture of the Samaritans*. Peabody, MA: Hendrickson, 2002.
Arav, Rami, and Richard A. Freund. *Bethsaida: A City by the North Shore of the Sea of Galilee*. Bethsaida Excavations Project 3, 4. Kirksville, MO: Truman State University Press, 2004, 2009.
Arnal, William E. "Galilee, Galileans." In *The New Interpreter's Dictionary of the Bible*, edited by Katherine Doob Sakenfield et al., 2:514–18. Nashville: Abingdon, 2007.
Ashton, John. "John and the Johannine Literature: The Woman at the Well." In *The Cambridge Companion to Biblical Interpretation*, edited by John Barton, 259–75. Cambridge: Cambridge University Press, 1998.
Baillie, Donald M. *Faith in God*. 2nd ed. London: Faber, 1964.
Barth, Karl. *The Epistle to the Romans*. Oxford: Oxford University Press, 1933.
Barton, John, editor. *The Cambridge Companion to Biblical Interpretation*. Cambridge, UK: Cambridge University Press, 1998.
Barton, Stephen, editor. *The Cambridge Companion to the Gospels*. Cambridge, UK: Cambridge University Press, 2006.
Batey, Richard A. *Jesus and the Forgotten City: New Light on the Urban World of Jesus*. Grand Rapids: Baker, 1991.
———. "Sepphoris and the Jesus Movement." *New Testament Studies* 47 (2001) 402–9.

Bibliography

Bauckham, Richard. "Eyewitnesses and Critical History: A Response to Jens Schröter and Craig Evans." *Journal for the Study of the New Testament* 31 (2008) 221–35.
———. *God Crucified*. Grand Rapids: Eerdmans, 1998.
———. "Historiographical Characteristics of the Gospel of John." *New Testament Studies* 53 (2007) 17–36.
———. *Jesus and the Eyewitnesses. The Gospels as Eyewitness Testimony*. Grand Rapids: Eerdmans, 2006.
———. *Jesus and the God of Israel: "God Crucified" and Other Studies on the New Testament's Christology of Divine Identity*. Grand Rapids: Eerdmans, 2008.
———. "The Scrupulous Priest and the Good Samaritan: Jesus' Parabolic Interpretation of the Law of Moses." *New Testament Studies* 44 (1998) 475–89.
Beare, F. W. *The Gospel according to Matthew*. San Francisco: Harper & Row, 1981.
Beasley-Murray, George R. *John*. Word Biblical Commentary 36. Waco, TX: Word, 1987.
Billings, J. Todd. *The Word of God for the People of God: An Entryway to the Theological Interpretation of Scripture*. Grand Rapids: Eerdmans, 2010.
Bird, Michael F. "The Criterion of Greek Language and Context: A Response to Stanley E. Porter." *Journal for the Study of the Historical Jesus* 4:1 (2006) 55–67.
——— *Crossing Over Sea and Land: Jewish Missionary Activity in the Second Temple Period*. Grand Rapids: Baker Academic, 2010.
———. "Jesus and the Gentiles after Jeremias: Patterns and Prospects." *Currents in Biblical Research* 4 (2005) 83–108.
———. *Jesus and the Origins of the Gentile Mission*. Library of New Testament Studies 331. London: T. & T. Clark, 2007.
———. "The Purpose and Preservation of the Jesus Tradition: Moderate Evidence for a Conserving Force in its Transmission." *Bulletin of Biblical Research* 15 (2005) 161–85.
Blakley, J. Ted. "Incomprehension or Resistance?: The Markan Disciples and the Narrative Logic of Mark 4:1—8:30." PhD diss., University of St. Andrews, 2008.
Blomberg, Craig L. *Jesus and the Gospels: An Introduction and Survey*. 2nd ed. Nashville: B. & H., 2009.
Bock, Darrell L. *Luke 9:51—24:53*. Baker Exegetical Commentary on the New Testament 2. Grand Rapids: Baker, 1996.
Bockmuehl, Markus. "God's Life as a Jew: Remembering the Son of God as Son of David." In *Seeking the Identity of Jesus: A Pilgrimage*, edited by Beverly Roberts Gaventa and Richard B. Hays, 60–78. Grand Rapids: Eerdmans, 2008.
Bockmuehl, Markus, and Alan J. Torrance, editors. *Scripture's Doctrine and Theology's Bible: How the New Testament Shapes Christian Dogmatics*. Grand Rapids: Baker Academic, 2008.
Boers, Hendrikus. *Neither on This Mountain nor in Jerusalem: A Study of John 4*. Society of Biblical Literature Monograph Series 5. Atlanta: Scholars, 1988.
Booth, R. P. *Jesus and the Laws of Purity: Tradition History and Legal History in Mark 7*. Journal for the Study of the New Testament: Supplement Series 13. Sheffield: University of Sheffield Press, 1986.
Boring, M. Eugene. "Matthew." In *The New Interpreter's Bible*, edited by Leander E. Keck, 8:87–505. Nashville: Abingdon, 2004.
Bosch, David J. "Hermeneutical Principles in the Biblical Foundation for Mission." *Evangelical Review of Theology* 17 (1993) 437–51.

———. *Transforming Mission: Paradigm Shifts in Theology of Mission*. Maryknoll, NY: Orbis, 1991.
Bovon, François. *Luke 1: A Commentary on the Gospel of Luke 1:1—9:50*. Hermeneia. Minneapolis: Fortress, 2002.
———. *Luke the Theologian: Fifty-Five Years of Research (1950-2005)*. Waco, TX: Baylor University Press, 2006.
Bowald, Mark Alan. "The Character of Theological Interpretation of Scripture." *International Journal of Systematic Theology* 12 (2010) 162–83.
Brenner, Athalya, Archie Chi Chung Lee, and Gale A. Yee, editors. *Genesis*. Texts@ Contexts. Minneapolis: Fortress, 2010.
Brodie, Thomas L. *The Gospel according to John: A Literary and Theological Commentary*. Oxford: Oxford University Press, 1993.
Brown, Raymond E. *The Gospel according to John*. Vol. 1. Anchor Bible 29. Garden City, NY: Doubleday, 1966.
Bruner, F. D. *Matthew: A Commentary*. 2 vols. Rev. ed. Grand Rapids: Eerdmans, 2004, 2007.
Burge, Gary M. *Encounters with Jesus: Uncover the Ancient Culture, Discover Hidden Meanings*. Grand Rapids: Zondervan, 2010.
———. *John: The NIV Application Commentary*. Grand Rapids: Zondervan, 2000.
Byrne, Brendan. *The Hospitality of God: A Reading of Luke's Gospel*. Collegeville, MN: Liturgical, 2000.
Cahnman, Werner J. *Jews and Gentiles: A Historical Sociology of Their Relations*. New Brunswick, NJ: Transaction, 2004.
Caldwell, Stuart. "Jesus in Samaria: A Paradigm for Church Planting among Muslims." *International Journal of Frontier Missions* 17 (2000) 25–31.
Calvin, John. *Matthew, Mark and Luke: A Harmony of the Gospels with Commentary*. Translated by A. W. Morrison. Grand Rapids: Eerdmans, 1989.
Carey, Greg. *Sinners: Jesus and His Earliest Followers*. Waco, TX: Baylor University Press, 2009.
Carrell, Peter. Review of *The Partings of the Ways* by James Dunn. *Reviews in Biblical Literature*, November 2007.
Carter, Warren. *Matthew and the Margins: A Sociopolitical and Religious Reading*. The Bible and Liberation. Maryknoll, NY: Orbis, 2000.
Cary, Phillip. *Jonah*. Brazos Theological Commentary on the Bible. Grand Rapids: Brazos, 2008.
Chancey, Mark A. *Greco-Roman Culture and the Galilee of Jesus*. Cambridge: Cambridge University Press, 2005.
———. "How Jewish Was Jesus' Galilee?" *Biblical Archaeology Review* 33/4 (July–August 2007) 42.
———. *The Myth of a Gentile Galilee*. Cambridge: Cambridge University Press, 2002.
Chancey, Mark A., and Eric M. Meyers. "Did Jesus Speak Greek?" *Biblical Archaeology Review* 26/4 (July–August 2000) 33.
Chapman, Alister, et al. *Seeing Things Their Way: Intellectual History and the Return of Religion*. Notre Dame, IN: University of Notre Dame Press, 2009.
Chapman, Colin. *Cross and Crescent: Responding to the Challenge of Islam*. 2nd ed. Downers Grove, IL: InterVarsity, 2008.
Charlesworth, James H., editor. *Jesus and Archaeology*. Grand Rapids: Eerdmans, 2006.

Bibliography

Charlesworth, James H., and Petr Pokorný. *Jesus Research: An International Perspective.* Grand Rapids: Eerdmans, 2009.
Childs, Brevard. *Biblical Theology of the Old and New Testaments.* London: SCM, 1992.
Chilton, Bruce, and Craig A. Evans. *The Missions of James, Peter, and Paul: Tensions in Early Christianity.* Supplements to Novum Testamentum 115. Leiden: Brill, 2005.
Coggins, R. J. *Samaritans and Jews: The Origins of Samaritanism Reconsidered.* Atlanta: John Knox, 1975.
Collins, John J., and Daniel C. Harlow. *Eerdmans Dictionary of Early Judaism.* Grand Rapids: Eerdmans, 2010.
Cosgrove, Charles H. "Did Paul Value Ethnicity?" *Catholic Biblical Quarterly* 68 (2006) 268–90.
Cotter, Wendy J. *The Christ of the Miracle Stories: Portrait through Encounter.* Grand Rapids: Baker Academic, 2010.
Cox, Harvey. *Many Mansions: A Christian's Encounter with Other Faiths.* 2nd ed. Boston: Beacon, 1992.
Crockett, Larrimore C. "Luke 4:25–27 and Jewish-Gentile Relations in Luke-Acts." *Journal of Biblical Literature* 88 (1969) 177–83.
Crook, Zeba. "Honor, Shame, and Social Status Revisited." *Journal of Biblical Literature* 128 (2009) 591–611.
Crossan, John Dominic. *The Historical Jesus: The Life of a Mediterranean Jewish Peasant.* San Francisco: HarperSanFrancisco, 1991.
Crossley, James G. *The New Testament and Jewish Law: A Guide for the Perplexed.* London: T. & T. Clark, 2010.
———. "Social-Sciences, Ideology and Christian Origins: Debating with Lloyd Pietersen." *Conversations in Religion & Theology* 7 (2009) 22–27.
———. *Why Christianity Happened: A Sociohistorical Account of Christian Origins (26–50 CE).* Louisville: Westminster John Knox, 2006.
D'Costa, Gavin. *The Meeting of Religions and the Trinity.* Faith Meets Faith. Maryknoll, NY: Orbis, 2000.
Das, Somen. *Christian Faith and Multiform Culture in India.* Bangalore: United Theological College, 1987.
Daube, David. "Jesus and the Samaritan Woman: The Meaning of *Sygchraomai.*" *Journal of Biblical Literature* 69 (1950) 137–47.
Davies, W. D., and Dale C. Allison Jr. *The Gospel according to Saint Matthew.* 3 vols. Edinburgh: T. & T. Clark, 1988, 1991, 1997.
Davis, E. F., and R. B. Hays. *The Art of Reading Scripture.* Grand Rapids: Eerdmans, 2003.
De Béthune, Pierre-François. *By Faith and Hospitality: The Monastic Tradition as a Model for Interreligious Encounter.* Leominster: Gracewing, 2003.
———. *Interreligious Hospitality: The Fulfilment of Dialogue.* Collegeville, MN: Liturgical, 2010.
Di Segni, Leah. "Early Christian Authors on Samaritans and Samaritanism: A Review Article." *Journal for the Study of Judaism* 37 (2006) 241–59.
Donaldson, Terence L. *Judaism and the Gentiles: Jewish Patterns of Universalism (to 135 CE).* Waco, TX: Baylor University Press, 2007.
———. *Paul and the Gentiles: Remapping the Apostle's Convictional World.* Minneapolis: Fortress, 2006.

———. "The Vindicated Son: A Narrative Approach to Matthean Christology." In *Contours of Christology in the New Testament*, edited by Richard N. Longenecker, 100–121. Grand Rapids: Eerdmans, 2005.
Downing, F. Gerald. "In Quest of First-Century C.E. Galilee." *Catholic Biblical Quarterly* 66 (2004) 78–97.
Drummond, Richard. *Toward a New Age in Christian Theology*. Maryknoll, NY: Orbis, 1985.
Dunn, James D. G. "Jesus and Purity: An Ongoing Debate." *New Testament Studies* 48 (2002) 449–67.
———. *Jesus Remembered*. Christianity in the Making 1. Grand Rapids: Eerdmans, 2003.
———. "Pharisees, Sinners and Jesus." In Jacob Neusner et al., *The Social World of Formative Christianity and Judaism*, 264–89. Philadelphia: Fortress, 1988.
Dupuis, Jacques. *Christianity and the Religions: From Confrontation to Dialogue*. Maryknoll, NY: Orbis, 2002.
———. *Toward a Christian Theology of Religious Pluralism*. Maryknoll, NY: Orbis, 1997.
Durber, Susan. "Political Reading: Jesus and the Samaritans—Reading in Today's Context." *Practical Theology* 4 (2002) 67–79.
Edwards, Douglas R. "Recent Work in Galilee: A Village and Its Region." Abstract of paper present at the Annual Meeting of the Society of Biblical Literature, November 18, 2006.
Esler, Philip F. "Jesus and the Reduction of Intergroup Conflict: The Parable of the Good Samaritan in the Light of Social Identity Theory." *Biblical Interpretation* 8 (2000) 325–56.
Fee, Gordon. "The New Testament and Kenosis Christology." In *Exploring Kenotic Christology: The Self-Emptying of God*, edited by C. Stephen Evans, 25–44. Oxford: Oxford University Press, 2006.
Fiensy, David. *Jesus the Galilean: Soundings in a First Century Life*. Piscataway, NJ: Gorgias, 2007.
Fitzmyer, Joseph A. "Did Jesus Speak Greek?" *Biblical Archaeology Review* 18/5 (September–October 1992) 58.
Flett, John G. *The Witness of God: The Trinity, Missio Dei, Karl Barth, and the Nature of Christian Community*. Grand Rapids: Eerdmans, 2010.
Fowl, Stephen E. *Engaging Scripture: A Model for Theological Interpretation*. Oxford: Blackwell, 1998.
France, R. T. *The Gospel of Matthew*. New International Commentary on the New Testament. Grand Rapids: Eerdmans, 2007.
Francis, Mariam. "The Samaritan Woman." *Asian Journal of Theology* 2 (1988) 147–48.
Franke, John R. "Still the Way, the Truth, and the Life." *Christianity Today*, December 2009. Online: http://www.christianitytoday.com/ct/2009/december/6.27.html.
Fredriksen, Paula. *Jesus of Nazareth, King of the Jews: A Jewish Life and the Emergence of Christianity*. New York: Knopf, 1999.
Freyne, Seán. "Archaeology and the Historical Jesus." In *Jesus and Archaeology*, edited by James H. Charlesworth, 64–83. Grand Rapids: Eerdmans, 2006.
———. "The Galilean Jesus and a Contemporary Christology." *Theological Studies* 70 (2009) 281–97.

Bibliography

———. "Galilee and Judaea in the First Century." In *The Cambridge History of Christianity: Origins to Constantine*, edited by Margaret M. Mitchell and Frances M. Young, 37–51. Cambridge: Cambridge University, 2006.
———. *Galilee and Gospel: Selected Essays*. Wissenschaftliche Untersuchungen zum Neuen Testament 125. Tübingen: Mohr, 2000.
———. "Galilee as Laboratory: Experiments for New Testament Historians and Theologians." *New Testament Studies* 53 (2007) 147–64.
———. *Galilee from Alexander the Great to Hadrian 323 B.C.E. to 135 C.E.: A Study of Second Temple Judaism*. Wilmington, DE: M. Glazier, 1980.
———. "Galilee, Jesus and the Contribution of Archaeology." *Expository Times* 119 (2008) 573–81.
———. *Galilee, Jesus and the Gospels: Literary Approaches and Historical Investigations*. Dublin: Gill and Macmillan, 1988.
———. "Galilee-Jerusalem Relations according to Josephus' *Life*." *New Testament Studies* 33 (1987) 600–609.
———. *Jesus, a Jewish Galilean: A New Reading of the Jesus-Story*. London: T. & T. Clark, 2004.
———. "Jesus and the 'Servant' Community in Zion: Continuity in Context." In *Jesus from Judaism to Christianity: Continuum Approaches to the Historical Jesus* edited by Tom Holmén, 10 9–24. New York, NY: T & T Clark, 2007.
———. "Jesus in Context: Galilee and Gospel." In *Jesus of Galilee: Contextual Christology for the 21st Century*, edited by Robert Lassalle-Klein, 1 7–38. Maryknoll, NY: Orbis, 2011.
Funk, Robert W. *Honest to Jesus: Jesus for a New Millennium*. San Francisco: HarperSanFrancisco, 1996.
Furstenberg, Yair. "Defilement Penetrating the Body: A New Understanding of Contamination in Mark 7.15." *New Testament Studies* 54 (2008) 176–200.
Garland, David E. *Reading Matthew: A Literary and Theological Commentary on the First Gospel*. Macon, GA: Smyth & Helwys, 2001.
Gaventa, Beverly Roberts. "Learning and Relearning the Identity of Jesus in Luke-Acts." In *Seeking the Identity of Jesus: A Pilgrimage*, edited by Beverly Roberts Gaventa and Richard B. Hays, 148–65. Grand Rapids: Eerdmans, 2008.
Gaventa, Beverly Roberts, and Richard B. Hays, editors. *Seeking the Identity of Jesus: A Pilgrimage*. Grand Rapids: Eerdmans, 2008.
———. "Seeking the Identity of Jesus," in Gaventa and Hays, *Seeking the Identity of Jesus*, 1–24.
Gench, Frances Taylor. *Back to the Well: Women's Encounters with Jesus in the Gospels*. Louisville: Westminster John Knox, 2004.
Gilbert, Gary. "Gentiles," In *Eerdmans Dictionary of Early Judaism*, edited by John J. Collins and Daniel C. Harlow, 670–73. Grand Rapids: Eerdmans, 2010.
Gillmayr-Bucher, Susanne. "'She Came to Test Him with Hard Questions': Foreign Women and Their View on Israel." *Biblical Interpretation* 15 (2007) 135–50.
Glaser, Ida. *The Bible and Other Faiths: Christian Responsibility in a World of Religions*. Downers Grove, IL: InterVarsity, 2005.
Glasser, Arthur F. *Announcing the Kingdom: The Story of God's Mission in the Bible*. Grand Rapids: Baker Academic, 2003.
Gorman, Michael J. "A 'Seamless Garment' Approach to Biblical Interpretation." *Journal of Theological Interpretation* 1 (2007) 117–28.

Grabbe, Lester L. *Judaic Religion in the Second Temple Period: Belief and Practice from the Exile to Yavneh.* New York: Routledge, 2000.
Gray, Timothy C. *The Temple in the Gospel of Mark: A Study in Its Narrative Role.* Tübingen: Mohr/Siebeck, 2008; Grand Rapids: Baker Academic, 2010.
Green, Joel B. *The Gospel of Luke.* New International Commentary on the New Testament. Grand Rapids: Eerdmans, 1997.
———. *Seized by Truth: Reading the Bible as Scripture.* Nashville: Abingdon, 2007.
Green, Joel B., editor. *Hearing the New Testament: Strategies for Interpretation.* 2nd ed. Grand Rapids: Eerdmans, 2010.
Green, Joel B., Scot McKnight, and I. Howard Marshall, editors. *Dictionary of Jesus and the Gospels.* Downers Grove, IL: InterVarsity, 1992.
Green, Michael. *The Message of Matthew.* Rev. ed. The Bible Speaks Today. Leicester, UK: Intervarsity, 2000.
Griffith, Sidney H. Review of *Allah* by Miroslav Volf. *First Things* 216 (October 2011) 56–58.
Griffiths, Paul, and Delmas Lewis. "On Grading Religions, Seeking Truth, and Being Nice to People—a Reply to Professor Hick." *Religious Studies* 19 (1983) 75–80.
Guelich, Robert A. *Mark 1—8:26.* Word Biblical Commentary 34A. Dallas: Word, 1989.
Gundry, Robert H. *Mark: A Commentary on His Apology for the Cross.* Grand Rapids: Eerdmans, 1992.
Haacker, K. "Samaritan, Samaria." In *New International Dictionary of New Testament Theology*, edited by Colin Brown, 3:449–67. Grand Rapids: Zondervan, 1986.
Hagner, Donald A. *Matthew.* 2 vols. Word Biblical Commentary 33A, B. Dallas: Word, 1993, 1995.
Hakola, Raimo. *Identity Matters: John, the Jews, and Jewishness.* Leiden: Brill, 2005.
Hare, Douglas R. A. *Matthew.* Interpretation. Louisville: John Knox, 1993.
Hare, Douglas R. A., and Daniel J. Harrington. "'Make Disciples of All the Gentiles' (Mt 28:19)." *Catholic Biblical Quarterly* 37 (1975) 359–69.
Harrington, Daniel J. *The Gospel of Matthew.* Sacra pagina. Collegeville, MN: Liturgical, 1991.
Harrington, Hannah. "Purity and the Dead Sea Scrolls—Current Issues." *Currents in Biblical Research* 4 (2006) 397–428.
———. *The Purity Texts.* Companion to the Qumran Scrolls 5. London: T. & T. Clark, 2004.
Hayes, Christine E. *Gentile Impurities and Jewish Identities: Intermarriage and Conversion from the Bible to the Talmud.* Oxford: Oxford University Press, 2002.
Hays, Richard B. "Can Narrative Criticism Recover the Theological Unity of Scripture?" *Journal of Theological Interpretation* 2 (2008) 193–211.
———. "Reading the Bible with Eyes of Faith: The Practice of Theological Exegesis." *Journal of Theological Interpretation* 1 (2007) 5–21.
Held, Heinz Joachim. "Matthew as Interpreter of the Miracle Stories." In *Tradition and Interpretation in Matthew*, by Günther Bornkamm, Gerhard Barth, Heinz Joachim Held, 165–299. London: SCM, 1963.
Hellerman, Joseph H. *Jesus and the People of God: Reconfiguring Ethnic Identity.* New Testament Monographs 21. Sheffield: Sheffield Phoenix, 2007.
Hengel, Martin. *The "Hellenization" of Judaea in the First Century after Christ.* London: SCM, 1989.
———. *Judaism and Hellenism.* Philadelphia: Fortress, 1974.

Bibliography

———. *Studies in the Gospel of Mark.* Philadelphia: Fortress, 1985.
Hick, John. "On Grading Religions." *Religious Studies* 17 (1981) 451–67.
Hjelm, Ingrid. "What Do Samaritans and Jews Have in Common?: Recent Trends in Samaritan Studies." *Currents in Biblical Research* 3 (2004) 9–59.
Holmén, Tom. *Jesus and Jewish Covenant Thinking.* Biblical Interpretation Series 55. Leiden: Brill, 2001.
Hoppe, Leslie J. "Capernaum and Its Synagogue." *Bible Today* 46 (2008) 254–59.
Horsley, Richard A. *Galilee: History, Politics, People.* Valley Forge, PA: Trinity, 1995.
Iverson, Kelly R. *Gentiles in the Gospel of Mark: "Even the Dogs under the Table Eat the Children's Crumbs".* Library of New Testament Studies 339. London: T. & T. Clark, 2007.
Jensen, Michael P. "'In Spirit and in Truth': Can Charles Taylor Help the Woman at the Well Find Her Authentic Self?" *Studies in Christian Ethics* 21 (2008) 325–41.
Jenson, Robert W. "Identity, Jesus, and Exegesis," In *Seeking the Identity of Jesus: A Pilgrimage*, edited by Beverly Roberts Gaventa and Richard B. Hays, 43–59. Grand Rapids: Eerdmans, 2008.
Jeremias, Joachim. *Jesus' Promise to the Nations.* Translated by S. H. Hooke. London: SCM, 1958.
———. *The Parables of Jesus.* Translated by S. H. Hooke. London: SCM, 1972.
Johns, Anthony. "Islam as a Challenge to Christianity." In *Christianity among World Religions*, edited by Hans Küng and Jürgen Moltmann, 13–21. Edinburgh: T. & T. Clark, 1986.
Kaminsky, Joel S. *Yet I Loved Jacob: Reclaiming the Biblical Concept of Election.* Nashville: Abingdon, 2007.
Kazen, Thomas. "The Good Samaritan and a Presumptive Corpse." *Svensk Exegetisk Å[set circle over A]rsbok* 71 (2006) 131–44.
———. *Jesus and Purity Halakhah: Was Jesus Indifferent to Impurity?* Coniectanea biblica: New Testament Series 38. Stockholm: Almqvist & Wiksell, 2002.
Kee, Howard C. "Early Christianity in the Galilee: Reassessing the Evidence from the Gospels." In *The Galilee in Late Antiquity*, edited by Lee I. Levine, 3–22. New York: Jewish Theological Seminary of America, 1992.
Keener, Craig S. *A Commentary on the Gospel of Matthew: A Socio-Rhetorical Commentary.* Rev. ed. Grand Rapids: Eerdmans, 2009.
———. *The Gospel of John: A Commentary.* Peabody, MA: Hendrickson, 2003.
———. *The Historical Jesus of the Gospels.* Grand Rapids: Eerdmans, 2009.
———. *The IVP Bible Background Commentary: New Testament.* Downer's Grove, IL: InterVarsity, 1993.
———. "Some New Testament Invitations to Ethnic Reconciliation." *Evangelical Quarterly* 75 (2003) 195–213.
Kelsey, David. *Proving Doctrine: The Uses of Scripture in Modern Theology.* Harrisburg, PA: Trinity, 1999.
Kingsbury, Jack Dean. "Observations on the 'Miracle Chapters' of Matthew 8–9." *Catholic Biblical Quarterly* 40 (1978) 559–73.
Kirk, J. Andrew. *Mission under Scrutiny: Confronting Current Challenges.* Minneapolis: Fortress, 2006.
"A Kiss of Heaven: Abraham, Global Blessing, and Civil Society." *Encounters Mission Journal* 17 (April 2007) 1–5. Online: http://www.redcliffe.org/SpecialistCentres/EncountersMissionJournal/vw/1/ItemID/43.

Klawans, Jonathan. *Impurity and Sin in Ancient Judaism*. Oxford: Oxford University Press, 2000.
Knowles, Michael P. "What Was the Victim Wearing?: Literary, Economic, and Social Contexts for the Parable of the Good Samaritan." *Biblical Interpretation* 12 (2004) 145–74.
Koester, Craig R. "The Savior of the World (John 4:42)." *Journal of Biblical Literature* 109 (1990) 665–80.
Koskie, Steven J. "Seeking Comment: The Commentary and the Bible as Christian Scripture." *Journal of Theological Interpretation* 1 (2007) 237–49.
Köstenberger, Andreas J. "Jesus the Good Shepherd Who Will Also Bring Other Sheep." *Bulletin for Biblical Research* 12 (2002) 67–96.
———. *John*. Grand Rapids: Baker Academic, 2004.
———. *A Theology of John's Gospel and Letters*. Grand Rapids: Zondervan, 2009.
Larsen, Kasper Bro. *Recognizing the Stranger: Recognition Scenes in the Gospel of John*. Biblical Interpretation Series 93. Leiden: Brill, 2008.
Lassalle-Klein, Robert, ed. *Jesus of Galilee: Contextual Christology for the 21st Century*. Maryknoll, NY: Orbis, 2011.
Lawrence, Jonathan D. *Washing in Water: Trajectories of Ritual Bathing in the Hebrew Bible and Second Temple Literature*. Society of Biblical Literature Academia Biblica 23. Leiden: Brill, 2006.
Lawrence, Louise Joy. *An Ethnography of the Gospel of Matthew: A Critical Assessment of the Use of the Honour and Shame Model in New Testament Studies*. Tubingen: Mohr/Siebeck, 2003.
Le Grys, Alan. Review of *Thiselton on Hermeneutics* by Anthony C. Thiselton. *Journal for the Study of the New Testament* 29 (2007) 163–64.
Levine, Amy-Jill. "Theory, Apologetic, History: Reviewing Jesus' Jewish Context." *Australian Biblical Review* 55 (2007) 57–78.
Loader, William R. G. *Jesus' Attitude towards the Law: A Study of the Gospels*. Grand Rapids: Eerdmans, 2002.
Lodahl, Michael. *Claiming Abraham: Reading the Bible and the Qur'an Side by Side*. Grand Rapids: Brazos, 2010.
Lohr, Joel N. *Chosen and Unchosen: Conceptions of Election in the Pentateuch and Jewish-Christian Interpretation*. Winona Lake, IN: Eisenbrauns, 2009.
Love, Stuart L. *Jesus and Marginal Women: The Gospel of Matthew in Social-Scientific Perspective*. Matrix: The Bible in Mediterranean Context 5. Eugene, OR: Cascade, 2009.
Luz, Ulrich. *Matthew 8–20: A Commentary*. Minneapolis: Fortress, 2001.
MacDonald, John. *The Theology of the Samaritans*. Philadelphia: Westminster, 1964.
Mack, Burton. *The Lost Gospel: The Book of Q and Christian Origins*. San Francisco: HarperCollins, 1993.
———. *A Myth of Innocence: Mark and Christian Origins*. Philadelphia: Fortress, 1988.
Magen, Yitzhak. "Bells, Pendants, Snakes and Stones." *Biblical Archaeology Review* 36/6 (November 2010) 29–30.
Malchow, Bruce V. "Wisdom's Contribution to Dialogue." *Biblical Theology Bulletin* 13 (1983) 111–15.
Malina, Bruce J. *The Social Gospel of Jesus: The Kingdom of God in Mediterranean Perspective*. Minneapolis: Fortress, 2001.

Bibliography

Malina, Bruce J., and Richard L. Rohbaugh. *Social Science Commentary on the Synoptic Gospels.* 2nd ed. Minneapolis: Fortress, 2003.

Marshall, I. Howard. *Luke: Historian and Theologian.* 3rd ed. Exeter, UK: Paternoster, 1998.

———. *New Testament Theology: Many Witnesses, One Gospel.* Downers Grove, IL: InterVarsity, 2004.

Marshall, I. Howard, et al., editors. *The New Bible Dictionary.* 3rd ed. Downers Grove, IL: InterVarsity, 1996.

Matera, Frank J. "New Testament Theology: History, Method, and Identity." *Catholic Biblical Quarterly* 67 (2005) 1–21.

McCullough, Ross. "Westernizing Islam and the American Right." *First Things* 214 (June–July 2011) 17–19.

McDermott, Gerald D. *Can Evangelicals Learn from World Religions?: Jesus, Revelation, and Religious Traditions.* Downers Grove, IL: InterVarsity, 2000.

McGrath, Alister E. *A Passion for Truth: The Intellectual Coherence of Evangelicalism.* Leicester, UK: Apollos, 1996.

McLaren, Brian D. *Everything Must Change: Jesus, Global Crises, and a Revolution of Hope.* Nashville: T. Nelson, 2007.

Medearis, Carl. *Muslims, Christians, and Jesus: Gaining Understanding and Building Relationships.* Minneapolis: Bethany House, 2008.

Meier, John P. "The Historical Jesus and the Historical Samaritans: What Can Be Said?" *Biblica* 81 (2000) 202–32.

———. *A Marginal Jew: Rethinking the Historical Jesus.* Vols. 2, 3. Garden City, NY: Doubleday, 1991, 2001.

Merino, Stephen M. "Religious Diversity in a 'Christian Nation': The Effects of Theological Exclusivity and Interreligious Contact on the Acceptance of Religious Diversity." *Journal for the Scientific Study of Religion* 49 (2010) 231–46.

Meyers, Eric M. "Jesus and His Galilean Context." In *Archaeology and the Galilee,* edited by Douglas R. Edwards et al., 57–66. Atlanta: Scholars, 1997.

Meyers, Eric M., and J. F. Strange. *Archaeology, the Rabbis, and Early Christianity.* Nashville: Abingdon, 1981.

Michaels, J. Ramsey. *The Gospel of John.* New International Commentary on the New Testament. Grand Rapids: Eerdmans, 2010.

Moberly, Walter. "Biblical Criticism and Religious Belief." *Journal of Theological Interpretation* 2 (2008) 71–100.

Muck, Terry C., and Frances S. Adeney. *Christianity Encountering World Religions: The Practice of Mission in the Twenty-First Century.* Grand Rapids: Baker Academic, 2009.

Munro, Winsome. "The Pharisee and the Samaritan in John: Polar or Parallel?" *Catholic Biblical Quarterly* 57 (1995) 710–28.

Neusner, Jacob, editor. *Dictionary of Judaism in the Biblical Period: 450 B.C.E to 600 C.E.* Peabody, MA: Hendrickson, 1966.

Newbigin, J. E. Lesslie. *The Open Secret: An Introduction to the Theology of Mission.* Grand Rapids: Eerdmans, 1994.

Neyrey, Jerome H. "What's Wrong with This Picture?: John 4, Cultural Stereotypes of Women, and Public and Private Space." In *A Feminist Companion to John,* edited by Amy-Jill Levine et al., 1:98–125. Feminist Companion to the New Testament and Early Christian Writings 4. Sheffield: Sheffield Academic, 2003.

Neyrey, Jerome H., Eric C. Stewart, editors. *The Social World of the New Testament: Insights and Models.* Peabody, MA: Hendrickson, 2008.
Nissen, Johannes. "Testament in Mission: The Use of the New Methodological and Hermeneutical Reflections." *Mission Studies* 21/2 (2004) 167–98.
Nolland, John. *The Gospel of Matthew: A Commentary on the Greek Text.* Grand Rapids: Eerdmans, 2005.
———. *Luke.* 3 vols. Word Biblical Commentary 35. Dallas: Word, 1989, 1993.
Oakman, Douglas E. Review of *Archaeology, History, and Society in Galilee* by Richard Horsley. *Catholic Biblical Quarterly* 60 (1998) 568–69.
O'Day, Gail R. "Surprised by Faith: Jesus and the Canaanite Woman." In *A Feminist Companion to Matthew,* edited by Amy-Jill Levine et al., 114–25. Feminist Companion to the New Testament and Early Christian Writings 1. Sheffield: Sheffield Academic, 2001.
Okure, Teresa. "Jesus and the Samaritan Woman (Jn 4:1–42) in Africa." *Theological Studies* 70 (2009) 401–18.
———. *The Johannine Approach to Mission: A Contextual Study of John 4:1–42.* Tübingen: Mohr, 1988.
Osiek, Carolyn. "Jesus and Galilee." *The Bible Today* 34 (1996) 153–59.
Padgett, Alan G. "The Canonical Sense of Scripture: Trinitarian or Christocentric?" *Dialog* 45 (2006) 36–43.
Paget, James C. "Some Observations on Josephus and Christianity." *Journal of Theological Studies* 52 (2001) 539–624.
Patte, Daniel. *The Challenge of Discipleship: A Critical Study of the Sermon on the Mount as Scripture.* Harrisburg, PA: Trinity, 1999.
Patte, Daniel, editor. *Global Bible Commentary.* Nashville: Abingdon, 2004.
Pazdan, Mary Margaret. "Nicodemus and the Samaritan Woman: Contrasting Models of Discipleship." *Biblical Theology Bulletin* 17 (1987) 145–48.
Perrin, Nicholas. *Jesus the Temple.* Grand Rapids: Baker Academic, 2010.
Pinnock, Clark. *A Wideness in God's Mercy: The Finality of Jesus Christ in a World of Religions.* Grand Rapids: Zondervan, 1992.
Poirier, John C. "Jesus as an Elijianic Figure in Luke 4:16–30." *Catholic Biblical Quarterly* 71 (2009) 349–63.
———. "Theological Interpretation and its Contradistinctions." *Tyndale Bulletin* 61/1 (2010) 105–18.
Porter, Stanley E. *The Criteria for Authenticity in Historical-Jesus Research: Previous Discussions and New Proposals.* Sheffield: Sheffield Academic, 2000.
———. "The Criterion of Greek Language and Its Context: A Further Response." *Journal for the Study of the Historical Jesus* 4 (2006) 69–74.
———. "Jesus and the Use of Greek in Galilee." In *Studying the Historical Jesus: Evaluations of the State of Current Research,* by Bruce Chilton et al., 123–54. Leiden: Brill, 1994.
———. "Luke 17.11–19 and the Criteria for Authenticity Revisited." *Journal for the Study of the Historical Jesus* 1 (2003) 201–24.
Prior, Michael. *Jesus the Liberator: Nazareth Liberation Theology (Luke 4:16–30).* The Biblical Seminar 26. Sheffield: Sheffield Academic, 1995.
Rae, Murray. "The Ethics of Jesus." *Cultural Encounters* 3/2 (Summer 2007) 47–64.
———. "Texts in Context: Scripture and the Divine Economy." *Journal of Theological Interpretation* 1 (2007) 23–45.

Bibliography

Räisänen, Heikki. *Beyond New Testament Theology: A Story and a Program.* 2nd ed. London: SCM, 2000.

Rapinchuk, Mark. "The Galilee and Jesus in Recent Research." *Currents in Biblical Research* 2 (2004) 197–222.

Ratzinger, Joseph. "Declaration 'Dominus Iesus' on the Unicity and Salvific Universality of Jesus Christ and the Church." Vatican Congregation for the Doctrine of the Faith. August 6, 2000. Online: http://www.vatican.va/roman_curia/congregations/cfaith/documents/rc_con_cfaith_doc_20000806_dominus-iesus_en.html.

Reed, Jonathan L. *Archaeology and the Galilean Jesus: A Re-Examination of the Evidence.* Harrisburg, PA: Trinity, 2000.

———. "Archeological Contributions to the Study of Jesus and the Gospels." In *The Historical Jesus in Context*, edited by Amy-Jill Levine, Dale C. Allison Jr., and John Dominic Crossan, 40–54. Princeton Readings in Religion. Princeton, NJ: Princeton University Press, 2006.

———. Review of *Herod Antipas in Galilee* by Morten H. Jensen. *Journal for the Study of Judaism* 38 (2007) 402–5.

Renan, Ernest. *Life of Jesus.* London: Kegan Paul, Trench, Trübner, 1893.

Rhoads, David. "Jesus and the Syrophoenician Woman in Mark: A Narrative-Critical Study." *Journal of the American Academy of Religion* 62 (1994) 343–75.

Ridderbos, Herman. *The Gospel according to John: A Theological Commentary.* Grand Rapids: Eerdmans, 1997.

Riley, Gregory J. *One Jesus, Many Christs: How Jesus Inspired Not One True Christianity but Many.* Minneapolis: Fortress, 2000.

Robinson, Bob. "Christian-Hindu Dialogue—Are There Persuasive Biblical and Theological Reasons for It?: A Critical Assessment." *Dharma Deepika* 10/2 (July–December 2006) 7–22.

———. *Christians Meeting Hindus: An Analysis and Theological Critique of the Hindu-Christian Encounter in India.* Regnum Studies in Mission. Carlisle, UK: Paternoster, 2004.

———. "A 'Fifth Gospel' Less Torn and More Legible?: On Recent Attempts to Retrieve Herodian Galilee." In *The Gospel and the Land of Promise*, edited by Philip Church et al., 86–102. Eugene, OR: Pickwick, 2011.

———. "What Exactly Is Meant by the 'Uniqueness of Christ'?—An Examination of the Phrase and Other Suggested Alternatives in the Context of Religious Pluralism." *Evangelical Review of Theology*, part 1, 25 (2001) 362–71; part 2, 26 (2002) 76–90.

Rowe, C. Kavin. *Early Narrative Christology: The Lord in the Gospel of Luke.* Grand Rapids: Baker Academic, 2009.

Ryken, Leland, et al., editors. *Dictionary of Biblical Imagery.* Downers Grove, IL: InterVarsity, 1998.

Saeed, Abdullah. "The Islamic Case for Religious Liberty: A Close Reading of the Qur'an and the Prophet Leads to Supporting Religious Tolerance." *First Things* 217 (November 2011) 33–36.

Sanders, E. P. *Judaism: Practice and Belief, 63 BCE–66 CE.* London: SCM, 1992.

Sanders, James A. "From Isaiah 61 to Luke 4." In *Luke and Scripture: The Function of Sacred Traditions in Luke-Acts*, edited by James A. Sanders and Craig A. Evans, 46–69. Minneapolis: Fortress, 1993.

Sawicki, Marianne. *Crossing Galilee: Architecture of Contact in the Occupied Land of Jesus.* Harrisburg, PA: Trinity, 2000.

Scalise, Charles J. "The Hermeneutical Circle of Christian Community: Biblical, Theological, and Practical Dimensions of the Unity of Scripture." *Journal of Theological Interpretation* 1 (2007) 209–27.

Schnabel, Eckhard J. *Early Christian Mission.* Vol. 1, *Jesus and the Twelve.* Downers Grove, IL: InterVarsity, 2004.

———. "Israel, the People of God, and the Nations." *Journal of the Evangelical Theological Society* 45 (2002) 35–57.

Schnackenburg, Rudolf. *The Gospel according to St. John.* Herder's Theological Commentary on the New Testament 1. New York: Herder, 1968.

Schnelle, Udo. *Theology of the New Testament.* Translated by M. Eugene Boring. Grand Rapids: Baker Academic, 2009.

Schuler, Mark T. "Recent Archaeology of Galilee and the Interpretation of Texts from the Galilean Ministry of Jesus." *Concordia Theological Quarterly* 71 (2007) 99–117.

Schwartz, Joshua. Review of *Judaism and the Gentiles* by Terence Donaldson. *Reviews in Biblical Literature,* March 2010. Online: http://www.bookreviews.org/pdf/7258_7898.pdf.

Senior, Donald. "Between Two Worlds: Gentiles and Jewish Christians in Matthew's Gospel." *Catholic Biblical Quarterly* 61 (1999) 1–23.

———. *Matthew.* Abingdon New Testament Commentaries. Nashville: Abingdon, 1988.

Siker, Jeffrey S. "'First to the Gentiles': A Literary Analysis of Luke 4:16–30." *Journal of Biblical Literature* 111 (1992) 73–90.

Smillie, Gene R. "'Even the Dogs': Gentiles in the Gospel of Matthew." *Journal of the Evangelical Theological Society* 45 (2002) 73–97.

Snodgrass, Klyne. *Stories with Intent: A Comprehensive Guide to the Parables of Jesus.* Grand Rapids: Eerdmans, 2008.

So, Damon W. K. *Jesus' Revelation of His Father: A Narrative-Conceptual Study of the Trinity with Special Reference to Karl Barth.* Milton Keynes, UK: Paternoster, 2006.

———. "The Missionary Journey of the Son of God into the Far Country." *Transformation* 23/3 (July 2006) 130–42.

Sperber, Daniel. *The City in Roman Palestine.* Oxford: Oxford University Press, 1998.

Spina, Frank Anthony. *The Faith of the Outsider: Exclusion and Inclusion in the Biblical Story.* Grand Rapids: Eerdmans, 2005.

Stein, Robert H. *Mark.* Baker Exegetical Commentary on the New Testament. Grand Rapids: Baker Academic, 2008.

Stibbe, Mark W. G. *John's Gospel.* New Testament Readings. London: Routledge, 1994.

Story, J. Lyle. "All Is Now Ready: An Exegesis of 'The Great Banquet' (Luke 14:15–24) and 'The Marriage Feast' (Matthew 22:1–14)." *American Theological Inquiry* 2/2 (2009) 67–79.

Stott, John R. W. *The Contemporary Christian.* Leicester, UK: InterVarsity, 1992.

Sumner, George R. *The First and the Last: The Claim of Jesus Christ and the Claims of Other Religious Traditions.* Grand Rapids: Eerdmans, 2004.

Swartley, Willard M. *Covenant of Peace: The Missing Peace in New Testament Theology and Ethics.* Grand Rapids: Eerdmans, 2006.

Talbert, Charles. *Matthew.* Paideia. Grand Rapids: Baker Academic, 2010.

Tcherikover, Victor. *Hellenistic Civilization and the Jews.* Translated by S. Appelbaum. New York: Athenium, 1970.

Theissen, Gerd. *Sociology of Early Palestinian Christianity.* Philadelphia: Fortress, 1978.

Bibliography

Theissen, Gerd, and Annette Merz. *The Historical Jesus: A Comprehensive Guide.* London: SCM, 1998.

Tilley, Terrence W. *Faith: What It Is and What It Isn't.* Maryknoll, NY: Orbis, 2010.

Tillich, Paul. *Dynamics of Faith.* New York: Harper and Row, 1957.

Treier, Daniel J. *Introducing Theological Interpretation of Scripture: Recovering a Christian Practice.* Grand Rapids: Baker Academic, 2008.

Turner, David L. *Matthew.* Baker Exegetical Commentary on the New Testament. Grand Rapids: Baker Academic, 2008.

Twelftree, Graham H. *Jesus the Miracle Worker: A Historical and Theological Study.* Downers Grove, IL: InterVarsity, 1999.

Udoh, Fabian E., et al. *Redefining First-Century Jewish and Christian Identities: Essays in Honor of Ed Parish Sanders.* Christianity and Judaism in Antiquity Series 16. Notre Dame, IN: University of Notre Dame Press, 2008.

Vale, Ruth. "Literary Sources in Archaeological Description: The Case of Galilee, Galilees, and Galileans." *Journal for the Study of Judaism* 18 (1987) 209–26.

Vanhoozer, Kevin J., editor. *The Trinity in a Pluralistic Age: Theological Essays on Culture and Religion.* Grand Rapids: Eerdmans, 1997.

Vanhoozer, Kevin J., et al., editors. *Dictionary for Theological Interpretation of the Bible.* Grand Rapids: Baker Academic, 2005.

Vanhoozer, Kevin J., et al., editors. *Theological Interpretation of the New Testament: A Book-by-Book Survey.* Grand Rapids: Baker Academic, 2008.

Vermes, Geza. *Jesus the Jew: A Historian's Reading of the Gospels.* Philadelphia: Fortress, 1973.

Verstraelen, Frans J., et al., editors. *Missiology: An Ecumenical Introduction.* Grand Rapids: Eerdmans, 1995.

Volf, Miroslav. *Allah: A Christian Response.* New York: HarperOne, 2011.

———. "Johannine Dualism and Contemporary Pluralism." *Modern Theology* 21 (2005) 189–217.

Wahlen, Clinton. *Jesus and the Impurity of Spirits in the Synoptic Gospels.* WUNT 2/185. Tübingen: Mohr/Siebeck, 2004.

Watson, Francis. "*Veritas Christi*: How to Get from the Jesus of History to the Christ of Faith without Losing One's Way." In *Seeking the Identity of Jesus: A PilgrimAge*, edited by Beverly Roberts Gaventa and Richard B. Hays, 96–114. Grand Rapids: Eerdmans, 2008.

Webster, John. "Editorial: Five Thoughts on Theological Interpretation of Scripture." *International Journal of Systematic Theology* 12 (2010) 116–17.

———. *Holy Scripture: A Dogmatic Sketch.* Cambridge, UK: Cambridge University Press, 2003.

Wenell, Karen J., *Jesus and Land: Sacred and Social Space in Second Temple Judaism.* Library of New Testament Studies 334. London: T. & T. Clark, 2007.

Wheatley, A. *Josephus on Jesus: The Testimonium Flavianum Controversy from Late Antiquity to Modern Times.* New York: P. Lang, 2003.

Whitacre, Rodney A. *John.* IVP New Testament Commentary Series. Downers Grove, IL: InterVarsity, 1999.

Williams, Rowan. "Looking for Jesus and Finding Christ." In *Biblical Concepts and Our World*, edited by D. Z. Philips and Mario von der Ruhr, 141–52. Basingstoke: Palgrave Macmillan, 2004.

Williams, Rowan. "The Finality of Christ in a Pluralist World." Lecture delivered March 2, 2010. Online: http://www.archbishopofcanterbury.org/2789.

Williamson, H. G. M., and Craig A. Evans. "Samaritans," In *Dictionary of New Testament Background: A Compendium of Contemporary Biblical Scholarship*, edited by Craig A. Evans and Stanley E. Porter, 1056–61. Downers Grove, IL: InterVarsity, 2000.

Wills, Lawrence M. *Not God's People: Insiders and Outsiders in the Biblical World*. Religion in the Modern World. Lanham, MD: Rowman and Littlefield, 2008.

Witherington, Ben. *The Christology of Jesus*. Minneapolis: Fortress, 1990.

Wright, Christopher J. H. "Interpreting the Bible among the World Religions." *Themelios* 25/3 (June 2000) 48–51.

———. *The Mission of God: Unlocking the Bible's Grand Narrative*. Downers Grove, IL: InterVarsity, 2006.

———. *Thinking Clearly about the Uniqueness of Christ*. Crowborough, UK: Monarch, 1997.

Wright, N. T. *Jesus and the Victory of God*. Christian Origins and the Question of God 2. Philadelphia: Fortress, 1996.

Wyckoff, Eric John. "Jesus in Samaria (John 4:4–42): A Model for Cross-Cultural Ministry." *Biblical Theology Bulletin* 25 (2005) 89–98.

Yarbro Collins, Adela. *Mark: A Commentary*. Hermeneia. Minneapolis: Augsburg Fortress, 2007.

Yong, Amos. *Hospitality and the Other: Pentecost, Christian Practices and the Neighbor*. Maryknoll, NY: Orbis, 2008.

———. "'Not Knowing Where the Wind Blows . . .': On Envisioning a Pentecostal-Charismatic Theology of Religions." *Journal of Pentecostal Studies* 14 (1999) 81–112.

———. "The Turn to Pneumatology in Christian Theology of Religions: Conduit or Detour?" *Journal of Ecumenical Studies* 35 (1998) 437–54.

Scripture Index

OLD TESTAMENT

Genesis
28:16–18   173

Exodus
22:27   45

2 Kings
17   170

Isaiah
61:1–2   22, 25, 27–31, 37, 261–62

NEW TESTAMENT

Matthew
8:5–12   83–92, 111–13
8:7   75
8:11–12   104, 111, 118, 121–22, 163–64, 259
8:28–34   151–52
10:5–6   100, 175, 179, 241
13:31–32   144–45
15:1–20   128–30, 132–33
15:21–28   96–101
15:24   100, 102, 104, 241
15:32–39   153–54
20:1–16   143–44
21:33–46   141–43
22:1–14   141

Mark
4–8   146–50
4:30–32   144–45
5:1–20   151–52
7:1–23   128–36
7:24–30   95–98
7:31–37   152–53
8:1–10   153–54
8:22–26   152–53
12:1–12   141–43

Luke
4:16–30   21–39, 229–30, 249, 261–62
7:1–10   83–87, 92–93
8:26–39   151–52
9:50   154, 175–76
9:51–56   175–76, 214
10:25–37   191–99
13:18–19   144–45
14:15–24   141
17:11–19   176
20:9–17   141–43

Scripture Index

John

4:4–42	177–91, 218–19, 248–49
4:24	256
4:42	183, 240, 242
4:46–54	94–95, 121
10:16	157
11:52	157
12:20–26	157–60

Philippians

2:5	7

1 John

2:6	7

Subject Index

Abraham (patriarch), 50, 220–23
   'tribes of', 210, 220
archaeology, 60–65, 70, 72–73
attitudes, Christian towards plurality, 1
banquet, messianic, 91–92, 122
Barth, Karl, 268–69
basilikos, 86
   faith of 115
Bauckham, Richard, 81–82
Bethsaida, 147–48
Bird, Michael, 24, 47, 79–80, 83, 85, 100, 109, 116, 124, 145, 154, 164
Blakley, Ted, 107–109, 146–50
blind man healed by Jesus, 152–53
Calvin, John, 268–69
Canaanite, woman described as, 99–100
Capernaum, 83–87
centurion, 85–88
   faith of, 111–13, 116
   healing of servant of, 83–95
   healing of servant, comparison of accounts, 85
centurion at the cross, 160
Chancey, Mark, 58, 74
Christ as exegete, 21–39
Christocentrism, 2–4
Christological implications of encounters, 160–63
Christology, as seen in encounters, 123–24, 242–54
   exemplary, 6–10, 34–37, 228–29, 250–54
   identity of Jesus and, 123–24, 242–54, 257–59

narrative and eschatological dimensions of, 23–25, 122–25
compassionate Samaritan, parable of, 191–99
   prophetic critique within, 195–96
conflict reduction, 199
conservative Christians, 5, 15, 117, 209, 223, 227, 237, 263
contextuality, 237–38
continuity and discontinuity between religions, 187–89, 232–33, 238–41, 265
conversion, 46–47
Cotter, Wendy, 250–53, 261
Cox, Harvey, 6
De Béthune, Pierre-François, 215–16
deaf mute healed by Jesus, 152–53
dialogue between religions, 189–90, 216–17, 233–34, 264–67
   not based on external 'markers', 197–98
   risks in, 265–66
   starting points, 233–34
dialogue, interpersonal, seen in Jesus' example and teaching, 236–38
disciple / discipleship, 83, 116, 120, 159, 241, 263; *see also* Jesus' disciples
discontinuity between religions, 238–41
Donaldson, Terence, 47, 51–52
Elijah, 22–32
Elisha, 22–32
eschatological understanding of Jesus' encounters, 124–25, 161–64, 253–54
eschatology and contested worship, 218–19, 262–63

Subject Index

Esler, Philip, 199
ethnic 'superiority', 196–97
Evangelicals, 4–5, 220, 227, 237
example of Jesus, with Gentiles and
    Samaritans, 34–37, 228–29,
    250–54, 268–69
  and attitudes towards Muslims,
    208–27
exemplary christology, 6–10, 34–37,
    228–29, 250–54
exorcisms, 163
faith and humility in 'outsiders', 26–27,
    90–91, 111–18, 159–60, 230–
    31, 260–61, 263
food laws, Jesus and, 126–36, 161
Freyne, Séan, 55, 59, 64–72, 121–23,
    130–31, 135–38, 259
Gadara, demon-possessed man in,
    151–52
Galilee, Herodian, 53–80, 243–44
  Hellenization and Romanization
    in, 55–64
  Jewish religious milieu, 63–69, 243
  regional variations in, 63
  unresolved issues concerning,
    67–69
Galilee, Sea of, 146–49
'Galilee of the Gentiles', 59
Gamla, 134–35
Gentile mission, in Mark, 146–54
Gentiles, 20–39
  ambivalent Jewish attitudes
    towards, 44–45
  among the crowds, 150–51
  as participants in Rule of God, 125
  capitalization of term? 41n3
  in parables, 140–45
  Jewish attitudes towards, 40–53
  Jewish eschatological perspectives,
    49–50
  Jewish interactions with, 47–48
  particular and universal
    perspectives concerning, 50–53
  Rabbinic attitudes towards, 48–49,
    234
Gilbert, Gary, ch 1 *passim*
God, character of, 37–38

Goldenberg, Robert, ch 1 *passim*
Greek, spoken by Jesus? 77–80
Greeks approach Jesus, 157–60
Hayes, Christine, 45–46, 48
hekatontarchos, 85–88
Hellenization, 53–63
Herod / Herod Antipas, 54, 71–72
Hertig, Paul, 54–55
Hindus, Hinduism, 5–6, 8, 254, 259
Hippos, 57–58, 134
historical Jesus, 243–44
historicity and Gospels, 81–83
hospitality and reconciliation, 215–16
imitation of Christ, 6–10, 250–54; see
    also exemplary Christology
inter-religious relations, 1–2, 109–25,
    164–66, 257–69
  'seeing heart' and, 198–199
Islam, and Samaritanism, thirteen
    common characteristics,
    200–208
  example of Jesus and, 208–27
  Jesus' encounter with Samaritans
    and, 208–27
Israel, extended definition of, 31, 110–
    11, 140, 145, 247–48
  Jesus and priority of, 104–5
Jerusalem, 49, 54, 56, 58, 68, 72, 77,
    136, 139, 156, 159–60, 173–76,
    180, 189, 203, 218, 249, 266
Jesus
  food laws and, 126–36, 161
  people of God and, 139, 142; see
    also Israel
  the Law and, 129–30, 133–34,
    245–46
  as Galilean, 69–73
  attitude to authority, 123, 244
  challenge of the person and identity
    of, 257–59
  commends some Gentiles and
    Samaritans, 229–31, 253
  compassion of, 259–61
  dialogue with religions, 236–38
  disciples of; see disciples
  example of, 6–10, 34–37, 250–54,
    268–69

Subject Index

Gentiles and, 73–80
Gentiles and Samaritans,
  conclusions from encounters,
  228–68
humanity of, 102–4
identity of, 123–24, 242–54, 257–59
missional intent of, 100–101,
  241–42, 249
priority of Israel and, 104–5
purity and, 126–36, 161
purity and Gentiles, 131–36
renunciation of vengeance and
  violence in, 261–62
Samaritans and, 167, 175–99,
  254–55
speaker of Greek? 77–80
Samaritan woman and, 177–91,
  185–87, 189, 208–9, 218–19,
  235–36
Temple and, 136–39, 161–62
'temple action' and, 136–39, 161–62
universality of, 259–61
Jesus and the religions, particularity,
  discontinuity and mission,
  238–42
universality and continuity, 231–36
Jesus' disciples, attitudes of, 75, 90–91,
  100, 106, 108–9, 111–12,
  116–17, 119, 133, 146–49,
  152–54, 165, 175, 182, 184, 188,
  209, 214, 230, 249, 254, 260–62,
  265–66
in encounter situations, 252–53,
  268
Jews and Samaritans, bitterness
  between, 174–75
Jonah, sign of, 155–57
Josephus, 43, 45, 60–62, 68, 72, 76, 86–
  87, 97, 136, 156, 168, 174, 204
Jotapata, 134–35
Kaminsky, Joel, 52–53
Kingdom of God; *see* Rule of God
Klawans, Jonathan, 45–46
Kreeft, Peter, 224–25, 264
Kurie, 89, 92–93
Law, Jesus' view of, 129–30, 133–34
love, universality of, 196–97

margins to center, from, 33, 111, 210,
  254–55, 267–68
marriage, Jewish with Gentiles, 48
McCullough, Ross, 223–14
meal imagery, 91–92, 122
methodologies employed, 10–20
miqva'ot, 65, 67, 135
mission, 4, 188–89
  seen in Jesus' example and teaching,
  100–101, 241–42, 249
Mt. Gerizim, 173
Muslims, 5, 231–33, 254, 260–62, 264,
  266; *see also* Islam
Naaman the Syrian, 22, 26–28, 31–32,
  34, 117
Nazareth, Jesus' synagogue address in,
  21–39, 253
Ninevites, 155–57, 164
nōkhri, 42
'other sheep', 157
'outsiders', 50–51, 217, 262–63
parables
  compassionate Samaritan, 191–99,
    234, 236
  Gentiles in, 140–45
  great banquet / marriage feast, 141
  marriage feast, 141
  mustard seed, 144–45
  vineyard and murderous tenants,
    141–43
  workers in vineyard, 143–44
particularities, religious, 211–12, 264
particularity, discontinuity and
  mission, seen in Jesus' example
  and teaching, 238–42
patris, 28–32
people of God, Jesus' view of, 139, 142,
  209–10, 219–20, 247–48; *see
  also* Israel
Porter, Stanley, 78–79
proselytes, 46–47
purity, Gentiles and, 45–46
  Jesus and, 126–36, 161
  Jewish views, 127
Queen of the South, 155–57, 164
Qumran community, 31, 46

291

Subject Index

rabbinic attitudes to Gentiles, 48–49, 234
reader-centered approaches, 12–17
reconciliation, hospitality and, 215–16
  enemies, 212–13, 262–64
  refusal to blame, 213–14
  refusal to denigrate, 213–14
religions, 18–20
  dialogue with, 264–67; *see also* dialogue
  understanding, 264–65
religious plurality, 25–26
religious superiority, 196–97
reversal, religious, 27–30, 118–19, 260–61, 266–67
Rule of God, and encounters, 17, 23, 111, 120, 124, 139–40, 144–45, 162–64, 166, 210, 228, 245–46, 249, 258, 267–68
Samaritan woman, and Jesus, 177–91
  cultural understanding of, 182–85
  historicity of acount, 177–79
  implications of encounter with, 182–91
Samaritanism, 170–73
  Islam and, thirteen common characteristics, 200–208
Samaritans, Jesus and, 167, 175–99, 254–55
  bitterness between Jews and, 174–75
  Christian encounter with Islam and, 200–227
  beliefs of and practices of, 167–73
  history of, 169–70
  secondary material in the Gospels on, 175–76
  terminology concerning, 167–69
'Savior of the world', 209, 236, 240, 242, 249
'scattered children', 157
Schnelle, Udo, 256
Schröter, Jens, 61–62, 69–70
second feeding of the crowds, 153–54
Sepphoris, 57–58, 71, 123, 134, 244

Sidon, 22
'sinners', 75–76
So Damon, 6
social-scientific analyses, 105–6
Sodom and Gomorrah, 155
soteriological implications of encounters, 162–63, 258–59
Spina, Frank, 50–51
stone purification jars, 65–66, 135
Syrophoenician / Canaanite mother, 95–109, 250–53
  faith of, 115–17
  rejected by Jesus? 101–2
Syrophoenician daughter's healing, as domestic parable of, 106–8
  as intentionally ironic, 108–09
Temple, compassionate Samaritan and, 246–47
  Jesus and, 136–39, 161–62
theological exegesis, 10–12, 34–36
Tiberias, 57–58, 71, 123, 134, 244
Trinitarian dimensions of encounters, 37–38, 255–56
Twelftree, Graham, 82
Tyre, 73, 97
Tyre and Sidon, 22, 97, 99, 150–51, 155, 265
universality, 30–33, 120–22, 236, 259–60
universality and continuity, seen in Jesus' example and teaching, 231–36
vengeance, exclusion of, 30–33, 120, 214–15
Vale, Ruth, 62–63
Volf, Miroslav, 225–26
Wannenwetsch, Bernd, 198–99
widow of Zarephath, 22, 26, 28, 31–32, 34, 117
wisdom, 122
worship, contested, 218–19, 248–49
zār, 42
Zion, 31, 49, 118, 121, 137–39, 172–73, 243, 249

www.ingramcontent.com/pod-product-compliance
Lightning Source LLC
Chambersburg PA
CBHW020608300426
44113CB00007B/562